Contemporary Debates in Childhood Education and Development

- What are the risks and benefits of non-parental care for young children?
- What are the short- and long-term effects of academically- vs. play-focused environments for learning?
- How and when should we teach reading?
- What are the purposes of education?
- What is the best way to teach mathematics to children, from preschool and beyond?

Contemporary Debates in Childhood Education and Development is a unique resource and reference work that brings together leading international researchers and thinkers, with divergent points of view, to discuss contemporary problems and questions in childhood education and developmental psychology. Through an innovative format whereby leading scholars each offer their own constructive take on the issue in hand, this book aims to inform readers of both sides of a variety of topics and in the process encourage constructive communication and fresh approaches.

Spanning a broad spectrum of issues, this book covers:

- Phonic and whole language reading approaches
- The developmental effect of non-parental childcare
- The value of preschool academic skill acquisition
- The most effective methods of teaching mathematics
- Standardized assessment – does it work?
- The role of electronic media and technology
- The pedagogical value of homework
- The value of parents' reading to children.

This book combines breadth of vision with cutting edge research and is a 'must have' resource for researchers, students and policy makers in the fields of education and child development.

Sebastian Suggate is currently working as a lecturer at the Institute of Psychology, Education and Sport Science at the University of Regensburg, Germany.

Elaine Reese is Associate Professor in the Department of Psychology at the University of Otago, New Zealand. Dr. Reese is the incoming editor of the *Journal of Cognition and Development*.

Contemporary Debates in Childhood Education and Development

Edited by
Sebastian Suggate and
Elaine Reese

Routledge
Taylor & Francis Group

LONDON AND NEW YORK

First published 2012
by Routledge
2 Park Square, Milton Park, Abingdon, Oxon OX14 4RN

Simultaneously published in the USA and Canada
by Routledge
711 Third Avenue, New York, NY 10017

Routledge is an imprint of the Taylor & Francis Group, an informa business

British Library Cataloguing in Publication Data
A catalogue record for this book is available from the British Library

Library of Congress Cataloging in Publication Data
Contemporary debates in childhood education and development / [edited] by
Sebastian Suggate and Elaine Reese.
p. cm.
Includes bibliographical references and index.
1. Early childhood education–Cross-cultural studies. 2. Child development–
Cross-cultural studies. I. Suggate, Sebastian. II. Reese, Elaine.
LB1139.23.C656 2012
372.21–dc23
2011049175

ISBN: 978-0-415-61489-4 (hbk)
ISBN: 978-0-415-61490-0 (pbk)
ISBN: 978-0-203-11555-8 (ebk)

Typeset in Bembo
by Saxon Graphics Ltd, Derby

MIX
Paper from
responsible sources
FSC
www.fsc.org   FSC® C004839

Printed and bound in Great Britain by
TJ International Ltd, Padstow, Cornwall

Contents

Acknowledgements   ix

Introduction   x

PART I
What are the purposes of education?   I

1   The purpose of education – a "post-liberal" perspective   3
    BO DAHLIN

2   Intellectual goals in the early years   13
    LILIAN G. KATZ

3   De Groot's lesson   19
    JOHN SWELLER

PART II
**What is the effect of non-parental childcare on child
development?**   25

4   Why non-maternal childcare can be good for children and families:
    research and policy implications   27
    LYNNE VERNON-FEAGANS AND ALLISON DE MARCO

5   Delegated parenting: some neuroendocrine reservations   38
    ARIC SIGMAN

PART III
**Is shared book-reading an indispensable ingredient
of responsible parenting?**   49

6   Shared book-reading: there is no downside for parents   51
    CATHERINE MCBRIDE-CHANG

7   The tyranny of shared book-reading   59
     ELAINE REESE

PART IV
**What should be done to foster children's mathematical
development in the preschool years?**   69

8   Mathematics for the whole child   71
     JULIE SARAMA AND DOUGLAS H. CLEMENTS

9   Fostering mathematical thinking through playful learning   81
     KELLY FISHER, KATHY HIRSH-PASEK, AND ROBERTA M. GOLINKOFF

PART V
What is the role of digital media in early education?   93

10   Extending opportunities for learning: the role of digital media
     in early education   95
     LYDIA PLOWMAN, JOANNA MCPAKE, AND CHRISTINE STEPHEN

11   The inappropriateness of ICT in early childhood: arguments from
     philosophy, pedagogy, and developmental research   105
     RICHARD HOUSE

PART VI
How is school readiness best fostered?   121

12   Promoting school readiness: an integrative framework   123
     FREDERICK J. MORRISON AND ANNEMARIE H. HINDMAN

13   School readiness and school's readiness: on the child's transition
     from preschool to school   133
     NIKLAS PRAMLING AND INGRID PRAMLING SAMUELSSON

PART VII
**Is academic skill acquisition important during
preschool and kindergarten?**   143

14   Understanding the contributions of early academic skills to
     children's success in school   145
     CHRISTOPHER J. LONIGAN AND BETH M. PHILLIPS

15   The importance of balance in early childhood programs   159
     REBECCA MARCON

PART VIII

**Is it important for children to acquire reading
skills in preschool and kindergarten?**   169

16 Why is it important for children to begin learning to read
    in kindergarten?   171
    LINNEA C. EHRI

17 Watering the garden before a rainstorm: the case of early
    reading instruction   181
    SEBASTIAN P. SUGGATE

PART IX

**What are the best ways to develop primary school
children's mathematical abilities?**   191

18 The importance of reasoning and of knowing the number system
    when children begin to learn about mathematics   193
    PETER BRYANT AND TEREZINHA NUNES

19 Towards proficiency: the Chinese method of teaching mathematics
    to children   204
    YUJING NI

PART X

**Is phonological awareness causally important in
the acquisition of reading and spelling?**   215

20 Re-impact of phonological awareness on the acquisition of literacy   217
    WOLFGANG SCHNEIDER AND NICOLE BERGER

21 Increasing awareness of phonological awareness –
    helpful or misleading?   227
    RENATE VALTIN

PART XI

**What form should reading instruction in kindergarten
and elementary school take?**   239

22 Contemporary reading acquisition theory: the conceptual basis for
    differentiated reading instruction   241
    ALISON W. ARROW AND WILLIAM E. TUNMER

23   Toward better teaching: revising the fundamentals of
     learning to read   250
     G. BRIAN THOMPSON AND CLAIRE M. FLETCHER-FLINN

PART XII
What is the pedagogical value of homework?   261

24   The changing debate: from assigning homework to
     designing homework   263
     JOYCE L. EPSTEIN AND FRANCES L. VAN VOORHIS

25   What the evidence says and what we need to investigate   275
     JULIAN ELLIOTT AND PETER TYMMS

PART XIII
**Is regular standardized assessment important for
childhood education?**   285

26   The benefits of regular standardized assessment in childhood
     education: guiding improved instruction and learning   287
     GAVIN T. L. BROWN AND JOHN HATTIE

27   Developments in standardized assessment: a perspective
     from the UK   293
     CHRISTINE MERRELL

PART XIV
**What is the role of the modern educator in fostering
moral values and virtues?**   305

28   On the educational value of moral virtues: some lessons from
     ancient philosophy   307
     DAVID CARR

29   The pursuit of virtue as an aim of education   316
     RICHARD PRING

Index   325

Acknowledgements

We are very grateful to Tamara Suggate for her help with conceptualising and editing this book. We also thank David Green for his advice on the cover art and Wolfgang Schneider for his encouraging and thoughtful contributions throughout the book's development. Simon Kuttner also provided cogent advice at the editing stage. A large part of the work on this book was completed while one of us (S. S.) was an Alexander-von-Humboldt research fellow at the University of Würzburg hosted by Wolfgang Schneider.

Our gratitude extends to all of the contributors of this book who have embraced the book's concept and shown their willingness for scholarly dialogue.

Introduction

It is better to stir up a question without deciding it than to decide it without stirring it up.
Joseph Joubert (1754–1824)

One of the many lessons from the dialogues of Plato, one of the founding fathers of the Age of Reason, is the power of dialogue and debate. Indeed, only fools, not scientists, shy away from debate, which at its best entails not only the skills of jousting and defending, respect and tolerance, knowledge and reason, but above all a regard for the workings of the world. Through debate, we seek and hope to gradually reveal universal secrets. Equipped with these virtues and undertaken in this spirit, debate becomes a veritable tool, through which we learn the ideas of our fellows and hone our own scientific understanding.

Unfortunately, several features of modern academic environments often mean that such noble and far-reaching debate is not possible. On simple logistical grounds alone, experts are often scattered across universities and continents, departments and disciplines. Where researchers gather in larger research teams, the human trait of preferring colleagues with similar views and expertise to oneself can reduce diversity.

Diversity, however, is a beast of burden in this increasingly complicated world. Just as research methods belong to developmental psychology, philosophy belongs to research methods, and all of these are, in turn, necessary for educational research. The application of education to real life necessitates sociology, economics, and politics – and this is surely only part of the picture still. It is critical for scientists to know not only what they study, measure, count, and weigh, but what they fail to measure and take into account. In this spirit, Johann Wolfgang von Goethe once bemoaned that the scientist seeking to study the rose has at once failed in his or her task the moment that she or he cuts the bud from the plant and brings it into a laboratory.

A further problem – that has not only yet to be solved, but multiplies by the month – is the exponential and bewildering increase in the number of journals, fields of studies, researchers, and research results. Thus many researchers are compelled to become specialized to such an extent that they end up neglecting the broader aspects to any given field of study, which are absolutely crucial for an integrated perspective. Conversely, one can aim for a broad perspective, but then a consequence is the loss of specialist expertise as one inevitably fails to keep abreast with swarms of new research findings. Indeed, one of us (S. S.) once read that the definition of an expert is one who knows ever more about an increasingly narrow field, such that the perfect expert knows absolutely everything about absolutely nothing! Equally, the perfect Jack-of-all-trades knows absolutely nothing about everything.

We believe that an appropriate mixture of diversity and expertise promotes debate and dialogue. Debate and dialogue are essential for progressing science because these promote the exchange of ideas, the broadening of research, and encourage researchers to critically examine, defend, and adapt their own views. Our concern at the lack of true dialogue and debate in educational and developmental science inspired us to prepare the present volume. We aim to bring diverse yet expert views together under one roof, so that readers can join the authors in grappling with the issues. By making the effort to do so, we hope that this book will provide a stimulus to students and researchers alike in their further work.

Our goal was to select topics that are pertinent and empirically contentious. In some instances we deliberately 'revive' topics on which many consider 'consensus' to have been reached because we are not necessarily convinced that such consensus is justified. In other words, we view consensus as having little to do with whether an issue has been adequately researched or not.

We also sought views on these topics from researchers representing a broad range of countries: the United States of America, the United Kingdom, New Zealand, Australia, Sweden, Germany, and China. Inevitably, our views of the research literature are shaped by our cultural, political, educational, and social environments. It is our hope that students, educators, and researchers will benefit from the diversity of views and interpretations expressed herein. Ultimately, we must each draw our own conclusions from the literature, ideally in a well-informed and measured way.

Some chapters in this volume adopt a more typical debate style, with a clear pro and contra. However, equally important in debates are topics that move beyond a clear pro versus contra position, often because the issues are complicated and the question cannot be dichotomously formulated. In such instances the chapters of this book represent a discussion in which the authors begin with quite different approaches; yet in some instances the two camps reach similar conclusions. Just as equally as one ought not fear debate, one ought marvel at how lines of inquiry often converge, despite being diverse.

It goes without saying that we have included only a handful of topics and authors from a rich field of developmental psychology and education. There are thus many worthy minds whose work is not presented here. Interestingly, even in the process of searching for topics for this book, we encountered tremendous gaps in the research. For example, many of the topics suffer outright from a dire lack of research. In other instances there appeared to be much consensus among researchers, even when it was clear that key questions had not been researched and diverse fields of inquiry integrated. This makes both the need for this book and the contribution that it can make all the greater.

We consider that specific educational questions cannot be satisfactorily answered without first considering what education seeks to achieve. Bo Dahlin begins by arguing that education needs to help citizens to find meaning for their life; however, far from slipping into one-sided subjectivism, he also discusses our duty to ground this meaning in reality, and thereby to help the individual relate to the world. Lilian Katz focuses on the early years and the need to provide genuinely rich and stimulating experiences for children. She specifically alludes to the development of skills, dispositions, feelings, and academic goals and emphasizes long-term benefits. John Sweller presents a more cognitive approach, derived from a careful analysis of Chess Grand Masters. He presents a compelling case for the importance of practice and memorization in learning and true problem solving.

Lynne Vernon-Feagans and Allison de Marco propose that in the face of high rates of maternal employment, non-parental childcare is a reality for many families in industrialized society. Given that reality, they turn the question to how to maximize the quality of non-parental childcare for all children, but especially for low-income children, for whom high-quality childcare can make all the difference. Aric Sigman presents a sobering alternative view for all mothers, and indeed all parents, to consider. The growing evidence on the neuroendocrine front is that young children, even those in high-quality childcare environments, evidence stress in the form of increased cortisol levels as a result of non-parental care. Sigman thus advocates that we err on the side of caution in the heated debate on the effects of childcare on young children.

Parents in industrialized countries are encouraged to read books with their young children. Yet is shared book-reading an indispensable ingredient of good parenting? Catherine McBride-Chang argues that it is, given the evidence that high-quality shared book-reading enhances young children's oral language development, and indirectly, their reading skills. Elaine Reese cautions against one-size-fits-all advice in favor of shared book-reading, presenting evidence that not all parents are comfortable sharing books with their young children. If parents do not like books themselves, perhaps it is better for them to engage in other types of interactions and conversations with the shared goal of advancing children's oral language and literacy skills.

Douglas Clements and Julie Samara present an inspiring argument for why mathematics is not boring. Adult prejudice aside, they argue that children are naturally interested in mathematics. Key for these authors is stimulating mathematics skills for preschool children to prevent disadvantaged children being ultimately excluded from future careers dependent on math skills. To do this, it is not enough to leave children to discover everything themselves; they need guidance. Kelly Fisher, Kathy Hirsh-Pasek, and Roberta Golinkoff present an equally compelling picture: rigid and memorization-oriented approaches bore and wrangle the interest out of mathematics. Accordingly, they arrive at a persuasive position toward mathematics, whereby interest and competence can be stimulated simultaneously, when done properly by allowing and encouraging playful learning.

The role of digital media in the education of young children is a highly controversial issue. Lydia Plowman, Joanna McPake, and Christine Stephen argue that when used thoughtfully, digital media can extend young children's learning at home and at school. The key is to integrate digital media into activities seamlessly, to allow children to learn basic technologies while simultaneously expressing themselves in innovative ways. In contrast, Richard House argues that there is too little research at present to know that digital media have positive or even benign effects on young children and their learning. Given the potential harmful effects of digital media on very young children's neurological and social development, House recommends that we err on the side of caution and keep digital media out of the nursery.

The important topic of school readiness is tackled in two different, compelling ways by the contributors. Frederick Morrison and Annemarie Hindman begin by acknowledging the conceptual and empirical difficulty in isolating the key ingredients of school readiness, alluding to how we can prepare children by focusing on these factors. Then they systematically work their way through key aspects of readiness, identifying factors that have a strong empirical and conceptual appeal. Taking a different approach, Niklas Pramling and Ingrid Samuelsson present evidence from different cultures and examine the kind of reasoning that children bring with them to school. Working from this understanding of the child's world, they argue that school readiness can entail the school being ready for the children, taking care to build upon what they bring instead of imposing criteria without regard to what is there first.

Christopher Lonigan and Beth Phillips build their argument for the importance of acquiring early academic skills on well-established predictors of later school performance. Arguing that there is considerable continuity in development, they emphasize the importance of using evidence-based interventions and programmes targeting children's early academic skills. Rebecca Marcon counters by alluding to the observable academization of kindergarten and stops to ask the question, what do preschoolers actually need? Her answer to this question is balanced and developmentally appropriate learning.

Linnea Ehri presents a strong case for beginning reading instruction at an early age. She argues that there is every advantage, and no disadvantage, to early reading instruction, especially for low-income children and those with potential reading disabilities. Sebastian Suggate disagrees, arguing instead that beginning reading instruction at age 4 or 5 is akin to watering the garden before a rainstorm. Suggate proposes instead that for most children, time spent strengthening oral language skills in the early years will produce equal or greater reading skills in a shorter period of time once formal reading instruction begins at age 6 or 7.

Peter Bryant and Terezhina Nunes, and Yujing Ni present different approaches to teaching numeracy skills in the primary school years. Based on the psychological literature, Bryant and Nunes argue that children's understanding of number involves both the ability to count single sets and the ability to compare sets in terms of number. Most research and early numeracy instruction focus on the counting of single sets alone, but relational understanding is another critical feature of a full understanding of cardinality. In a fascinating counterpoint to the U.S. mathematics educational system, Ni presents evidence that the highly coherent Chinese 'two-basics' method of instruction can advance children's mathematical skill during the school years. Yet Ni acknowledges that the downside to such a standardized approach is that older children and adolescents may suffer low self-competence in the mathematics arena, despite their considerable skill.

Addressing the still-controversial question of whether phonemic awareness is causally involved in reading and spelling development, Wolfgang Schneider and Nicole Berger adopt a probabilistic account of causality and argue that, beyond reasonable doubt, there are indeed good empirical grounds to believe that phonemic awareness is causally related to reading and spelling. Counter to this position, Renate Valtin calls into question the interpretation of correlational data and points to actual errors made by children during reading and spelling. She also scrutinizes definitions and understanding of the concept of phonemic awareness and finishes by arguing that a broader early training is more important for children than phonemic awareness alone.

The focus of the next section is on the important and still raging debate about how to best to teach beginning reading. Alison Arrow and William Tunmer present a case for teaching explicit relations between phonemes and graphemes, particularly with children entering school with inadequate foundations. They argue that it is key for many readers – particularly those who will later struggle – to receive explicit training on phonics skills. Presenting a counter-argument in the next chapter, Brian Thompson and Claire Fletcher-Flinn introduce their Knowledge Sources Theory, according to which explicit instruction in phonics is not necessary because children acquire these relations implicitly. Highlights of this contribution are their critical challenges for previous research and models and their discussion of data showing that children can exhibit decoding in the absence of phonics reading instruction.

Homework is the bane of many children and more than a few parents. Yet what is its pedagogical value? Joyce Epstein and Frances van Voorhis consider the debate on the merits of homework closed, with resounding evidence in favor of homework. They believe it is time to shift the research question to the design of innovative homework that will motivate and facilitate the learning of all students. Julian Elliott and Peter Tymms begin their chapter with a radically different proposition – that the evidence for the merits of homework is surprisingly limited. The benefits of homework instead depend upon the age and intellectual level of the child, and the family's socioeconomic background. Elliott and Tymms advocate the need for more sophisticated research designs that take these factors into account. Yet Elliott and Tymms arrive at a similar conclusion to Epstein and van Voorhis, which is to encourage researchers and teachers to improve the type of homework assigned. In particular, they suggest that homework that is better integrated with classroom learning is essential.

Gavin Brown and John Hattie present a cogent and concise argument for the value of standardized assessment in education. They simply argue that well-designed and appropriately developed and applied standardized tests have an important role to play in education. Christine Merrell agrees that assessment can be important and delineates conditions for its intelligent usage, including dangers of misclassification, false comparisons, and teacher and child stress caused by school and classroom comparisons. She finishes by pointing out the kind of information that is often not captured by tests, the role of bias, and pitfalls in semi-standardized observations.

In many ways, we have saved the most provocative section for last. Both David Carr and Richard Pring provide rich and pertinent critiques of the role of virtue in education. Taking different routes, one through Aristotle and the other through the study of literature, they both reach the conclusion that values cannot be neglected in education. Many pearls of wisdom are contained in these chapters; the nature of virtue, the trappings of not heeding this, consequences of running schools like businesses and the importance of seeing virtue as more than rule following. As well as providing educators with much to ponder, both chapters serve as an inspiration to examine the role of virtue more closely.

We hope that our attempt at debate is a constructive one that will encourage students and researchers into being unafraid to provoke and to be provoked. We want researchers to tackle the big questions, even when (and perhaps especially when) the answers do not fit with conventional wisdom, or when the answers raise new questions. In the most heated debate, however, we must remember to be respectful of other points of view and to argue fairly. We must never forget that at the heart of the debate lies the future of all of our children and grandchildren.

Part I

What are the purposes of education?

[T]he most general purpose of education is to help human beings find individual fulfilment and meaning in life ... I would add that true meaning and fulfilment in life is surely not possible to find "outside reality" ... So education must be "to reality"; this must be part of the ultimate and overriding purpose. That reality in our postmodern times is actually a contested concept (Anderson, 1992) does not take anything away from this obligation of the older to the younger generation. But it makes it a greater moral challenge than ever before.

Bo Dahlin

[E]arly childhood curriculum and teaching methods are best when they address children's lively minds so that they have frequent opportunities to be fully intellectually engaged as well as to engage in spontaneous play, and not just cutting and pasting and producing "refrigerator art".

Lilian Katz

Understanding means memorising. It is knowledge held in long-term memory that results in understanding and it is the same knowledge that in an appropriate form and under appropriate conditions results in the problem-solving skill exhibited by chess masters and anyone else who has acquired problem-solving skill ... Long-term memory and its characteristics tend to be ignored or in many cases even derided by educationists insisting that its only function is to allow students to rote learn information. In fact, it is a central, possibly *the* central structure relevant to learning.

John Sweller

Chapter 1

The purpose of education – a "post-liberal" perspective

Bo Dahlin

Rudolf Steiner University College, Norway & Karlstad University, Sweden

Introduction

The question of the purpose of education has a long history among educational thinkers; on European grounds our literal tradition goes back at least to Plato and the ancient Greeks. However, it has been noted that writings about the aims of education are now less common than 2–3 decades ago. This has made it easier for utilitarian and purely instrumental conceptions of education to become commonplace (Standish, 2006). Standish even quotes a 1996 White Paper from the European Commission, *Teaching and learning: towards the learning society*, in which it is poignantly stated that the arguments about the aims of education are now finished: the purpose of education is simply to serve the economy. And that appears to be how many, even a majority of people, today actually think. Another reason for the lack of discussion of educational aims may be the one-sided focus on *learning* in present educational discourses, academic as well as non-academic (Biesta, 2010). The focus on learning itself and how to enhance it blinkers out the question of the ends of learning, of *what* is to be learnt and *why*.

My personal view is that the most general purpose of education is to help human beings find fulfilment and meaning in life. This view can of course be contested in many ways. It is nevertheless a rational and arguable point of view, which will be implicitly or explicitly present throughout this paper. I will begin by putting the question in a socio-political context, relating it to the issue of state versus state-independent schooling as well as to the social function of the educational system. Thereafter I will discuss the traditional liberal perspective on the purpose of education as illustrated by Winch and Gingell (2004) and what I consider to be a critical transformation of that view presented by Biesta (2010). I will end with a short discussion of the German philosopher Robert Spaemann's idea of "education for reality", which I find to be close to my own conception.

The question of freedom in education

Let us begin with Aristotle, who in his work on *Politics* is noted to say the following:

> That education should be regulated by law and should be an affair of state is not to be denied, but what should be the character of this public education, and how young persons should be educated, are questions which remain to be considered. As things are, there is disagreement about the subjects. For mankind are by no means agreed about the things to be taught, whether we look to virtue or the best life. Neither is it

clear whether education is more concerned with intellectual or with moral virtue. The existing practice is perplexing; no one knows on what principle we should proceed – should the useful in life, or should virtue, or should the higher knowledge, be the aim of our training; all three opinions have been entertained. Again, about the means there is no agreement; for different persons, starting with different ideas about the nature of virtue, naturally disagree about the practice of it.

(*Politics*, 8: II)

It seems that the issues dealt with in this quote have not changed much since Aristotle's time. That education should be regulated by law and therefore is a question of state policy is almost common sense today. That it should also be *carried out* by the state is less self-evident but still strongly believed by educational thinkers and those fractions of the population who oppose the so-called neo-liberal "marketization" of schooling. However, the present author belongs to those who do *not* see this as self-evident (cf. Dahlin, 2010). Since this issue is highly relevant to the question of the aim of education, let us pursue it further.

State versus state-independent schooling

It is a commonly accepted historical fact that the rise of state funded and state run educational institutions did not happen only out of sheer altruism, but mainly because it was in the interest of the ruling classes to form loyal citizens and to develop the economy of the nation (Green, 1990). But the state did not always succeed in this; neither was it always open about its real intentions but concealed them under more idealistic discourses. Of course, particular individualities were probably completely honest in their engagement for educational rights, ideals and values. Considering these facts, it is no surprise to find that there are many conceptions of education and its aims, depending on the social, historical, political and cultural contexts in which they are conceived and the social/cultural/political interests behind them. An educational conception is unavoidably ethical in character; it is inseparable from values and ideas of "the good life" (Winch and Gingell, 2004). Apparently this was so already in ancient Greece, as indicated by Aristotle in the quote above. Naturally, the education that was implemented by the state in actual practice would also bear inevitable traits of a particular educational conception, constituted by cultural and political forces.

If this was so historically, is it any different today? One could expect it to be *somewhat* different in democratic states, where governments are forced to take more than one interest, ideology or conception into account when formulating its educational policies and national curriculum plans. However, even in democratic states there is the problem of "the tyranny of the majority"; that it may be more or less impossible for minorities (ethnical, cultural or religious) to institute their own educational ideals because of government decisions based on the will of the majority (Winch and Gingell, 2004, p. 6). There is also the strong tendency that the values of the elite or higher classes determine the educational conception of state run schools (Winch and Gingell, 2004). Hence, it would seem that in the name of justice people should be allowed to form their own schools and run them according to their own educational ideals. And this they have been allowed to do, as there are now so-called state-independent schools in all democratic countries. The question, however, is how much independent of the state these schools really are? Under the present almost global politics of "performativity" (cf. Ball, 2003) the margins of freedom for both the non-state schools and each individual state school are rapidly diminishing. National governments increasingly hold the idea that the aims and goals of education are for the state to decide, whereas *how* these aims are realized in practice is up to the schools. "Pedagogical freedom" is thus reduced to the freedom to choose the means for implementing the goals decided by the state. This would perhaps not be a complete mockery of pedagogical professionalism if goals and aims were explicated only for the last grade of obligatory schooling (15–16 years old in most countries). However, as a result of the growing importance of international comparisons like *Trends in Mathematics and Science Study* (TIMSS), *Progress in International Reading Literacy Studies* (PIRLS) and OECD's *Program for International Student Assessment* (PISA), aims are now often explicitly formulated already from grade 1 in order to make test results comparable across countries. What consequences does this have for the freedom and the possibility to choose a different educational conception than the one propagated by the state? If grade specific goals are made obligatory for all schools, public or "state-independent" – which is now the case in many countries – this freedom is severely restricted.

Arguments against a complete freedom in educational choices often include the following (cf. Winch and Gingell, 2004):

- the *interests* of the state or the society *as a whole* will not be taken account of
- many people are not "knowledgeable, committed and responsible enough to make the right decision" (Winch and Gingell, p. 14)
- there are problems which require co-operation directed by a central agency.

The "interests" referred to are presumably those of economy and social cohesion. But, concretely, in what way does an educational system based on freedom not take these interests into account? Winch and Gingell (2004) themselves point out that ideas about what is a good or "strong economy" differ. Thus, if the state is going to take economical interests into account it has to decide which model of a "strong economy" is the right one, against the interest of those who disagree. As for social cohesion, it might be argued that a school system consisting of many different ethnically, culturally or religiously based schools will increase difficulties of mutual understanding between sub-cultural sections of the population and hence potentially undermine social cohesion. However, the principle of freedom in education does not preclude the state from constituting a minimal set of *laws* to which all schools must abide (laws are different from aims and goals). One such law could forbid dogmatic and indoctrinating approaches in religious and political views – a law or regulation that is already in place in many countries.[1] One could also prescribe the duty to teach other religious and political systems than that of one's own cultural group. Here it is also worth noting that social-psychological studies of tolerance indicate that the more authentically one is grounded in one's own culture, the more open and tolerant one can be towards people of other cultural beliefs and values (Hornsey and Hogg, 2000; Moghaddam and Solliday, 1991).

Thus, even in democratic states there is a problem that the values of the majority, the elite or the higher classes determine the educational conception of state run schools. Traditional liberalism has tried to solve this problem by maintaining that the liberal state stands only for the values of autonomy or personal liberty and political equality; regarding all other norms and values the state is/should be neutral (Winch and Gingell, 2004,

p. 141). However, *can* the state be neutral regarding conceptions of "the good life"? Under present conditions the answer is definitely no, considering that there is a strong link between the state and the economic system. Historically the state has intervened in education for two reasons: to develop faithful citizens and to develop the economy of the nation (Green, 1990; Winch and Gingell, 2004, p. 11). Although government intolerance for non-patriotism has obviously decreased in most democratic states, the economic interests of the state have not. The growth of the GNP is now virtually the overriding goal of all politics. This, together with the idea of the so-called knowledge economy (Neef, 1998), is what makes PISA, PIRLS and TIMSS so important. Economic interests become educational interests and education becomes "an affair of the state", an issue of power and politics, not of freedom and creativity.

The conclusion of my argument in this section is that from a social and political point of view, the question of the purpose of education is always already answered by the actual practice of educational institutions – and this practice is virtually determined by social, political and economic power relations. At present there is hardly any freedom in the educational sphere because of state dictates about what standards ought be reached and when. From *this* point of view, the question of the purpose of education is rather much like a so-called academic question: our answer to it has little practical meaning in the current climate.

The social function of education

There is another perspective from which we could have reached the same conclusion. By referring to the functionalistic school of sociology the question of the purpose of education would be transformed into the question of the function of education in society. Looking at a phenomenon like education, one has to ask what function it has in the social system as a whole. The answer to this question was formulated decades ago; the function of the educational system is twofold: to reproduce the social structure and to "sort" the future citizens so that each one finds their "right place" in an increasingly differentiated labour market (Bourdieu and Passeron, 1977). Hence, from this point of view also, the question of the purpose of education is too idealistic. We can debate over it as much as we want, the educational system will unaffectedly go on performing its functions – at least as long as our economical and working life is organised according to present principles. The early Marxist vision of a more humane society where we can be craftsmen in the morning, hunters in the afternoon and philosophers in the evening (or something of that sort) would require substantial changes of these principles.

Nevertheless, we continue to discuss aims and purposes of education and our ideas in this field are not without significance. The functionalistic view is only partially true and there are still some greater or smaller margins of freedom left. Even though educational thought has not affected the basic function of the educational system, it has in many places severely reduced the function's inhumane consequences, for instance by counteracting the social predetermination of life trajectories that was so prevalent in the past. The idea that all children have the right to a common education that develops their inherent abilities, talents and interests for at least nine years is one example.[2] With that in mind, it still seems worthwhile to reflect on the aims of education in a more philosophical way, in spite of the fact that the functions of education are not likely to change unless the whole social system in which education takes place is radically transformed.

Aims of education: some suggestions

It may first be noted that there is a distinction to be made between process aims and outcome aims. Education is a process leading up to certain results in terms of acquired knowledge and capabilities, and we may aim for the process itself to manifest certain qualities. Even though the distinction is not always possible to uphold in practice – especially when it comes to complex aims such as "critical thinking" or "democratic attitudes and values" – this essay will focus specifically on the wished-for results of the educational process.

It has been noted that the issue of the purpose of education is basically related to how we understand what it means to be human (Standish, 2006), an insight that goes back to Aristotle (Reeve, 2000). If, furthermore, education is conceived as a "preparation for life" (Winch and Gingell, 2004) – probably the most general formulation of its aim (and therefore so empty that almost nobody can disagree) – then the next question to arise is: what is a genuinely *human* life? From the Enlightenment liberalism point of view (a perspective that has been fundamental for the democratic development of Western societies) human life and its preparation entails three basic aspects: liberal, civic, and vocational (Winch and Gingell, 2004). These three aspects render three corresponding aims of education. The liberal aim is the most personal or individually oriented. It encompasses such abilities as to appreciate one's culture and to make choices about the direction in which one wants one's life to go. The civic aim has to do with becoming a responsible citizen of one's society and the vocational aim relates to one's ability to take care of one's economical and material needs.

Liberal and vocational education have often been seen as antagonistic, the first being based on intrinsic, the second on extrinsic/instrumental values. But, as Standish points out, there is no reason why "the ultimate usefulness of certain activities should make them any less intrinsically rich" (2006, p. 224). Furthermore, it has been suggested that the arts and artistic exercises – typically considered as belonging to the liberal aspect of education – are becoming more and more useful in developing the competencies needed in modern working life (Brater, 2008). These competencies are often based on a dialogical-explorative approach, where perception and feeling play significant roles. Such an approach to work is similar to that of the creative artist. However, limiting ourselves to the basic, comprehensive education of children and youth, we may take the vocational aim as of relatively less importance in the sense that comprehensive schooling does not aim at specific vocations. It is only vocational to the degree that it is *preparing* for the acquisition of specific vocational competencies.

As for civic education, Martha Nussbaum (1997) and others have argued that *empathy* is a basic virtue of future democratic citizens, which should be *citizens of the world*, not merely formal citizens of their own nation. Empathy is largely based on the ability to imagine oneself "in the shoes of another". Imagination is developed by, among other things, the reading of literature. Hence literary studies, a traditional liberal arts subject, are also related to civic education. In fact, liberal, civic and vocational educational aims all belong together like organs in an organism; they cannot be taken as independent and isolated from each other. If education is based on the idea that they belong to isolated realms it risks being flawed.[3]

Biesta (2010) makes another threefold distinction regarding education and its aims that is interesting in this context: he calls them qualification, socialisation and subjectification.

There is a certain parallel between these three dimensions of education and the vocational, civic and liberal aims discussed above: qualification is for working life, socialisation is for adaptation to society and subjectification has to do with becoming a "subject", developing a sense of self and identity. All three dimensions are always more or less involved in any educational process, but there are also potential conflicts between them. Today, Biesta maintains, subjectification is – or should be – the centre of gravity, that which so to speak holds education together, because it has to do with democracy and freedom. Because of its connection to freedom, subjectification, like the liberal aims discussed above, links back to Kant and the Enlightenment idea of personal autonomy. Kant may therefore be seen as one of the first philosophers that made it possible to distinguish socialisation from subjectification, or external adaptation from inner freedom. (But the distinction has an obvious forerunner in the words of Christ: "Be in the world but not of the world"). However, within twentieth-century philosophy a certain dissociation from all forms of humanism has taken place, because – it is argued – they are all based on a necessarily exclusivist definition of the human essence. For instance, Kant and Enlightenment humanism (which constitutes much of the basis for classical political liberalism) sees *Reason* as the essence of human beings, thereby in effect excluding "non-reasonable" individuals from humanity (and in extreme cases justifying their extinction). By letting subjectification replace autonomy Biesta dissociates himself from such ideas, emphasising a completely open-ended human *becoming* instead of *being*. Perhaps it could be said that Biesta suggests a new, "post-liberal" humanism, for which the open-ended becoming of human subjectivity is the central issue.[4]

The examples above, illustrating that liberal education is related both to civic and to vocational educational aims (or that subjectification is related to qualification and socialisation), suggest that the liberal aspect, or subjectification, is actually the most basic aim of education. This is certainly an idea that takes more than a few examples to verify or make plausible; I nevertheless contend that it is so. It is a view of education that has certain links back to the German and Continental European idea of *Bildung* (often related to liberal or "liberal arts" education in Anglophone countries). The idea of *Bildung* has been central to German educational thought (Westbury *et al.*, 2000). It is – or was originally with the early Romantics (Beiser, 2000; 2006) – a *spiritual* concept of education and its aim. Now, the UK Education Reform Act of 1988 explicitly says that one of the general purposes of the school curriculum is to promote the "spiritual" development of pupils, in addition to "moral, cultural, mental and physical development". But all of these, except the physical, could actually be taken as aspects of spiritual development.

However, the Reform Act does not give any definition of "spiritual", which has caused some debate over the possible meaning of the term. Various definitions or descriptions have been put forward, most of them trying to distinguish spirituality from religion. Religion is then seen as based on confessional belief in a dogma handed down by tradition and the adherence to a particular congregation of faith, whereas spirituality is open to many different religious ideas and does not necessarily adhere to one particular congregation. Critics, however, maintain that it is impossible to come to a consensus of the meaning of spirituality and therefore it is meaningless to state it as an aim in the national curriculum plan. Perhaps it is even against the ethical neutrality of a secular democratic state to endorse such an educational aim (Watson, 2000). Against the latter view one could argue that surveys have showed that a substantial part of the population in modern societies agree they have had spiritual experiences of one form or another, in

UK and USA as much as 30 percent (Rolph, 1991). Why should state school curricula not reflect this fact about their citizens?

Winch and Gingell for their part hold that spiritual aims for education are unrealistic: "one can be well educated as we currently understand it and, at the same time, neurotic, selfish and incapable of sustaining relationships" (2004, p. 32). But they also put forward the "liberal aims" of education as reasonable and these aims they say encompass such abilities as *to appreciate one's culture* and *to make choices about the direction in which one wants one's life to go*. Such choices are difficult to make if one is at the same time "neurotic, selfish and incapable of sustaining relations". On the other hand, to be mentally sound, unselfish, and capable of sustaining relations are qualities of soul and spirit that help one to appreciate one's culture and make important life choices. Spirituality is therefore actually the basis of the liberal aims of education.

Education for reality

I will end these reflections on the aims of education by considering the idea of the German philosopher Robert Spaemann, that education (German *Erziehung*) does not really have an aim (Speamann, 1987/88). *Teaching* and *instruction* have aims, but not education, because education is part of life, and life does not have any other purpose than to be lived. We learn throughout life, but what we learn is a secondary "outcome" of living, it is not intentionally planned. The paradigmatic example of education for Spaemann is learning to talk one's mother tongue. Of course there may be more or less frequent instances where parents or other adults explicitly teach the child words and grammar, but these are nevertheless exceptions. Spoken language is generally acquired as a *side effect* as the child simply *partakes of life* in and outside of the family.

In former times, Spaemann admits, there could be general aims of education, but different for different social groups and classes; for instance, the ideal of the Knight, the Gentleman, or the Housewife. In a democratic, pluralistic society this is no longer possible. It seems that Spaemann here thinks mainly of what Biesta (2010) calls the socialisation and qualification aspects of education. Nevertheless (and somewhat contradictory) Spaemann also suggests that there *is* a general purpose to education, which he calls "*Erziehung zur Wirklichkeit*", translatable as *education for reality*. (Perhaps the contradiction dissolves if education primarily happens through participation in life, as Spaemann maintains.) Reality is actually not real to all people, Spaemann claims. That is, the world is not seen as it is objectively, but as distorted by personal opinions, interests, likes, and dislikes. The claim that there actually is, or could be, an objective view of reality is of course an outrage to present constructivist and post-structural epistemological sensibilities, but Spaemann simply does not adhere to these modes of thinking.

Since "education for reality" has something to do with the correction of subjective distortions, or the prevention of their arising, it necessarily involves self-reflection. Self-reflection in turn has to do with identity and meaning, that is, with subjectification. Subjectification may seem to contradict objectivity but the contradiction is only apparent, if we accept the insights of existential phenomenology and post-structural strands of thought that we and the world, subject and object, *mutually constitute each other* (cf. Tarnas, 2006).[5]

Einstein is reported saying that "reality is not a given, it is a task" – a task of education and of life, we could add. But for Spaemann, this task is not scientific but primarily social and moral: it has to do with love. Only through love does the Other become real for me. An education for reality is therefore an education to love. Children first of all need to *be loved* in order to become real to themselves. That is the basis out of which they learn to love others.

Love makes me real. When I am real, others are real and the world is real. When the world is real we face its beauty as well as its horror. This usually inspires moral ideals and the wish to do good. But in order to act fruitfully we need knowledge and understanding, even wisdom. So we set out to learn more about the world and about ourselves.

Schools that emphasise liberal education or the arts and humanities more than the acquisition of "useful" knowledge (qualification) are often considered to be alien to life or "unrealistic" – maybe because reality in our culture is very often understood in a Freudian manner. Reality, for Freud, is that which *frustrates* our dreams and desires. Children, therefore, have to learn that the real world is bound to frustrate their innermost dreams, and school is a good place to learn that. The so-called "reality principle" has to replace the childish "pleasure principle". But reality for Spaemann is not that which frustrates our desires, on the contrary: reality is that which fulfils our deepest human/ spiritual desires or needs; it is the unity of Beauty and Truth.

I began by saying that the most general purpose of education is to help human beings find individual fulfilment and meaning in life – a purpose that is obviously related to the "liberal aims" of education. Now with Spaemann I would add that true meaning and fulfilment in life is surely not possible to find "outside reality", in an understanding of the world based on illusions and deceptions. So education must be "to reality"; this must be part of the ultimate and overriding purpose. That reality in our postmodern times is actually a contested concept (Anderson, 1992) does not take anything away from this obligation of the older to the younger generation. But it makes it a greater moral challenge than ever before. Reality is no longer a neutral fact but a deeply moral question.

Notes

1   In Sweden, religious education has been non-confessional since the 1950s and other countries have later followed this idea.
2   Johann A. Comenius propagated the idea of a common free schooling for all children as early as the 17th century (Comenius, 1967). Educational ideas and ideals often take a long time to be realized in practice.
3   The three aims of liberal, civic and vocational education can be seen in a larger social context by relating them to the three basic spheres of society or culture, state and "market" or economy, called by some the institutional metaphors of the modern world (Scott, 1998). Rudolf Steiner, the inaugurator of the now worldwide Steiner-Waldorf school movement, diagnosed the problem of modern social structure as the imbalance between these spheres, which ideally should be (relatively) autonomous. His idea of a general schooling for all children up to 18 years old was related to this social vision (Steiner, 1997). From Steiner's point of view education itself belongs essentially to the cultural sphere, and liberal education is for culture. The cultural sphere, which includes science, is the realm where freedom should reign because freedom is necessary for creativity to flourish. It is also the realm where individuals can seek and find "the good life" for themselves. Civic education is for the state. The basic value in the state sphere is equality: as citizens we should all have the same rights and the same obligations as far as ability allows, a principle that is recognized in all democratic states. Vocational education is for economy. Ideally, in the economical sphere "brotherhood" or solidarity should be the basic value, not profit and competition as under present capitalist conditions – but this issue is too comprehensive to consider here (cf. Dahlin, 2010).

4 It is however questionable whether Biesta's (and others') critique of philosophical humanism is altogether justifiable. It seems partly based on a conflation of the ideas of particular philosophers and the socio-political reception and "implementation" of these ideas. See also Laverty (2009) for a critique of Biesta's critique of Kant.

5 Tarnas is concerned with the cultural bias of traditional Western knowledge but also with preserving what has been accomplished within this tradition:

> The remarkable modern capacity for differentiation and discernment that has been so painstakingly forged must be preserved, but our challenge now is to develop and subsume that discipline in a more encompassing, more magnanimous intellectual and spiritual engagement with the mystery of the universe. Such an engagement can happen only if we open ourselves to a range of epistemologies that together provide a more multidimensionally perceptive scope of knowledge. To encounter the depths and rich complexity of the cosmos, we require ways of knowing that fully integrate the imagination, the aesthetic sensibility, moral and spiritual intuition, revelatory experience, symbolic perception, somatic and sensuous modes of understanding, empathic knowing. Above all, we must awaken to and overcome the great hidden anthropocentric projection that has virtually defined the modern mind: the pervasive projection of soullessness onto the cosmos by the modern self's own will to power. (2006, p. 55; italics in original)

References

Anderson, W. T. (1992). *Reality isn't what it used to be: Theatrical Politics, Ready-to-wear Religion, Global Myths, Primitive Chic and Other Wonders of the Postmodern World*. San Francisco, CA: Harper San Francisco.

Ball, S. J. (2003). The teacher's soul and the terrors of performativity. *Journal of Education Policy, 18*, 215–228.

Beiser, F. C. (2000). A romantic education: the concept of *Bildung* in early German Romanticism. In A. Oksenberg-Rorty (Ed.), *Philosophers on education. Historical perspectives* (pp. 130–142). London & New York: Routledge.

——(2006). Romanticism. In R. Curren (Ed.), *A companion to philosophy of education* (pp. 130–142). Oxford: Blackwell.

Biesta, G. (2010). *Good Education in an Age of Measurement: Ethics, Politics, Democracy*. Boulder, Colo: Paradigm Publishers.

Bourdieu, P. and Passeron, J. (1977). *Reproduction in Education, Society and Culture*. London: Sage.

Brater, M. (2008). Wie kann eine Hochschule berufliche Handlungskompetenz ausbilden? Anmerkungen zur Hochschuldidaktik. In J. Schieren (Ed.), *Bildungsmotive in Kunst und Wissenschaft* (pp. 137–162). Oberhausen, DE: Athena.

Comenius, J. A. (1967). *The Great Didactic*. New York: Russell & Russell.

Dahlin, B. (2010). Steiner Waldorf education, social three-folding and civil society: education as cultural power. *RoSE – Research on Steiner Education, 1*(1); 49–59.

Green, A. (1990). *Education and State Formation*. London: Macmillan.

Hornsey, M. J. and Hogg, M. A. (2000). Intergroup similarity and subgroup relations: some implications for assimilation. *Personality and Social Psychology Bulletin, 26*, 948–958.

Laverty, M. J. (2009). Gert J. J. Biesta, Beyond Learning: Democratic Education for a Human Future. *Studies in Philosophy and Education, 28*, 569–576.

Moghaddam, F. M. and Solliday, E. A. (1991): 'Balanced multiculturalism' and the challenge of peaceful coexistence in pluralistic societies. *Psychology and Developing Societies, 3*, 51–72.

Neef, D. (Ed.). (1998). *The Knowledge Economy*. Oxford: Butterworth-Heinemann.

Nussbaum, M. C. (1997). *Cultivating Humanity: A Classical Defense of Reform in Liberal Education*. Cambridge, Mass.: Harvard University Press.

Reeve, C. D. C. (2000). Aristotelian education. In A. Oksenberg-Rorty (Ed.), *Philosophers on Education. Historical Perspectives* (pp. 51–65). London & New York: Routledge.

Rolph, J. (1991). Can there be quality in teacher education without spirituality? *Assessment & Evalutaion in Higher Education, 16*, 49–55.

Scott, P. (1998). Decline or transformation? The future of the university in a knowledge economy and a post-modern age. In P. Baggen, A. Tellings and W. van Haaften (Eds.), *The University and the Knowledge Society* (pp. 13–30). Bemmel/London/Paris: Concorde Publishing House.

Spaemann, R. (1987/88). Erziehung zur Wirklichkeit. *Scheidewege, 17*, 136–146.

Standish, P. (2006). The nature and purposes of education. In R. Curren (Ed.), *A Companion to the Philosophy of Education* (pp. 221–231). Oxford: Blackwell.

Steiner, R. (1997). *Education as a Force for Social Change. Lectures.* New York: Anthroposophic Press.

Tarnas, R. (2006). *Cosmos and Psyche: Intimations of a New Worldview.* New York: Viking Press.

Watson, J. (2000). Whose model of spirituality should be used in the spiritual development of school children? *International Journal of Children's Spirituality, 5*, 91–101.

Westbury, I., Hopmann, S. and Riquarts, K. (Eds.). (2000). *Teaching as a Reflective Practice: The German Didaktik Tradition.* Mahwah, N.J.: Lawrence Erlbaum.

Winch, C. and Gingell, J. (2004). *Philosophy & Educational Policy. A Critical introduction.* London & New York: RoutledgeFalmer.

Intellectual goals in the early years

Lilian G. Katz

Clearinghouse on Early Education and Parenting, Editor,
Early Childhood Education and Parenting,
University of Illinois, Urbana-Champaign

All teachers at all levels of education have to address the question: What should be learned? Their answers to this question are based on their understanding of the main purposes of education. What are the main purposes of education in the early years? How should teachers of our youngest children answer this question? The education of young children can address a wide range and long list of purposes.

The field of early education has a long history of dissention concerning appropriate goals, curriculum and teaching methods. Sometimes the dissention was phrased as "Child-centered versus teacher-centered" or "Progressive versus traditional". However, these contrasts over-simplify the issues teachers must address when considering the purposes of their own work with young children. I suggest that when it comes to the main purposes of education – at all levels and not just the early years – it is useful to focus on four basic goals, (a) knowledge (and understanding), (b) skills, (c) dispositions, and (d) feelings.

The goal of helping children to acquire knowledge (as well as understanding) is placed at the top of the list not because it is more important than the other listed goals of long-term development, but because the acquisition of important knowledge is a goal uniquely assigned to educational institutions. I have added also the concept of "understanding" to emphasize that a major accomplishment in the early years is the development of deeper and more accurate understanding of what may only be superficially understood at first (e.g. early understanding of the calendar).

During the early years, educational and child-care settings are also expected to help the young to acquire important developmentally appropriate skills. Such skills include social skills, physical skills (fine and gross motor skills), cognitive skills, literacy skills, and numerous others. Indeed, depending upon how specific we want to be, the number of skills to be acquired in the first five or six years of life is a very large one.

Dispositions are difficult to define. They are often thought of as habits of mind that are associated with motives as well as some emotions. There are many social dispositions (e.g. being friendly or unfriendly, bossy or cooperative, generous, competitive, etc.) and many intellectual dispositions as well (e.g. expressing curiosity, creativity, being analytical, observant, etc.). Feelings refer to emotions such as joy, anxiety, fear, love, and many others. These four kinds of educational goals are discussed in greater detail below.

Four kinds of learning goals

Many discussions about desirable goals or purposes of education refer to what children should "know and be able to do". Rarely is any reference made to the idea that the children should not only know, but also that they also understand what they know. I am reminded of an incident reported to me by a kindergarten teacher about her five-year-old grandson who was in his sixth month of attendance at a school in a distant city. He called her to report that his teacher had "messed up the calendar today! She put a number 1 on the blackboard instead of 32 for the number!" His judgment of the teacher's behavior indicated a gap between his knowledge and his understanding of the calendar and the dates it signifies.

During the early childhood years, knowledge includes a wide range of facts, concepts, vocabulary, stories, songs, ideas, and many other aspects of children's culture. As already suggested, the goal concerning knowledge should also emphasize the gradual deepening of *understanding* the facts, concepts, and ideas as they arise. Thus the role of parents and teachers as well as older siblings and friends is to offer answers to young children's questions, to probe their thinking, and to provide clarifications and explanations for events and phenomena that interest them. In other words, one of the main purposes of early education is to help the children to make fuller and more accurate and deeper sense of their own experiences and environment.

Skills

The term *skills* usually refers to small units of action that occur in a relatively short period of time and are fairly easily observed or inferred from observation or from examining its products (e.g. graphic skills indicated by a child's observational drawing). Physical, social, verbal, reading, counting, and drawing skills are among a few of the almost endless number of skills being learned during the early years. Skills can be learned from direct instruction or by imitation when observing others in the action of applying them.

Dispositions

As already suggested, dispositions can be thought of as habits of mind or tendencies to respond to certain kinds of situations in particular ways. Curiosity, friendliness, bossiness, generosity, meanness, and creativity are just a few examples of dispositions, rather than kinds of knowledge, understanding, or skills. Accordingly, it is useful for us as teachers of young children to keep in mind that we want children to acquire significant and useful knowledge, understandings, and skills, and *at the same time* to develop and strengthen the dispositions to use them. For example, we want children to learn the essential knowledge and understandings and skills to enable them to read; but we also want them, at the same time, to acquire the disposition to be readers. It is not just a matter of learning to enjoy reading; rather it is having the habit of reading so that as children grow into adulthood they have the disposition to read in order to gain information and knowledge. If the experiences involved in acquiring the necessary knowledge, understandings, and skills to be able to read are too painful or boring, the learner may master them, but resolve never to use the reading skills outside of the setting in which they have been learned! In other words, answers to the question of what are purposes of education and what should be learned should include: the knowledge, understandings, and skills required to become a competent reader *plus* at the same time, a strong disposition to be a reader.

Dispositions are not learned through instruction or drill. The dispositions that children need to acquire or to strengthen, for example, curiosity, creativity, cooperation, and friendliness, are learned primarily from being around people who exhibit them. It is unfortunate that some dispositions, such as to be curious – that is most likely in-born in all children, though probably stronger in some than in others – are rarely displayed by adults in front of the children. Furthermore, for dispositions to be strengthened and maintained, they must be used fairly frequently, and appreciated by those adults whose responses matter to the children.

Feelings

Feelings are not easy to define, but they are experiences of which we all are aware and can recognize. They are probably best thought of as subjective emotional states, many of which are innate, but many of which are learned from experience. Among these are feelings of competence, or feelings of incompetence, similarly feelings of belonging or not belonging, and so forth. Feelings about school, teachers, learning, and peers are also learned in the early years.

Academic versus intellectual goals

To return to the matter of the main purposes of education, a strong trend has emerged in the US and several other countries to emphasize supporting young children's readiness for school by introducing academic instructional activities during the preschool years. These trends represent a return to teacher-centered tradition purposes and instructional methods as well. However, I want to suggest that the issue involved is not a simple matter of making a choice between emphasizing academic instruction *versus* traditional spontaneous play activities. The main argument here is that much of the discussion and debate about appropriate early years curricula is based on a misleading dichotomy – between offering young children formal academic instruction versus child-centered play, cutting and pasting. I suggest that a more useful way of looking at the choices involved in the early years curriculum approaches is to examine the distinctions between *academic* and *intellectual* goals and activities, especially during the early years.

Academic goals

Academic goals are those concerned with acquiring small discrete bits of disembedded information, usually related to pre-literacy skills that must be practiced in drills, and worksheets, and other kinds of exercises designed to prepare them for later literacy and numeracy learning. In an academic curriculum the items learned and practiced require correct answers, rely heavily on memorization, on the application of formulae versus understanding. The activities consist largely of giving the teacher the correct answers that the children know she awaits. Although one of the traditional meanings of the term *academic* is "of little practical value," these bits of information are essential components of reading and other academic competences. The question here is not whether academic skills matter; rather it is: *When* does their acquisition matter?

Intellectual goals and their related activities, on the other hand, address the life of the mind in its fullest sense, including a range of aesthetic and moral sensibilities. The formal definition of the concept of *intellectual* emphasizes reasoning, hypothesizing, predicting, the quest for understanding and conjecturing as well as the development and analysis of ideas. An appropriate curriculum for young children focuses on supporting their in-born intellectual dispositions, for example, the disposition to make the best sense they can of their own experience and environment. An appropriate curriculum in the early years is one that encourages and motivates children to seek mastery of basic academic skills, for example, beginning writing skills *in the service of their intellectual pursuits*. The children should be able to sense the purposefulness of their efforts to master a variety of academic skills and to appreciate their usefulness and their various purposes.

There are at least two points to emphasize in connection with the importance of intellectual goals. The first is that it is easy to mistakenly assume that because some young children have not been exposed to the knowledge and skills associated with "school readiness" they lack the basic intellectual dispositions – such as to make sense of experience, to analyze, hypothesize, predict – as do their peers of more affluent backgrounds. Children of very low-income families may not have been read to or held a pencil at home. But I suggest that it is a good idea to assume that they too have lively minds. Indeed, the intellectual challenges many children face in coping with precarious environments are likely to be substantial and often complex.

Second, while intellectual dispositions may be weakened or even damaged by excessive and premature formal instruction, they are also not likely to be strengthened by many of the trivial if not banal activities frequently offered in child care and other early years programs. The main point here is that in our early years practices we are not caught between a curriculum largely focused on formal academic lessons or, on the other hand, the fairly mindless cutting and pasting "refrigerator art" activities as along with spontaneous play time. I visited a school district in one of our Western states not long ago in which the kindergartens had adopted as a theme for the year "Teddy Bears". In the classroom visited, each of the children was expected to "show and tell" about his or her own teddy bears, to count a collection, to measure their lengths and obtain their weights and make up stories with them as main characters. While such activities are probably not harmful and may even be fun for the children, they are not intellectually engaging or stimulating.

By contrast, when young children engage in projects in which they conduct investigations of significant objects and events around them for which they have developed the research questions, their intellectual capacities are provoked and used. In the course of these investigations that are a part of their curriculum, the children's minds are fully engaged as they themselves find out how things work, what things are made of, where they come from, who does what, what tools they use, and in general what people around them do to contribute to their well-being, as can be seen in many reports of project work in the early years (see reports of projects in each issue of *Early Childhood Research and Practice* http://ecrp.uiuc.edu). Furthermore, the usefulness and importance of being able to read, write, measure and count, and make charts, become self-evident in the course of good project work (Katz and Chard, 2000; Helm and Katz, 2001).

Another factor to consider here is that frequently, academic instruction puts children in a passive and receptive role, whereas during the investigations conducted in project work the children are in an active, assertive role; they take initiative and responsibility in determining the research questions to be answered, and what data to collect and how and where to go to obtain the relevant data and how to represent and document it (see Katz and Chard, 2000).

The distinction between short-term versus long-term effects of early academic instruction

While many academic skills are both useful and essential, the question to raise here again is a developmental one, namely: at what point in the course of development are academic exercises most appropriate? We all agree with the proposition that learning to read – and in the process, acquiring the disposition to be readers – is a major educational goal during the early years. But just *when* this instruction and processes should be started and with what intensity raises many questions among those concerned with our youngest children.

No doubt one of the factors accounting for increasing interest in formulating clear outcomes and standards for preschool programs may be the recent and growing recognition of the role of stimulation in early brain development. However, Blair's analysis of neurological research does not imply that formal academic instruction is the way to optimize early brain development (Blair, 2002). On the contrary, Blair proposes a neurobiological model of school readiness based on his analysis of recent neurological data, the implications of which are that early years programs are best when they focus on social, emotional, and intellectual goals rather than on drill on narrow academic skills. On the basis of his model, an *intellectually*, rather than *academically* focused, approach is most likely to yield desirable "school readiness" as well as longer term benefits. Blair's analysis emphasizes the positive role of early experiences that provoke self-regulation, initiative, and what he calls synchronous interaction in which the child is interactive with others rather than a mere passive recipient of isolated bits of information.

Furthermore, the common sense notion that "earlier is better" is not supported by longitudinal studies of the long-term effects of different kinds of preschool curriculum models. On the contrary, a number of longitudinal follow-up studies indicate that while formal instruction produces good test results in the short term, early years curriculum and teaching methods emphasizing children's interactive roles and providing frequent opportunities for them to exercise initiative, while not so impressive in the short term, yield better school participation and achievement in the long term (Golbeck, 2001; Marcon, 2002).

There are two points to emphasize about the implications of these data concerning the effects of different early years curricula. One is that only in the long term are the disadvantages of early formal instruction apparent. The disadvantages are not usually observable in the short term. To some unknowable extent the apparent short-term benefits of formal instruction are related to the extent to which the curriculum prepares the children to respond to the items on the tests! Obviously, preschoolers who do not have formal academic instruction related to items on the tests are less likely to perform well on them.

The second point is that early formal instruction, in the long term, is apparently more damaging to boys than to girls. Explanations for this finding are not entirely clear. One interpretation of this finding may be that in most cultures, girls generally learn to accept a passive role (the essence of academic instruction) early and accept it more easily than do boys. On the whole, boys appear to prefer active and interactive experiences, and in most cultures are expected to be more visibly assertive than girls. Another possible explanation is the well-known fact that girls mature neurologically slightly earlier than boys, but that they catch up with each other around the age of eight years.

Conclusion

Taken together, these goals and sets of distinctions suggest that formal academic instruction may not be an appropriate purpose of education in the early years, and may not be in the best interests of many of our young children, and in fact, may be damaging *in the long term*. However, early childhood curriculum and teaching methods are best when they address children's lively minds so that they have frequent opportunities to be fully intellectually engaged as well as to engage in spontaneous play, and not just cutting and pasting and producing "refrigerator art". The incorporation of the Project Approach can provide young children with ample opportunities to strengthen their intellectual dispositions as they learn a great deal about their own environments.

References

Blair, C. (2002). School readiness: integrating cognition and emotion in a neurological conceptualization of child functioning at school entry. *American Psychologist, 57,* 111–127.

Goldbeck, S. L. (2001). Instructional models for early childhood: in search of child-regulated/teacher guided pedagogy. In Goldbeck, S. (Ed.) *Psychological Perspectives on Early Childhood Education: Reframing Dilemmas in Research and Practice* (pp. 153–189). NY: Erlbaum.

Helm, J. H. and Katz, L. G. (2011). *Young Investigators. The Project Approach in the Early Years.* NY: Teachers College Press.

Katz, L. G. and Chard, S. C. (2000) *Engaging Children's Minds. The Project Approach.* Stamford, CT: Ablex Publishing Corporation.

Marcon. R. A. (2002) Moving up the grades: the relationship between preschool model and later school success. *Early Childhood Research & Practice, 4*(1). Retrieved from: http:ecrp.uiuc.edu/v4n1/marcon.html (accessed 25 January 2012).

Chapter 3

De Groot's lesson

John Sweller

University of New South Wales

There have been many findings in cognitive psychology that are relevant to instruction. Arguably, one of the most important was de Groot's (1965) finding on memory of chess board configurations. That work was not merely a breakthrough; it changed our understanding of human cognition and indeed our understanding of ourselves. We have, more or less routinely, seen ourselves as being differentiated from the rest of the animal kingdom by our ability to solve problems. We knew we were skilled at problem solving but we did not really know why because the cognitive machinery required was a mystery. De Groot's work has played a very large part in de-mystifying and describing that machinery. As a consequence of our knowledge of what constitutes problem-solving skill, we also are in a position to determine instructional procedures that can facilitate skill acquisition. There is considerable evidence that the skills identified by de Groot translate directly to educationally relevant domains (Chiesi *et al.*, 1979; Egan and Schwartz, 1979; Jeffries *et al.*, 1981; Sweller and Cooper, 1985). I will begin by reviewing de Groot's findings.

De Groot was concerned with the factors that permit chess grand-masters to always defeat weekend players. Chess is a problem-solving game with the best problem solver winning. It was easy to conclude that chess grand-masters were better problem solvers than weekend players but what did that mean? What did grand-masters do, what did they know to always defeat weekend players?

De Groot began by testing two, closely related hypotheses. The first was that better chess players engaged in a greater search in depth. That means that before making a move, they considered more moves ahead. For example, rather than planning ahead by 3 moves they might look 6 moves ahead. The more moves ahead that a player considers, the greater the probability of finding a good series of moves. While it was plausible to hypothesise that looking more moves ahead might account for differential chess skill, that hypothesis was not supported. De Groot found that chess grand-masters did not look ahead more moves than weekend players.

All was not lost in de Groot's investigation of chess players because there is an equally plausible, related hypothesis. Rather than engaging in a greater search in depth, chess grand-masters might engage in a greater search in breadth. That means that they might consider a greater range of possible moves at each point. For example, rather than considering 3 alternatives moves whenever it was their turn to make a move, they might consider 6 alternative moves. Again, if more moves are considered, the chances of generating a good move should be increased. Unfortunately, the hypothesis that differential search in breadth could account for differential chess skill turned out to be no more valid than differential search in depth. Chess grand-masters did not consider a greater range of moves than weekend players. Differential ability to search for novel moves did not distinguish chess masters from less able players and so did not explain why grand-masters defeated weekend players.

At this point, the mystery had merely deepened. Chess grand-masters always defeat weekend players but they seemed not to do anything cognitively to effect this outcome. The next test of de Groot's chess players finally established a difference, although it was in many ways a strange difference. Both grand-masters and weekend players were shown a chess-board configuration, for about 5 seconds, consisting of pieces taken from a real game. The board then was removed and participants were asked to replace the pieces in the configuration that they had just seen. Grand-masters were particularly good at this task, replacing the pieces with an accuracy rate of about 70 percent. In contrast, weekend players had an accuracy rate of about 30 percent on the same task.

Chase and Simon (1973) replicated this result and in addition, ran the experiment again using random board configurations rather than configurations taken from real games. For random configurations, the superiority of chess-grand-masters disappeared. Both grand-masters and weekend players had an accuracy rate of about 30 percent for random board configurations. The superior memory of grand-masters applied only to board configurations taken from real games. While a basic difference between more and less able chess players had finally been established, what did it mean?

Cognitive implications of de Groot's work

De Groot's findings raise several questions: (a) why can chess grand-masters remember board configurations taken from real games so well, (b) why does their ability to remember board configurations taken from real games disappear when the configurations are random, and (c) what do these results tell us about the human cognitive system? First, de Groot's (1965) and Chase and Simon's (1973) work provides us with an explanation of those aspects of problem-solving skill that can be acquired. We can learn to recognise problem states and the best move or moves associated with those states. Chess grand-masters could readily reproduce board configurations taken from real games because they had seen those configurations before, probably on numerous occasions. They recognised those configurations and they understood the "meaning" of those configurations in the sense that they had learned which move sequences could lead to an advantageous outcome and which would not. All of that knowledge was stored in long-term memory and was activated when they saw a familiar configuration. They could not reproduce random board configurations better than weekend players because they had no more seen them before than anyone else. The superiority of grand-masters applied only to familiar configurations.

It may, of course, be argued that grand-masters could not possibly remember the huge number of configurations that they encounter but that would be missing the point. It takes at least 10 years of practice to become a chess grand-master (Ericsson and Charness, 1994). During that time, chess grand-masters not only play many games, they spend most of their waking hours studying previous games, especially important and famous games. They analyse why a particular configuration requires a particular move and the consequences of that move. Gradually, they build up a large repertoire of familiar configurations and the moves associated with those configurations. As a consequence, when shown a configuration from a real game, it is very likely to be a familiar configuration that they can readily reproduce. Over the years they may become familiar with literally tens of thousands of such configurations (Simon and Gilmartin, 1973). They win games because during a game, most of the configurations that they encounter are familiar ones for which they know the best move. Their opponents, with much less familiarity with the various problem states encountered, must engage in the difficult task of attempting to devise a problem-solving strategy. Chess grand-masters do not have to devise a strategy because they know the best moves that should be made. They can make a move quickly and without a great deal of conscious, cognitive processing.

These results explain some of the surprising skills of chess grand-masters. For example, they can simultaneously play a dozen weekend players and defeat all of them. We may ask how they possibly can devise a dozen game plans and keep track of all of them simultaneously. Such a cognitive feat is surely beyond even elevated human capacity. Indeed it is, but chess grand-masters playing simultaneous chess have knowledge that enables them to use a far simpler, far more plausible strategy. They do not need to remember and execute multiple, novel game plans. As they come to each board, they merely need to recognise the configuration and recall the best move associated with that configuration. Once that move is made they can temporarily forget about that particular game and move onto the next game, repeating the process. No more sophisticated planning is required. The hard work had been carried out years earlier when studying and practicing. It is their opponents, without the same information held in long-term memory, who must engage in the complex, on-the-spot planning processes associated with devising a viable game plan. The relatively low likelihood of *finding* the best move and defeating an opponent who *knows* the best move leads to a near inevitable result.

The major cognitive implication of this work is the central importance of long-term memory to cognition in general and problem-solving in particular. In the field of education, we tend to disparage the importance of long-term memory. Frequently, it is associated with "rote-learning" that, rightly, is seen as highly undesirable. While long-term memory can be used to rote learn information, rote learning is not the major function of long-term memory in human cognition. Instead, long-term memory is used to store complex, integrated information that permits us to appropriately process analogous incoming information and to determine appropriate action. I will use an example from simple arithmetic to demonstrate the process and simultaneously indicate the difference between learning by rote and learning with understanding. The role of long-term memory is critical to both.

Assume a student is learning to multiply two numbers such as $3 \times 4 = 12$. The student may rote learn that $3 \times 4 = 12$, which means that he or she has stored this fact in long-term memory. Assume the student does not understand the meaning of $3 \times 4 = 12$ at this point. Understanding begins only after more information has been memorised and stored in long-term memory. The first step may be to learn that 3×4 means 3 lots of 4 added together, i.e. $4 + 4 + 4$. At this point the student may have stored in long-term memory not just the element that $3 \times 4 = 12$, but the more complex element that $3 \times 4 = 4 + 4 + 4 = 12$. Note that the only factor that has changed cognitively is that the student has substituted a more complex element for a less complex element in long-term memory. No new cognitive process has occurred, just the storage of a relatively complex element in long-term memory. Understanding involves memorisation in the same manner as rote learning with the only difference being that more needs to be memorised.

Does the learner who has memorised $3 \times 4 = 4 + 4 + 4 = 12$ now "understand" the multiplication of 3×4? Of course not. Understanding is part of a continuum, not a category. We rarely move from rote learning to understanding in one step. Our student may next learn that $3 \times 4 = 12$ not only means that $3 \times 4 = 4 + 4 + 4 = 12$, but also means $3 \times 4 = 3 + 3 + 3 + 3 = 12$. More related information must be stored in long-term memory. Next, the student needs to learn that if $3 \times 4 = 4 + 4 + 4 = 12$ and $3 \times 4 = 3 + 3 + 3 + 3 = 12$, then $3 \times 4 = 4 + 4 + 4 = 3 + 3 + 3 + 3 = 12$. Further steps in the process of understanding require the student to relate multiplication not only to addition but to subtraction and division. Critically, each step involves the memorisation of ever larger, ever more complex sets of relations. The end result of this process of understanding is that the student holds in long-term memory a very complex set of relations that generalise to an infinite set of numbers. It can be suggested that exactly the same process applies to every curriculum area.

Understanding means memorising. It is knowledge held in long-term memory that results in understanding and it is the same knowledge that in an appropriate form and under appropriate conditions results in the problem-solving skill exhibited by chess masters and anyone else who has acquired problem-solving skill. None of this process would be possible without the huge long-term memory that constitutes a central component of human cognitive architecture. Long-term memory and its characteristics tend to be ignored or in many cases even derided by educationists insisting that its only function is to allow students to rote learn information. In fact, it is a central, possibly *the* central structure relevant to learning. By ignoring its critical function, I believe we have crippled the field of instructional design.

What de Groot did not find

De Groot's findings are critical to our understanding of human cognition. What he did not find is, in some ways, equally important. He did not find that chess grand-masters' superiority stems from the possession of complex, sophisticated general problem-solving strategies. Not only did de Groot fail to find such strategies, neither has anyone else in the subsequent decades. To this day, we have no evidence of a teachable/learnable general problem-solving strategy that improves learning and problem-solving. There is no evidence that chess grand-masters use such strategies and furthermore, the superior ability of masters seems to be fully explained by the long-term memory assumptions outlined above. If a sophisticated general problem-solving strategy ever is found we would need to establish that chess experts used it and we would need to explain why it was needed given the sufficiency of the long-term memory explanation for chess skill.

Not only is there no evidence that chess grand-masters use sophisticated general problem-solving strategies, there is no evidence that they use any unusual, complex, sophisticated cognitive strategies of any sort that could explain their superior skills. The absence of such strategies and skills casts into doubt their existence in a learnable/teachable form. De Groot's work in indicating both what does and does not constitute problem-solving expertise has substantial instructional implications.

It also should be noted that de Groot's findings do not necessarily indicate that chess experts have a better ability to store information in long-term memory than less able players. They simply have spent more time storing the relevant information. We all have stored large amounts of information in long-term memory related to areas in which we are skilled, as discussed in the next section.

Instructional implications

De Groot's lesson is that higher cognitive processes such as problem solving are inextricably associated with long-term memory. We are skilled in an area to the extent that we have acquired a large, domain-specific knowledge-base relevant to the area and stored it in long-term memory. Without that knowledge, we are unskilled.

As might be expected, de Groot's findings apply equally to common curriculum areas as to the game of chess. For example, findings analogous to those obtained in chess have been obtained in areas such as understanding and remembering text (Chiesi *et al.*, 1979), electronic engineering (Egan and Schwartz, 1979), programming (Jeffries *et al.*, 1981), and algebra (Sweller and Cooper, 1985). In all areas, more experienced learners who are presented with problem states taken from the area are more likely to be able to reproduce those states than less experienced learners. Competence in any area requires learners to have stored innumerable problem states and the best moves associated with those states in long-term memory and it is that knowledge that constitutes expertise.

Furthermore, the same arguments that apply to chess also apply to instructional areas commonly taught within an educational context. Not only does long-term memory explain competence, it may be sufficient to fully explain the learnable aspects of skill. If other general cognitive, as opposed to domain-specific knowledge, can be acquired, the required strategies first need to be described followed by evidence that they can be taught. Within an educational context, that evidence needs to include randomised, controlled experiments that test the effects of teaching students general problem-solving or cognitive strategies on far transfer problems. Far transfer problems are required as a test in order to eliminate the possibility that students are simply acquiring domain-specific knowledge. Despite decades of effort, there is no body of evidence supporting either the teachability of or even the existence of such skills. Until the required evidence becomes available, instructional procedures should concentrate on domain-specific knowledge rather than cognitive skills. As is the case for the game of chess, domain-specific skills may be the only ones that can be taught. Of course, just because domain-specific knowledge is critical for skilled performance does not mean that teachable, domain-general, cognitive skills do not exist. Nevertheless, the fact that domain-knowledge can explain acquired, skilled performance must call into question the function and necessity of putative, general cognitive skills that can be acquired.

Accordingly, the major purpose of instructional design is to facilitate the acquisition of knowledge. Cognitive load theory (Sweller, 2011; Sweller *et al.*, 2011) has been devised with this purpose in mind. While the theory is not only concerned with long-term memory but rather, with the entire human cognitive system as it applies to instructional design (Sweller, 2003; 2012), long-term memory and its relations to working memory are central. Long-term memory changes the characteristics of working memory. When dealing with novel information, working memory is very limited in terms of capacity (Cowan, 2001; Miller, 1956) and duration (Peterson and Peterson, 1959). That explains Chase and Simon's (1973) finding that chess players have a poor memory for random board configurations irrespective of levels of expertise. In contrast, when dealing with familiar information stored in long-term memory, there are no known capacity or duration limits. The lack of working memory limitations when dealing with familiar information stored in long-term memory explains the superiority of chess masters over weekend players when memorising board configurations taken from real games.

From an instructional perspective, cognitive load theory uses this cognitive architecture to devise instructional procedures intended to reduce working memory load. A reduced working memory load can be expected to facilitate the transfer of information to long-term memory. Once information is stored in long-term memory, we are transformed. Because of the reduction of working memory load attendant on information stored in long-term memory, we are able to carry out tasks including solving problems that we otherwise would have no possibility of completing. That education is transformational is, of course, a truism. De Groot's findings and their extension to instructional design explain why.

References

Chase, W. G. and Simon, H. A. (1973). Perception in chess. *Cognitive Psychology, 4*, 55–81.

Chiesi, H., Spilich, G. and Voss, J. (1979). Acquisition of domain-related information in relation to high and low domain knowledge. *Journal of Verbal Learning and Verbal Behaviour, 18*, 257–273.

Cowan, N. (2001). The magical number 4 in short-term memory: a reconsideration of mental storage capacity. *Behavioral and Brain Sciences, 24*, 87–114.

de Groot, A. (1965). *Thought and Choice in Chess*. The Hague, Netherlands: Mouton. (Original work published 1946).

Egan, D. E. and Schwartz, B. J. (1979). Chunking in recall of symbolic drawings. *Memory & Cognition, 7*, 149–158.

Ericsson, K. A. and Charness, N. (1994). Expert performance; its structure and acquisition. *American Psychologist, 49*, 725–747.

Jeffries, R., Turner, A., Polson, P. and Atwood, M. (1981). Processes involved in designing software. In J. R. Anderson (Ed.), *Cognitive Skills and their Acquisition* (pp. 255–283). Hillsdale, NJ: Erlbaum.

Miller, G. A. (1956). The magical number seven, plus or minus two: some limits on our capacity for processing information. *Psychological Review, 63*, 81–97.

Peterson, L. and Peterson, M. J. (1959). Short-term retention of individual verbal items. *Journal of Experimental Psychology, 58*, 193–198.

Simon, H. and Gilmartin, K. (1973). A simulation of memory for chess positions. *Cognitive Psychology, 5*, 29–46.

Sweller, J. (2003). Evolution of human cognitive architecture. In B. Ross (Ed.), *The Psychology of Learning and Motivation* (Vol. 43, pp. 215–266). San Diego: Academic Press.

——(2011). Cognitive load theory. In J. Mestre and B. Ross (Eds.), *The Psychology of Learning and Motivation: Cognition in Education* (Vol. 55, pp. 37–76). Oxford: Academic Press.

——(2012). Human cognitive architecture: why some instructional procedures work and others do not. In K. Harris, S. Graham and T. Urdan (Eds.), *APA Educational Psychology Handbook* (Vol. 1, pp. 295–325). Washington, D.C.: American Psychological Association.

Sweller, J. and Cooper, G. (1985). The use of worked examples as a substitute for problem-solving in learning algebra. *Cognition & Instruction, 2*, 59–89.

Sweller, J., Ayres, P. and Kalyuga, S. (2011). *Cognitive Load Theory*. New York: Springer.

Part II

What is the effect of non-parental childcare on child development?

Given that most mothers of young children in industrialized countries are working, with 57 percent to 60 percent of mothers with children under 5 years of age working outside the home in both Britain and the United States (Crosby & Hawkes, 2007), the actual question is not: "Is non-maternal childcare positive for children?", but rather, "How can we insure that non-maternal care is a positive force in children's development?"

Lynne Vernon-Feagans and Allison De Marco

[T]here is a paucity of understanding of what it *feels* like for the child while they are actually *in* daycare. This gap is partly due to the inherent difficulty in gauging such an internal experiential phenomenon at an age when infants and children have such a limited ability to describe their inner landscape … However, research methods from the biosciences have started to provide an illuminating glimpse of this landscape … [a]nd this voice is often singing a very different tune to that presented by the daycare establishment: There is something about attending daycare for an extended time … that often elicits stress in young children.

Aric Sigman

Chapter 4

Why non-maternal childcare can be good for children and families

Research and policy implications

Lynne Vernon-Feagans and Allison De Marco

The University of North Carolina at Chapel-Hill

Introduction

The use of non-parental childcare, or more accurately non-maternal care, became an issue in the United States and elsewhere as women/mothers began entering the paid workforce in large numbers in the 1970s. Even though this influx of women/mothers into the labor market happened more than 30 years after the Great Depression, the family values of that era still dominated American life, even as these values were inconsistent with the reality of the 1970s when more and more women/mothers began entering the paid workforce outside of the home. Because of these depression era values, women who worked outside the home were viewed as putting their families at risk. During the Great Depression, women were expected to turn down jobs that men could perform so that men could support their family (Anderson, 2001). In addition, it was thought that women who worked might jeopardize their bond with their children and the children might develop behavioral and other problems as a consequence. These traditional views of women in the larger culture of the United States clashed with the growing numbers of women who wanted or needed to work in the 1970s; and this clash created controversies about how society might address this change and about the effect on children's development.

In this chapter, we briefly describe the history of non-maternal care as the background for concerns in the United States about women, and especially mothers, working outside the home. This history helps to lay the groundwork for why maternal employment and especially non-maternal care for young children has become so controversial. We will elucidate how the research and scholarly community reacted to these societal concerns about non-maternal care, mostly in the United States, and argue that even under poor parental leave and subsidy policies, research results demonstrate that medium- to high-quality non-parental care is not detrimental to most children. Moreover, for almost all children, and certainly for our most at-risk children, the benefits of good non-parental care can be substantial in the areas of school readiness, academic success, and social/emotional adjustment. However, given that most mothers of young children in industrialized countries are working, with 57 to 60 percent of mothers with children under 5 years of age working outside the home in both Britain and the United States (Crosby and Hawkes, 2007), the actual question is not: "Is non-maternal childcare positive for children", but rather, "How can we insure that non-maternal care is a positive force in children's development?"

History of women's work in the United States

Women have always worked, but until the mid-twentieth century middle-class women's work was relegated to the home where they worked taking care of children, cooking, cleaning, and generating other resources for the family. Almost all of that work was unpaid. Low-income and minority women had always worked outside the home while still trying to raise children and keep their families together; however, their experience was not reflected in the mainstream cultural values about women and work and was largely ignored by the wider culture. By the time of the Great Depression, the traditional values about middle-class women's work were further solidified with so many men out of work. At that time, over 80 percent of Americans believed that women should not work outside the home if their husbands had a job (Yellin, 2004). Laws were even proposed that would prohibit married women from working. Both women and men believed that married women should leave their paid jobs if their husbands wanted them to (Yellin, 2004).

During World War II, women were needed to enter the paid workforce to do the jobs left vacant by men who were off fighting in the war in both the United States and Europe. Norman Rockwell's image on the cover of the *Saturday Evening Post* in 1943 was the first widely publicized pictorial representation of "Rosie the Riveter," and was used as a symbol of the need for women to work during the war as a patriotic gesture. Women responded to this call to work and thousands of women entered jobs that men had previously filled. During the war "Rosie" often found her job satisfying and challenging (Yellin, 2004), even though it was temporary: most of these women were generally let go from their jobs at the end of World War II as men returned home. Although most women went back to working in the home, their work experiences during World War II laid the groundwork for the next generation of women raised by "Rosie" and her peers. In the 1970s when Rosie's daughters began entering the paid workforce in large numbers, they were likely benefiting from their mothers' experiences during World War II.

Yet this new generation of young women/mothers in the 1970s faced considerable challenges because there were inadequate policies in place to accommodate their need for childcare and other supportive services. Most of these women entered the workforce out of necessity. Many of the young mothers wanted the opportunity to stay at home with their young children, but economically this was not possible. Other young women wanted the challenge of working outside of the home, coupled with having young children. Whatever the reason, beginning in the 1970s, the dramatic rise in non-maternal care for children, and especially young children, was unprecedented. For instance, in 1947, 12 percent of mothers with children younger than 5 were employed outside the home; today that figure is 64 percent. One quarter of women with children younger than 18 were employed in 1947 and now three-quarters of mothers are in the workforce (US Congress Committee on Ways and Means, 2000). This rise in maternal work was paralleled in European countries. For instance, in Britain, 39 percent of women were in the paid workforce after World War II but by 1997, this number had risen to 66 percent (Walsh and Wrigley, 2001). Yet, both values and policies in the United States and elsewhere have been slow to change in accommodating women's new status.

The central issue related to non-maternal care

The central issue related to non-maternal care is not whether women need to or will stay home to care for their young children, but rather how society can provide the resources (particularly high-quality childcare) necessary to ensure that all children develop optimally. Western societies, as a whole, were concerned that children who spent large parts of their day outside of the home environment might not be provided with the emotional support and resources available in the home setting. The reaction to women entering the paid workforce differed from country to country in the Western world, depending on the cultural values about maternal work. In the United States, the previously held cultural values regarding maternal work outside the home as detrimental to the family no doubt influenced the lack of supportive policies for women with young children. Since the 1970s few women have had access to maternal leave with or without pay at their child's adoption or birth, and few resources have been provided by employers or government agencies to subsidize childcare and/or provide high-quality childcare for young children. In a comparison of 31 Western countries, the United States ranked near the bottom on all parental leave and subsidy policies for working mothers (Ray *et al.*, 2009). These US policies have led many mothers to resort to a patchwork of childcare for their children while they worked, as well as shouldering the tasks of homemaker and mother (Clarke-Stewart and Allhusen, 2005).

On the other hand, countries like Sweden and Denmark addressed the issue of maternal work quite differently by providing long maternal/paternal leave policies, child subsidies, and generous sick leave and other leave to support families in which the mother worked. In Sweden, government-mandated paid parental leave has been available to both mothers and fathers since 1974 along with a host of other support services for families (Sundström, 1991). These Swedish policies were a reflection of the political and social forces in Sweden that aimed at gender equity and the preservation of families (Sundström, 1991). Thus, the controversy in many Scandinavian countries did not revolve around whether non-maternal care was good or bad but rather how society should accommodate maternal work by establishing policies that would enhance children's development. France, whose women only gained the right to vote in 1944, has become the unlikely leader in support of mothers' work because of the provision of universal free childcare for young children. Thirty-five percent of two-year-olds are enrolled in free all-day care and 100 percent of 3- to 6-year-old children receive free all-day care (Morgan, 2003). Thus, the proportion of mothers who work is higher in France than in any other European country and this is especially true for single mothers. Thus, while the Scandinavian countries and other European countries like France have moved forward to accommodate women's work, the United States has spent years debating the merits of maternal work, without addressing the central issue of the quality of care that children were receiving when mothers were forced to or chose to work outside the home.

Research on non-maternal childcare

Amount of childcare

In the first generation of research on non-maternal care, one of the major issues was the number of hours that children were spending in non-maternal care. Belsky and Rovine

(1988) published one of the first influential articles that suggested that children who spent more than 20 hours per week in childcare might develop suboptimal social/emotional functioning. This finding has been reframed and refined in more recent childcare work, suggesting that although children in care for more than 20 hours a week are rated by their teachers as displaying more behavior problems, they also experience positive influences on their cognitive and language development (NICHD ECCRN, 2003). Some research continues to indicate that more childcare hours are associated with more negative behavioral outcomes (Brooks-Gunn *et al.*, 2010; Loeb *et al.*, 2007; NICHD, 2004); however, in the NICHD (2004) study, the higher externalizing problems were not in the clinical or at-risk range and became nonsignificant by the time the child was in sixth grade (Belsky *et al.*, 2007).

A more nuanced examination of care hours now focuses not only on hours but also whether these hours are during regular work hours (7:00 a.m. to 6:00 p.m.), or whether they are during non-standard work hours, where mothers work non-traditional shifts and night work and have unpredictable work schedules that change from week to week or month to month (De Marco *et al.*, 2009). There has been recent evidence that this may be more detrimental to children, but it is not clear if this has to do with the lack of quality care available at these non-standard work hours and/or to the changing caregivers that often may be employed to manage such difficult work schedules (Han, 2007).

Type of care

There are three primary types of non-maternal childcare: relatives, family daycare homes/babysitters, and formal childcare centers. For many families, relatives take care of their children while parents work outside the home. These relatives might be a grandmother or non-resident father but could also be an older sibling or aunt, etc. Studies of type of care have provided mixed results, largely based on the age of the child. Studies that have examined infant childcare have found that grandmothers and fathers exhibit higher quality caregiving behaviors than family daycare homes and center-based care. On the other hand, most center-based care across the preschool years is related to better child outcomes for children in language and readiness skills, while children who are cared for at home have better behavioral outcomes (NICHD ECCRN, 2000).

Center-based care

Most of the research has examined center-based care in two different ways. Important long-term studies of childcare interventions for poor, minority or disabled children, using the best research designs such as randomized control trials, have clearly shown the benefits of early and later childcare experiences on children's achievement and adult life success (Campbell and Ramey, 1994; Vernon-Feagans, 1996). Children in these studies were in childcare five days a week, 50 weeks a year, with little controversy at the societal level about the children's lack of non-maternal care. This is largely due to the fact that these early intervention studies, including Head Start and Early Head Start, were aimed at helping poor and minority children whose families were deemed unable to provide them with the resources they needed to be successful in our society. Research assessing the Chicago Child-Parent Centers found that participation in these early intervention programs by children from high-poverty neighborhoods had effects into adolescence and beyond (Reynolds, 2000; Reynolds *et al.*, 2011). Participation prevented grade retention, high school dropout, and substance abuse while promoting higher educational attainment and income. In addition, benefits of quality childcare reach beyond individual children. The Perry Preschool Study found that every $1 spent on good-quality early childhood programs saved $7 in future costs related to welfare use, juvenile delinquency, and remedial education (Karoly *et al.*, 1998). Clearly, non-maternal care in these studies had very positive effects for both society and the children served.

On the other hand, studies of mixed groups of low-income and middle-income children have not always shown clear positive outcomes. For instance, the NICHD Study of Early Childcare and Youth Development that examined non-maternal care in 10 sites around the United States found that non-maternal care was positively related to children's development in language and cognition but produced mixed results with respect to behavioral outcomes, although even these slight negative behavioral outcomes were not of clinical significance (NICHD ECCRN, 2003).

Quality of childcare

Because, to a large extent, the US childcare system is designed as a work support for parents, high-quality care is not at the forefront and thus, overall, childcare quality is not high. High-quality childcare is defined as care that supports attachment and optimal learning and development (Howes *et al.*, 1992; Marshall, 2004). Childcare programs that do focus on quality, such as Head Start, do not reach all eligible children and do not meet the needs of working families who need care beyond the limited Head Start schedule. Furthermore, many young children are in childcare arrangements that are subject to little regulation, such as care by babysitters, relatives, and small family childcare homes (Phillips and Adams, 2001), particularly prevalent in rural communities (De Marco, 2008; Maher *et al.*, 2008; Whitener *et al.*, 2002). For arrangements that are regulated, such as large family childcare homes and centers, regulations are difficult to enforce due to the high cost of maintaining staffing sufficient to monitor all regulated childcare facilities. Phillips and Adams (2001) report that in most large-scale childcare studies approximately 20 percent of settings fall below minimal thresholds of adequate care. Three-quarters of caregivers provide only minimal cognitive and language stimulation, while one-fifth interacted in moderately or highly detached ways. Less than 25 percent of infants receive care from highly sensitive caregivers. Furthermore, in a study looking across the preschool period and using a largely working-class and middle-income sample, the NICHD (2004) has reported that observed childcare quality was generally not of high quality. In fact, only 17 percent of children experienced excellent-quality care across the preschool years while 11 percent of children experienced terrible-quality care. Thus, it appears that the United States has a long way to go in making sure all children receive quality care during the preschool years.

A substantial body of research has assessed quality in all types of childcare arrangements, finding high- and low-quality care across the board (Burchinal and Cryer, 2003; NICHD; 2002a; NICHD and Duncan, 2003; Phillips and Adams, 2001). A significant amount of research has also been conducted to assess the effect of childcare quality on child development (NICHD and Duncan, 2003; Belsky *et al.*, 2007). The Cost, Quality, and Outcome Study began following children in childcare centers, finding that high-quality care could ensure that children entered school ready to learn (Peisner-Feinberg *et al.*,

1999). Children in high-quality programs performed better on measures of cognitive skill, social skills, and displayed fewer problem behaviors during the transition to school. Most of these effects persisted through kindergarten and second grade.

Interrelated factors that contribute to quality are defined as either structural factors or process factors. Structural factors include child-to-caregiver ratio, group size, provider education level, and caregiver stability (Ceglowski and Davis, 2004; Marshall, 2004). These indicators are more easily regulatable and most states have set minimal standards. Conversely, process factors that characterize the quality of interactions between caregivers and children (e.g. more cognitive stimulation, more warmth, and more responsiveness) are not subject to regulation and are more difficult to measure. In terms of structural factors, a teacher who provides care to a smaller group of children is more able to tailor care to the particular needs of each child (Helburn and Howes, 1996; Larner et al., 2001). When ratios are lower, caregivers are more likely to be sensitive and warm (process factors) in their interactions with children, children are more likely to be emotionally attached to their caregivers and to be socially competent with peers (De Schipper et al., 2006; Vandell et al., 2000). Better ratios and higher caregiver education and training have been associated with children's increased language, cognitive, and social skills (Vernon-Feagans et al., 2007) while training in early childhood education was the most important factor in ensuring positive interactions between caregivers and children (Burchinal et al., 2002; NICHD, 2002b; Raikes et al., 2005; Honig and Hirallal, 1998).

The relationship between structural quality indicators and child outcomes is mediated by higher childcare process factors (sensitivity and responsiveness of caregivers) with lasting effects after one year, at kindergarten, and in the 2nd grade, though magnitudes declined.

Quality matters more for children with less

Although at the beginning of this chapter we mentioned that the early childcare intervention literature suggested that children from low-income and minority families benefit in many ways from early intervention in the form of full-time childcare (Campbell and Ramey, 1994), these carefully designed studies only included children who were at risk and were thus not able to draw conclusions about the effect of childcare on children who were more mainstream and middle-income. Some recent work has examined a more diverse group of children and childcare quality. These studies have reported that children from lower-quality home environments may be buffered against poorer outcomes by the provision of high-quality childcare (Burchinal et al., 2000; Dearing et al., 2009; Magnuson et al., 2004; McCartney et al., 2007; NICHD ECCRN, 2000). For instance, McCartney and colleagues (McCartney et al., 2007; Dearing et al. 2009), in a series of papers using the NICHD Study of Early Childcare, have explored whether childcare quality might benefit low-income children more than other children in predicting a variety of language and academic outcomes. They found that high-quality childcare buffered children from the negative effects of poverty with respect to receptive and expressive language skills. A variety of other preschool and prekindergarten studies have also supported this finding that high-quality care may be more important for children from riskier home environments. Using data from three different childcare samples, Burchinal et al. (2000) found some evidence for the buffering effect of high-quality childcare, especially for African American children's language development. In a follow-up of this work, Burchinal et al. (2006)

found that childcare quality buffered African American children from the negative effects of social risk on later math and problem behaviors in elementary school. In an even larger and more comprehensive study of 11 state prekindergarten programs, childcare quality had positive effects on subsequent academic achievement for all children, but the effects were greater for children from impoverished backgrounds and with other risks, such as low maternal education, single parent status and non-English speaking families (Magnuson et al., 2004).

Thus, the quality of care, both structural and process, appears to be the most critical aspect of the issue of non-maternal care. It is vital to assure that low-income and minority children receive high-quality care because it matters more for their development. In the discussion we will suggest some solutions to this pressing issue.

Quality versus quantity of parenting in the home

As the NICHD Study of Early Childcare demonstrated, childcare accounts for a rather modest percentage of the variance in child outcomes compared to parenting. In fact, the effect sizes for parenting are four times that for childcare (NICHD ECCRN, 2008). Thus, the home environment and the parenting children experience suggest that the home is critical for children's development, with effect sizes between .8 and .9. Both SES and home environments are strong predictors of children's cognitive development (e.g. Dumas et al., 2005; Johnson et al., 2008). Thus, we need to put the effects of non-maternal care in perspective. Even when mothers are in the paid workforce and place their children in non-maternal care, the influence of their parenting is still substantial and needs to be recognized as the most important influence on children's development.

Conclusion

The question should not be whether or not non-parental/maternal childcare is good for children, but rather what we can do to provide a more family-friendly society that supports all families, whatever choices parents make regarding labor force participation. Many families do not have the option of staying home with their children but are often faced with few good choices about where to place their children given the limited options available. First, policies should be put in place to create more flexible workplaces that provide flexible hours, childcare subsidies, onsite workplace childcare, paid leave, and paid sick leave. All of these workplace policies are associated with home and family well-being, including parenting and child behavior (Hill et al., 2008). Parents whose jobs are characterized by high levels of support report an increased ability to meet family obligations and reduced distress, both for working men and women (Roxburgh, 1996). Further, parents with less flexible work environments reported they were less able to be involved with their children at school (Yoshikawa et al., 2007), had difficulties arranging childcare, and reported having insufficient time to spend with their children (Glass and Estes, 1997).

Secondly, efforts must be made to improve the quality of childcare available to all families through increased investments in provider education and training, increases in provider pay to reduce turnover, and initiatives to enable lower-income families to access the high-quality care that their more affluent counterparts can already buy into. This increase in the quality of childcare not only helps the poor; it also helps solve a major dilemma in the American educational system: the achievement gap between the rich and poor, between the most educated and the least educated families. *The Future of Children* (Rouse *et al.*, 2005) tackled the issue of the racial and economic achievement gap in this country with the conclusion: "For the present, however, we believe that by far the most promising strategy is to increase access to high-quality center-based early childhood education programs for all low-income three- and four-year-olds" (p. 12).

The US childcare system should adopt the dual goals of supporting parental work *and* fostering optimal child development. These efforts are essential, as London and his colleagues (2004) note: "if women's increased absence from the home is not compensated for in ways that are beneficial to children (e.g. high-quality childcare) then we might expect any potential gains for children [accruing from mothers' increased self-esteem and decreased depression related to work] to be short-lived" (p. 156).

References

Anderson, K. (2001) *Wartime Women: Sex Roles, Family Relations, and the Status of Women during World War II*. New York: Berkley Books.

Belsky, J. and Rovine, M. J. (1988). Nonmaternal care in the first year of life and the security of infant-parent attachment. *Child Development, 59*, 157–167. Available at: http://www.jstor.org/stable/1130397 (accessed 27 January 2012).

Belsky, J., Vandell, D. L., Burchinal, M., Clarke-Stewart, K. A., McCartney, K., Owen, M. T. and The NICHD Early Childcare Research Network. (2007). Are there long-term effects of early childcare? *Child Development, 78*, 681–701. doi: 10.1111/j.1467-8624.2007.01021.x

Brooks-Gunn, J., Han, W. and Waldfogel, J. (2010). First-year maternal employment and child development in the first 7 years: I. Introduction. *Monographs of the Society for Research in Child Development, 75*(2), 1–19.

Burchinal, M. R. and Cryer, D. (2003). Diversity, childcare quality, and developmental outcomes. *Early Childhood Research Quality, 18*, 401–426. doi:10.1016/j.ecresq.2003.09.003

Burchinal, M., Howes, C. and Kontos, S. (2002). Structural predictors of childcare quality in childcare homes. *Early Childhood Research Quarterly, 17*, 87–105. doi: 10.1016/S0885-2006(02)00132-1

Burchinal, M. E., Roberts, J. E., Riggins, R., Zeisel, S. A., Neebe, E. and Bryant, D. (2000). Relating quality of center-based childcare to early cognitive and language development longitudinally. *Child Development, 71*, 339–357. doi: 10.1111/1467-8624.00149

Burchinal, M. E., Roberts, J. E., Riggins, R., Zeisel, S. A., Hennon, E. A. and Hooper, S. (2006). Social risk and protective child, parenting, and childcare factors in early elementary school years. *Parenting: Science and Practice, 6*, 79–113. doi: 10.1207/s15327922par0601_4

Campbell, F. A. and Ramey, C. T. (1994). Effects of early intervention on intellectual and academic achievement: a follow-up study of children from low-income families. *Child Development, 65*, 684–698. doi: 10.1111/j.1467-8624.1994.tb00777.x

Ceglowski, D. and Davis, E. (2004). Assessing structural indicators of childcare quality at the local level: lessons from four Minnesota counties. *Child & Youth Care Forum, 33*, 71–93. doi: 10.1023/B:CCAR.0000019632.64327.a9

Clarke-Stewart, A. and Allhusen, V. (2005). *What We Know About Childcare*. Cambridge, MA: Harvard University Press.

Crosby, D. A. and Hawkes, D. D. (2007). Cross-national research using contemporary birth cohort studies: a look at early maternal employment in the UK and USA. *International Journal of Social Research Methodology: Theory & Practice, 10*, 379–404. doi: 10.1080/13645570701677151

Dearing, E., McCartney, K. and Taylor, B. A. (2009). Does higher quality early childcare promote low-income children's math and reading achievement in middle childhood? *Child Development, 80*, 1329–1349. doi: 10.1111/j.1467-8624.2009.01336.x

De Marco, A. (2008). A qualitative look at childcare selection among rural Welfare-to-Work participants. *Journal of Children and Poverty, 14*, 119–138. doi: 10.1080/10796120802336191

De Marco, A., Crouter, A. C. and Vernon-Feagans, L. (2009). The relationship of maternal work characteristics to childcare type and quality in rural communities. *Community, Work, & Family, 12*, 369–387. doi: 10.1080/13668800802528249

De Schipper, E. J., Riksen-Walraven, J. M. and Geurts, S. A. E. (2006). Effects of child–caregiver ratio on the interactions between caregivers and children in child-care centers: an experimental study. *Child Development, 77*, 861–874. doi: 10.1111/j.1467-8624.2006.00907.x

Dumas, J. E., Nissley, J., Nordstrom, A., Smith, E. P., Prinz, R. J. and Levine, D. W. (2005). Home chaos: sociodemographic, parenting, interactional, and child correlates. *Journal of Clinical Child and Adolescent Psychology, 34*, 93–104. doi: 10.1207/s15374424jccp3401_9

Glass, J. L. and Estes, S. B. (1997). The family responsive workplace. *Annual Review of Sociology, 23*, 289–313.

Han, W. J. (2007). *Nonstandard Work Schedules and Work-family Issues.* Boston, MA: Sloan Work and Family Research Network, Boston College. Available at: http://wfnetwork.bc.edu/encyclopedia_entry.php?id=5854&area=All (accessed 27 January 2012).

Helburn, S. W. and Howes, C. (1996). Childcare cost and quality. *The Future of Children, 6*, 62–82. Princeton, New Jersey: Woodrow Wilson School of Public and International Affairs at Princeton University & The Brookings Institution.

Hill, J. E., Grzywacz, J. G., Allen, S., Blanchard, V. L., Matz-Costa, C., Shulkin, S. and Pitt-Catsouphes, M. (2008). Defining and conceptualizing workplace flexibility. *Community, Work & Family, 11*, 149–163. doi: 10.1080/13668800802024678

Honig, A. S. and Hirallal, A. (1998). Which counts more for excellence in childcare staff – years in service, education level or ECE coursework? *Early Child Development and Care, 145*, 31–46. doi: 10.1080/0300443981450103

Howes, C., Phillips, D. A. and Whitebook, M. (1992). Thresholds of quality: Implications for the social development or children in center-based childcare. *Child Development, 63*, 449–460. doi: 10.1111/j.1467-8624.1992.tb01639.x

Johnson, A. D., Martin, A., Brooks-Gunn, J. and Petrill, S. A. (2008). Order in the house! Associations among household chaos, the home literacy environment, maternal reading ability, and children's early reading. *Merrill-Palmer Quarterly, 54*, 445–472. doi: 10.1353/mpq.0.0009

Karoly, L. A., Greenwood, P. A., Everingham, S. S., Hoube, J., Kilburn, M. R. C., Rydell, P., Sanders, M. and Chiesa, J. (1998). *Investing In Our Children: What We Know and Don't Know About the Costs and Benefits of Early Childhood Interventions.* Santa Monica, CA: RAND Corporation, 1998. Available online: http://www.rand.org/pubs/monograph_reports/MR898 (accessed 27 January 2012).

Larner, M., Behrman, R. E., Young, M. and Reich, K. (2001). Caring for infants and toddlers: analysis and recommendations. *Future of Children, 11*, 7–20. Princeton, New Jersey: Woodrow Wilson School of Public and International Affairs at Princeton University & The Brookings Institution.

Loeb, S., Bridges, M., Bassok, D., Fuller, B. and Rumberger, R. (2007). How much is too much? The influence of preschool centers on children's social and cognitive development. *Economics of Education Review, 26*, 52–66.

London, A. S., Scott, E. K., Edin, K. and Hunter, V. (2004). Welfare reform, work-family tradeoffs, and child well-being. *Family Relations, 53*, 148–158. doi: 10.1111/j.0022-2445.2004.00005.x

Magnuson, K., Meyers, M., Ruhm, C., and Waldfogel, J. (2004). Inequality in preschool education and school readiness, *American Educational Research Journal, 41*, 115–157. doi: 10.3102/00028312041001115

Maher, E. J., Frestedt, B. and Grace, C. (2008). Differences in childcare quality in rural and non-rural areas. *Journal of Research in Rural Education, 23*(4), 1–13.

Marshall, N. L. (2004). The quality of early childcare and children's development. *Early Childcare and Development, 13*, 165–168. doi: 10.1111/j.0963-7214.2004.00299.x

McCartney, K., Dearing, E., Taylor, B. A. and Bub, K. L. (2007). Quality childcare supports the achievement of low-income children: direct and indirect pathways through caregiving and the home environment. *Journal of Applied Developmental Psychology, 28*, 411–426. doi: 10.1016/j.appdev. 2007.06.010

Morgan, K. (2003). The politics of mothers' employment: France in comparative perspective. *World Politics, 55*, 259–289. doi: 10.1353/wp.2003.0013

National Institute of Child Health and Development Early Childcare Research Network (NICHD) (2002a). Early childcare and children's development prior to school entry: Results from NICHD Study of Early Childcare. *American Educational Research Journal, 39*, 133–164. doi: 10.3102/00028312039001133

——(2002b). The interaction of childcare and family risk in relation to child development at 24 and 36 months. *Applied Developmental Science, 6*, 144–156. doi: 10.1207/S1532480XADS0603_4

National Institute of Child Health and Development (NICHD) & Duncan, G. J. (2003). Modeling the impact of childcare quality on children's preschool cognitive development. *Child Development, 74*, 1454–1475. doi: 10.1111/1467-8624.00617

National Institute of Child Health and Development. (NICHD) (2004). Type of childcare and children's development at 54 months. *Early Childhood Research Quarterly, 19*, 203–230. doi: 10.1016/j. ecresq.2004.04.002

National Institute of Child Health and Development Early Childcare Research Network (NICHD ECRN) (2003). Does amount of time spent in childcare predict socioemotional adjustment during the transition to kindergarten? *Child Development, 74*, 976–1005. doi: 10.1111/1467-8624.00582

——(2008). Mothers' and fathers' support for child autonomy and early school achievement. *Developmental Psychology, 44*, 895–907. doi: 10.1037/0012-1649.44.4.895

National Institute of Child Health and Human Development Early Childcare Research Network (NICHHD ECCRN) (2000). The relation of childcare to cognitive and language development. *Child Development, 71*, 960–980. doi: 10.1111/1467-8624.00202

Peisner-Feinberg, E. S., Burchinal, M. R., Clifford, R. M., Yazejian, N., Culkin, M. L., Zelazo, J. *et al.* (1999). *The Children of the Cost, Quality, and Outcomes Study Go to School – Executive Summary.* Chapel Hill, North Carolina: Frank Porter Graham Child Development Center.

Phillips, D. A. and Adams, G. (2001). Childcare and our youngest children. *Future of Children, 11*, 35–51. Princeton, New Jersey: Woodrow Wilson School of Public and International Affairs at Princeton University & The Brookings Institution.

Raikes, A., Raikes, H. and Wilcox, B. (2005). Regulation, subsidy receipt and provider characteristics: what predicts quality in childcare homes? *Early Childhood Research Quarterly, 20*, 164–184. doi: 10.1016/j.ecresq.2005.04.006

Ray, R., Gornick, J. C. and Schmitt, J. (2009). *Parental Leave Policies in 21 Countries: Accessing Generosity and Gender Equality* (2nd edn). Report prepared for the Center for Economic Policy and Research, Washington, DC.

Reynolds, A. (2000). *Success in Early Interventions: The Chicago Child-Parent Centers.* Lincoln, NE: University of Nebraska Press.

Reynolds, A. J., Temple, J. A., Ou, S. R., Arteaga, I. A. and White, B. A. (2011). School-based early childhood education and age-28 well-being: effects by timing, dosage, and subgroups. *Science, 333*, 360–364. doi: 10.1126/science.1203618

Rouse, C., Brooks-Gunn, J. and McLanahan, S. (2005). School readiness: closing racial and ethnic gaps. *The Future of Children, 15.* Princeton, New Jersey: Woodrow Wilson School of Public and International Affairs at Princeton University & The Brookings Institution.

Roxburgh, S. (1996). Gender differences in work and well-being: effects of exposure and vulnerability. *Journal of Health and Social Behavior, 37*, 265–277. doi: 10.2307/2137296

Sundström, M. (1991). Sweden: Supporting work, family, and gender equality. In S. B. Kamerman, A. J. Kahn, S. B. Kamerman, A. J. Kahn (Eds.), *Childcare, Parental Leave, and the Under 3s: Policy Innovation in Europe* (pp. 171–199). New York, NY England: Auburn House Publishing Co.

US Congress Committee on Ways and Means (2000). *Background Material and Data on Programs within the Jurisdiction of the Committee on Ways and Means.* Washington, DC: US Government Printing Office.

Vandell, D. L., Dadisman, K. and Gallagher, K. (2000). Another look at the elephant: childcare in the nineties. In R. D. Taylor and M. C. Wang (Eds.) *Resilience Across Contexts: Family, Work, Culture, and Community* (pp. 91–120). Mahwah, NJ: Lawrence Erlbaum.

Vernon-Feagans, L. V. (1996). *Children's Talk in Communities and Classrooms.* Cambridge, MA: Blackwell Publishers.

Vernon-Feagans, L., Hurley, M. M., Yont, K. M., Wamboldt, P. M. and Kolak, A. (2007). Quality of childcare and otitis media: relationship to children's language during naturalistic interactions at 18, 24, and 36 months. *Journal of Applied Developmental Psychology*, 28, 115–133. doi:10.1016/j.appdev.2006.12.003

Walsh, M. and Wrigley, C. (2001). Womanpower: the transformation of the labour force in the UK and the USA since 1945. *ReFresh 30*, 1–4. Available at: http://www.ehs.org.uk/othercontent/Walsh30a.pdf (accessed 27 January 2012).

Whitener, L. A., Duncan, G. J. and Weber, B. A. (2002). *Reforming Welfare: What Does It Mean For Rural Areas?* (Food Assistance and Nutrition Research Report Number 26-4). Washington, DC: United States Department of Agriculture.

Yellin, E. (2004). *Our Mother's War: American Women at Home and at the Front during World War II.* New York: Free Press.

Yoshikawa, H., Lowe, E. D., Bos, J. M., Weisner, T. S., Nikulina, V. and Hsueh, J. (2007). Do pathways through low-wage work matter for children's development? In H. Yoshikawa, T. S. Weisner and E. D. Lowe (Eds.), *Making It Work: Low-wage Employment, Family Life, and Child Development* (pp. 54–74). New York: Russell Sage Foundation.

Chapter 5

Delegated parenting
Some neuroendocrine reservations

Aric Sigman

Non-parental care in the form of daycare, practiced in industrialized societies, is an evolutionary novelty. Segregating children by age is new. Throughout most of human history, people lived in small foraging groups and children rarely had playmates of the same age. Socialization involved interacting with people of all ages, from infants to grandparents (Konner, 2005). In foraging groups and village-based societies today, children play in multi-age playgroups (Hewlett and Lamb, 2005) and may be watched over by various carers, including older sisters and grandmothers (Hrdy, 2005).

In traditional societies offered up as examples of care by the "extended family", the situation bears no resemblance whatsoever to daycare arrangements in industrialized societies. Children are cared for by a hierarchy of long-standing attachment figures, most of whom are biologically related to the child. Furthermore, the children often remain in or near their own homes: hut/tent, which is closely connected to a village. And the disposition and behaviour of the babies and toddlers is often of note. One of many examples is of the Dogon in West Africa which found a complete absence of anxious-avoidant attachment, attributed to the community's infant care practices which involve responsiveness, constant closeness to mothers and immediate breastfeeding in response to signs of stress (McMahan *et al.*, 2001). I have visited many of these traditional societies including the Dogon and have seen precisely this.

The assumption that we as Western industrialized parents and researchers – who have comparatively few children and spend relatively few hours in close proximity to them – have a *better* sense of a young child's emotional needs than mothers from traditional "developing" cultures who have more children and spend more time with them, is unjustified.

When visiting many traditional communities within cultures including Republic of Congo, Bhutan, North Korea, Mali, Borneo, Tonga, Burma, West Papua, Turkmenistan, Laos, Iran, Vietnam, Bolivia, Burkina Faso, Far Eastern Siberia, Sumatra, and Cambodia, I have mentioned to the local people the growing belief in and reliance on daycare in Western culture ... to the frowns and astonishment of highly experienced mothers who instinctively feel non-familial care, especially daycare, does not offer the best circumstances for the well being of their young children. But are these merely the concerns of "superstitious, ignorant, unemancipated tribal peasants" who can perhaps be forgiven for not knowing any better? Or do they actually know something that we don't?

Although Vernon-Feagons and De Marco's chapter in this book discusses the perceived benefits of daycare, the explicit intention in this chapter is to provide readers with some of the neuroendocrine evidence, which is conspicuous by its absence in discussions of daycare (Sigman, 2011). I argue that this research has often been overlooked and therefore I seek to draw attention to this – regardless of how well it fits with today's political climate – because it provides a wider and perhaps more subtle understanding of daycare.

The HPA way

Much of the research on daycare generally emanates from the fields of child education and social work. And much of the discussion has focused on "outcomes" in terms of "school readiness", academic achievement, and overt behavioural problems, the so-called "daycare proof". Society has been unaware of the distinction between the effects of daycare on children of low socio-economic status whose mothers have low levels of education, and children of middle-class socio-economic status with professional mothers of higher educational background. On closer inspection, the benefits widely extolled are often a description of the *remedial* use of daycare as an "intervention" for deprived children. However, for middle-class children it is often a case of: take a privileged mother out of the home, and some of the privileges leave with her.

At the same time, there is a paucity of understanding of what it *feels* like for the child while they are actually *in* daycare. This gap is partly due to the inherent difficulty in gauging such an internal experiential phenomenon at an age when infants and children have such a limited ability to describe their inner landscape.

However, research methods from the biosciences have started to provide an illuminating glimpse of this landscape, with children's neuroendocrine responses serving as the voice of their experience. And this voice is often singing a very different tune to that presented by the daycare establishment. There is something about attending daycare for an extended time, whether small-scale and home-based or large-scale and centre-based, that often elicits stress in young children (Gunnar *et al.*, 2010).

The hypothalamic–pituitary–adrenocortical (HPA) axis is a system intricately involved in a child's capacity to respond to threat such as that triggered by fear or uncertainty. Neuroendocrine research of stress in infants and small children has used salivary samples to measure cortisol, the steroid end-product of the HPA axis. Therefore, by examining cortisol levels in children in daycare environments, especially those who cannot yet talk, we gain unique insight into how stressful they find these environments.

Cortisol levels undergo a diurnal cycle; the level peaks in the early morning, declining across the day to reach the lowest level at about midnight to 4 am, or three to five hours after falling asleep. Infants are born without a diurnal rhythm in cortisol and they acquire it during their first year of life.

Under certain circumstances, a rise in cortisol as an appropriate stress response is a healthy and necessary part of life. After a perceived danger has passed, the body then tries to return to normal. However, when stress is chronic, high levels of cortisol remain active in the system. These high levels of cortisol can have significant biological consequences in adulthood. For example, increased cortisol exposure is independently linked to higher numbers of plaques in and artherosclerosis of the carotid arteries (Dekker *et al.*, 2008). And high cortisol levels strongly predict cardiovascular death, even in people who have no pre-existing cardiovascular disease (Vogelzangs *et al.*, 2010).

Dysregulations of the HPA axis are now implicated in the pathophysiology of stress-related disorders, such as depression and anxiety. Ellenbogen *et al.* (2011) recently reported that cortisol levels at age 17 have been used to predict the development of psychiatric disorders during the subsequent 2.5 years of these adolescents' lives. Vreeburg *et al.* (2010) suggested that a higher cortisol awakening response (CAR) – an increase occurring 20 to 30 minutes after waking in the morning in healthy people – indicates a trait marker for an underlying biological vulnerability for the development of depressive and anxiety disorders. Chen *et al.* (2010) point to HPA dysregulation as a biological explanation for why children living in a low socioeconomic environment (SES) may be more vulnerable to developing psychiatric and physical illnesses later in life. Over a 2-year period, cortisol rose almost twice as much in low-SES compared with high-SES children.

Attachment, copresence and cortisol

There is a close relation between maternal care, proximity to child (called copresence), and infant cortisol levels. A Swedish study examined diurnal cortisol levels among infants, and mothers who remained at home with their children, 93 percent of whom were breast-feeding. Strong correlations were identified between mother and child cortisol levels on all sampling occasions, while weaker correlations were found between father and child levels and only in the afternoon and the evening samples (Stenius *et al.*, 2008). Demonstrating further the role of copresence, Waynforth (2007) reported lower cortisol levels among 3- to 8-year-old children who had slept in their parent(s)' rooms, and also those children who attended less daycare in the first 4 years of life.

As well as being in close proximity, attachment style has been linked with waking cortisol levels in healthy female children and adolescents aged 9 to 18 years. Those with a more anxious attachment style had higher levels on awakening and an attenuated cortisol awakening response, compared to those who were securely attached. It has been pointed out that this is the same cortisol dysregulation pattern linked with disorders in adulthood (Oskis *et al.*, 2011). Crucially, adolescents' attachment orientation also influences their blood pressure responses to everyday social interactions.

It has been suggested that children who experience less nurturance early in life may be less securely attached as adolescents and adults with greater vulnerability to stress compared to children who experience consistent, nurturing caregiving (Gallo and Mathews, 2006). In a prospective study comparing different child-rearing environments, Stenius *et al.* (2010) found low salivary cortisol levels in infants of families with an "anthroposophic lifestyle". This lifestyle is considered an alternative, more natural holistic approach thought to provide environmental conditions for the infant aimed at reducing stress, compared to infants in families with more conventional lifestyles. Based on the above evidence, it would be a reasonable guess that copresence reduces cortisol and boosts attachment.

HPA programming in the early years

In the past decade, a body of animal and human research has revealed a profound influence of early-life parenting on HPA axis regulation in adulthood. Early-life parental care has been shown to influence the development of the brain's hippocampus and modify the cortisol awakening response (Engert *et al.*, 2010).

In rats, the quality and sheer amount of the mother's care causes changes in the brain's structural neuroplasticity and alters brain cell functioning and the response to anti-inflammatory hormones (including cortisol) and stress.

In controlled experiments involving rats, highly significant reductions in the length and density of the branches of pyramidal brain cells are found in the hippocampi of adult offspring with mothers who were less attentive (Champagne *et al.*, 2008). In human grey matter, the quality of a mother's care in early childhood is a factor thought to modulate the size of the hippocampus (Buss *et al.*, 2007). Attachment insecurity has now been significantly linked to reduced brain size and cell density within the hippocampus (Quirin *et al.*, 2010).

The mechanisms by which the child's early care experiences are translated into neuroendocrine, dispositional, and behavioural changes are thought to involve epigenetic imprinting: modifying how easily a gene can be read. Maternal care or a deficiency of it plays a key role: maternal care can produce semi-permanent changes in gene expression in brain regions vital in stress response, thereby providing a potential mechanism for early childhood programming of stress-induced disease in adults (Tara *et al.*, 2009). In rats, the degree of maternal care alters the offspring epigenome at a glucocorticoid receptor in cells of the hippocampus, as well as altering the HPA axis response to stress (Weaver *et al.*, 2004; Weaver, 2009). Stress occurring during sensitive periods of development might therefore cause lasting changes in the settings and function of the child's HPA axis (Murgatroyd *et al.*, 2009; Mesquita *et al.*, 2009). There is now an emerging association in human literature between deficiencies in the post-natal environment and negative consequences on adult HPA axis responsivity and stress-related disease.

Elevated levels of stress in young children are particularly of concern because a range of developing systems is put at risk, including HPA programming. Concern is not restricted to high cortisol levels; it includes any *dysregulation* of the diurnal cycle or the HPA axis in general. Therefore, a key aspect in the early care environment for young children is the ability of adults to be available to respond appropriately to stress reactions triggered (inevitably) by normal day-to-day events. Given the lower child-to-carer ratios when children stay at home, and the mother's soothing effect on cortisol levels, it is unlikely that daycare environments best offset the effects of stressors.

Daycare and HPA function

Attending a daycare centre, and the consequent separation from parents, is a significant source of stress for many young children. A review and meta-analysis of nine studies concluded:

> Our main finding was that at daycare children display higher cortisol levels compared to the home setting. Diurnal patterns revealed significant increases from morning to afternoon, but at daycare only. … We examined all papers on possible associations between cortisol levels and quality of care, and the influences of age, gender, and children's temperament. Age appeared to be the most significant moderator of this relation. The effect of daycare attendance on cortisol excretion was especially notable in children younger than thirty-six months. We speculate that children in center daycare show elevated cortisol levels because of their stressful interactions in a group setting.
>
> (Vermeer and van IJzendoorn, 2006, p. 390)

Sumner *et al.* (2010) compared children aged 16 to 24 months on two childcare days versus two non-childcare days and found significantly different patterns of cortisol secretion on childcare days characterized by an afternoon increase in cortisol levels. This was not the case on non-childcare days. Other studies have compared home-based and center-based childcare. In one, 71 children from childcare homes and 45 children from childcare centers in the 20–40 months age range were monitored. The authors concluded "children displayed higher cortisol levels at childcare than at home, irrespective of type of care" (Groenveld et al., 2010, p. 502).

Again suggesting the importance of the mother, similar patterns of results on HPA function have been found for full-time home-based day care. Gunnar and colleagues (2010) examined 151 children (3.0–4.5 years) in full-time home-based daycare. "Compared to cortisol levels at home, increases were noted in the majority of children (63%) at daycare, with 40% classified as a stress response" (p. 851), even in daycare homes where there were only one or two children.

The HPA axis and the immune system are functionally linked. So, a recent study at Cornell University examined both cortisol levels and antibody secretion among 3- to 5-year-old children "attending very high quality, full-time childcare centers" (Watamura et al., 2010, p. 1156). Salivary antibody provides a critical line of defense against pathogens entering children's bodies via the mouth. Saliva samples were taken across the day at home and in childcare, to examine the relationship between salivary cortisol concentration and antibody secretion – secretory IgA (SIgA) – and their relationships with child illnesses. Researchers identified rising cortisol levels at daycare, driven by higher afternoon levels, which predicted lower antibody levels on the subsequent weekend. Of particular note was "a declining daily pattern in SIgA on weekend and daycare days for older [preschool children]" and they concluded that "elevated cortisol in children during childcare may be related to both lowered antibody levels and greater illness frequency" (Watamura et al., 2010, p. 1156).

In addition to lowering antibody levels, daycare related stress may activate immune cells in a child's skin, resulting in inflammatory skin diseases such as eczema (Joachim et al., 2008). Cramer et al. (2011) used a German birth cohort study to determine the incidence and prevalence of eczema up to the age of 6. Of 11 possible risk factors, only daycare attendance during the first two years of life was significantly associated with later eczema. "Daycare centre attendance is associated with an increased prevalence and incidence of eczema. Regional differences in eczema prevalence could be explained by regional differences in utilization of early daycare" (p 68).

Others have found that between ages 2 and 3 the differences in cortisol levels between home and daycare are transient, diminishing over a period of a year. At 3 years of age, children displayed higher cortisol levels at daycare only if they had a "later entry", defined as starting after 16 months, while children with more daycare experience, entering before 8 months, showed higher levels at home (Ouellet-Morin et al., 2010). Although this suggests some form of adaptation, it is important to realize that the one year elapsing between ages 2 and 3 constitutes one-third of a child's life, incidentally during the greatest period of brain volume growth and at a time when experiences affect the way genes are expressed in the developing brain. And so even if cortisol rises diminish within a year, there has been some systematic HPA axis dysregulation, such that subtle lasting effects may have already been set in motion.

Additionally, the effects of daycare also appear long lasting. A large-scale study in 2009 involving nine institutions followed approximately 1,000 children from 1 month through mid-adolescence to examine the effects of childcare in children's first few years of life on later development. The researchers observed children in and out of their homes. When the children were 15, they measured their levels of awakening cortisol. Children who, during their first three years "spent more time in center-based childcare – whether of high or low quality – were more likely to have the atypical pattern of lower levels of cortisol just after awakening when they were 15 years of age, which could indicate higher levels of early stress" (Roisman et al., 2009, press release). Abnormal cortisol patterns were observed regardless of the child's gender or ethnicity, the family's income level, the mother's level of education, or the sensitivity the parents exhibited towards the children as teenagers. It is thought that these children may be more prone to stress in their teen years (Roisman et al., 2009).

Many from the social sciences and education are aware of findings by Brooks-Gunn et al. (2010) on effects of first-year maternal employment reporting that "later cognitive, social, and emotional outcomes are neutral because negative effects, where present, are offset by positive effects" (p. 9). The study involved assessing these variables at age 3, age 4.5 and in first grade. Most crucially, on closer inspection, the "emotional outcomes" were almost exclusively behavioural measures involving a Child Behavior Checklist, subscales of social skills and peer competence and child compliance on a "clean-up" task. Unlike Roisman et al. (2009), this study had an outcome age of less that half of the other two and focused on overt behavioural outcomes, not emotional ones, and certainly not physiological outcomes. Thus, it is a different animal altogether.

Interestingly, Vandell et al. (2010) found that the effects of daycare from birth to 4.5 years extend to age 15 years. Both quality and quantity of daycare were linked to adolescent functioning: "More hours of nonrelative care predicted greater risk taking and impulsivity at age 15" (p. 737). Although the clinical significance of the effects is still being debated, the very fact that such long-term reliable differences have been found is illuminating.

Quality of care and cortisol

The quality of care has been found to mediate some – but not all – of the relationship between daycare attendance and cortisol dysregulation. In the study above by Groenveld et al. (2010) in home-based childcare, lower caregiver sensitivity was associated with higher levels of cortisol during the day. In center-based childcare, lower global quality of care was associated with an increase in cortisol between 11am and 3pm. The authors concluded that the quality of care is an important factor in young children's wellbeing and HPA stress reactions.

Interestingly, higher cortisol levels of caregivers in daycare centres have "predicted lower-quality caregiver behaviour" (Schipper et al., 2009, p. 55), even when other obvious predictors – higher physical workload, more children under two years to care for, and lower caregiver age – were taken into account.

Gunnar et al.'s (2010) study on home-based daycare also found that cortisol increases over the day were larger in settings where children moved frequently between activities, were given relatively little time for free play, and spent long periods of time in structured activities (learning letters, numbers, and colours) led by the carers. The researchers reported that the behavior of the care provider is linked with both how well children function at daycare, and how much their cortisol rises.

It is not surprising that when (a) the carer-to-child ratio is higher, (b) carer sensitivity is greater and (c) children are not pushed, that cortisol elevation may be less pronounced. However, cortisol elevation still occurs, and for long periods of time.

Clinical significance of HPA dysregulation

It is clear that early childcare experiences are associated with endocrine changes in the HPA axis. Some argue that repeated separation stress between infant and mother can produce better child outcomes with the child being more resilient to later stress, and less fearful. These beliefs are based on a misinterpretation of studies of monkeys whereby increased cortisol that was caused by episodes of separation of an infant monkey from its mother was associated with better outcomes in terms of resilient brain structure and function. What advocates of such studies are unaware of, or reluctant to consider, is that these studies actually involve free-living foraging monkeys that are biologically independent and only then separated from their mothers for only an hour a week for only 10 weeks (Parker et al., 2004; Katz et al., 2009). This scenario is not at all comparable to breast-feeding babies and small toddlers in daycare for 35 hours a week.

The University of Minnesota College of Education and Human Development reports that in some cases "70–80 percent of children in center-based care show ever-increasing levels of cortisol across the day, with the biggest increases occurring in toddlers" yet by age 5, "children don't show these stress reactions to being with other children all day" (Gunnar, 2010).

Sustained or increased glucocorticoid exposure can have adverse effects on the hippocampus, which causes decreases of synapses and decreased production of new neurons. Elevations of cortisol can lead to structural alterations in the amygdala (Sharpley and Bitsika, 2010). Overexposure to cortisol also negatively affects the prefrontal cortex. Such damage might progressively reduce the control of the HPA axis and lead to increased stress responses (Arborelius et al., 1999; Fuchs and Gould, 2000). HPA dysregulation and its effects may be subtle and nuanced but still may be highly significant, particularly so since the structure and function of the brain is developing in children. Given that cortisol exposure can be neurotoxic, with adverse effects on both specific neurons and entire neural systems, and that some children are incurring elevated cortisol levels at daycare during the first three years of life when the brain will reach approximately 80 percent its of adult size, any consideration of daycare must take these factors into account.

The early rearing environment and a less secure infant-mother attachment are now associated with earlier puberty in girls (Belsky et al., 2010), as is absence of the biological father. Deardoff et al. (2010) found this to be the case only among higher income families and posited that "higher income families without fathers are more likely to have a single mother who works long hours and is not as available for caregiving" (press release). The study pointed to "neuroendocrine pathways that influence development" (p. 5), especially cortisol release.

Unique maternal-child interaction

I argue that a credible attempt to understand the effects of daycare must compare this with *parental* care and in particular maternal care. In both areas, science has the difficult task of accounting for the intricate and unique interactions known to take place between mothers and young children. I have already presented neuroendocrine evidence that suggests a uniqueness of the mother-child bond at ages when many children are in daycare. Before concluding, I now present some other research showing the uniqueness of this bond from different perspectives.

When a baby suckles at a mother's breast, it starts a chain of events that leads to a surge of the "trust" hormone oxytocin in the mother's brain, which in turn strengthens the bond between mother and child. Rossoni et al. (2008) identified an unprecedented neuropeptide feedback system, which coordinates a "swarm" of oxytocin factories, which generate extremely intense and recurring bursts of oxytocin. This does not happen between baby and care worker.

Tactile, olfactory, auditory, visual, and perhaps other types of sensory stimuli contribute to the adaptive changes in both mother and infant. For example, the dark area around a mother's nipple warms suddenly at the sound of her crying baby and pheromones are released from the surrounding skin glands. Schaal et al. (2006) found that these pheromones speed the time it takes the newborn infant to locate the breast and begin suckling. Babies turn toward the odor of their mother's breast as opposed to another woman's (including a care worker's) lactating breast (Wyatt, 2003).

Across cultures foetuses can remember and recognize their biological mother's voice before they are even born and then prefer it after birth to that of other females, including care workers. Newborns will even change their behaviour to elicit their mother's voice. Kisilevsky and colleagues (Kisilevsky et al., 2003) found that experiences in the womb have an impact on newborn/infant behaviour and development and that recognising the mother's voice may play a role in mother-infant attachment. They believe in–utero neural networks sensitive to the mother's voice and native-language speech are being formed (Kisilevsky et al., 2009).

And neurophysiological research finds only the biological mother's voice preferentially activates the parts of the baby's brain responsible for learning language, even when babies listened regularly pre-birth, to a nurse who was also a mother and whose voice was matched to be similar to the mother (Beauchemin et al., 2010). These researchers see the findings as showing, "scientifically speaking, that the mother's voice is special to babies … This research confirms that the mother is the primary initiator of language…" (Beauchemin et al., 2010, press release).

And there is a reciprocal effect. New mothers seem to be primed with a linguistic advantage for their children. When hearing a recording of infant-directed speech ("Motherese"), only mothers with young infants exhibit increased brain activity in areas known to govern language. This enhanced activation is not observed in any other group, including mothers of children who had advanced beyond the preverbal stage (Matsuda et al., 2010).

Years later, a mother's voice continues to have neuroendocrine effects on her child. When children and young adolescents who are experiencing anxiety and elevated cortisol levels hear their mother's voice on the telephone, there is a dramatic change: a rapid rise in oxytocin and dramatic reduction in salivary cortisol levels (Seltzer et al., 2010). It should not be surprising to learn that the maternal-child interaction is now being elevated to a clinical status. Editorial papers in critical care medical journals are now calling for recognition and use of "the therapeutic effects of a mother's voice" on seriously ill patients (Alspach, 2010, p. 13).

The principle of precaution

It appears that maternal presence, or lack of it, during the early years has biological implications ranging from the epigenetic to the neuroendocrine to the neuroanatomical. Daycare is now a part of this equation. Yet understanding the effects of daycare obviously involves more than mere neuroendocrine studies. Moreover, many fundamental aspects of a child's developmental wellbeing are not accessible to current methods of assessment: they are simply too nuanced or unsuitable. Understanding the effects daycare has on children continues to be hindered by bitter politicised arguments involving women's rights, governmental desire for economic growth, a disproportionate sensitivity to maternal guilt, and the media's portrayal of daycare study findings.

In other areas of child health and development, when considering the potential effects of profound new developments, our society instinctively adopts a principle of precaution. Perhaps in the case of early childcare we should remind ourselves that when it comes to an issue of such fundamental importance we must invoke the Hippocratic medical principle of "first do no harm", and for the time being, assume that Mother knows best.

References

Alspach, G. (2010). Editorial: should selected aspects of family-centered care be moved from the margins to the center? *Critical Care Nurse, 30*(4), 13–16.

Arborelius, L., Owens, M. J., Plotsky, P. M. and Nemeroff, C.B. (1999). The role of corticotrophin releasing factor in depression and anxiety disorders. *Journal of Endocrinology, 160*, 1–12.

Beauchemin, M., González-Frankenberger, B., Tremblay, J., Vannasing, P., Martínez-Montes, E., Belin, P., Béland, R., Francoeur, D., Carceller, A., Wallois, F. and Lassonde, M. (2010). Mother and stranger: an electrophysiological study of voice processing in newborns. *Cerebral Cortex*, published online December 13, 2010. doi: 10.1093/cercor/bhq242. And press release. Mom's voice plays special role in activating newborn's brain. *News*, University of Montreal, 16 December 2010.

Belsky, J., Houts, R.M. and Fearon. P. (2010). Infant attachment security and the timing of puberty: testing an evolutionary hypothesis. *Psychological Science, 21,* 1195–1201.

Brooks-Gunn, J., Han, W. and Waldfogel, J. (2010). First-year maternal employment and child development in the first 7 years. *Monographs of the Society for Research in Child Development,* September.

Buss, C., Lord, C., Wadiwalla, M., Hellhammer, D. H., Lupien, S. J. and Meandey, M. J. (2007). Maternal care modulates the relationship between prenatal risk and hippocampal volume in women but not in men. *The Journal of Neuroscience, 27*, 2592–2595.

Champagne, D. L., Bagot, R. C., van Hasselt, F., Ramakers, G., Meaney, M. J., *et al.* (2008). Maternal care and hippocampal plasticity: evidence for experience-dependent structural plasticity, altered synaptic functioning, and differential responsiveness to glucocorticoids and stress. *The Journal of Neuroscience, 28*, 6037–6045.

Chen, E., Cohen, S. and Miller, G. E. (2010). How low socioeconomic status affects 2-year hormonal trajectories in children. *Psychological Science, 21*, 31–37.

Cramer, C., Link, E., Bauer, C.-P., Hoffmann, U., Von Berg, A., Lehmann, I., Herbarth, O., Borte, M., Schaaf, B., Sausenthaler, S., Wichmann, H.-E., Heinrich, J., Krämer, U. and LISAplus study group. (2011). Association between attendance of day care centres and increased prevalence of eczema in the German birth cohort study LISAplus. *Allergy, 66*, 68–75. doi: 10.1111/j.1398-9995.2010.02446.x

Deardorff, J., Ekwaru, J. P., Kushi, L. H., Ellis, B. J., Greenspan, L. C., Mirabedi, A., Landaverde, E. G. and Hiatt, R. A. (2010). Father absence, Body Mass Index, and pubertal timing in girls: differential effects by family income and ethnicity. *Journal of Adolescent Health*. doi: 10.1016/j.jadohealth.2010.07.032 And press release: Father absence linked to earlier puberty among certain girls. UC Berkley News Center. In S. Yang, *Media Relations*, 17 September 2010.

Dekker, M. J. H. J., Koper, J. W., van Aken, M. O., Pols, H. A. P., Hofman, A., de Jong, F. H., Kirschbaum, C., Witteman, J. C. M., Lamberts, S. W. J. and Tiemeier, H. (2008). Salivary cortisol is related to atherosclerosis of carotid arteries. *The Journal of Clinical Endocrinology & Metabolism, 93*, 3741–3747.

Ellenbogen, M. A., Hodginsb, S., Linnena, A. and Ostiguya, C. S. (2011). Elevated daytime cortisol levels: a biomarker of subsequent major affective disorder? *Journal of Affective Disorders, 132,* 265–269. doi: 10.1016/j.jad.2011.01.007

Engert, V., Efanov, S. I., Dedovic, K., Duchesne, A., Dagher, A. and Pruessner, J. C. (2010). Perceived early-life maternal care and the cortisol response to repeated psychosocial stress. *Journal of Psychiatry Neuroscience, 35*(6), 370–377.

Fuchs, E. and Gould, E. (2000). Mini-review: in vivo neurogenesis in the adult brain: regulation and functional implications. *European Journal of Neuroscience, 12,* 2211–2214.

Gallo, L. C. and Matthews, K. A. (2006). Adolescents' Attachment Orientation influences ambulatory blood pressure responses to everyday social interactions. *Psychosomatic Medicine, 68,* 253–261.

Groeneveld, M. G., Vermeer, H. J., van IJzendoorn, M. J. and Linting, M. (2010). Children's well being and cortisol levels in home-based and center-based childcare. *Early Childhood Research Quarterly, 25,* 502–514.

Gunnar, M. R., Kryzer, E., Van Ryzin, M. J. and Phillips, D. A. (2010). The rise in cortisol in family day care: associations with aspects of care quality, child behavior, and child sex. *Child Development, 81, 851–869. And press release.*

Gunnar, M. (2010). How young children manage stress. *Research Works.* University of Minnesota. http://www.cehd.umn.edu/research/highlights/Gunnar/ (accessed 25 January 2012).

Hewlett, B. S. and Lamb, S. E. (Eds.) (2005). *Hunter-gatherer Childhoods: Evolutionary, Developmental and Cultural Perspectives.* New Brunswick, NJ: Transaction Publishers.

Hrdy, S.B. (2005). Comes the child before the man: how cooperative breeding and prolonged postweaning dependence shaped human potential. In B. S. Hewlett and S. E. Lamb (Eds.), *Hunter-gatherer Childhoods: Evolutionary, Developmental and Cultural Perspectives.* New Brunswick, NJ: Transaction Publishers.

Joachim, R. A., Handjiski, B., Blois, S.M., Hagen, E., Paus, R., Arck, P.C. (2008). Stress-induced neurogenic inflammation in murine skin skews dendritic cells towards maturation and migration: Key role of ICAM1/LFA-1 interactions. *American Journal of Pathology, 173,* 1379–1388.

Katz, M., Liu, C., Schaer, M., Parker, K. J., Ottet, M., Epps, A., *et al.* (2009) *Prefrontal Plasticity and Stress Inoculation-Induced Resilience. Developmental Neuroscience, 31,* 293–299.

Kisilevsky, B. S., Hains, S. M. J., Brown, C. A., Lee, C. T., Cowperthwaite, B., *et al.* (2009). Fetal sensitivity to properties of maternal speech and language. *Infant Behavior & Development, 32,* 59–71.

Kisilevsky, B. S., Hains, S. M. J., Lee, K., Xie, X., Huang, H., Ye, H.-H., *et al.* (2003). Effects of experience on fetal voice recognition. *Psychological Science, 14,* 220–224.

Konner, M. (2005). Hunter-gatherer infancy and childhood: The !Kung and others. In B. S. Hewlett and S. E. Lamb (Eds.), *Hunter-gatherer Childhoods: Evolutionary, Developmental and Cultural Perspectives.* New Brunswick, NJ: Transaction publishers.

McMahan, T. M., Pisani, L. and Oumar, F. (2001). Infant–mother attachment among the Dogon of Mali. *Child Development, 72,* 451–1466. doi: 10.1111/1467-8624.00359

Matsuda, Y., Ueno, K., Waggoner, R. A., Erickson, D., Shimura, Y., Tanaka, K., Cheng, K. and Mazuka, R. (2010). Processing of infant-directed speech by adults. *Neuroimage.* doi: 10.1016/j.neuroimage.2010.07.072

Oskis, A., Loveday, C., Hucklebridge, F., Thorn, L. and Clow, A. (2011). Anxious attachment style and salivary cortisol dysregulation in healthy female children and adolescents. *Journal of Child Psychology & Psychiatry, 52,*111-118. doi: 10.1111/j.1469-7610.2010.02296.x.

Parker, K. J., Buckmaster, C. L., Schatzberg, A. F., Lyons, D. M. (2004). Prospective investigation of stress inoculation in young monkeys. *Archives of General Psychiatry,* 61, 933-941.

Ouellet-Morin, I., Tremblay, R. E., Boivin, M., Meaney, M., Kramer, M. and Côté, S. M. (2010), Diurnal cortisol secretion at home and in child care: a prospective study of 2-year-old toddlers. *Journal of Child Psychology and Psychiatry, 51,* 295–303.

Quirin, M. Gillath, O., Pruessner, J. C. and Eggert L. D. (2010). Adult attachment insecurity and hippocampal cell density. *Social Cognitive & Affective Neuroscience, 5,* 39–47.

Roisman, G. I., Susman, E., Barnett-Walker, K., Booth-LaForce, C., Owen, M. T., Bradley, R. H., *et al.* (2009). Early family and childcare antecedents of awakening cortisol levels in adolescence. *Child Development, 80,* 907–920. Accompanying press release, *Child Development* (Issue 3) 15 May 2009.

Rossoni, E., Feng, J., Tirozzi, B., Brown, D., Leng, G., *et al.* (2008). Emergent synchronous bursting of oxytocin neuronal network. PLoS *Computarional Biology, 4*(7), e1000123. doi:10.1371/journal.pcbi.1000123

Schaal, B., Doucet, S., Sagot, P., Hertling, E. and Soussignan, R. (2006). Human breast areolae as scent organs: morphological data and possible involvement in maternal-neonatal coadaptation. *Developmental Psychobiology, 48,* 100–110. doi: 10.1002/dev.20122

Schipper, E. J. de, Riksen-Walraven, J. M., Geurts, S. A. E. and de Weerth, C. (2009). Cortisol levels of caregivers in child care centers as related to the quality of their caregiving. *Early Childhood Research Quarterly, 24,* 55–63 doi: 10.1016/j.ecresq.2008.10.004

Seltzer, L. J., Ziegler, T. E. and Pollak, S. D. (2010). Social vocalizations can release oxytocin in humans. *Proceedings of the Royal Society B: Biological Sciences, 277,* no. 1694, 2661–2666. doi: 10.1098/rspb.2010.0567

Sharpley, C. F. and Bitsika, V. (2010). Joining the dots: neurobiological links in a functional analysis of depression. *Behavioral and Brain Functions, 6,* 73. doi: 10.1186/1744-9081-6-73

Sigman, A. (2011). Mother Superior?: The biological effects of daycare. *The Biologist, 58*(3), 28–32.

Stenius, F., Theorell, T., Lilja, G., Scheynius, A., Alm, J. and Lindblad, F. (2008). Comparisons between salivary cortisol levels in six-months-olds and their parents. *Psychoneuroendocrinology, 33,* 352–359.

Stenius, F., Swartz, J., Lindblad, F., Pershagen, G., Scheynius, A., Alm, J., Theorell, T. (2010). Low salivary cortisol levels in infants of families with an anthroposophic lifestyle. *Psychoneuroendocrinology, 35,* 1431–1437.

Sumner, M., Bernard, K. and Dozier, M. (2010). Young children's full-day patterns of cortisol production on child care days. *Archives Pediatric & Adolescent Medicine, 164,* 567-571.

Tara, K., Craft, S. and DeVries, A. C. (2009). Vulnerability to stroke: implications of perinatal programming of the hypothalamic-pituitary-adrenal axis. *Frontiers in Behavioral Neuroscience,* December, 1–12.

Vandell, D. L., Belsky, J., Burchinal, M., Steinberg, L., Vandergrift, N. and NICHD Early Child Care Research Network (2010). Do effects of early child care extend to age 15 years? Results From the NICHD Study of Early Child Care and Youth Development. *Child Development, 81,* 737–756. doi: 10.1111/j.1467-8624.2010.01431.x

Vermeer, H. J. and van IJzendoorn, M. H. (2006). Children's elevated cortisol levels at daycare: A review and meta-analysis. *Early Childhood Research Quarterly, 21,* 390–401.

Vogelzangs, N., Beekman, A. T. F., Milaneschi, Y., Bandinelli, S., Ferrucci, L. and Penninx, B. W. J. H. (2010). Urinary cortisol and six-year risk of all-cause and cardiovascular mortality. *Journal of Clinical Endocrinology & Metabolism,* August 25. doi: 10.1210/jc.2010-0192

Vreeburg, S. A., Hartman, C. A., Hoogendijk, W. J. G., van Dyck, R., Zitman, F. G., Ormel, J., Penninx, B. W. J. H. (2010). Parental history of depression or anxiety and the cortisol awakening response. *The British Journal of Psychiatry, 197,* 180–185.

Watamura, S. E., Coe, C.L., Laudenslager, M.L., Robertson, S.S. (2010). Child care setting affects salivary cortisol and antibody secretion in young children. *Psychoneuroendocrinology, 35,* 1156–1166.

Waynforth, D. (2007). The influence of parent–infant cosleeping, nursing, and childcare on cortisol and SIgA immunity in a sample of British children. *Developmental Psychobiology, 49,* 640–648. doi: 10.1002/dev.20248

Weaver, I. C. (2009). Epigenetic effects of glucocorticoids. *Seminars Fetal Neonatal Medicine, 14,*143-50.

Weaver I. C. G., Cervoni, N., Champagne, F. A., D'Alessio, A. C., Sharma, S., Seckl, J. R. *et al.* (2004) Epigenetic programming by maternal behavior. *Nature Neuroscience, 7,* 847–54

Wyatt, T. D. (2003). *Pheromones and Animal Behaviour: Communication By Smell and Taste.* Cambridge University Press, Cambridge.

Part III

Is shared-book reading an indispensable ingredient of responsible parenting?

The cumulative developmental advantages of routine shared-book reading are so great that several research teams have focused on it as a core parenting goal, at least in relation to subsequent language and, perhaps indirectly, reading achievement ... Shared-book reading thus provides both a cognitive and an emotional context in which children can hone their earliest language and, indirectly, literacy skills. For these reasons, then, shared-book reading is an indispensable ingredient of responsible parenting.

Catherine McBride-Chang

Once we have escaped the tyranny of shared-book reading, new avenues for extended conversation with low-income and middle-income children alike may open up for us. Susan Sonnenschein (personal communication, April 2011), for instance, claimed that mealtimes in Head Start and many other childcare settings are usually a wasted opportunity for engaging in high-quality conversation with young children. And Bond and Wasik (2009) have developed a wonderful technique called "conversation stations" with young children in which an adult in a childcare setting helps a child to create a rich story about a past event. In other words, keep sharing books with young children, but be creative about it. A little cheese sauce on the broccoli goes a long way, and a side of edamame beans wouldn't hurt either.

Elaine Reese

Chapter 6

Shared-book reading

There is no downside for parents

Catherine McBride-Chang

Department of Psychology,
The Chinese University of Hong Kong

Introduction

Shared-book reading is an essential aspect of responsible parenting because of both the cognitive and the emotional and motivational benefits it affords. Many of these benefits are long lasting and likely cumulative. At the same time, how a given adult approaches this important task of book reading with a child is perhaps equally important, as is the skill level of the child (e.g. Reese and Cox, 1999). For example, those who benefit most from shared-book reading tend to be younger children. The cumulative developmental advantages of routine shared-book reading are so great that several research teams have focused on it as a core parenting goal, at least in relation to subsequent language and, perhaps indirectly, reading achievement (e.g. Adams, 1990; Snow *et al.*, 1998; Wells, 1985). This is true across families. The idea of shared-book reading in bilingual families, though only rarely researched, also suggests some benefits of shared-book reading in a second language. In the following, I attempt to summarize the benefits of shared-book reading by parents cross-culturally.

Shared-book reading promotes language skills

Across meta-analyses, shared-book reading appears to be at least moderately associated with children's language skills (Bus *et al.*, 1995; Mol and Bus, 2011; Sénéchal *et al.*, 2008; Van Steensel *et al.*, 2011). Although most of the studies that have focused on this issue have come from North America or Europe, similar phenomena have been demonstrated in Asia, both in studies involving questionnaire data related to parents' reading practices (Kim, 2009; Lau and McBride-Chang, 2005) and experimental studies (e.g. Chow and McBride-Chang, 2003; Chow *et al.*, 2008). The most commonly demonstrated benefits of shared-book reading center on vocabulary and grammar skills development (Reese and Cox, 1999). It is important to note that although the benefits of shared-book reading are almost always associated with language skills across studies, the most convincing evidence comes from intervention studies that trace the effects of shared-book reading across time (e.g. Mol *et al.*, 2008; Whitehurst *et al.*, 1994; Whitehurst *et al.*, 1988). Such studies demonstrate a causal association between shared-book reading in children and accelerated language abilities in children.

Shared-book reading depends upon reading technique

Moreover, to maximize the utility of shared-book reading, reading technique itself is clearly important (e.g. Reese and Cox, 1999). For example, early cognitive benefits of shared-book reading appear to be stronger when parents adopt a dialogic reading approach (e.g. Whitehurst *et al.*, 1994; Whitehurst, *et al.*, 1988; Whitehurst and Lonigan, 1998). The dialogic reading technique deliberately focuses on scaffolding children's shared-book reading experiences. With the dialogic reading technique, children are prompted to interact with their parents in relation to the storybook. Parents may ask children to anticipate actions in the story (e.g. "What do you think will happen next?"), evaluate the story in some particular way (e.g. "Who was your favorite character? Why?"), relate to the actions (e.g. "Did you ever feel the way this little mouse felt? When?"), and engage children in other ways during the storytelling session to prompt children to talk about the story. Parents then respond to the child's comments by extending them, following them up, asking for clarifications, or using other communication techniques that further parent-child interactions surrounding the story. In one study, this dialogic reading technique accelerated American two-year-old children's language skills on different dimensions by 6 to 8.5 months across a four-week intervention period, and these vocabulary gains were maintained in a follow-up of the children nine months later (Whitehurst *et al.*, 1988). We have found evidence for enhanced vocabulary skills associated with similar programs in Hong Kong for typically developing (Chow *et al.*, 2008; Chow and McBride-Chang, 2003) and hearing impaired preschool and early primary school children (Fung *et al.*, 2005).

Shared-book reading promotes a novel focus

One might argue that this talk surrounding shared-book reading, rather than a focus on the book itself, is the crucial element of such parent-child interactions, leading to children's vocabulary enhancement. In other words, shared-book reading is not in and of itself important; rather, parents should simply talk, in depth insofar as this is possible, to their children. Though I know of no research that has actually tested this possibility, in some ways, this is a plausible argument when considering parent-child interactions in a vacuum. Parents with lots of ideas and motivation to introduce their children to many elements of the world might encourage similar interactions by going to the zoo or a garden or a shipyard or just around the house and talking extensively about what they see.

However, practically, this is more difficult to keep up than is shared-book reading. Perhaps more importantly, one of the most striking elements of shared-book reading *per se* is the fact that books "transport" families to contexts they will never encounter in daily life. Even a zoo or a garden or a shipyard or one's own house may not introduce children to all the animals, plants, vessels, or foods that exist in the world. Books can better facilitate such encounters on a regular basis. The richness of context in books is crucial for introducing new scenarios and vocabulary to learn about. In addition, even the syntax or sentence structures of language in books is plausibly likely to be more complex or rhythmic than is the speech of daily life, enriching children's knowledge and awareness of various aspects of language.

Shared-book reading promotes interest in reading

Another important factor in shared-book reading has to do with children's interest in reading. Such reading interest has been associated with more advanced language skills even from the age of two in some studies (e.g. Deckner *et al.*, 2006; Lyytinen *et al.*, 1998). Such effects are likely bidirectional. For example, those children who tend to show greater interest in shared-book reading are also the ones who are more likely to be read to by parents over time (e.g. Lyytinen *et al.*, 1998; Scarborough and Dobrich, 1994). As one research team (Bus *et al.*, 1995) stated, "A child who has the desire to learn to read, who is interested in literacy-related activities, and who voluntarily engages in them will – everything else being equal – elicit more or better reading by the parent" (p. 3). These patterns may evolve and reinforce one another over time. In our own research in Hong Kong (Lau and McBride-Chang, 2005), for example, we found that second graders' self-rated enjoyment of shared-book reading with mothers was significantly moderately associated with children's Chinese vocabulary knowledge. Moreover, in that study, children's self-efficacy related to literacy skills (e.g. feeling good about their skills in book-reading and writing) was uniquely associated with actual word recognition, even with mothers' education level, children's ages, number of books at home, and children's own vocabulary knowledge statistically controlled. It is likely that these developmental trajectories are complex and multi-faceted. Nevertheless, there is at least limited evidence that both children's interest in reading (e.g. Deckner *et al.*, 2006; Lau and McBride-Chang, 2005) and oral language skills (e.g. Whitehurst and Lonigan, 1998) may independently facilitate subsequent reading achievement.

Parents' own attitudes about reading are also important in fostering children's interest in literacy-related activities (e.g. Weigel *et al.*, 2006). A focus on reading practices often centers on parents' responses to questionnaires about their reading habits, including a simple measure of number of books at home. In our study of over 199,000 15-year-olds across 43 cultures (Chiu and McBride-Chang, 2006), parents' number of books in the home was uniquely associated with adolescents' reading achievement, even with many other demographics variables statistically controlled. Importantly, students' own interests in reading were also independently associated with their reading achievement in that study. Such findings are noteworthy because they suggest that even at much older ages than those typically targeted in shared-book reading, attitudes about reading activities within the family are fundamental for ultimate reading acquisition (e.g. Adams, 1990).

Shared-book reading expands some, but not all, literacy related skills in children

However, the mechanisms by which such skills are ultimately acquired via book reading are not always clear. For example, during shared reading sessions, young children rarely look at print in books (Evans and Saint-Aubin, 2005). Thus, the act of reading together does not automatically facilitate print awareness or reading skill. Indeed, family literacy practices surrounding shared-book reading are distinguishable, with a focus on print teaching being associated with literacy acquisition and a focus on story elements within a book being associated with vocabulary building over time (e.g. Aram and Levin, 2002; Hood *et al.*, 2008; Sénéchal, 2006). Several models of this developmental process have been put forward (e.g. Sénéchal and LeFevre, 2002; Whitehurst and Lonigan, 1998). These models share in common the basic idea that parents who expand and share language with their children in the context of shared-book reading promote their children's language development. However, only with some explicit focus on elements of print, such as the letters of the alphabet or individual characters of Chinese, will children's knowledge of the print of their native orthography expand (e.g. Aram and Levin, 2002).

At the same time, however, preschool vocabulary knowledge is uniquely associated with subsequent reading comprehension (Muter *et al.*, 2004; Roth *et al.*, 2002; Sénéchal *et al.*, 2006; Tong *et al.*, 2009). Reading comprehension ultimately forms the foundation for all school learning (e.g. Adams, 1990). Broadly, shared-book reading may also sensitize children to story structures or other general characteristics of any narrative of expository piece of writing. With this sense, developed over many instances of shared reading, children enter school confident in one of the main tools of schooling, the use of text itself. This effect alone is enough to recommend shared-book reading to all families of young children, particularly given the fact that early success or failure in school often predicts subsequent success or failure, a phenomenon sometimes referred to as "Matthew Effects" in reading (Stanovich, 1986).

In addition, it is entirely possible that teaching of print takes place primarily in the context of shared-book reading for very young children (e.g. "Oh, look! There is the letter T! Your name starts with T too!"). Stephenson *et al.* (2008) made this point by noting that 90 percent of the parents who indicated on a questionnaire teaching of aspects of print to children aged two to four years, including letter identification or word reading itself, said that they read to their children at least once daily. For very young children, perhaps one of the most meaningful contexts in which to explore print might be in the context of their own books. This issue may also be related to individual differences in children's skills and even interests, as well as the styles of book reading adopted by parents in this process (e.g. Reese and Cox, 1999).

Shared-book reading depends on the genre of the books, parents' own educational levels, and first vs second language approach

Because the discussion between parents and children about concepts in books is such a fundamental aspect of shared book experiences, two other aspects of such experiences are also important to mention. First, the genre of the books to be read is important to consider in relation to both interest and knowledge levels. Second, parents' own educational levels in approaching the stories are likely to make a difference.

The genre of books as a key to successful shared-book reading is clear to anyone who has ever actually read to a child. Children have preferences for topics, illustrations, and styles of language that spark their interests and imaginations in particular ways from the earliest ages. At a broad level, Wagemaker *et al.* (1996), for example, noted that, across 32 cultures, reading achievement differed strongly between girls and boys depending upon the text to be read. In that study, girls tended to excel in reading narratives, whereas the sexes differed much less in comprehension of expository writing and document texts (at ages 9 and 14). These are gross generalizations about preferences on a particular dimension. However, it is clear to all parents that individual children's preferences emerge early. On another dimension, some children seem more interested in rhyming books and repetition than do others, though the widespread success of *Dr. Seuss* books suggests that this element of language has a certain universal appeal at some points in development. The transition to learning about print, which most researchers agree is by no means inevitable, nor perhaps even likely, from shared-book reading alone (e.g. Evans and Saint-Aubin, 2005) may also be related to genre. For example, there are many books in English devoted to thinking about the alphabet. Children who have an interest in this issue may, conceivably, make more progress in learning the letters of the alphabet earlier via parent-child book reading than do those without this interest.

In the context of genre, it is important to note that the majority of the world's children are learning more than one language from a very early age. Thus, one question that has arisen in relation to shared parent-child book reading focuses on the extent to which parents reading to children in a second language facilitate their second language learning. Previous work showed a correlation between parents' reports of reading in a second language for English language skill development among both Indian (Kalia, 2007) and Spanish (Patterson, 2002) preschoolers. Korean children who were engaged in a shared-book reading program with their teachers at school also improved in English language skills (Kim and Hall, 2002). In terms of parent-child interventions, we (Chow *et al.*, 2010) found that Hong Kong Chinese children whose parents participated in a shared-book reading intervention improved significantly in word reading in English over those who did not. Moreover, among families trained to use the dialogic reading technique specifically, children made greater gains in phonological awareness in both Chinese and English as compared to both the group engaged in typical (i.e. not dialogic) storybook reading in English and the control group.

We interpreted these findings based on the Hong Kong context, in which English is typically taught to Chinese children from the age of three from textbooks. Indeed, in Hong Kong, learning the English language and learning to read/spell English are often considered to be synonymous. At the same time, spontaneous English exchanges among native speakers of Chinese within a family may be awkward and somewhat slow, so that vocabulary knowledge in English from shared-book reading in English did not improve. Interestingly, however, phonological awareness did improve in the dialogic reading group only, perhaps indicating that these families engaged in more verbal exchanges than did the other groups over the reading intervention time, although this pattern requires future studies to establish definitively since this was not found in a previous study of dialogic reading in a first language (Whitehurst *et al.*, 1994). Although a comprehensive understanding of shared-book reading in a second language is likely years away, with issues of parents' own competency in the second language being of great importance when considering the utility of this focus (e.g. Tabors and Snow, 2001), in certain contexts, such as Hong Kong, in which (English) second language learning is required in school, this approach is worth considering. In particular, one might imagine scenarios in which pictures or subjects of such books, accompanied by a few minutes of precious time with parents focused on these, might serve to pique the interest of young children who are sometimes inundated with less attractive copying exercises as the main avenue through which a second language is typically learned, as is often the case in Hong Kong.

Parents' own educational backgrounds may also be an important factor in influencing the effects of shared-book reading on children's development (e.g. Chaney, 1994; Korat *et al.*, 2006). Parents' lower education levels tend to be associated with more limited reading achievement in children across cultures (e.g. Aram and Levin, 2002; Chiu and McBride-Chang, 2006; Rauh *et al.*, 2003). Part of this effect may be that parents with higher levels of education tend to be particularly successful in both asking more questions of children in the course of shared reading (e.g. Tracey and Young, 2002), a key element to the relatively successful dialogic reading technique, and in communicating to young children, quite literally, the joy of print (e.g. Sonnenschein *et al.*, 1997).

Family motivation is key for shared-book reading for all

Thus, beyond the purely cognitive aspects of shared-book reading as enhancing children's language skills and academic readiness, children's motivation for reading may also be important to consider in fully understanding the importance of shared-book reading. The process through which motivation develops may be related to parents' interactions with their children. For example, Bus and van IJzendoorn (1995) showed that in parent-child dyads in which attachment was less secure (determined via behavioral observations), shared-book reading occurred less frequently as well. The process of book reading often begins very early and is important in building up a safe and warm environment in which to enjoy literacy activities (e.g. Bus and van IJzendoorn, 1995; 1997).

Happily, shared-book reading appears to have approximately equivalent effects on children's language growth across families with different socioeconomic statuses (e.g. Bus *et al.*, 1995). However, given the fact that children with mothers with lower socioeconomic statuses often have more limited vocabularies than do those from higher such statuses (e.g. Hoff, 2003), shared-book reading may be a particularly important element of parenting among those who have enjoyed fewer educational opportunities in order to facilitate their own children's ultimate success in school.

Conclusion

Taken together, the bulk of the research in the area of shared-book reading thus indicates that this is an essential aspect of early parenting. Shared-book reading provides an early foundation from which advanced vocabulary and syntactical structures are encountered in a motivating environment. A key element of this focus is the fact that interactions between the child and the parent are shared in this context. Thus, the child often has some autonomy in deciding what books to read and how. Dialogic reading, an optimal approach to shared-book reading, additionally ensures that children and parents will discuss the books in some measure. Such sharing may indirectly encourage children to begin to think about print in some contexts, such as the reading of an alphabet book itself. However, a direct transition from shared-book reading to print knowledge is not typical. At the same time, shared-book reading provides some familiarity with the context of literacy learning, so young children who have enjoyed shared-book reading with their children can transition to text reading in school with some sense of what print knowledge is and what kinds of narrative structures are typical in books. This early sensitization is longitudinally linked to subsequent reading comprehension gains (e.g. Sénéchal and LeFevre, 2002), one ultimate skill throughout schooling. Shared-book reading thus provides both a cognitive and an emotional context in which children can hone their earliest language and, indirectly, literacy skills. For these reasons, then, shared-book reading is an indispensable ingredient of responsible parenting.

References

Adams, M. J. (1990). *Beginning to Read: Thinking and Learning about Print.* Cambridge, MA: MIT Press.

Aram, D. and Levin, I. (2002). Mother-child joint writing and storybook reading: relations with literacy among low SES kindergartners. *Merrill-Palmer Quarterly, 48*, 202–224.

Bus, A. G. and van IJzendoorn, M. H. (1995). Mothers reading to their 3-year-olds: the role of mother-child attachment in becoming literate. *Reading Research Quarterly*, 30, 998–1015.

——(1997). Affective dimension of mother-infant picturebook reading. *Journal of School Psychology*, 35, 47–60.

Bus, A. G., van IJzendoorn, M. H. and Pellegrini, A. D. (1995). Joint book reading makes for success in learning to read: a meta-analysis on intergenerational transmission of literacy. *Review of Educational Research*, 65, 1–21.

Chaney, C. (1994). Language development, metalinguistic awareness, and emergent literacy skills of 3-year-old children in relation to social class. *Applied Psycholinguistics*, 15, 371–394.

Chiu, M. M. and McBride-Chang, C. (2006). Gender, context, and reading: a comparison of students across 43 countries. *Scientific Studies of Reading*, 10, 331–362.

Chow, B. Y.-W. and McBride-Chang, C. (2003). Parent-child book reading as an intervention technique for preschoolers in Hong Kong. *Early Education and Development*, 14, 233–248.

Chow, B. Y.-W., McBride-Chang, C. and Cheung, H. (2010). Parent-child reading in English as a second language: effects on language and literacy development of Chinese kindergarteners. *Journal of Research in Reading*, 33, 284–301.

Chow, B. W.-Y., McBride-Chang, C., Cheuk, C. and Cheung, H. (2008). Dialogic reading and morphology training in Chinese children: effects on language and literacy. *Developmental Psychology*, 44, 233–244

Deckner, D. F., Adamson, L. A. and Bakeman, R. (2006). Child and maternal contributions to shared reading: effects on language and literacy development. *Applied Developmental Psychology*, 27, 31–41.

Evans, M. A. and Saint-Aubin, J. (2005). What children are looking at during shared storybook reading: evidence from eye movement monitoring. *Psychological Science*, 16, 913–920.

Fung, P. C., Chow, B. W.-Y. and McBride-Chang, C. (2005). The impact of a dialogic reading program on deaf and hard-of-hearing kindergarten and early primary school-aged students in Hong Kong. *Journal of Deaf Studies and Deaf Education*, 10, 82–95.

Hoff, E. (2003). The specificity of environmental influence: socioeconomic status affects early vocabulary development via maternal speech. *Child Development*, 74, 1368–1378.

Hood, M., Conlon, E. and Andrews, G. (2008). Preschool home literacy practices and children's literacy development: a longitudinal analysis. *Journal of Educational Psychology*, 100, 252–271.

Kalia, V. (2007). Assessing the role of book reading practices in Indian bilingual children's English language and literacy development. *Early Childhood Education Journal*, 35, 149–153.

Kim, D. and Hall, J. K. (2002). The role of an interactive book reading program in the development of second language pragmatic competence. *The Modern Language Journal*, 86, 332–348.

Kim, Y.-S. (2009). The relationship between home literacy practices and developmental trajectories of emergent literacy and conventional literacy skills for Korean children. *Reading & Writing*, 22, 57–84.

Korat, O., Klein, P. and Segal-Drori, O. (2006). Maternal mediation in book reading, home literacy environment, and children's emergent literacy: a comparison between two social groups. *Reading and Writing*, 20, 361–398.

Lau, J. H.-Y. & McBride-Chang, C. (2005). Home literacy and Chinese reading in Hong Kong Children. *Early Education and Development*, 16, 5–22.

Lyytinen, P., Laakso, M.-L. and Poikkeus, A.-M. (1998). Parental contribution to child's early language and interest in books. *European Journal of Psychology of Education*, 13, 297–308.

Mol, S. E. and Bus, A. G. (2011). To read or not to read: a meta-analysis of print exposure from infancy to early adulthood. *Psychological Bulletin*, 137, 267–296.

Mol, S. E., Bus, A. G., de Jong, M. T. and Smeets, D. J. H. (2008). Added value of dialogic parent-child book readings: a meta-analysis. *Early Education and Development*, 19, 7–26.

Muter, V., Hulme, C., Snowling, M. J. and Stevenson, J. (2004). Phonemes, rimes, vocabulary, and grammatical skills as foundations of early reading development: evidence from a longitudinal study. *Developmental Psychology*, 40, 665–681.

Patterson, J. L. (2002). Relationships of expressive vocabulary to frequency of reading and television experience among bilingual toddlers. *Applied Psycholinguistics*, 23, 493–508.

Rauh, V. A., Lamb-Parker, F., Garfinkel, R. S., Perry, J. and Andrews, H. F. (2003). Biological, social, and community influences on the third-grade reading levels of minority head start children: a multi-level approach. *Journal of Community Psychology*, 31, 255–278.

Reese, E. and Cox, A. (1999). Quality of adult book reading affects children's emergent literacy. *Developmental Psychology*, 35, 20–28.

Roth, F. P., Speece, D. L. and Cooper, D. H. (2002). A longitudinal analysis of the connection between oral language and early reading. *Journal of Educational Research*, 95, 259–272.

Scarborough, H. S. and Dobrich, W. (1994). On the efficacy of reading to preschoolers. *Developmental Review*, 14, 245–302.

Sénéchal, M. (2006). Testing the home literacy model: parent involvement in kindergarten is differentially related to grade 4 reading comprehension, fluency, spelling, and reading for pleasure. *Scientific Studies of Reading*, 10, 59–87.

Sénéchal, M and LeFevre, J. (2002). Parental involvement in the development of children's reading skill: a five-year longitudinal study. *Child Development*, 73, 445–460.

Sénéchal, M., Oullette, G. and Rodney, D. (2006). The misunderstood giant: on the predictive role of early vocabulary to future reading. In S. B. Neuman & D. Dickinson (Eds.) *Handbook of Early Literacy Research*, Volume 2 (pp. 173–182). New York: Guilford Press.

Sénéchal, M., Pagan, S., Lever, R. and Ouellette, G. P. (2008). Relations among the frequency of shared reading and 4-year-old children's vocabulary, morphological and syntax comprehension, and narrative skills. *Early Education and Development*, 19, 27–44.

Snow, C. E., Burns, M. S. and Griffin, P. (Eds.) (1998). *Preventing Reading Difficulties in Young Children*. Washington, DC National Academy Press.

Sonnenschein, S., Baker, L., Serpell, R., Scher, D., Truitt, V. G. and Munsterman, K. (1997). Parental beliefs about ways to help children learn to read: the impact of an entertainment of a skills perspective. *Early Child Development and Care*, 127-128, 111–118.

Stanovich, K. (1986). Matthew effects in reading: some consequences of individual differences in the acquisition of literacy. *Reading Research Quarterly*, 21, 360–407.

Stephenson, K. A., Parrila, R. K., Georgiou, G. K. and Kirby, J. R. (2008). Effects of home literacy, parents' beliefs, and children's task-focused behavior on emergent literacy and word reading skills. *Scientific Studies of Reading*, 12, 24–50.

Tabors, P. O. and Snow, C. E. (2001). Young bilingual children and early literacy development. In S. B. Neuman and D. K. Dickinson (Eds.), *Handbook of Early Literacy Research*. New York: Guilford Press, 159–178.

Tong, X., McBride-Chang, C., Shu, H. and Wong, A. M.-Y. (2009). Morphological awareness, orthographic knowledge, and spelling errors: keys to understanding early Chinese literacy acquisition. *Scientific Studies of Reading*, 13(5), 426–452.

Tracey, D. H. and Young, J. W. (2002). Mothers' helping behaviors during children's at-home oral-reading practice: effects of children's reading ability, children's gender, and mothers' educational level. *Journal of Educational Psychology*, 94, 729–737.

Van Steensel, R., McElvany, N., Kurvers, J. and Herppich, S. (2011). How effective are family literacy programs? Results of a meta-analysis. *Review of Educational Research, 81,* 69–96.

Wagemaker, H. Taube, K., Munck, I., Kontogiannopoulou-Polydorides, G. and Martin, M. (1996). *Are Girls Better Readers?* Amsterdam: IEA.

Weigel, D. J., Martin, S. S. and Bennett, K. K. (2006). Contributions of the home literacy environment to preschool-aged children's emerging literacy and language skills. *Early Child Development & Care*, 176, 357–378.

Wells, G. (1985). *Language Development in the Preschool Years*. New York: Cambridge University Press.

Whitehurst, G. J., Epstein, J. N., Angell, A. L., Payne, A. C., Crone, D. A. and Fischel, J. E. (1994). Outcomes of an emergent literacy intervention in Head Start. *Journal of Educational Psychology*, 86, 542–555.

Whitehurst, G. J., Falco, F. L., Lonigan, C. J., Fischel, J. E., DeBaryshe, B. D., Valdez-Menchaca, M. C. and Caulfield, M. (1988). Accelerating language development through picture book reading. *Developmental Psychology*, 24, 552–559.

Whitehust, G. J. and Lonigan, C. J. (1998). Child development and emergent literacy. *Child Development*, 69, 848–872.

Chapter 7

The tyranny of shared book-reading

Elaine Reese

Department of Psychology, University of Otago

The image of a young child curled up in her father's arms while he reads a book to her is a hard one to fault. The child (let us call her Sophie), soothed by the sound of her father's storytelling voice, is fully absorbed in the experience. As her father reads and talks about the book, Sophie looks at the pictures steadfastly, pulling her thumb out of her mouth on occasion to provide an answer, ask a question herself, or make a comment.

But is this image a reality? Sometimes, and for some children, yes. And when shared book-reading works, it is a wondrous experience for all involved. For many children, however, this image is an airbrushed ideal. The reality of shared book-reading for many young children, in particular toddlers, is quite a different picture. Imagine instead an active toddler (let's call him James) climbing on the couch cushions as his mother attempts to interest him in a storybook. She points to a picture of a dog in the book and says, "Look at this one, James. What is this animal called?" James briefly looks at the book and then proceeds to stomp over his mother's legs and clamber down off the couch to retrieve his toy truck. He noisily zooms the truck across the carpet. His mother turns the page and says "Me-oooow. James, what animal says 'meow'?" James looks up at his mother and laughs, then zooms his truck behind the couch. "Beep beep!"

Shared book-reading is not always the idyllic experience portrayed in parenting books and pamphlets in the doctor's waiting room. Does that mean that parents and educators should not persist in attempting to create positive shared book-reading experiences with young children? Scarborough and Dobrich (1994) argued that for some children, shared book-reading was about as enjoyable as eating broccoli. They proposed that for these children, perhaps we should not force-feed them books, just as we would not force them to eat broccoli. Is book-reading like broccoli to some children? Should we force them, or even gently encourage them, to share books with us whether they like it or not?

To complicate the issue, an abundance of research now demonstrates the value of shared book-reading for children's oral language skills and for some aspects of their literacy skills. I will consider the research evidence for all of these established and potential benefits of shared book-reading.

Yet I will argue that shared book-reading is not the only way to access these benefits for children. The zealous promotion of shared book-reading by early childhood educators, librarians, medical professionals, and the media as a panacea for young children's learning and future success in school, and even for the future well-being of society, has led to an overemphasis on this single activity to the neglect of other important conversations between adults and children. I will present research showing that these other conversations have many of the same benefits, as well as some new benefits, for children's development. I will also review evidence that for some children in some cultures, these other conversations may even be a better way of achieving those benefits in comparison to shared book-reading. Ultimately a tyrannical view of shared book-reading results in a loss for middle-income and lower-income children alike of a diverse range of conversations and interactions with parents, grandparents, and teachers. Along with the broccoli, perhaps we should be serving up some butternut squash, beetroot, and kale.

The benefits of shared book-reading

Benefit #1: Shared book-reading advances children's language development

The benefits of shared book-reading are perhaps most robustly established for young children's language skill. This link was first indicated in studies of the reported quantity of shared book-reading with preschoolers (see Bus *et al.*, 1995; Scarborough and Dobrich, 1994 for reviews). In these studies, parents estimated how often they read books with their preschoolers, and researchers assessed the children's language development. Some of these studies were longitudinal, with language outcomes measured at a later point in time. In a meta-analysis, Bus *et al.* estimated an effect size of $d = .67$ for the role of book-reading frequency on children's language growth. About 10 percent of children's language growth could be explained by the amount of book-reading they received in the preschool years. Of course, many other factors that co-vary with the quantity of book-reading (e.g. maternal education; total amount of child-directed speech) could potentially explain such a correlation. Unfortunately, most of this correlational research has failed to account for genetic and other environmental contributors to children's language skill besides shared book-reading.

Fortunately, excellent experimental research also exists on the effects of shared book-reading on children's language development. The best-known experimental studies are those in which a particular style of book-reading, called *dialogic reading*, is contrasted to naturally occurring styles of book-reading or to various non-reading control groups (see Mol *et al.*, 2008 for a review). Dialogic reading is a style in which adults are encouraged to interact frequently with young children during storybook reading. In fact, reading the text is not essential; the critical features of dialogic reading are to ask open-ended questions on each page, and to follow up children's responses with praise or correction, an expansion, and ideally, a new but related open-ended question. The specific details of dialogic reading depend on the age of the child, with a more advanced style comprised of more difficult open-ended and abstract questions recommended for older preschoolers. Still, the main point of dialogic reading – to engage the child in the book-sharing and to get them talking – is the same throughout early childhood.

Although many studies of dialogic reading exist, only a few of these studies have compared dialogic reading to a control group in which parents or other adults engaged in their typical reading style (e.g. Whitehurst *et al.*, 1988). Findings from these studies are valuable in informing us of the added value of reading dialogically to typically occurring book-reading. These studies demonstrate benefits of dialogic reading over other styles of reading for young children's language skills (cf. Reese and Cox, 1999), and in particular for their expressive vocabulary skills.

Other dialogic reading studies that compare dialogic reading to a non-reading control group can inform us of the value of shared book-reading over other adult-child interactions, such as art projects, for children's expressive language (Lever and Sénéchal, 2011; Valdez-Menchaca and Whitehurst, 1992). It is true that book-reading as a conversational context is more linguistically complex than adult-child talk in some other contexts, such as toy play, feeding, and caregiving (see Hoff, 2006 for a review). However, when compared to other demanding conversational contexts, mothers' language during shared book-reading is *less* complex and literate than their talk during a storytelling context, in which they reminisced about a past event (Curenton *et al.*, 2008). These reminiscing conversations are a good contrast to shared book-reading because, like book-reading, they are decontextualized conversations – the topic is about another place and time, not about the here-and-now. Thus, reminiscing conversations are a fairer comparison to shared book-reading because they are more demanding, both cognitively and linguistically, for children than talk that occurs during an art project or during free play with toys. Reminiscing conversations also occur frequently (albeit briefly) between parents and children in all cultures studied to date (e.g. Miller *et al.*, 1990). When mothers are trained to reminisce more elaboratively, their children's expressive language skills benefit (Taumoepeau and Reese, 2012, Manuscript under review).

Thus, shared book-reading advances children's oral language skills, but it is possible that other demanding conversations that do not involve a book boost children's oral language to a similar degree.

Benefit #2: Shared book-reading can promote children's phonological development

Phonological awareness is children's knowledge of the separate sounds that make up words, whether those sounds are at the level of the syllable or phoneme. Phonological awareness develops rapidly in early childhood, prior to reading instruction, and is causally linked to children's reading achievement (Bradley and Bryant, 1983; Lonigan *et al.*, 2009; cf chapters in this book).

As it is typically practiced in the home or preschool, shared book-reading is not uniquely linked to growth in young children's phonological awareness skills. When reading a storybook with their children, parents hardly ever talk explicitly about the sounds of words (Stadler and McEvoy, 2003). Other types of interactions besides shared storybook reading appear to contribute instead to children's growing phonological awareness. When parents read alphabet books with their children, for instance, they focus more on the sounds of words (Stadler and McEvoy, 2003). Foy and Mann (2003) noted direct links between children's phonological awareness and other aspects of the home literacy environment, such as the children's exposure to electronic print media, but did not find a link between children's phonological awareness and estimates of shared book-reading frequency. Any link between book-reading frequency and children's phonological awareness appears to be indirect, via the well-established effect of book-reading on children's vocabulary growth. For instance, Metsala (1999) proposed that increases in vocabulary advance children's phonological awareness by creating denser "neighborhoods" of words that sound alike, which in turn forces children to discriminate amongst similar sounding words (e.g. "dog" vs "dig").

Nor does dialogic reading on its own promote children's phonological awareness (see Mol *et al.*, 2009; but cf. Lonigan *et al.*, 1999; Chow *et al.*, 2010). However, it is possible to practice book-reading in a way that does advance children's phonological awareness by focusing on the sounds of words. For instance, Chow *et al.* (2008) designed a metalinguistic awareness intervention for Hong Kong parents in which they brought children's attention to the morphemes in Chinese words during book-reading. In contrast to a dialogic reading-only intervention, which promoted the children's vocabulary development, the dialogical reading plus metalinguistic awareness intervention also developed children's recognition of Chinese characters, which would be analogous to letter recognition in English.

However, because discussions during shared storybook reading naturally gravitate toward content (Stadler and McEvoy, 2003), perhaps these interactions promoting phonological awareness are best situated in shared reading of alphabet or rhyming books.

Benefit #3: Shared book-reading can promote the acquisition of print skills

During a typical book-reading interaction, preschool children only look at the print about 4 percent of the time (Justice *et al.*, 2008). It is therefore not surprising that correlational studies find no link between the frequency of typically occurring shared book reading and children's print skills (e.g. Sénéchal and LeFevre, 2002). Nor does dialogic reading promote children's print skills except when add-on activities focusing on print are included in a broader intervention (see review by Mol *et al.*, 2009). In fact, in one large-scale study in which preschool teachers were trained in interactive reading, the intervention even had a negative effect on children's letter knowledge by the end of the school year (see Wasik *et al.*, 2006).

However, when adults talk explicitly about print or point to the words in the book, children respond accordingly and pay significantly more attention to print during shared book-reading (Justice *et al.*, 2008). Experimental work bears out the potential use of shared book-reading as a context for promoting children's print skills (Justice and Ezell, 2002). In an intervention with preschool teachers, children from classrooms whose teachers were trained to reference print explicitly during shared storybook reading over the school year advanced faster in their print skills than children from classrooms in which teachers engaged in their typical reading styles (Justice *et al.*, 2010). Importantly, this effect of reading style on print skills was not moderated by child factors such as SES, age, or initial print awareness, nor was it moderated by type of school program or teacher experience. Nor did these advances in print skills occur at the cost of children's language development – the two reading styles were indistinguishable in their effects on children's language growth across the school year.

It appears that both parents and teachers can be trained to read storybooks in ways that advance children's print knowledge, even though their typically occurring reading styles do not result in these benefits.

The limitations of shared book-reading

Shared book-reading is therefore a highly flexible context that can be tailored to promote different skills: vocabulary and oral language expression; phonological awareness; and print awareness. Yet is it the panacea for children's language and literacy development that it appears?

Limitation #1: The benefits of shared book-reading for children's language extend to only some children, some of the time

Mol *et al.* (2008) conducted a meta-analysis on parent-led dialogic reading with preschoolers of different ages and socioeconomic levels. Only with younger preschoolers was dialogic reading effective in advancing children's language skills, and it was more effective for their expressive than receptive language. For older preschoolers, even in studies that had used the more demanding style of dialogic reading, the effects of parents' dialogic reading on children's language were weak to non-existent. Cutspec (2004) reached the same conclusion in her review of the literature: Dialogic reading is primarily beneficial for two- to three-year-old children's language development. Moreover, parent-led dialogic reading worked primarily with children whose parents were middle-class and of European descent. For children from low-income families, who also tended to be of non-European descent, results of parent-only dialogic reading programs were not effective.

Our experimental study (Reese and Cox, 1999) of three book-reading styles (a lower-level dialogic style vs. two more demanding styles) clarified the benefits of a dialogic style of reading. The researcher-led dialogic-type style only worked to boost the vocabulary of younger preschoolers and those who started out the study with lower vocabulary levels. For older preschoolers and those with more advanced language skills, a more demanding style of reading in which the book was discussed in-depth at the end was more effective in boosting their vocabularies. Similarly, Lever and Sénéchal's (2011) successful dialogic reading intervention for kindergarteners' expressive vocabulary and narrative skills was also led by researchers and included an add-on narrative elaboration component.

Shared book-reading is also more frequent with girls and firstborn children than boys and laterborns (Raikes *et al.*, 2006; Westerlund and Lagerberg, 2008), but experimental studies of interactive reading do not find different effects on girls' and boys' language development. Child temperament does not appear to be a strong factor in shaping parents' book-reading frequency, at least for mothers (Karrass *et al.*, 2003; Westerlund and Lagerberg 2008). Karrass *et al.* did identify differences in father-child book reading with their eight-month-olds as a function of child temperament.

On the whole, though, the main limitations for the effects of shared book-reading on children's language development appear to be children's age, language level, and socioeconomic and cultural background.

Limitation #2: The benefits of shared book-reading are limited by the quality of the interaction and sometimes by group size

In a meta-analysis of interactive reading programs in preschools, Mol *et al.* (2008) noted that when experimenters rather than teachers led the book-reading sessions, children were much more likely to demonstrate language growth. Experimenters may be more faithful to the intervention protocol than are teachers. When experimenters conducted the reading, however, the effectiveness of the program for children's oral language also decreased linearly with group size (cf. Karweit and Wasik, 1996). In contrast, Justice *et al.*'s (2010) teacher-led intervention of print-focused reading in large groups found strong effects on children's print skills. Thus, the size of the group may be less important than the qualities and training of the person leading the group, and the targeted outcome. Teachers may feel more comfortable with large groups and manage those interactions better than do other adult readers, who may feel more comfortable with one-on-one or small-group interactions. Moreover, large-group book-reading may be most effective for promoting children's print rather than language skills.

Limitation #3: In some cultures, shared book-reading is not a natural activity

For adults from some cultures and socioeconomic classes, it is not normal or natural to interact with a child during storybook reading, or indeed to read storybooks at all with their children (Heath, 1982; Melzi and Caspe, 2005). Put simply, educated and European mothers are much more likely to read to their children than are less educated mothers and those who are Hispanic (Raikes *et al.*, 2006).

Fortunately, it turns out that other conversational contexts may be just as effective at promoting most of the skills that interactive reading develops. For instance, Beals (2001) noted that parents who engaged in extended narratives about the past and future during mealtime conversations had children with more advanced receptive vocabulary and story comprehension skills in kindergarten. In a comparative study, I demonstrated that parent-child reminiscing about past events predicted children's language and literacy as well or better than did parent-child book-reading throughout early childhood (Reese, 1995). The features of parent-child reminiscing that best predicted children's language and literacy were the degree to which parents elaborated on past events and linked those events to other experiences in the child's life. Likewise, the features of parent-child book-reading that best predicted children's later language and literacy were the degree to which parents asked high-level questions and comments about the book (e.g. inferring or predicting events). In other words, a similar focus on rich, cognitively demanding conversation was linked to children's language and literacy, whether those conversations occurred during book-reading or reminiscing. We (Leyva *et al.*, 2011) extended these findings by comparing parents' reminiscing conversations to their interactions with children during a writing task. Parents' elaborative talk during reminiscing was uniquely correlated with children's writing skills, even after controlling for parents' support during the writing task itself and for children's language and literacy skills. We believe that parents' elaborative talk during reminiscing, because it is a decontextualized conversation, is helping children's metalinguistic and metacognitive skills. These analytical skills are in turn promoting children's reading and writing development.

My colleagues and I garnered further support for these patterns in an intervention study of low-income US families from diverse cultural backgrounds whose children were attending Head Start. In these families, parents' elaborative talk during reminiscing at pretest was concurrently correlated with their children's language and literacy (Sparks and Reese, in press). In contrast, parents' elaborative talk during shared book-reading at pretest was not at all correlated with their children's language and literacy levels. After this baseline phase of the study, we began the intervention phase in which we randomly assigned parents to read dialogically with their preschoolers in comparison to an elaborative reminiscing training and a control group (Reese *et al.*, 2011). The main outcome of the intervention was that children whose parents were trained to reminisce elaboratively had better oral narrative skills at the end of Head Start in comparison to children whose parents were trained to read dialogically. In conjunction with the baseline findings that parents' book-reading styles were not correlated with their children's language and literacy, we interpret these findings to mean that for these parents, book-reading may not have been a natural occurrence in the home. Even though the parents reported at the start of the study that they read books frequently to their children, they may have overestimated their reading frequency, given the societal dictum that shared book-reading is necessary for children's school success. Or perhaps they did read books frequently with their children, but they did not do so in an interactive way.

It will be important in future research to explore other types of conversations between parents and children that are promising arenas for children's language and literacy development. For instance, we are finding that parents' interactions with their children in which they play with the sounds of words (through rhyming, singing, or other soundplay) are strongly predictive of children's phonological awareness (Reese *et al.*, 2011; Schaughency *et al.*, 2011). These interactions may be brief and hard to capture, but are nonetheless an important contrast to shared book-reading and other extended conversations, especially because these lengthier and more prototypical conversations are not strongly linked to children's phonological awareness.

Other promising conversations to explore for children's language and literacy development include parents' talk with their children during dramatic play or about their children's imaginary companions (see Trionfi and Reese, 2009). These conversations are for the most part unmapped with respect to their contributions to children's language and literacy development, and they have not yet been compared at all to shared book-reading.

Implications for the care and education of young children

What are the implications of this enlarged view of the benefits of adult conversation that goes beyond shared book-reading? Those of us parenting and teaching young children should keep reading books with them, but we should do so carefully, with an eye to pitching the interaction to critical characteristics of the child: especially their age and language level. We should read interactively with children when they are younger and at lower language levels to advance their vocabulary development, but as children grow older, they need higher-level, and perhaps less interrupting interactions, to stay engaged and to process the overall structure of the story. Because it is extremely hard to tailor your book-reading style to children's language levels when reading with more than one or two children, we might consider reserving teacher-led reading with groups of children as a way of advancing other skills besides language. Large-group reading led by preschool teachers, for instance, appears to be a perfectly viable option for advancing children's print development, regardless of the child's initial print skills (Justice *et al.*, 2010).

Moreover, we should supplement shared book-reading with a rich range of other types of conversations and language interactions. Shared book-reading can be an important part of a child's conversational diet, but it should not dominate to the exclusion of other forms of conversation, especially those conversations that extend children's language and thought. It is vitally important for educators and practitioners working with low-income parents to avoid the suggestion that shared book-reading with children is the only way, or even the best way, to help advance children's language skill. Janes and Kermani (2001) provide a cautionary tale of a family literacy program they conducted with Latino immigrant parents. As part of the program, parents were trained to read commercially available storybooks in Spanish interactively with their young children. Families enrolled in the program with great enthusiasm, but by the end of the first year, the dropout rate was 70 percent. Comments from parents at exit interviews were illuminating: "Reading was always a punishment when I was small" and "I don't like books" (p. 460). The authors describe the resulting *castigo* (punishment) style of book-reading as one characterized by the parent sitting physically apart from the child, without eye contact, reading with flat intonation and few pauses, and interrupting the reading frequently to issue behavioral directives. Parents' responses to the intervention improved when they were encouraged to create their own home-made books for their children, but only a minority of the caregivers who remained in the program were able to develop an interactive reading style with their children. For parents who have not had positive experiences with reading, a conversational intervention may be a much more natural and successful way of advancing children's language development than a book-reading intervention.

Once we have escaped the tyranny of shared book-reading, new avenues for extended conversation with low-income and middle-income children alike may open up for us. Susan Sonnenschein (personal communication, April 2011), for instance, claimed that mealtimes in Head Start and many other childcare settings are usually a wasted opportunity for engaging in high-quality conversation with young children. And Bond and Wasik (2009) have developed a wonderful technique called "conversation stations" with young children in which an adult in a childcare setting helps a child to create a rich story about a past event.

In other words, keep sharing books with young children, but be creative about it. A little cheese sauce on the broccoli goes a long way, and a side of edamame beans wouldn't hurt either.

References

Beals, D. (2001). Eating and reading: links between family conversations with preschoolers and later language and literacy. In D. K. Dickinson and P. O. Tabors (Eds.), *Beginning Literacy with Language* (pp. 75–92). Baltimore, MD: Paul H. Brookes Publishing Co.

Bond, M. A. and Wasik, B. A. (2009). Conversation stations: promoting language development in young children. *Early Childhood Education Journal, 36,* 467–473.

Bradley, L. and Bryant, P.E. (1983). Categorizing sounds and learning to read: a causal connection. *Nature, 301,* 419–421.

Bus, A. G., van IJzendoorn, M. H. and Pellegrini, A. D. (1995). Joint book-reading makes for success in learning to read: a meta-analysis on intergenerational transmission of literacy. *Review of Educational Research, 65,* 1–21.

Chow, B. W-Y., McBride-Chang, C. and Cheung, H. (2010). Parent-child reading in English as a second language: effects on language and literacy development of Chinese kindergarteners. *Journal of Research in Reading, 33,* 284–301.

Chow, B. W-Y., McBride-Chang, C., Cheung, H. and Chow, C. S-L. (2008). Dialogic reading and morphology training in Chinese children: effects on language and literacy. *Developmental Psychology, 44,* 233–244.

Curenton, S. M., Craig, M. J. and Flanigan, N. (2008). Use of decontextualized talk across story contexts: how oral storytelling and emergent reading can scaffold children's development. *Early Education and*

Development, 19, 161–187.

Cutspec, P. A. (2004). Influences of dialogic reading on the language development of toddlers. *Bridges: Practice-Based Research Syntheses, 2(2),* 1–12.

Foy, J. G. and Mann, V. (2003). Home literacy environment and phonological awareness in preschool children: differential effects for rhyme and phoneme awareness. *Applied Psycholinguistics, 24,* 59–88.

Heath, S. B. (1982). What no bedtime story means: narrative skills at home and school. *Language in Society, 11,* 49-76.

Hoff, E. (2006). How social contexts support and shape language development. *Developmental Review, 26,* 55–88.

Janes, H. and Kermani, H. (2001). Caregivers' story reading to young children in family literacy programs: pleasure or punishment? *Journal of Adolescent and Adult Literacy, 44,* 458–466.

Justice, L. M. and Ezell, H. K. (2002). Use of storybook reading to increase print awareness in at-risk children. *American Journal of Speech-Language Pathology, 11,* 17–29.

Justice, L. M., McGinty, A. S., Piasta, S. B., Kaderavek, J. N. and Fan, X. (2010). Print-focused read-alouds in preschool classrooms: intervention effectiveness and moderators of child outcomes. *Language, Speech, and Hearing Services in Schools, 41,* 504–520.

Justice, L. M., Pullen, P. C. and Pence, K. (2008). Influence of verbal and nonverbal references to print on preschoolers' visual attention to print during storybook reading. *Developmental Psychology, 44,* 855–866.

Karrass, J., VanDeventer, M. C. and Braungart-Rieker, J. M. (2003). Predicting shared parent-child book-reading in infancy. *Journal of Family Psychology, 17,* 134–146.

Karweit, N. and Wasik, B. A. (1996). The effects of story reading programs on literacy and language development of disadvantaged preschoolers. *Journal of Education for Students Placed at Risk, I,* 319–348.

Lever, R. and Sénéchal, M. (2011). Discussing stories: on how a dialogic reading intervention improves kindergartners' oral narrative construction. *Journal of Experimental Child Psychology, 108,* 1–24.

Leyva, D., Reese, E. and Wiser, M. (2011). Early understanding of the functions of print: parent-child interaction and preschoolers' notating skills. *First Language.* doi: 10.1177/0142723711410793

Lonigan, C. J., Anthony, J., Bloomfield, B., Dyer, S. and Samuel, C. (1999). Effects of two shared-reading interventions on emergent literacy skills of at-risk preschoolers. *Journal of Early Intervention, 22,* 306–322.

Lonigan, C. J., Anthony, J. L., Phillips, B. M., Purpura, D. J., Wilson, S. B. and McQueen, J. D. (2009). The nature of preschool phonological processing abilities and their relations to vocabulary, general cognitive abilities, and print knowledge. *Journal of Educational Psychology, 101,* 345–358.

Melzi, G. and Caspe, M. (2005). Variation in maternal narrative styles during book reading interactions. *Narrative Inquiry, 15,* 101–125.

Metsala, J. (1999). Young children's phonological awareness and nonword repetition as a function of vocabulary development. *Journal of Educational Psychology, 91,* 3–19.

Miller, P. J., Potts, R., Fung, H., Hoogstra, L. and Mintz, J. (1990). Narrative practices and the social construction of self in childhood. *American Ethnologist, 17,* 292–311.

Mol, S. E., Bus, A. G. and de Jong, M. T. (2009). Interactive book reading in early education: a tool to stimulate print knowledge as well as oral language. *Review of Educational Research, 79,* 979–1007.

Mol, W. E., Bus, A. G., de Jong, M. T. and Smeets, D. J. H. (2008). Added value of parent-child dialogic readings: a meta-analysis. *Early Education and Development, 19,* 7–26.

Raikes, H., Pan, B. A., Luze, G., Tamis-LeMonda, C. S., Brooks-Gunn, J., Constantine, J., Tarullo, L. B., Raikes, H. A. and Rodriguez, E. T. (2006). Mother-child book-reading in low-income families: correlates and outcomes during the first three years of life. *Child Development, 77,* 924–953.

Reese, E. (1995). Predicting children's literacy from mother-child conversations. *Cognitive Development, 10,* 381–405.

Reese, E. and Cox, A. (1999). Quality of adult book reading affects children's language and literacy. *Developmental Psychology, 35,* 20–28.

Reese, E., Divers, S. and Robertson, S-J. (2011). *Having Pun with your Kids: The Role of Parents' Wordplay in Children's Phonological Development*. Paper presented at the Australasian Human Development Conference, Dunedin, New Zealand.

Reese, E., Leyva, D., Sparks, A. and Grolnick, W. (2010). Maternal elaborative reminiscing increases low-income children's narrative skills relative to dialogic reading. *Early Education and Development, 21,* 318–342.

Scarborough, H. and Dobrich, W. (1994). On the efficacy of reading to preschoolers. *Developmental Review, 14,* 245–302.

Schaughency, E., Lau, R. and Reese, E. (2011). *Predicting Children's Literacy from Mother-child Interactions and Sleep Quality*. Paper presented at the Australasian Human Development Conference, Dunedin, New Zealand.

Sénéchal, M. and LeFevre, J. A. (2002). Parental involvement in the development of children's reading skill: a five-year longitudinal study. *Child Development, 73,* 445–460.

Sparks, A. and Reese, E. (in press). From reminiscing to reading: home contributions to children's developing language and literacy. *First Language*.

Stadler, M. A. and McEvoy, M. A. (2003). The effect of text genre on parent use of joint book reading strategies to promote phonological awareness. *Early Childhood Research Quarterly, 18,* 502–512.

Taumoepeau, M. and Reese, E. (2012), Manuscript under review. *Parental reminiscing and children's theory of mind: a longitudinal intervention*.

Trionfi, G. and Reese, E. (2009). A good story: children with imaginary companions create richer narratives. *Child Development, 80,* 1310–1322.

Valdez-Menchaca, M. C. and Whitehurst, G. J. (1992). Accelerating language development through picture book reading: a systematic extension to Mexican day care. *Developmental Psychology, 28,* 1106–1114.

Wasik, B. A., Bond, M. A. and Hindman, A. (2006). The effects of a language and literacy intervention on Head Start children and teachers. *Journal of Educational Psychology, 98,* 63–74.

Westerlund, M. and Lagerberg, D. (2008). Expressive vocabulary in 18-month-old children in relation to demographic factors, mother and child characteristics, communication style and shared reading. *Child: Care, Health, and Development, 34,* 257–266.

Whitehurst, G. J., Falco, F., Lonigan, C. J., Fischel, J. E., DeBaryshe, B. D. and Valdez-Menchaca, M. C. (1988). Accelerating language development through picture-book reading. *Developmental Psychology, 24,* 552–558.

Part IV

What should be done to foster children's mathematical development in the preschool years?

How important is it that math is often not present in today's early childhood classrooms? We have shown that mathematical thinking comes naturally to children. Is not that enough? Not at all. Children do not develop that thinking unless it is intentionally supported.

Julie Sarama, Ph.D. and Douglas H. Clements, Ph.D.

Based on learning sciences theory and research, we show that playful learning experiences are intrinsically motivating and allow children to develop conceptual and procedural math knowledge through meaningful engagement and "sense-making" processes.

Kelly Fisher, Kathy Hirsh-Pasek, and Roberta M. Golinkoff

What should be done to foster children's mathematical development in the preschool years

Chapter 8

Mathematics for the whole child

Julie Sarama, Ph.D. and Douglas H. Clements, Ph.D.
University at Buffalo, SUNY

ALETHA: Math is just inappropriate for preschool. Children need to play, not memorize facts and drill on skills. It's not like language, which you can help kids develop, well, more naturally or informally. Math you have to teach directly.

BRENDA: I agree, but that doesn't make it inappropriate. Especially my preschoolers, who come from low-resource communities – they need that kind of direct instruction in math. Otherwise, they'll be behind forever.

CATHY: It may be important, but do you need to teach it that way? I mean, aren't they doing math when they build with blocks?

Which teacher do you agree with? Or do you have another opinion? What role is there for math early education? Should math be more teacher-directed or more child-centered? What are the best strategies to ensure all children are successful?

If you are similar to most people in the US, including most early childhood teachers, you have a firm ("gut") feeling that math is hard, abstract, and at the opposite end of a spectrum from a vision of early childhood that features children at play, curious and creative. When mathematics is discussed in or out of school, it is likely you filter everything said through these feelings.

You are not alone. Although it is *not* true through its history (see Cohen, 1982), the US culture has become inhospitable for the development of positive attitudes and beliefs about mathematics. As just one example, all it takes to raise math anxiety in approximately 17 percent of the US population is … to show them "17%" (Ashcraft, 2006)!

Many adults believe "too much" mathematics is inappropriate for young children. Because they often struggled with mathematics themselves – frequently in badly taught, boring mathematics lessons – they believe that mathematics is difficult and inappropriately abstract. Further, their biases lead them to believe that mathematical experiences stand in opposition to play-based experiences.

There is some good news. These biases and the resultant fears have no basis in young children. Observe them learning mathematics in high-quality settings, or in their play, and you see that they love it.

Surprisingly, such fears and misunderstandings have been with our country for a long time. Let's take a short historical trip.

Early math in the past

Frederick Froebel invented kindergarten. Kindergarten originally included a range of ages, so he invented present-day kindergarten *and* preschool. Froebel originally was a crystallographer – he studied the shape and structure of crystals. Almost every aspect of his kindergarten crystallized into beautiful mathematical forms – the "universal, perfect, alternative language of geometric form" (Brosterman, 1997). Its ultimate aim was to instill in children an understanding of the mathematically generated logic underlying creation. Froebel used "gifts" to teach children the geometric language of the universe. Cylinders, spheres, cubes, and other materials were arranged and moved to show geometric relationships. His "occupations" (activities children engaged in with the gifts) included explorations (e.g. spinning the solids in different orientations, showing how, for example, the spun cube can appear as a cylinder), puzzles, paper folding, and constructions. Children covered the faces of cubes with square tiles, and peeled them away to show parts, properties, and congruence. Shapes were arranged and rearranged on grids etched into each of the children's tables, creating shifting, symmetric patterns or geometric borders.

Cubes that children had made into the chairs, ovens, and the like would be made into geometric design on these grids, and later laid into two rows of four each and expressed as "4 + 4." In this way, connections were key: the "chair" became an aesthetic geometric design, which became a number sentence.

Unfortunately, not everyone *observed* the children engaged with and motivated to learn mathematics. Instead, with no real experience, based only on broad social theories, they drove mathematics out of the curriculum as "inappropriate" (Balfanz, 1999).

Bureaucratic and commercial imperatives emerging from the institutionalization of early childhood education quashed most of the promising mathematical movements. For example, Edward Thorndike wished to emphasize health, so he replaced the first gift (small spheres) with a toothbrush and the first mathematical occupation with "sleep" (Brosterman, 1997). And thus the mathematics was diluted and lost.

Consider another example. Many believe children should be playing, not doing mathematics. They should be building with blocks. Again, this reflects an unfortunate misunderstanding and loss of the historical root of those very blocks. The inventor of today's unit blocks, Caroline Pratt (1948), designed them to teach mathematics (that's why they have "units" and "double" and "half" units, and so forth). She tells of children making enough room for a horse to fit inside a stable. The teacher told Diana that she could have the horse when she had made a stable for it. She and Elizabeth began to build a small construction, but the horse did not fit. Diana had made a large stable with a low roof. After several unsuccessful attempts to get the horse in, she removed the roof, added blocks to the walls to make the roof higher, and replaced the roof. She then tried to put into words what she had done. "Roof too small." The teacher gave her new words, "high" and "low," and she gave a new explanation to the other children.

Children create forms and structures that were planned, by Pratt and others, to embody mathematical relationships. For example, children may struggle with length relationships in finding a roof for a building. Length and equivalence are involved in substituting two shorter blocks for one long block. Children also consider height, area, and volume.

At least they *may* do so, implicitly and intuitively. Teachers such as Diana's, who observe children and understand the mathematics, help children reflect on and further develop these intuitive ideas by discussing them, giving birth to explicit concepts and giving words to their actions. For example, children can be helped to distinguish between different quantities such as height, area, and volume. Three preschoolers made towers and argued about whose was the biggest. Their teacher asked them if they meant whose was tallest (gesturing) or widest, or used the most blocks? The children were surprised to find that the tallest tower did not have the most blocks.

Thus, those who actually observe preschoolers engaging in high-quality mathematics see that they are naturally interested in and drawn to mathematics activities, situations, and problems. They love to engage in and play with mathematics. Those who quelled or vitiated mathematics in the curriculum were those who did *not* observe or interact with children (Balfanz, 1999). Just as we flower the preschool environment with books even before most children can read, just as we delight if a child wants to write her own name, we can easily ensure that mathematics is a joy throughout the preschool day.

Early math in the present: missing in action

Not much math learning happens in early childhood settings

Observations of the full day of 3-year-olds' lives, across all settings, revealed remarkably few mathematics activities, lessons, or episodes of play with mathematical objects, with 60 percent of the children having no experience across 180 observations (Tudge and Doucet, 2004). Factors such as race-ethnicity, socio-economic status (SES), and setting (home or child care) did not significantly affect this low frequency. A study of four pre-K teachers from two settings revealed that little mathematics was presented, either directly or indirectly (Graham *et al.*, 1997). Only one instance of informal mathematical activity with physical materials and few instances of informal or formal mathematics teaching was observed. Teachers stated that they believed that mathematics was important and that they engaged in mathematical discussions. It appears that selection of materials and activities such as puzzles, blocks, games, songs, and finger plays constituted mathematics instruction for these teachers.

How about the effects of programs that are ostensibly "complete" programs but fundamentally built upon literacy goals? In the OWL (*Opening the World of Learning*) curriculum, which includes mathematics in its all-day program, for every 360-minute day, only 58 seconds were devoted to math (Farran *et al.*, 2007). No children gained math skills, and those beginning with higher scores lost math skills over the year.

Little math is a big mistake

How important is it that math is often not present in today's early childhood classrooms? We have shown that mathematical thinking comes naturally to children. Is not that enough? Not at all. Children do not develop that thinking unless it is intentionally supported.

Further, the mathematics achievement of American students compares unfavorably with the achievement of students from several other nations, even as early as first grade and kindergarten (Stigler *et al.*, 1990). Some cross-national differences in informal mathematics knowledge appear as early as three to five years of age (Yuzawa *et al.*, 1999). The knowledge gap is most pronounced in the performance of US children living in economically deprived urban communities (e.g. Griffin *et al.*, 1994; Siegler, 1993).

These gaps are more important than previously realized. Early knowledge strongly affects later success in mathematics (Denton and West, 2002). Specific quantitative and numerical knowledge in the years before first grade has been found to be a stronger predictor of later mathematics achievement than tests of intelligence or memory abilities (Krajewski, 2005). What children know early affects them for many years thereafter, into high school (National Mathematics Advisory Panel, 2008).

Thus, *all* children need a firm foundation in mathematics in the early years. This is especially true of children who live in poverty and who are members of linguistic and ethnic minority groups, because most have had significantly fewer opportunities to learn mathematics (Arnold and Doctoroff, 2003; Denton and West, 2002; Griffin *et al.*, 1995; Jordan *et al.*, 1992). Differences start early and widen (Alexander and Entwisle, 1988). If these children do not receive the best mathematics education possible, they are trapped in a trajectory of failure (Rouse *et al.*, 2005) that closes the door to opportunities in all technical and most professional fields.

Play "vs." mathematics – the tragic – and false – dichotomy

As described, educators of the past did not argue whether children should engage in play *or* mathematics – they created toys that embodied mathematics and taught mathematics. Further, children organically see the work through mathematical lenses. Researchers videotaped 90 4- to 5-year-old children, some from low-income families, others from middle-income families, as they played (Seo and Ginsburg, 2004). For example, a boy takes out all the beads in a box and puts them on a table. He states, "Look! I got one hundred!" He starts counting them to check that assertion. Others join in the counting and they do count up to one hundred, with minimal errors.

The range of mathematics is impressive: they classified, counted, and created patterns and shapes. Even more so is the frequency children engaged in math activities. About 88 percent of children engaged in at least one math activity during their play. Overall, the children showed at least one instance of mathematical activity during 43 percent of the minutes during which they were observed. Of course, these actions may have been just a brief episode within the observed minute of play, but there is little doubt that children are involved in mathematics during a considerable portion of their free play.

What does all this mean regarding children's development? Such everyday *foundational* experiences form the intuitive, implicit conceptual foundation for later mathematics. Later, children represent and elaborate on these ideas – creating models of an everyday activity with mathematical objects, such as numbers and shapes; mathematical actions, such as counting or transforming shapes; and their structural relationships. We call this process "mathematization" (Sarama and Clements, 2009). That is, when children play a game and recognize that they cannot win on the next move, because they need a 7 and the largest number they can roll is a 6, they have represented the game situation with numbers and used mathematical reasoning. Children who recognize that a floor can be tiled with regular hexagons because "the angles fit together" have modeled an aspect of their world with geometry.

Further, recognizing the difference between *foundational* and *mathematized* experiences is necessary to avoid confusion about the type of activity in which children are engaged (Kronholz, 2000). Providing preschoolers with building blocks invites children to have foundational experiences with three-dimensional shapes. Asking them which blocks stack and which roll engages them in mathematizing those experiences, thinking about the properties of those blocks in geometric terms. Children need both types of experiences.

Unfortunately, adults often do not encourage children to reflect on the foundational experiences, using mathematical ideas and language, as we saw.

Surprisingly, such math instruction actually increases the quality of young children's play. Children in classrooms with stronger emphasis on literacy or math were more likely to be engaged at a higher quality level during free choice (play) time. Those in classrooms with an emphasis on both literacy and math were more likely to be engaged at a high quality level than those in classrooms with only one, or no, such emphasis (Aydogan *et al.*, 2005). Thus, high-quality instruction in math *and* high-quality free play do not have to "compete" for time in the classroom. *Doing both* makes each richer, and children benefit in every way. Unfortunately, many adults believe that "open-ended free play" is good and "lessons" in math are not (Sarama, 2002; Sarama and DiBiase, 2004). They do not believe that preschoolers need specific math teaching (Clements and Sarama, 2009). They do not realize that they are depriving their children both of the joy and fascination of mathematics, and of higher-quality free play as well.

These and other examples bring us to the final fascinating and usually overlooked type of play: *mathematical play*. Here we do not mean play that involves mathematics – we've been talking about that throughout this article. We mean *playing with mathematics itself.*

Just after her fourth birthday, Abby is playing with three of the five identical toy train engines her father had brought home. Passing by, her mother asked, "Where are the other trains?" Although she left, Abby spoke to herself. "Oh, I have five. Ummm … [pointing to each engine] you are one, two, three. I'm missing 'four' and 'five' – two are missing! [She played with the trains for another minute.] No, I have 'one,' 'three,' and 'five.' I'm missing 'two' and 'four.' I gotta find them two" (Clements and Sarama, 2009).

When Abby first figured out how many she was missing, she was using math in her play. But when she decided that she would renumber the three engines she had with her 'one,' 'three,' and 'five' and the missing engines 'two' and 'four' she was *playing with the notion that the assignment of numbers to a collection of objects is arbitrary*. She was also counting not just objects, but counting words themselves. She counted the words "four, five" to see there were two missing, and then figured that counting the renumbered counting words "two" and "four" *also* yielded the result of "two." She was *playing with the idea that counting words themselves could be counted*. Teachers well-versed in mathematics education will find and build on children's boundless creativity in playing with mathematics itself.

Laissez-faire math is not enough

Although math can and should be playful and joyous, this does *not* mean that "letting children play" provides high-quality, or even barely adequate, mathematics education. Teachers who do not understand mathematics and how children learn mathematics are not able to recognize or enhance children's spontaneous mathematical thinking.

That is unfortunate because *mathematization* is critical and is often neglected. Consider one more example. Teachers, even in middle school, approach the topics of parallelism and perpendicularity with trepidation. Then consider a preschool boy who is making the bottom floor of a block building. He lays two long blocks down, going in the same direction. Then he tries to bridge across the two ends with a short block. It does span across the long blocks, so he moves an end of one of the long block so it will reach. However, before he tries the short block again, he carefully adjusts the other end of the long block. *He seems to understand that parallel lines are the same distance apart at all points.* He then confidently places the short block and quickly places many short blocks, creating the floor of his building (Seo and Ginsburg, 2004). Like this boy, many children intuitively use ideas that are *theorems in action* (Vergnaud, 1978). The boy even seemed to understand – in his actions – that parallel lines are always the same distance apart. Unfortunately, students often do not "understand" these concepts when they arrive in middle school. If teachers never help them to *mathematize* their theorems in action, to *describe their understandings with the language of mathematics*, the concepts will not become theorems in thought.

Further, even rich, everyday mathematics, properly discussed, are inadequate alone and must be complemented by intentional and sequenced instruction, especially for children who have not had many opportunities to learning math out of school. Traditional approaches to early childhood, such as "developmentally appropriate practice" (DAP) do not appear to increase children's mathematics learning (Van Horn *et al.*, 2005). Programs based only on an "everyday" or "play" approach to mathematics education frequently show negligible gains. We need ways to keep the probable benefits of DAP, such as socio-emotional growth (Van Horn *et al.*, 2005), and yet infuse the young child's day with interesting, equally appropriate, opportunities to engage in mathematical thinking (cf. Peisner-Feinberg *et al.*, 2001). Teaching math indirectly through everyday activities does not predict achievement gains, whereas sequential, intentional group work does (Klein *et al.*, 2008). *Mathematization is requisite to basic mathematical ability.* Adults must help children discuss and think about the mathematics they learn in their play. Further, mathematics is a hierarchical subject. *Intentional teaching using a sequenced mathematics curriculum is an essential complement to rich, scaffolded free play.* This is especially important for children from low-resource communities.

High-quality, explicit, and sequential teaching should be the core of children's mathematical experiences. This helps children learn, helps teachers see the mathematical potential of other, everyday activities, and, as we have seen, even promotes higher-quality play.

Everyone wins.

Learning trajectories: the mathematics of children

The backbone of high-quality teaching and learning is the use of research-based *learning trajectories*. Children generally follow natural developmental trajectories in learning mathematics. When teachers understand these trajectories, and sequence activities based on them, they can build powerful mathematics learning environments.

Each learning trajectory has three parts: a goal, a developmental progression, and instructional activities. To attain a certain mathematical competence in a given topic or domain (the goal), children learn each successive level (the developmental progression), aided by tasks (instructional activities) designed to build the mental actions-on-objects that enable thinking at each higher level (Clements and Sarama, 2009; Sarama and Clements, 2009).

For example, research has revealed a developmental progression of children's ability to compose geometric shapes, both in 2-dimensional puzzle play and free play (Clements and Sarama, 2009; Sarama and Clements, 2009). Children at first are unable to combine shapes and can solve only the simplest puzzles, in which individual shapes only touch at

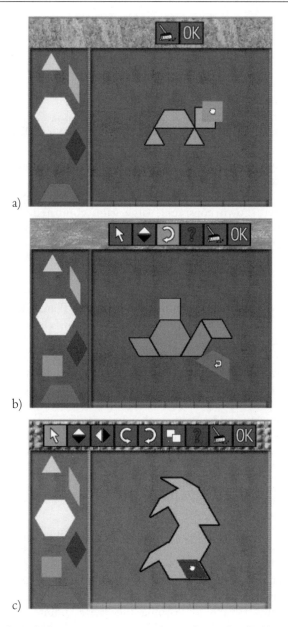

a)

b)

c)

Figure 8.1 Examples of shape composition activities from the Building Blocks curriculum (Clements and Sarama, 2007a)

their corners (Figure 8.1a). They gradually learn to see both individual pieces and a "whole" and learn that parts can make a whole and still remain parts (Figure 8.1b). Most preschoolers can solve puzzles by trial and error, and make pictures with shapes placed next to one another. With experience, they gradually learn to combine shapes to make larger shapes. They become increasing intentional, building mental images of the shapes and their attributes, such as side length and angles (Figure 8.1c). They should do this with physical blocks and computer shapes. (Only the latter are pictured in Figure 8.1, but both are important.) Computer versions do have advantages, including giving immediate feedback, such as highlighting shapes that do not fit and making those shapes transparent so children can see the outline puzzle "underneath" them. Further, children often talk more and explain more of what they are doing on computers than when using other materials (Clements and Sarama, 2009).

Teachers who understand this learning trajectory can provide puzzles and other tasks and environments that are truly developmentally appropriate – challenging but achievable. They can see the advance of children's thinking in free play in 2D and 3D (block building) contexts and promote it with challenges (e.g. "You ran out of those rectangular blocks. Can you make more by combining some of these?").

Curricula based on such learning trajectories, such as *Building Blocks* (Clements and Sarama, 2007a), have shown consistent, large gains compared to other curricula and approaches (Clements and Sarama, 2007b; 2008). This is true even when scaled up to entire school districts (Clements *et al.*, 2011; Sarama *et al.*, 2008).

Final words

Is it true that the experiences of R. Buckminster Fuller, Frank Lloyd Wright, and Paul Kale in Froebelian kindergartens are the foundation of all their creative work, as Brosterman (1997) claimed? Whether or not this is true, it is clear that mathematics in the early years is not a recent invention. But over centuries those without knowledge of children have eliminated these opportunities for young children. Today, many adults have biases against mathematics, and these adults militate against mathematics for their children.

But those who observe children can see they love mathematics. Given the opportunity, children organically see the world through mathematical eyes. They explore, discover, and discuss mathematics. They also show mathematics in their play and *play with mathematics*. They do so more if their teachers use a comprehensive, research-based mathematics curriculum. Just as important, children whose teachers use intentional teaching and sequenced mathematics curricula *engage in more high-level social dramatic play* then children whose teachers do not.

Children in preschool can learn more mathematics, in multiple ways that honor their unique ways of thinking, than was previously thought possible. Learning trajectories can support children's learning, as well as assessment and curriculum development and enactment. Children whose teachers use research-based learning trajectories demonstrate higher levels of mathematical reasoning. They help children learn the language of mathematics. Current research in learning trajectories points the way toward more effective and efficient, yet creative and enjoyable mathematics learning through culturally relevant and developmentally appropriate curricula and assessment.

Acknowledgements

This chapter was based upon work supported in part by the Institute of Education Sciences (US Dept. of Education) under Grant No. R305K05157. Work on the research was also supported in part by the National Science Foundation under Grants No. DRL-1019925 and DRL-1020118. Any opinions, findings, and conclusions or recommendations expressed in this material are those of the authors and do not necessarily reflect the views of the funding agencies.

References

Alexander, K. L. and Entwisle, D. R. (1988). Achievement in the first 2 years of school: patterns and processes. *Monographs of the Society for Research in Child Development, 53*(2, Serial No. 157).

Arnold, D. H. and Doctoroff, G. L. (2003). The early education of socioeconomically disadvantaged children. *Annual Review of Psychology, 54*, 517–545.

Ashcraft, M. H. (2006). *Math Performance, Working Memory, and Math Anxiety; Some Possible Directions For Neural Functioning Work*. Paper presented at the The Neural Basis of Mathematical Development, Nashville, TN.

Aydogan, C., Plummer, C., Kang, S. J., Bilbrey, C., Farran, D. C. and Lipsey, M. W. (2005). *An Investigation of Prekindergarten Curricula: Influences on Classroom Characteristics and Child Engagement*. Paper presented at the NAEYC, Washington, DC.

Balfanz, R. (1999). Why do we teach young children so little mathematics? Some historical considerations. In J. V. Copley (Ed.), *Mathematics in the Early Years* (pp. 3–10). Reston, VA: National Council of Teachers of Mathematics.

Brosterman, N. (1997). *Inventing Kindergarten*. New York: Harry N. Abrams.

Clements, D. H. and Sarama, J. (2007a). *Building Blocks –SRA Real Math, Grade PreK*. Columbus, OH: SRA/McGraw-Hill.

——(2007b). Effects of a preschool mathematics curriculum: summative research on the *Building Blocks* project. *Journal for Research in Mathematics Education, 38*, 136–163.

Clements, D. H. and Sarama, J. (2008). Experimental evaluation of the effects of a research-based preschool mathematics curriculum. *American Educational Research Journal, 45*, 443–494.

——(2009). *Learning and Teaching Early Math: The Learning Trajectories Approach*. New York, NY: Routledge.

Clements, D. H., Sarama, J., Spitler, M. E., Lange, A. A. and Wolfe, C. B. (2011). Mathematics learned by young children in an intervention based on learning trajectories: a large-scale cluster randomized trial. *Journal for Research in Mathematics Education, 42*(2), 127–166.

Cohen, P. C. (1982). *A Calculating People: The Spread of Numeracy in Early America*. Chicago: University of Chicago Press.

Denton, K. and West, J. (2002). *Children's Reading and Mathematics Achievement in Kindergarten and First Grade* (Vol. 2002). Washington, DC: US Department of Education, National Center for Education Statistics.

Farran, D. C., Lipsey, M. W., Watson, B. and Hurley, S. (2007). *Balance of Content Emphasis and Child Content Engagement in an Early Reading First Program*. Paper presented at the American Educational Research Association, Chicago, IL.

Graham, T. A., Nash, C. and Paul, K. (1997). Young children's exposure to mathematics: the child care context. *Early Childhood Education Journal, 25*, 31–38.

Griffin, S., Case, R. and Capodilupo, A. (1995). Teaching for understanding: the importance of the Central Conceptual Structures in the elementary mathematics curriculum. In A. McKeough, J. Lupart and A. Marini (Eds.), *Teaching For Transfer: Fostering Generalization in Learning* (pp. 121–151). Mahwah, NJ: Lawrence Erlbaum Associates.

Griffin, S., Case, R. and Siegler, R. S. (1994). Rightstart: providing the central conceptual prerequisites for first formal learning of arithmetic to students at risk for school failure. In K. McGilly (Ed.), *Classroom Lessons: Integrating Cognitive Theory and Classroom Practice* (pp. 25–49). Cambridge, MA: MIT Press.

Jordan, N. C., Huttenlocher, J. and Levine, S. C. (1992). Differential calculation abilities in young children from middle- and low-income families. *Developmental Psychology, 28*, 644–653.

Klein, A., Starkey, P., Clements, D. H., Sarama, J. and Iyer, R. (2008). Effects of a pre-kindergarten mathematics intervention: a randomized experiment. *Journal of Research on Educational Effectiveness, 1,* 155–178.

Krajewski, K. (2005). *Prediction of Mathematical (Dis-)abilities in Primary School: A 4-year German Longitudinal Study from Kindergarten to Grade 4.* Paper presented at the Biennial Meeting of the Society for Research in Child Development, Atlanta, GA.

Kronholz, J. (2000). See Johnny jump! Hey, isn't it math he's really doing? *The Wall Street Journal,* May 16, p. A1; A12.

National Mathematics Advisory Panel. (2008). *Foundations for Success: The Final Report of the National Mathematics Advisory Panel.* Washington D.C.: US Department of Education, Office of Planning, Evaluation and Policy Development.

Peisner-Feinberg, E. S., Burchinal, M. R., Clifford, R. M., Culkins, M. L., Howes, C., Kagan, S. L. and Yazejian, N. (2001). The relation of preschool child-care quality to children's cognitive and social developmental trajectories through second grade. *Child Development, 72,* 1534–1553.

Pratt, C. (1948). *I Learn From Children.* New York: Simon and Schuster.

Rouse, C., Brooks-Gunn, J. and McLanahan, S. (2005). Introducing the issue. *The Future of Children, 15,* 5–14.

Sarama, J. (2002). Listening to teachers: planning for professional development. *Teaching Children Mathematics, 9,* 36–39.

Sarama, J. and Clements, D. H. (2009). *Early Childhood Mathematics Education Research: Learning Trajectories For Young Children.* New York, NY: Routledge.

Sarama, J. and DiBiase, A.-M. (2004). The professional development challenge in preschool mathematics. In D. H. Clements, J. Sarama and A.-M. DiBiase (Eds.), *Engaging Young Children in Mathematics: Standards For Early Childhood Mathematics Education* (pp. 415–446). Mahwah, NJ: Lawrence Erlbaum Associates.

Sarama, J., Clements, D. H., Starkey, P., Klein, A. and Wakeley, A. (2008). Scaling up the implementation of a pre-kindergarten mathematics curriculum: teaching for understanding with trajectories and technologies. *Journal of Research on Educational Effectiveness, 1,* 89–119.

Seo, K.-H. and Ginsburg, H. P. (2004). What is developmentally appropriate in early childhood mathematics education? In D. H. Clements, J. Sarama and A.-M. DiBiase (Eds.), *Engaging Young Children in Mathematics: Standards For Early Childhood Mathematics Education* (pp. 91–104). Mahwah, NJ: Lawrence Erlbaum Associates.

Siegler, R. S. (1993). Adaptive and non-adaptive characteristics of low income children's strategy use. In L. A. Penner, G. M. Batsche, H. M. Knoff and D. L. Nelson (Eds.), *Contributions of Psychology to Science and Mathematics Education* (pp. 341–366). Washington, DC: American Psychological Association.

Stigler, J. W., Lee, S.-Y. and Stevenson, H. W. (1990). *Mathematical Knowledge of Japanese, Chinese, and American Elementary School Children.* Reston, VA: National Council of Teaching of Mathematics.

Tudge, J. R. H. and Doucet, F. (2004). Early mathematical experiences: observing young Black and White children's everyday activities. *Early Childhood Research Quarterly, 19,* 21–39.

Van Horn, M. L., Karlin, E. O., Ramey, S. L., Aldridge, J. and Snyder, S. W. (2005). Effects of developmentally appropriate practices on children's development: a review of research and discussion of methodological and analytic issues. *Elementary School Journal, 105,* 325–351.

Vergnaud, G. (1978). The acquisition of arithmetical concepts. In E. Cohors-Fresenborg and I. Wachsmuth (Eds.), *Proceedings of the 2nd Conference of the International Group for the Psychology of Mathematics Education* (pp. 344–355). Osnabruck, Germany.

Yuzawa, M., Bart, W. M., Kinne, L. J., Sukemune, S. and Kataoka, M. (1999). The effects of "origami" practice on size comparison strategy among young Japanese and American children. *Journal of Research in Childhood Education, 13*(2), 133–143.

Chapter 9

Fostering mathematical thinking through playful learning

Kelly Fisher and Kathy Hirsh-Pasek

Temple University

Roberta M. Golinkoff

University of Delaware

> It is, in fact, nothing short of a miracle that the modern methods of instruction have not yet entirely strangled ... curiosity; for this delicate little plant, aside from stimulation, stands mainly in need of freedom. Without this it goes to wrack and ruin without fail.
>
> Albert Einstein

Albert Einstein – one of the greatest mathematical minds the world has ever known – struggled as a young student. In his memoirs, Einstein recalled how mechanical teaching methods, rote memorization, and exams in school stifled learning and evoked his rebellious attitude (Neffe, 2007). He sought refuge at home, where his budding interest in math flourished in puzzle and block play, solving word problems, building houses out of cards, reading books, and conversing with others about science and philosophy (Winteler-Einstein, 2000). Young Einstein's early playful learning experiences might have been a key catalyst for his ingenious discoveries in mathematics and theoretical physics later in life.

While Einstein was most certainly a unique child, his lament rings true for many children today. Reports show that numerous kindergarten and early elementary classrooms have replaced playful experiences with scripted curricula that directly link to state education standards and assessments at the expense of recess and free time (e.g. Miller and Almon, 2009; Pellegrini, 2009). Across classrooms, we see rote learning and a narrow curricular focus contribute to children's increased anxiety in school as well as their waning interest, motivation, and academic achievement in mathematics (Frenzel *et al.*, 2007; Renninger and Su, in press; Stipek *et al.*, 1995; Turner *et al.*, 2002). Moreover, recent reports reveal that only 39 percent of fourth graders and 26 percent of twelfth graders are proficient in mathematics (National Center for Educational Statistics, 2010a, 2010b) and that US students continue to rank significantly below international averages in math literacy and problem-solving (Fleischman *et al.*, 2010).

The National Mathematics Advisory Panel (2008) issued a formal report warning that US children are not acquiring the mathematical competencies necessary to be successful in the twenty-first century. The Panel argues that "the eminence, safety, and well-being of nations have been dependent on its citizens' ability to deal with sophisticated quantitative ideas for centuries ... [and that] without substantial and sustained changes to its educational system, the United States will relinquish its leadership in the 21st century" (p. xi). Accordingly, more preschool practices must promote interest and mathematical competencies in early childhood in ways that will facilitate later academic achievement and lifelong success (Ginsburg *et al.*, 2008; National Academies, 2006). In this chapter we argue that the optimal early learning environment fosters mathematical thinking through a playful learning approach. Based on learning sciences theory and research, we show that playful learning experiences are intrinsically motivating and allow children to develop conceptual and procedural math knowledge through meaningful engagement and 'sense-making' processes.

The math wars: theoretical perspectives

The "math wars" reflect a contentious debate between traditional and progressive reform movements that defined the educational landscape in the United States (Klein, 2003; Schoenfeld, 2004). This contention arises from fundamentally different ideological perspectives concerning *how* children develop mathematic concepts. Traditionalists maintain that children must be taught basic skills and computational methods for solving math problems explicitly, in a step-by-step fashion. Through repeated practice (e.g. worksheets, recitations, exams), they will develop fast, automatic recall of math facts that will facilitate problem-solving in real-world contexts (Becker and Jacob, 2000). In other words, it is assumed that mastery (and automaticity) of skills will lead to conceptual understanding and transfer of knowledge.

Evidence shows that children can – and do – learn under direct instruction (Stockard and Englemann, 2008). But this begs the question – *what* do they learn? Some argue that explicit instruction methods encourage children to view mathematics as a set of facts and procedures rather than a reasoning process – which ultimately result in children focusing on imitating behaviors (Battista, 2002). For example, if a child states "2 + 6 = 8," does this mean that she understands the problem or even the solution she generated? Researchers and philosophers alike would say 'not necessarily' (Griffin, 2003; Ma, 2010). Consider philosopher John Searle's classic "Chinese Room Argument" as a powerful illustration of how one may demonstrate knowledge in the absence of understanding:

> Imagine a native English speaker, let's say a man, who knows no Chinese is locked in a room with boxes of Chinese symbols … together with a book of instructions for manipulating the symbols … Imagine that people outside the room send in other Chinese symbols which, unbeknownst to the person in the room, are questions in Chinese … by following the instructions in the book, the man in the room is able to pass out Chinese symbols which are correct answers to the questions.
>
> (Searle, 2001, p. 115)

While Searle's argument was not directly related to mathematical learning, it aptly demonstrates how following procedural rules does not necessarily reflect conceptual knowledge. The man appeared to understand Chinese to all of the others outside of the room while he, in fact, had no knowledge of the Chinese language or the concepts that were being conveyed. Similarly, children can memorize step-by-step procedures and arrive at the "right answer" on a test but may not understand the symbolic nature of the numbers or the interrelations between them (Griffin, 2003). Moreover, studies show that procedural practice and memorization impedes children's later attempts at conceptual understanding (e.g. Hiebert and Carpenter, 1992; Schoenfeld, 1992).

Progressive reformists suggest that education must foster conceptual understanding through child-centered and inquiry-based experiences (Saracho and Spodek, 2009). This view presupposes that children seek meaning in all that they do and that they actively construct their knowledge through exploration and discovery (e.g. "constructivism" or "discovery learning," von Glasserfeld, 2006; Piaget, 1970). In particular, children interpret new experiences through their current understanding of the world and the construction of new concepts is provoked when their current beliefs do not adequately explain or accommodate the novel experience. In order for children to understand mathematics – and to use it in meaningful ways – they must engage in personally meaningful activities that facilitate the learning process (Donovan and Bransford, 2005; National Research Council, 2000).

Play, in particular, represents a *medium* for promoting interest and mathematical thinking in a developmentally appropriate manner (Bergen, 1988). Research shows that children naturally incorporate math concepts during free play, such as estimating how many blocks are needed to build the tallest skyscraper or translating the number on the die to the Chutes and Ladders board game (e.g. Ginsburg *et al.*, 2001). In such contexts, children do not merely learn that "4" is a number between "3" and "5," but that it represents a quantitative concept that *they* may symbolize in a variety of ways (e.g. four blocks to build a tower, four spaces on the game-board, four fingers). Moreover, evidence suggests that play-based learning experiences promote a cadre of cognitive and socioemotional skills beyond math, including attention, self-regulation, and sharing (see Hirsh-Pasek *et al.*, 2009, for a review).

The constructivist view is not without critics. Some argue that children's play with well-planned educational materials and toys alone does not guarantee children will learn the intended concept or mathematical skill (Klahr, 2009). A child playing with blocks, for example, may learn how to build a tower instead of developing number sense. Evidence also suggests that the nature of the materials may actually impede children's ability to learn the underlying concept (e.g. children may focus on texture or color of the materials rather than the numerical concept; Brown *et al.*, 2009). Findings emerging from the learning sciences reveal that multiple factors influence the quality of children's learning in child-centered contexts and that a more nuanced view of constructivist teaching practices is necessary (Fisher *et al.*, 2008; 2010; Wood, 2009).

Fostering mathematical thinking through playful learning

The proverbial pendulum has swung back and forth between these two perspectives over the last century. Many educators have come to believe that they must choose to teach *or* let children play (Kochuk and Ratnaya, 2007; Hirsh-Pasek and Golinkoff, in press). This is simply a false dichotomy. In the proceeding sections we argue that playful learning practices – those that include free- and guided play – represent the middle ground between these competing perspectives. Based on a growing body of scientific evidence, we will show that playful learning facilitates mathematical thinking, procedural fluency, and interest beyond traditional instruction methods. Moreover, we suggest that when we view mathematics as a way of thinking rather than a set of facts and procedures to be learned, we gain a broader perspective on what specific cognitive skills underlie math achievement and *how* play-based experiences foster such skills (e.g. Griffin, 2003; Schoenfeld, 1992).

Mathematics – or mathematical thinking?

To understanding how playful learning is a conduit for mathematical thinking, we must explore the nature of mathematics itself. For over a century mathematics has largely been viewed as a fixed body of knowledge involving the manipulation of numbers via rules and algorithms (Battista, 2002). While these are key elements, contemporary mathematicians and philosophers argue that analyzing problems and generating solutions is the fundamental goal of mathematics (Schoenfeld, 1992). Mathematical thinking does not merely represent a specific way of solving particular types of problems; rather, it is a way of thinking and sense-making that helps us generate solutions to novel, complex problems we face in the world. It requires one to explore, observe, and analyze situations, think flexibly and symbolically, identify inherent structures and structural relations and, others argue, some old-fashioned tinkering around, insight, and discovery. Furthermore, mathematical thinking is inherently intertwined with spatial cognition (Cross *et al.*, 2009; Newcombe, 2010). Our ability to understand, represent, and reason about space (e.g. shape, size, symbols, formulas) underlies our ability to measure, graph, and solve problems symbolically.

Understanding the nature of mathematical thinking provides insight into what content, skills, and cognitive processes should be promoted in educational settings and how to best promote these competencies. Mathematical thinking is not fostered through a finite set of math facts and memorization of procedures; rather, it *develops through the dynamic interaction* of procedural skills, conceptual knowledge, and specific cognitive competencies that accumulate over time (Battista, 2002; Clements and Sarama, 2009; Cross *et al.*, 2009). Well-planned playful learning experiences that encourage children to actively engage and explore materials, reason about what they see and do, think flexibly, try out ideas, and symbolize the world around them facilitate mathematical thinking beyond methods that focus on procedural skills and facts (e.g. Baroody and Dowker, 2003; Stipek *et al.*, 1995). Indeed, a closer look at the international assessments reveals a telling story: at a time when direct instruction dominates mathematics education, only 27 percent of US students engage in advanced mathematical thinking and reasoning (e.g. integrate/symbolize different mathematical representations, reason flexibly; Fleischman *et al.*, 2010).

The environmental context also plays a critical role in initially triggering and maintaining children's interests in mathematics, which, in turn, influences academic achievement. According to Renninger and Su (in press), children's interests are initially piqued when they are engaged in active learning experiences that are grounded in meaningful contexts, such as those found in play. Interest is initially situational, in which children's curiosity is sparked by materials, the teacher/peers, or other conditions in the context. Children's interest transitions from being situationally based to becoming individualized when they re-engage with the materials, when others help them discover connections among their skills, knowledge, and prior experiences, and when they have positive feelings during the learning process. Eventually teachers move from helping children make 'connections' to encouraging them to fully engage, explore, and work within the content area. Through this process children develop knowledge, competence, and a sense of value of the content domain, which in turn, facilitates academic motivation (Deci, 1992; Schiefele, 1991).

Thus, active, playful learning experiences that facilitate mathematical thinking and "sense-making" may facilitate longer-term interest and later success. In the following section we explore what is meant by "playful learning" and how we might enact this process in and out of the classroom.

Defining playful learning

Playful learning is a constructivist approach that promotes academic, socio-emotional, and cognitive competencies (Resnick, 2007). For the purpose of this chapter, we will focus on how playful learning approaches facilitate mathematical thinking. For a more thorough definition and review of the diverse benefits of playful learning, please see Fisher *et al.* (2010).

Playful learning is a broad construct that encapsulates both free and guided play. *Free play* reflects a wide array of child-initiated activities, including object play, pretend and socio-dramatic play, games, and rough-and-tumble play. While play is a relatively elusive construct that evades precise definition, contemporary play researchers generally agree that free play activities are fun, voluntary, flexible, have no extrinsic goals, involve active engagement of the child, and often contain an element of make-believe (e.g. Johnson *et al.*, 1999).

Guided play is a discovery learning approach at the midpoint between didactic instruction and free play experiences (Bergen, 1988; Epstein, 2007; Hirsh-Pasek *et al.*, 2009). Teachers create flexible, interest-driven, child-centered experiences that encourage children's natural curiosity and mathematical thinking. In particular, teachers are seen as collaborative partners who actively facilitate the 'sense-making' process in at least two ways (e.g. Berk, 2001; Vygotsky, 1978). First, adults might enrich the environment with objects/toys or games that provide experiential learning opportunities infused with curricular content ("contextual scaffolding"). To promote shape concepts, for example, teachers may imbed shapes with varying sizes and angles into play environments that enable children to discover and practice the basic principles of math.

Second, teachers might facilitate "sense-making" through a variety of socio-cognitive scaffolding techniques, including commenting on children's discoveries, co-playing with the children, asking open-ended questions about what children are finding, suggesting ways to explore and play with the materials in ways that children might not have thought to do, or creating games (e.g. Cross *et al.*, 2009). Expanding on our previous example, teachers may facilitate geometric shape concepts by encouraging children to play a game called "Seek the Shapes," in which children locate shapes throughout the classroom (e.g. blocks, other toys, windows, doors, tables, etc). The teacher scaffolds their understanding by prompting discovery of shape properties (e.g. What makes all of these triangles even though they look different? How many sides do you see?).

During guided play the teacher mediates the acquisition and mastery of mathematical concepts while respecting the child's autonomy and control over the discovery learning process (Fisher *et al.*, under review; Karpov, 2005). Effective teachers recognize that children operate according to their own developmental rhythms and may take different learning paths to reach the same curricular goal. Some children may quickly catch on to the learning objective while others may require additional time to explore materials, to strategize or problem-solve, or need additional adult guidance. Furthermore, teachers are inherently sensitive to the line between child-centered learning activities and direct instruction. They must continually evaluate and adapt their behaviors to foster learning, yet not become overly intrusive or directive (e.g. "hovering" over children's play activities, interjecting too much). Multiple child factors influence whether adult presence is more or less obtrusive during play activities (e.g. children's learning ability and even their socioeconomic status), all of which require additional research (e.g. Rubin *et al.*, 1976).

Importantly, teachers must also be well versed in mathematical thinking in order to effectively facilitate children's developmental progress (Battista, 2002). To teach children that numbers represent quantities, for example, they must understand how to symbolize and compare quantities themselves; however, evidence suggests that teachers may need additional training in mathematical thinking (Ma, 2010). Post *et al.* (1991) found that only 50 percent of teachers were able to put the following fractions in the correct ascending order: 2/3, 5/8, 1/4, 3/5, 3/10, 1/8. Findings reveal that for the remaining 50 percent of teachers, "the numbers in the problems were not associated with particular quantities, did not have a magnitude that could be visualized or imagined, and thus could not be easily rank ordered" suggesting that the ability to connect numbers to quantities was not well understood or meaningful to them (Griffin, 2003, p. 9). This finding also suggests that teacher training may require re-education in mathematical thinking processes beyond (or in replacement of) traditional secondary education practices.

Furthermore, teachers must also have a deep understanding of how children's mathematical concepts typically evolve over time and what specific experiences facilitate children's discovery and conceptual evolution (Baroody and Dowker, 2003; Sarama and Clements, 2002, 2009). For example, children demonstrate a concrete-to-abstract shift in their understanding of shapes in which they start out categorizing shapes by visual similarity and orientation irrespective of their definitional properties (e.g. triangles = shapes with points on tops and flat bottoms) and later shift to abstract, rule-based concepts (e.g. triangles = shapes with three sides and three corners; Satlow and Newcombe, 1998). During play activities teachers thoughtfully observe children, gauge their current understanding of concepts and uses of the materials, and facilitate learning in appropriate ways.

Thus, guided play is considered a dynamic, evolving learning process guided by the active participation of *both* the teacher and the child. Although it is a structured and teacher-facilitated activity, guided play is simultaneously child-centered, in which the child is allowed to make choices, decisions, and errors; is able to engage according to her own pace and developmental rhythms; and she is respected as autonomous and competent learner. In other words, guided play helps children *develop* the cognitive tools to become independent thinkers and mathematic problem-solvers in a supportive, social atmosphere.

A brief review of the playful learning evidence

Early mathematical thinking undergoes substantial development during the preschool and primary years. Developmental theory and research suggest that the building blocks of mathematical thinking arise from a variety of free play and guided play activities (Geary, 2006; Ginsburg, Lee, and Boyd, 2008). In the following sections we briefly review the literature that links playful learning activities to mathematical thinking processes.

Free play

Observational research shows that children spend substantial amounts of self-directed, free play experience in exploring and practicing math concepts (Bjorkland, 2008). Ginsburg *et al.* (2001), for example, examined the frequency of mathematic-related activities in four- and five- year-old children's free play period in daycare. During this time, children engaged in a variety of activities. Over half of children's playtime was spent in mathematic reasoning activities; 25 percent was spent examining patterns and shapes; 13 percent on magnitude comparisons; 12 percent on enumeration; 6 percent on dynamic change; 5 percent on spatial relations (e.g. height, width, location); and 2 percent on classifying objects. Findings suggest that free play is a rich experience for children to practice and expand their foundational math and spatial knowledge.

The frequency and complexity of math-related play has been linked to increases in mathematical knowledge and achievement (e.g. Caldera *et al.*, 1999). A longitudinal study by Wolfgang *et al.* (2001) indicated that complexity of block play in preschool was significantly related to number of math courses taken, number of honors courses, mathematics grades achieved, and weighted mathematics points' scores in high school. Complex block play may be one mode in which children practice rudimentary math knowledge; however, we must be cautious of drawing causal conclusions from correlational research, in that other variables not accounted for, such as interest in block play or spatial skills, may significantly influence the observed findings.

Guided play

Research also shows that the integration of math-related materials into children's early free play environments promotes math-relevant behaviors (e.g. Arnold *et al.*, 2002; Whyte and Bull, 2008; Ness and Feranga, 2007). When preschoolers' pretend play environments are enriched with artifacts emphasizing number symbols, children engage in more talk and activity related to mathematical concepts (Cook, 2000). Similarly, playful learning curricular programs facilitate mathematical thinking through games and guided play activities (e.g. Kamii and Kato, 2006; Ginsburg *et al.*, 2003; Siegler and Ramani, 2009). Experimental research by Sarama and Clements (2009) revealed that low-income preschoolers who experienced *Building Blocks*, a play-based learning program, showed substantially greater year-end gains in math concepts and skills, including counting, sequencing, arithmetic computation, and geometry compared to matched age-mates who experienced other educational programs.

The big picture: pedagogical comparisons

Even more substantive findings are revealed in the comparative program research. Playful learning programs promote mathematical competencies beyond those attained in traditional, academically focused programs in mastery of information, long-term retention, and academic motivation (e.g. Alfieri *et al.*, 2010; Barnett *et al.*, 2008; Burts *et al.*, 1993; Campbell *et al.*, 2001; Diamond *et al.*, 2007; *Fisher et al.*, under review; Lillard and Else-Quest, 2006; Stipek *et al.*, 1995). One of the most telling of these stories was a longitudinal study conducted by Marcon (1993; 2002) that found children who were exposed to playful, child-centered preschool environments at age four showed enhanced academic performance in mathematics and other academic subjects as well as higher intrinsic motivation than children who experienced more direct instruction.

Concluding thoughts

Taken together, research suggests that playful learning experiences prime children's early mathematical thinking and reasoning. Children's interest is piqued through active, engaging experiences that facilitate mathematical "meaning-making" and conceptual understanding. The data suggest that if we want to groom children who are more interested in math, more motivated to learn, have the ability to see relations in the world around them and who can better reason symbolically about those relations, playful learning might provide an optimal pedagogy.

Acknowledgements

This research was supported by Temple University's Center for Re-Imagining Children's Learning and Education NICHD grant 5R01HD050199; Spatial Intelligence Learning Center NSF grant SBE-0541957; NSF grant BCS-0642529; NIH grant 1RC1HD0634970-01.

References

Alfieri, L., Brooks, P. J., Aldrich, N. J. and Tenenbaum, H. R. (2010). Does discovery-based instruction enhance learning? *Journal of Educational Psychology, 103,* 1–18. doi: 10.1037/a0021017

Arnold, D., Fisher, P., Doctoroff, G. and Dobbs, J. (2002). Accelerating math development in Head Start classrooms. *Journal of Educational Psychology, 94,* 762–770.

Barnett, W. S., Jung, K., Yarosz, D. J., Thomas, J., Hornbeck, A., Stechuk, R. and Burns, S. (2008). Educational effects of the Tools of the Mind curriculum: a randomized trial. *Early Childhood Research Quarterly, 23,* 299–313.

Baroody, A. J. and Dowker, A. (2003). The development of arithmetic concepts and skills: constructing adaptive expertise. In A. Schoenfeld (Eds.), *Studies in Mathematics Thinking and Learning Series.* Mahwah, NJ: Lawrence Erlbaum Associates.

Battista, M. T. (2002). Research and reform in mathematics education. In T. Loveless (Ed.), *The Great Curriculum Debate: How Should We Teach Reading and Math?* (pp. 42–84). Washington, DC: Brookings Institution Press.

Becker, J. and Jacob, B. (2000). The politics of California school mathematics: the anti-reform of 1997–99. *Phi Delta Kappan, 81,* 527–539.

Bergen, D. (1988). Using a schema for play and learning. In D. Bergen (Ed.), *Play as a Medium for Learning and Development* (pp. 169–179). Portsmouth, NH: Heinemann Educational Books.

Berk, L. E. (2001). *Awakening Children's Minds: How Parents And Teachers Can Make a Difference.* New York: Oxford University Press.

Bjorklund, C. (2008). Toddlers' opportunities to learn math. *International Journal of Early Childhood, 40,* 81–95.

Brown, M. C., McNeil, N. M. and Glenberg, A. M. (2009). Using concreteness in education: real problems, potential solutions. *Child Development Perspectives, 3,* 160–164.

Burts, D. C., Hart, C. H., Charlesworth, R. and DeWolf, M. (1993). Developmental appropriateness of kindergarten programs and academic outcomes in first grade. *Journal of Research in Childhood Education, 8,* 23–31.

Caldera, Y. M., Culp, A. M. D., O'Brien, M., Truglio, R. T., Alvarez, M. and Huston, A. C. (1999). Children's play preferences, construction play with blocks, and visual-spatial skills: are they related? *International Journal of Behavioral Development, 23*, 855–872.

Campbell, F. A., Pungello, E. P., Miller-Johnson, S., Burchinal, M. and Ramey, C. T. (2001). The development of cognitive and academic abilities: growth curves from an early childhood education experiment. *Developmental Psychology, 37,* 231–242.

Clements, D. H. and Sarama, H. (2009). *Learning and Teaching Early Math: The Learning Trajectories Approach.* New York, NY: Routledge.

Cook, D. (2000). Voice practice: social and mathematical talk in imaginative play. *Early Child Development and Care, 162,* 51–63.

Cross, C. T., Woods, T. A. and Schweingruber, H. A. (Eds.), Committee on Early Childhood Mathematics & National Research Council. (2009). *Mathematics Learning in Early Childhood: Paths Toward Excellence and Equity.* Washington, DC: The National Academies Press.

Deci, E. L. (1992). The relation of interest to the motivation of behavior: a self-determination theory perspective. In A. Renninger, S. Hidi and A. Krapp (Eds.), *Interest in Learning and Development* (pp. 43–70). Hillsdale, NY: Erlbaum.

Diamond, A., Barnett, W. S., Thomas, J. and Munro, S. (2007). Preschool program improves cognitive control. *Science, 317,* 1387–1388.

Donovan, M. S. and Bransford, J. D. (Eds). (2005). *How Students Learn: Mathematics in the Classroom. A Targeted Report For Teachers.* Division of Behavioral and Social Sciences and Education, National Research Council of the National Academies. Washington, DC: National Academies Press.

Epstein, A. S. (2007*). The Intentional Teacher: Choosing The Best Strategies For Young Children's Learning.* Washington, DC: National Association for the Education of Young Children.

Fisher, K., Hirsh-Pasek, K., Golinkoff, R. M. and Glick Gryfe, S. (2008). Conceptual split? Parents' and experts' perceptions of play in the 21st century. *Journal of Applied Developmental Psychology, 29,* 305–316.

Fisher, K., Hirsh-Pasek, K., Golinkoff, R. M., Berk, L. and Singer, D. (2010). Playing around in school: implications for learning and educational policy. In A. Pellegrini (Ed), *Handbook of the development of play* (pp. 341–362). New York, NY: Oxford Press.

Fleischman, H. L., Hopstock, P. J., Pelczar, M. P. and Shelley, B. E. (2010). Highlights from PISA 2009: performance of US 15-year-old students in reading, mathematics, and science literacy in an international context (NCES 2011-004). Education, National Center for Education Statistics. Washington, DC: US Government Printing Office.

Frenzel, A. C., Goetz, T., Reinhard, P. and Watt, H. M. G. (2007). Development of mathematics interest in adolescence: influences of gender, family, and school context. *Journal of Research on Adolescence, 20,* 507–537.

Geary D. C. (2006). Development of mathematical understanding. In W. Damon and R. M. Lerner (Eds.), *Handbook of Child Psychology (V. 2): Cognition, Perception, and Language.* (6th edn). Hoboken, NJ: Wiley.

Ginsburg, H. P., Greenes, C. and Balfanz, R. (2003). *Big Math For Little Kids.* Parsippany, NJ: Dale Seymour Publications.

Ginsburg, H. P., Lee, J. S. and Boyd, J. S. (2008). *Mathematics Education For Young Children: What It Is and How To Promote It.* Social Policy Report (Volume XXII, Number I). Washington DC: SRCD.

Ginsburg, H. P., Pappas, S. and Seo, K. (2001). Everyday mathematical knowledge: asking young children what is developmentally appropriate. In S. L. Golbeck (Ed.), *Psychological Perspectives on Early Childhood Education: Reframing Dilemmas in Research and Practice* (pp. 181–219). Mahwah, NJ: Lawrence Erlbaum Associates.

Griffin, S. (2003). The development of mathematic competence in the preschool and early school years. In J. Royer (Ed.), *Mathematical Cognition* (pp. 1–32). Charlotte, NC: Information Age Publishing.

Hiebert, J. and Carpenter, T. (1992). Learning and teaching with understanding. In D. Grouws (Ed.), *Handbook of Research on Mathematics Research and Teaching.* (pp. 65–100). New York: MacMillan.

Hirsh-Pasek, K., Golinkoff, R. M., Berk, L. E. and Singer. D. G. (2009). *A Mandate For Playful Learning in School: Presenting the Evidence.* New York, NY; Oxford University Press.

Hirsh-Pasek, K. and Golinkoff, R. M. (in press) The great balancing act: optimizing core curricula through playful learning. To appear in E. Zigler, S. Barnett and W. Gilliam (Eds.) *The Preschool Education Debates.*

Johnson, J. E., Christie, J. F. and Yawkey, T. D. (1999). *Play and Early Childhood Development.* New York, NY: Addison Wesley Longman.

Kamii, C. and Kato, Y. (2006). Play and mathematics at ages one to ten. In D. P. Fromberg and D. Bergen (Eds.), *Play From Birth to Twelve: Contexts, Perspectives, and Meanings* (pp. 187–198). New York, NY: Routledge.

Karpov, Y. (2005). *The Neo-Vygotskian Approach to Child Development.* New York, NY: Cambridge University Press.

Klahr, D. (2009). "To every thing there is a season, and a time to every purpose under the heavens": what about direct instruction? In S. Tobias and T. M. Duffy (Eds.), *Constructivist Theory Applied to Instruction: Success or Failure?* (pp. 291–310). New York, NY: Taylor & Francis.

Klein, D. (2003). A brief history of American K-12 mathematics education in the 20th century. In J. Royer (Ed), *Mathematical Cognition* (pp. 175–225). Greenwich, CT: Information Age Publishing.

Kochuk, N. and Ratnayaka, M. (2007). *NCLB/ESEA: It's Time For a Change! Voices From America's Classrooms.* National Education Association.

Lillard, A. and Else-Quest, N. (2006). Evaluating Montessori education. *Science, 313,* 1893–1894.

Ma, L. (2010). *Knowing and Teaching Elementary Mathematics: Teachers' Understanding of Fundamental Mathematics in China and the United States.* New York, NY: Routlege.

Marcon, R. (1993). Socioemotional versus academic emphasis: impact on kindergartners' development and achievement. *Early Child Development and Care, 96,* 81–91.

——(2002). Moving up the grades: relationships between preschool model and later school success. *Early Childhood Research and Practice, 4,* 517–530.

Miller, E. and Almon, J. (2009). *Crisis in the Kindergarten: Why Children Need to Play in School.* Alliance for Childhood: College Park, MD.

National Academies (2006). *Rising Above the Gathering Storm: Energizing and Employing America for a Brighter Economic Future.* Washington, DC: National Academies Press.

National Center for Education Statistics (2010a). *The Nation's Report Card: Grade 12 Reading and Mathematics 2009 National and Pilot State Results* (NCES 2011–455). Institute of Education Sciences, US Department of Education, Washington, D.C.

——(2010b). *The Nation's Report Card: Grades 4 and 8 Mathematics 2009* (NCES 2010–451). Institute of Education Sciences, US Department of Education, Washington, D.C.

National Mathematics Advisory Panel. (2008). *Foundations for Success: The Final Report of the National Mathematics Advisory Panel,* US Department of Education: Washington, DC.

National Research Council. (2000). *Eager to Learn: Educating Our Preschoolers.* Washington, DC: National Academy Press.

Neffe, J. (2007). *Einstein: A Biography* (Shelley Frisch, Trans.). New York, NY: Farrar, Straus and Giroux.

Ness, D. and Farenga, S. J. (2007). *Knowledge Under Construction: The Importance of Play in Developing Children's Spatial and Geometric Thinking.* Lanham, MD: Rowman & Littlefield Publishers, Inc.

Newcombe, N. (2010). Picture this! Improving math and science learning by improving spatial thinking. *American Educator, Summer,* 29–43.

Pellegrini, A. D. (2009), Research and policy on children's play. *Child Development Perspectives, 3,* 131–136.

Piaget, J. (1970). *Science of Education and the Psychology of the Child.* New York: Orion Press.

Post, T., Harel, G., Behr, M. and Lesh, R. (1991). Intermediate teachers' knowledge of rational number concepts. In E. Fennema, T. Carpenter and S. Lamon (Eds.), *In Integrating Research on Teaching and Learning Mathematics* (pp. 177–198). Albany, NY: State University of New York.

Renninger, K. A. and Su, S. (in press). Interest and its development. In R. Ryan (Ed.), *Oxford Handbook of Motivation*, Oxford University Press.

Resnick, M. (2007). *All I Really Need To Know (About Creative Thinking) I Learned (By Studying How Children Learn) In Kindergarten.* Paper presented at the ACM Creativity & Cognition conference, Washington DC.

Rubin, K., Maioni, T. and Horung, M. (1976). Free play behaviors in middle- and lower-class preschoolers: Parten and Piaget revisited. *Child Development, 47*, 414–419.

Saracho, O. N. and Spodek, B. (2009). Educating the young mathematician: the twentieth century and beyond. *Early Childhood Educational Journal, 36*, 305–312.

Sarama, J. and Clements, D. H. (2002). Building blocks for young children's mathematical development. *Journal of Educational Computing Research, 27*, 93–110.

——(2009). *Early Childhood Mathematics Education Research: Learning Trajectories For Young Children.* New York, NY: Routledge.

Satlow, E. and Newcombe, N. (1998). When is a triangle not a triangle? Young children's conceptions of geometric shapes. *Cognitive Development, 13*, 547–559.

Schiefele, U. (1991). Interest, learning, and motivation. *Educational Psychologist, 26*, 299–323.

Schoenfeld, A. H. (1992). Learning to think mathematically: problem solving, metacognition, and sense-making in mathematics. In D. Grouws (Ed.), *Handbook for Research on Mathematics Teaching and Learning* (pp. 334–370). New York: MacMillan.

——(2004). The math wars. *Educational Policy, 18*, 253–286.

Searle, J. (2001). The Chinese room argument. In R. A. Wilson and F. C. Keil (Eds), The MIT *Encyclopedia of the Cognitive Sciences* (pp. 115–116). Boston, MA: MIT Press.

Siegler, R. S. and Ramani, G. B. (2009). Playing linear number board games – but not circular ones – improves low-income preschoolers' numerical understanding. *Journal of Educational Psychology, 101*, 545–560.

Stipek, D. J., Feiler, R., Daniels, D. and Milburn, S. (1995). Effects of different instructional approaches on young children's achievement and motivation. *Child Development, 66*, 209–223.

Stockard, J. and Engelmann, K. (2008). *Academic Kindergarten and Later Academic Success: The Impact of Direct Instruction* (Technical Report 2008–7). Eugene, OR: National Institute for Direct Instruction.

Turner, J., Midgley, C., Meyer, D., Gheen, M., Anderman, E., Kang, Y., *et al.* (2002). The classroom environment and students' reports of avoidance strategies in mathematics: a multi-method study. *Journal of Educational Psychology, 94*, 88–106.

Von Glasserfeld, E. (2006). A constructivist approach to experiential foundations of mathematical concepts revisited. *Constructivist Foundations, 1*, 61–72.

Vygotsky, L. S. (1978). *Mind and Society: The Development of Higher Mental Processes.* Cambridge, MA: Harvard University Press.

Whyte, J. C. and Bull, R. (2008). Number games, magnitude representation, and basic number skills in preschoolers. *Developmental Psychology, 44*, 588–596.

Winteler-Einstein, M. (2000). Albert Einstein a biographical sketch. *Resonance, 5*, 111–120.

Wolfgang, C. H., Stannard, L. L. and Jones, I. (2001). Block play performance among preschoolers as a predictor of later school achievement in mathematics. *Journal of Research in Childhood Education, 15*, 173–180.

Wood, E. (2009). Conceptualizing a pedagogy of play: international perspectives from theory, policy, and practice. In D. Kuschner (Ed.), *From Children to Red Hatters; Diverse Images and Issues of Play: Vol. 8. Play & Culture Studies.* New York, NY: University Press of America.

Part V

What is the role of digital media in early education?

In their early years, children learn to use digital media by watching others, by trying things out themselves, and by wanting to be able to do the kinds of things which these technologies offer, including entertainment, opportunities to learn, ways of communicating with others, and forms of self-expression. These activities are interwoven with other typical childhood pastimes: playing outside, helping to cook, joking with friends, going shopping, reading stories, dancing and singing. ... With the proviso that quality content and design is paramount, there is potential for digital media to extend the possibilities for children's learning and to transform our expectations of what children of this age have the capacity to do.

Lydia Plowman, Joanna McPake and Christine Stephen

Contrary to the conventional "wisdom" found in some of the pro-ICT literature, those who advocate the kinds of views proposed here are very far from being reactionary "conservatives", or uncritical "moral panickers" (Buckingham, 2007), or nostalgic, over-sentimental "commentators romanticizing a non-technological past" ... and we take great exception to being so condescendingly and dismissively labelled. What we *are* "guilty" of is bringing a radical, critically reflective capacity to the breathless momentum of modern technological developments, a concern with taking a paradigmatic, contextualizing meta-view of the place of technology in the evolution of human consciousness, and a passionate wish to protect what is fundamentally human from the march of "the inhuman".

Richard House

Part V

What is the role of digital media in early education?

Extending opportunities for learning

The role of digital media in early education

*Lydia Plowman, Joanna McPake, and
Christine Stephen*

Many people believe that children need to become competent users of digital media to avoid disadvantage or marginalisation and to become assured, discriminating, and effective members of society. For others, the ubiquity of these technologies has led to concerns about the ways in which they are seen to exert influence on the lives of young children. Like it or not, most people would agree that children's experiences with technology – whether for play, learning, or communication – will have significant implications for their future lives. We prefer to engage with this transformation rather than seek to establish a technology-free version of the past in the present. Nevertheless, we are aware that some of these changes are driven by the marketisation of education (Selwyn, 2011), a rhetoric of progress through technology (Plowman *et al.*, 2011) and sometimes inflated claims by media and technology industries. Later in this chapter we describe some of our concerns about the use of digital media in preschool settings. We are not inclined to base a general denunciation on these shortcomings, but prefer to consider the contribution that thoughtful use can make to young children's learning and how this might be achieved, while recognising the need for balance in children's activities.

The research studies

By taking cognisance of parents' and children's perspectives and looking at practices in preschool and home in some detail we aim to inform choices. For parents and the wider public this means supporting decisions about how we want to bring up children in a technologised world. For early education professionals and policy-makers it is to provide the wherewithal to make informed choices about how (or whether) to integrate digital media into pedagogical practice and curriculum design.

All of the target children in our studies were either three or four years old. Children of this age are generally the subject of close parental attention and their worlds revolve around home and family. By the age of eight, the changes in their lives – increased independence, more highly developed literacy, a wider social group – mean that children's digital media habits shift (Gutnick *et al.*, 2011). The term "digital media" refers to digital devices (such as computers and mobile phones) and to products or outputs (DVDs, websites, games, interactive stories) that are viewed, read, played, or created on these devices. By the time they started school, nearly all of the children in our case studies had encountered a range of digital media, such as mobile phones, interactive television, games consoles, DVD and MP3 players, as well as desktop and notebook computers. We also include toys such as play mobile phones and laptops in our discussion as they provide a means for children to engage in role-play about how these devices are used in everyday life. These get less attention than the technologies that have more obvious educational potential but they are an important part of the technological landscape in which children grow up.

Given its centrality in the lives of young children and the level of public interest, it is surprising that there has not been more research on the topic of the role of digital media in early education: what does exist tends to look at technology rather narrowly, concerning itself primarily with the use of computers and to use by older children. Our research on the role of digital media in early education began in preschools and involved educators in thinking about how to enhance pedagogy. As a result of this work, it became increasingly apparent that we needed to expand our sphere of interest to the ways in which young children experienced technology in their homes.

Most of our work is based on detailed case studies of families or particular technologies. This provides rich detail about how and why technologies are used but we acknowledge that we cannot claim that all families are like the ones we visit: the choices available to families are influenced by factors such as their geographical location, the experiences and values of the parents, and the preferences of the children. It is also influenced by household income, and one of the motivations for our research into children's experiences with technology at home was to establish whether children from low-income households were at a disadvantage when compared with more affluent families (McPake and Plowman, 2010). The implications of digital divides – the notion that certain sectors of the population might have restricted access and fewer opportunities to make use of technologies than others – are important for a discussion of the role of digital media in early education, but are beyond the scope of this chapter.

This chapter uses evidence collected during a sequence of research projects (see appendix) conducted in preschools and in homes to answer some key questions which address the question of the role of digital media in early education:

- Is it important that young children learn to use digital media?
- Which digital media are best suited to their needs?
- Can digital media provide opportunities for learning?

Is it important that young children learn to use digital media?

Much of the research we do is descriptive rather than evaluative. In other words, we aim to describe children's everyday lives and the technological and social landscapes in which they live with a level of verisimilitude consistent with the amount of time we are able to spend with them, their families, and the staff who care for them. In the research reported here, we don't set out to evaluate specific technologies or make judgements about the ones that we think work best, although we have made more general recommendations about the forms of technology suitable for preschool settings as part of *Interplay*, a more interventionist study. Nevertheless, in the context of the question of whether it is important that young children learn to use digital media it is incumbent upon us to be explicit about our own position and some of the conclusions we have drawn.

One response to the question of whether it is important that young children learn to use digital media is a pragmatic one: we live in a technological age so it follows that children need the skills, competences, and enthusiasms to function and flourish in the world in which they are growing up. This is not really contentious: our evidence to date suggests that using digital media requires the development of roughly analogous techniques such as learning to use a keyboard as well as how to hold a pencil and that this leads to an expansion rather than contraction of skills.

A greater challenge is to frame the question in terms of whether digital media actually change the *process* of learning in some way. Our studies are not designed to answer this question but Howard-Jones (2011) has conducted an analysis of research in neuroscience and psychology that looks at the impact of digital technologies on human wellbeing. He reminds us that all learning brings about changes in the brain and it is clear that some forms of digital media can be used to improve working memory or to provide mental stimulation that helps to slow cognitive decline. The multimodality of digital media (i.e. using different forms, such as image, text, audio, or touch, to present content) can enhance learning. However, he cautions (2011, p. 64) that the design of materials is of central importance and that "the developing brain is more susceptible to environmental influence than an adult's". As "children are at the forefront of the technological revolution" it is important to focus on those risks to children's development that are likely to be most significant. He judges these to be an increase in aggressive response from playing violent video games, interference with psychosocial wellbeing and attention, and the potential for disrupted sleep. However, these are based on excessive use and exposure to violent content and we have no evidence at all to suggest that preschool children are at risk from either of these. Nevertheless, whether a child enjoys dressing up, playing with toys, running around outside, or drawing and painting most parents would prefer them to enjoy a balanced range of activities rather than spend all of their time on any one of these and it is the same for technology. This is a matter of common sense rather than ideology.

Associated with the question of whether technology changes the process of learning is whether it provides benefits that are unavailable from other sources. On this, we have more evidence to bring to the discussion. In terms of recording children's learning, for instance, the possibilities opened up by digital cameras make it easier for practitioners to involve children in recording and tracking their own learning as they allow children to represent what they think is interesting about their world and to use this as a form of pre-literate communication. Technological toys and technologies such as computers and games consoles, televisions, DVD players, and the "real life" technologies that children have access to, such as digital cameras or mobile phones, have extended the range of possibilities for learning and playing. We return to this in our discussion of whether digital media can provide opportunities for learning.

When we asked parents whether it was important that young children learn to use digital media the answers we received varied. Many parents were convinced of the importance of technological skills, in particular those associated with using computers, and that this imperative was likely to be more pronounced by the time their children had grown up. They did not want their children to miss out in future, either at school or at work, by failing to become confident users of technologies while they were young. For a minority of parents, however, such benefits were questionable. Aware that the technological landscape had changed dramatically over the last decade and, in some cases, that skills they themselves had acquired in earlier times were now obsolete, they were sceptical as to whether early familiarity with technology would be of particular value. These parents believed that their children would acquire the skills they needed at the right time, a perception often accompanied by a view that other activities were more appropriate for the early years. For these parents, the question was whether their children would miss out on important aspects of childhood if they spent time with digital media now.

Amongst preschool practitioners there was a consensus that it was important for children to learn to use digital media, both as preparation for their imminent transition to school and for their future employment. The question for them was how this should be integrated into playroom practice and relate to other aspects of the early years curriculum. Generally, they interpreted this learning as developing operational skills, in large part because their definition of digital media (generally described as ICT or information and communication technology in UK schools) meant a rather mechanistic approach to using computers and interactive whiteboards. Where preschools engaged children in activities with a broader range of digital devices, particularly video and still cameras, microscopes, and pedometers, there was scope for more imaginative, creative, and collaborative activities.

As a result, the children in our studies were starting school at age five with different kinds of technological competences, most acquired at home, although some were introduced at preschool. Basic operational skills were widespread: they could use remote controls and other push-button controllers, and many were familiar with icons and onscreen menus, though their ability to use these with ease tended to be limited by their emergent literacy. Depending on the kinds of technology available in their homes, their opportunities to observe others using them or to participate in these activities themselves, their experiences of digital media for communication, learning, creative activities or entertainment were likely to be quite varied. Although this was not the focus of our studies, this variation in skills and experiences did not seem to make a difference at entry to school because most teachers saw the incoming children as a blank slate rather than building on existing competencies.

Which digital media are best suited to the needs of young children?

Both in the home and in preschool settings children are most likely to develop competences that are relevant to them when digital media are recognised as having a useful role to play, rather than treated as in some way different or special. This approach is more likely in the home than in preschool as children have opportunities to observe family members using digital media for their own purposes. Although children may, fleetingly, have an interest in pushing buttons just to see what happens – and many simple technological toys are based on this premise – their main interest in a television remote control is not button pressing *per se,* but rather a desire to choose their own television programmes or DVDs and to watch them when they please. Thus in the home, the development of operational skills is inextricably linked with an understanding of what the technology facilitates.

Our observations in preschool settings revealed that desktop computers can be difficult for young children to use because, as a workplace technology, their physical construction and interface are designed for bigger, more literate users and much of the software is more suited to the office than the playroom. This was exacerbated given that staff tended to set up an activity at the computer but not oversee it closely and children were reluctant to seek help from adults when needed. Some staff seemed to work on the reasonable basis that products specifically designed for young children and described as developmentally appropriate meant that close supervision was not needed. But while some children needed considerable support in their interactions with a computer, others were confident users. With digital media, perhaps more than with other types of educational resource, children can often do more than their parents or teachers might expect: we had many examples of this during our home visits (such as three-year-old children understanding and using specialised technical terms, controlling a DVD to watch it in slow motion, or resizing windows on a computer screen). Limiting children to what is considered to be developmentally appropriate can mean inhibiting the potential for learning and restricting their creativity and curiosity: games designed for children's consoles are often mundane educational tasks disguised as entertainment and the "magic" pen which reads a book aloud one word at a time is meant to support the development of early word recognition skills rather than the pleasure of hearing a story read aloud. Though young children may still be developing their motor skills and are in the early stages of becoming literate, their interests are often much more wide-ranging and ambitious than the kinds of activities that many children's technologies currently permit.

As an example of the kind of interactivity that could be promoted, let us take the low-tech example of an experienced reader sharing a picture book with a child by joining in the pleasures of the text and image as well as drawing out from the child both explicit and tacit knowledge. As pointed out in an article on designing educational interactive media (Plowman, 1996), this scenario can provide a model for the design of digital media for young children. More than fifteen years later, the technology has advanced considerably but the quality of design has not kept pace, so that some of the applications (or apps) designed for tablet computers simply reproduce tired versions of electronic books rather than exploit the affordances of the medium. In order to be confident about what a toy or software package has to offer, practitioners need to know if the model of learning and teaching matches their preferred practice and fits with the pedagogical strategies used to support the children in their playrooms. All educational materials, digital or not, have a model of the teaching and learning process implicit in their design, manifested by how the child is conceptualised, how content is presented, whether and how learning is assessed, the level of adaptivity, and the use of feedback. Unfortunately, this model is rarely made explicit and, in any case, is more complex to interpret in preschool contexts where the emphasis is on a child-centred model of learning through play rather than instruction. Although there can be some problems with the manual dexterity required to operate some devices it is the quality of the content that is the key issue here, whatever the platform, rather than the technology itself.

There follows a wish list of features most children and adults would want from digital media to support learning in the early years. In large part, these are the same qualities that we want from other media created for children of this age, such as printed books. The classics of children's literature (*The Very Hungry Caterpillar*, *The Gruffalo*, *The Cat in the Hat* amongst others) provide many of these features but, so far, there is no equivalent "classic" digital content or software. In no particular order, the digital media best suited to the needs of children provide challenge, delight, enchantment, play value, and adventure. Materials should be compelling, encourage creativity, develop curiosity, bear repeated re-use, be accessible for all children, and promote interaction with and away from the technology, and with others. Taking design seriously means that there is potential for digital media to meet the needs of young children but, with some exceptions, this has so far largely been unrealised.

Can digital media provide opportunities for learning?

Analysis of preschool educators' accounts of practice, combined with observation in the playroom, suggested that digital media could support three main areas of learning:

- *Acquiring operational skills* refers to understanding the functions of items such as the mouse as well as the ability to operate them, which often relies on motor skills. Operational competence also develops children's concepts of technological interactivity and demonstrates their understanding that taking an action can produce a response. Children usually needed adults to help them acquire specific operational skills, after which they could move on to become independent users.
- *Extending knowledge and understanding of the world* includes what is described as subject knowledge in schools. It encompasses learning in areas such as mathematics, language, and knowledge about living things and places such as animals or volcanoes, typically gained through software, websites and talking books.
- *Developing dispositions to learn* encompasses a range of affective, social, and cognitive features of learning to learn which were given high priority in preschool settings. Our interviews suggested that the practitioners mainly conceptualised learning as supporting children's development as confident and self-directed learners and that this was a fundamental part of practice. Using computers was perceived to have a role to play in this by increasing self-esteem and the confidence gained from success, as well as supporting independence and persistence in the face of initial difficulties.

These categories were not intended to be exhaustive and they do not include, for instance, learning through physical activity. Although we saw some examples of this, such as children using a dance mat or movement games performed in front of a Sony EyeToy (a camera attached to a PlayStation), these were exceptional. The introduction of the Nintendo Wii has led to interest in the potential for technology to encourage physical activity but this is more common in homes so far. Of these categories, the first (learning how to switch equipment on and off, and to record, store, retrieve, and select) is perhaps the least significant inasmuch as its acquisition is a fairly straightforward matter. Nevertheless, it is this learning that schools and preschools currently privilege.

It was during our research visits to homes that we identified another dimension of learning:

- *Understanding the role of technology in everyday life* includes learning about the role of technology for a range of social and cultural purposes. These may include communication, employment, study, self-expression, and entertainment in family and community contexts. This form of learning can be developed as an onlooker or as a participant.

For example, one three-year-old boy enjoyed taking photographs with the digital camera and his sister helped him to download these onto the computer, from where some were selected to send to relatives in Australia. Although he could not write, he liked to add emoticons such as smiley faces to these emails. These activities with other members of his family were not associated with typical preschooler needs or interests, catered for by age-appropriate toys or tools for early learning. Rather, he was being inducted into practices of value and significance to his family, including oral, visual, and written communication with relatives, maintaining family bonds at a distance and commemorating his immediate family's life through photographs. In this way we can see how his experiences have ensured that he has learned how to *use* digital media, has also learned *through* the technologies (which are supporting early literacy and self-expression) and has learned the *role* of digital media in the culture of his own family and the wider community. The domestic context offered more opportunities to prepare children for a life in which digital media would play an important role and to develop an awareness of these cultural practices. In contrast, but not surprisingly, preschool practitioners tended to focus on what they saw as the overtly educational gains to be made – the acquisition of basic operational skills (learning to use a mouse was frequently mentioned), certain learning dispositions such as taking turns, and the learning arising from the content of the activity.

Families acquired different technologies for different purposes. The children were thus being inducted into various cultural practices ranging from talking to relatives on mobile phones, to taking and printing digital photos of the family pets, sharing memories by watching family video recordings of special events, or using old computers and non-functioning mobile phones as props for play in imaginary offices, shops, and schools. Whether children were directly involved in these activities or observers of them, they could lead to the development of an understanding of the cultural role of technologies as well as operational competences. However, parents tended to underestimate this aspect of their children's learning because much of what they were picking up (using the telephone, putting on a DVD) was, in their eyes, unremarkable (Plowman *et al.*, 2008).

Discussion: how can educators recognise and extend children's experiences with digital media?

Parents and practitioners often lack confidence in extending children's learning with digital media. Some feel that their role is almost superfluous because they assume the interactivity means that children have their own, digital tutor and so adult guidance is not necessary. However, our research suggests that adults and other more able partners, such as older siblings, have a critical role in developing children's learning with computers and other digital media because children of this age are not usually able to derive maximum benefit without additional assistance. This support does not necessarily mean showing a child how to use a particular device. It can also mean providing support in ways that adults often do unthinkingly: showing interest, asking questions, making suggestions, or just being there. Practitioners and parents can also provide support by making available suitable resources and setting up appropriate activities. Most adults are also unaware that their own use of digital media provides support as children learn by watching and copying. The term we use to describe these various ways of providing support for learning with technology is guided interaction (Plowman and Stephen, 2007; Stephen and Plowman 2008).

The principles of playroom practice are based on child-led activities in which children learn through play and exploration, supported by practitioners who monitor and facilitate rather than teach or direct. While this approach has many strengths, playroom practice is sometimes incompatible with getting the most out of encounters with digital media. Practitioners are expert at providing responses which are intuitive and finely attuned to children's specific circumstances and abilities – when children are baking cakes or dressing up, for example – but they can find this more challenging when digital media are involved.

Most of the preschool settings we visited conducted the activities involving digital media (emailing, printing newsletters, searching websites for resources, downloading photographs) in an office, out of sight of children in the playroom, with the result that children rarely saw or participated in adults' authentic practices. This was very different from their home experiences where most children were aware of the ways in which their parents, older siblings, and other relatives made use of technology, even if they themselves were not always able to take part at this stage. By understanding more about how children experience digital media in the home context, practitioners are more likely to be able to incorporate them into the cultural practices of the playroom. This means developing existing mechanisms to support links between home and school so that discussions with parents systematically include children's experiences with digital media. Staff can build on this information, shifting the current focus on skills towards a broader range of competencies and dispositions and recognising that children will start school with diverse experiences of using digital media, involving not only computers but also a wide range of domestic leisure technologies and interactive toys.

The limitations on the technologies available in most preschool settings and the lack of use by staff meant that children's awareness of the different cultural and work-related uses of digital media was restricted. Children may not have been able to operate some of the technologies they saw in use at home, but they had an awareness of their function because the activities were culturally embedded in family members' day-to-day lives. Even in households with relatively limited access to technology, the home provided a much richer mix than many preschool settings, as well as providing opportunities for children to observe and participate in authentic activities. If schools are able to recognize and build on the wide range of competencies and dispositions children bring from home and from preschool education they will be better able to support children's learning in ways that have implications for their future, increasingly technologised, education.

Curriculum guidance for the early years emphasises the importance of supporting children in all aspects of their emotional, social, cognitive, and physical development in ways that will enable them to become increasingly independent, responsible, and eager to progress in their learning. The desired outcomes are confident, capable, and self-assured children who are accomplished communicators and who enjoy loving and secure relationships and enabling environments. These aspirations are compatible with the examples of playing and learning with technology at home that we have described above, less so if there is an emphasis on computers and operational skills. Preschool staff often express a need for professional development on the ways in which digital media can enhance children's learning but, as Stephen *et al.* (in press) point out, this requires learning about the child in the context of the family learning cultures and practices that influence their experiences outside the playroom and shape their expectations of learning.

In their early years, children learn to use digital media by watching others, by trying things out themselves, and by wanting to be able to do the kinds of things which these technologies offer, including entertainment, opportunities to learn, ways of communicating with others, and forms of self-expression. These activities are interwoven with other typical childhood pastimes: playing outside, helping to cook, joking with friends, going shopping, reading stories, dancing and singing. Some adults find it surprising that children pick up the skills needed to use digital media without seeming to need instruction. For the children themselves, the demands of using a television remote control, a mouse, a controller, or onscreen instructions are not necessarily more (or less) of a challenge than other tasks they need to master, such as getting dressed, tying shoelaces, using a pencil, learning the shapes of letters and numbers, or crossing the road safely. These are the kinds of skills they need in their daily lives and they are learnt by a mixture of instruction, observation, and practice. By describing and examining children's experiences at home and in preschool settings we have identified how factors such as their own preferences, the people in their lives, and the cultural practices of the different environments in which they spend time shape their encounters with technology. With the proviso that quality content and design is paramount, there is potential for digital media to extend the possibilities for children's learning and to transform our expectations of what children of this age have the capacity to do.

Acknowledgements

The research on which this chapter is based would not be possible without the children, families, and practitioners who welcomed us into their homes and workplaces. We are grateful for their willing participation. Olivia Stevenson and Claire Adey were valued members of the research team on the most recent study, *Young children learning with toys and technology at home*. The authors also gratefully acknowledge receipt of support from the Economic and Social Research Council (grant RES-062-23-0507).

References

Gutnick, A. L., Robb, M., Takeuchi, L. and Kotler, J. (2011). *Always Connected: The New Digital Media Habits of Young Children*. New York: The Joan Ganz Cooney Center at Sesame Workshop.

Howard-Jones, P. (2011). *The Impact of Digital Technologies on Human Wellbeing: Evidence from the Sciences of Mind and Brain*. Oxford: Nominet Trust. Available at www.nominettrust.org.uk [accessed 1 September 2011].

McPake, J. and Plowman, L. (2010). At home with the future: influences on young children's early experiences with digital technologies. In. N. Yelland (Ed.), *Contemporary Perspectives on Early Childhood Education* (pp. 210-226). Maidenhead: Open University Press.

Plowman, L. (1996). Designing interactive media for schools: a review based on contextual observation. *Information Design Journal*, 8 258–266.

Plowman, L. and Stephen, C. (2007) Guided interaction in pre-school settings. *Journal of Computer Assisted Learning*, 23 14–21.

Plowman, L., McPake, J. and Stephen, C. (2008). Just picking it up? Young children learning with technology at home. *Cambridge Journal of Education*, 38 303–319.

Plowman L., Stephen C. and McPake, J. (2010). *Growing Up with Technology: Young Children Learning in a Digital World*. London: Routledge.

Plowman, L., Stevenson, O., McPake, J., Stephen, S. and Adey, C. (2011). Parents, preschoolers, and learning with technology at home: some implications for policy. *Journal of Computer Assisted Learning*, 24 361–371.

Scottish Government (2010) *Pre-school and Childcare Statistics 2009*. Available at www.scotland.gov.uk/Publications/2010/09/28130623/1 [accessed 31 March 2011].

Selwyn, N. (2011). *Schools and Schooling in the Digital Age*. Abingdon, Oxon: Routledge.

Stephen, C. and Plowman, L. (2008). Enhancing learning with ICT in pre-school. *Early Child Development and Care*, 178 637–654.

Stephen, C., Stevenson, O. and Adey, C. (in press). Young children engaging with technologies at home: the influence of family context. *Journal of Early Childhood Research*.

Appendix – Summaries of the four research projects on which this chapter is based

All of the children in our studies attended preschool in central Scotland, typically for a half-day session, with a minority of children attending for a full working day. Preschool education in Scotland is provided for children aged between three and five, with 96 percent of four-year-old children in part-time preschool education funded by the government and provided by the public, private or voluntary sectors (Scottish Government 2010). Families were recruited from nurseries which served disadvantaged populations and selected by us, initially by postcode, to meet predetermined criteria. We refer to parents throughout this paper but in some cases this refers to adult caregivers who took a parental role in the household. *Already at a Disadvantage* was funded by Becta. The other three studies were funded by the Economic and Social Research Council. More information about all of these studies is available in *Growing Up with Technology: Young children learning in a digital world* (Plowman et al., 2010).

Interplay: Play, Learning and ICT in Pre-school Education investigated the ways in which children's learning with technology can be supported and enhanced in preschool settings. The study was based in eight preschools which represented a range of types of provision and served 400 families with a broad range of socioeconomic status. Researchers visited each setting on seven occasions and produced baseline information, a technology audit, field notes, focused observations, and video recordings. Over the course of a school year, each site implemented and evaluated two small-scale projects, identifying the ways in which guided interaction could be enacted. We interviewed the participating practitioners before and after the interventions and a questionnaire on competence and attitudes was distributed to all forty practitioners in these settings. Conversations with children about their use of technology in the playroom were recorded on an opportunistic basis.

Already at a Disadvantage? Children's access to ICT at home and their preparation for primary school ran in parallel with *Interplay* and provided case studies of 16 children from nurseries involved in that project, enabling us to look at their experiences across home and preschool. It also featured interviews with primary school teachers about their expectations of children's ICT competences as they enter school, their knowledge of children's experiences with technology at nursery and at home, and how this influences formal provision. "Disadvantage" was defined as households with an income which was less than 60 percent of the national average.

Entering e-Society: Young children's development of e-literacy investigated parents' expectations and aspirations for their children's futures as users of technology, provided observations of children using technology at home, and considered the extent to which a digital divide is emerging between young children who have opportunities to make use of technology and those who do not. The project included consultation with a range of education professionals on the implications of the project's findings for early years education.

Young children learning with toys and technology at home focused on play at home, particularly with technological and traditional toys. It produced in-depth case studies and traced children's play experiences at home over the course of a minimum of nine rounds of data collection based on visits to fourteen households. Each round had a specific focus, such as parental recollections of their own childhoods, a toy audit, conversations with children, parental perceptions of their child's play and learning, and family interviews about the changes brought about by the transition to school.

The inappropriateness of ICT in early childhood

Arguments from philosophy, pedagogy, and developmental research

Richard House

Department of Psychology, University of Roehampton

> The senses become disordered when too much of a simulated world is inserted between our body and the surrounding world.
>
> (Robert Sardello and Cheryl Sanders, 1999)

> Technology ... the knack of so arranging the world that we don't have to experience it.
>
> Max Frisch, architect (quoted in Honoré, 2008: 97)

The philosophical and cultural context is crucial when considering technological and ICT experience in early childhood. Commentators on and advocates of ICT in the early years (e.g. Galloway, 2009; Hayes and Whitebread, 2006; O'Hara, 2004; Siraj-Blatchford and Morgan, 2009; Tyler, 2010) commonly neglect, or completely ignore, philosophical and paradigmatic perspectives on these questions. I believe this to be a very serious error of omission. Much of what follows is strongly informed by this wider contextualizing *Zeitgeist*, in which critical perspectives on the "e-generation", many of them very recent (e.g. Bauerlein, 2009; Carr, 2010; Jackson, 2009; Lanier, 2010; Naydler, 2008, 2011; Watson, 2010); philosophical understandings of technology as a cultural and historically specific phenomenon (e.g. Habermas, 1971; Heidegger, 1977; Heim, 1994; Idhe, 2010; Misa *et al.*, 2003); and paradigmatic critiques of technological "modernity" more generally (e.g. Bauman, 2000; Oliver *et al.*, 2002; Postman, 1992; Sikorski, 1993; Winner, 1977) – all are seen as being central to any consideration of the appropriateness or otherwise of ICT and digital technologies in early childhood.

I will searchingly address the many shibboleths underpinning ICT early-years education, adopting three broad approaches to the question of ICT digital technologies in early childhood: namely,

- a *philosophical*, paradigmatic approach
- a *theoretical* approach grounded in child-development theory
- a *research-based* approach.

I argue that there are very compelling reasons to conclude that ICT technologies are harmful for young children's development and learning. This, at the very least, necessitates a strict *precautionary principle* where young pre-school` children are exposed to these technologies, lest we end up playing grossly irresponsible Russian Roulette with their future well-being.

To the extent that the arguments in this chapter are either ignored or have negligible impact will illustrate just how powerful are the vested interests that are driving the incursion of these "inhuman" technologies (Sim, 2001) into the lives of young children. My arguments developed here are not primarily about the *content* of these technologies, but rather about *the experience* of the technologies per se. A whole host of other, very powerful arguments can also be developed – and have been by a number of commentators (e.g. Large, 2003; Sigman, 2005) – that challenge the appropriateness of the *content* of these technologies. I make the much stronger claim that these technologies themselves are *intrinsically* inappropriate for, and harmful to, young children. If I make my case successfully, then the argument about the *content* is short-circuited, and becomes superfluous.

An uncritical and often unwitting ideology routinely dominates the field of children's early adult-derived ("educational") learning, with the quite unwarranted assumption being made that "earlier is better" (House, 2011), and that it somehow confers a developmental advantage upon young children if they learn certain things at the earliest "deliverable" age. Not only is there no evidence for such a view, but all of the evidence points to quite the opposite conclusion – that is, that if children are coaxed or led into learning that is developmentally inappropriate for their age, then major harm can be done in the long run (House, 2009b, 2011) – and quite possibly for a lifetime (Corrigan and Gordon, 1995). On this view, it is essential that young children consolidate knowledge about, and confidence with, what is *concrete* through *unhurried* experiential learning (cf. Reed, 1996), rather than rushing to more representational, abstract modes of learning. These arguments will be developed in depth later.

There is therefore an urgent need for educators and psychologists fully to engage with the complex subtleties of child development, and the crucial place that *balance* and *developmental appropriateness* need to take, if we are not to risk perpetrating a kind of "developmental violence" upon young children (e.g. Sardello and Sanders, 1999; Goddard Blythe, 2005, 2011a, 2011b). The kind of "holistic developmental" approach advocated a century ago by educationalist Rudolf Steiner (Steiner, 1988) is central here – an approach which grapples with the complexities of holistic body-mind-soul-spirit development which ICT advocates completely ignore. I argue that those advocating ICT experiences for young children are imposing "adult-centric" experiences in a wholly uncritical way that is dominated by "the ideology of modernity", depicting an absence of critical reflexivity about the technocratic paradigm in which we are all caught up.

In the last few years there has been an explosion of literature raising very challenging questions about the current and ever-accelerating (Gleick, 1999) ICT revolution in which we are all immersed (e.g. Jackson, 2009; Lanier, 2010; Carr, 2010; Watson, 2010). Although we need to be beware of the kind of "moral panics" and uncritical demonizing of technology discussed by Buckingham (2007), I see this literature as symptomatic of a wider paradigmatic concern that our technological competencies may be far outstripping our human capacity to mature in relation to those technologies – and this should be of particular concern in the case of early child development. As the great scientist Albert Einstein famously remarked, "It has become appallingly obvious that our technology has exceeded our humanity ... Technological progress is like an axe in the hands of a pathological criminal."

To illustrate the extent of the uncritical embracing of these technologies, we find Siraj-Blatchford and Whitebread, for example, setting the techno-scene when they write:

> In supporting children in their development of an early understanding of ICT we are concerned to support them in learning about a wide range of *products* that are used to manipulate, store, retrieve, transmit or receive information ... Computer education is now widely considered to be a priority for young children as it is considered to be the technology of the future ... We should provide [young children] with the *essential* early experiences *that they must have* if they are to go on to understand and be empowered by technology in their later lives.
>
> (Siraj-Blatchford and Whitebread, 2003, pp. 1, 2, 14, my italics)

According to Poulter and Basford (2003), "to deny [young children] access to such a powerful, all-pervasive device [i.e. the computer] would be wrong" (p. 7). Plowman, Stephen and McPake (2010) quote Don Tapscott in claiming that "What we know for certain is the children without access to the new media will be developmentally disadvantaged" (p. 18). Little surprise, therefore, when we find them asking, "How can pre-school practitioners ... *extend* children's experiences with technology?" (Plowman *et al.*, 2010, p. 140, my italics), and O'Hara (2004) titling a chapter "*The drive* to include ICT in early years practice". From the plethora of early-years ICT literature available (including those of multiple commercial interests), it certainly seems to be quite a hard "drive".

Whilst exceptions to the ignoring of the "technologization of early childhood" can be found (e.g. Plowman, Stephen and McPake, 2010; Plowman, McPake, and Stephen, 2010), nonetheless the level of critique in even these studies leaves much to be desired. Thus, Plowman, Stephen, and McPake (2010)[1] commit the logical non-sequitur of assuming that merely because there have arguably been "moral panics" throughout history in the face of major technological change, that what is happening today in the "toxic childhood" movement (Palmer, 2006) can be similarly categorized and written off.

In the British early childhood weekly *Nursery World* (7 October, 2010), one of the most prominent advocates of early ICT, John Siraj-Blatchford (2010), proposed a case for the importance of computer technology in the pre-school environment. This constitutes perhaps the most recent rationale that has been made in the literature for early ICT.[2] A litany of unsubstantiated assertion and uncritical lip-service paid to so-called "scientific research" litter the article. First, Siraj-Blatchford completely ignores the searching concerns of a long roll-call of distinguished critics of technology, including many of the greatest philosophers of recent centuries – Wittgenstein, Heidegger, Habermas, Adorno, and more recently, Jean-François Lyotard, Theodore Rozak, and Jeremy Naydler – not to mention the many feminist critics of what is argued to be a technocratic worldview dominated by patriarchal values. For Ludwig Wittgenstein, for example, it was "by no means obvious" that the dominance of science and technology was not "the beginning of the end of humanity" (quoted in Heaton, 2000, p. 43). And for Heidegger (1977, p. 4),

> Everywhere we remain unfree and chained to technology, whether we passionately affirm or deny it. But we are delivered over to it in the worst possible way when we regard it as something neutral; for this conception of it, to which today we particularly like to do homage, makes us utterly blind to the essence of technology.

Lyotard's notion of "the inhuman" is also instructive here, for it goes right the heart of what it means to be human, with:

> a deliberate blurring of the lines between human beings and machines ... The inhuman has infiltrated our daily existence to a quite remarkable degree – in the sense of the supersession of the human by the technological ... *We have internalised the dynamics of modernity into our very being*, as if that were the only possible way to behave.
> (Sim, 2001, pp.15, 6, 13, respectively; my italics; cf. Naydler, 2008)

Naydler (2011) compellingly highlights humanity's losing touch with the virtue of *gratitude* towards the earth and nature, and our associated despoliation of our environment, which he directly relates to the growth of technologies *which have no recognisable connection with nature*. It is surely no coincidence that many commentators are emphasizing the centrality that nature should have in the experience of young children (e.g. Schweizer, 2009) – and that the incursion of the potentially addictive technologies of narcissistic instantaneity into young children's experiential worlds cannot but have a compromising impact upon their developmental "rite of passage" into the human world of virtuous living (cf. Sardello, 2002). The development in young children of other quintessentially human virtues, like those of discernment, selflessness, compassion, and love, might well also be subject to a similar fate, if they are immersed into an inhuman machine-dominated world at too young and vulnerable an age.

Siraj-Blatchford also "cherry-picks" crassly positivistic research evidence to make his case for early ICT. In any reputable approach to psychosocial research, it is essential to tease out the underlying metaphysical axioms that inform, and often unwittingly direct, one's conceptualization of the key research questions. One grave danger in this particular field, for example, is that televisual and ICT technologies are becoming so culturally ubiquitous and taken-for-granted that they are treated uncritically as a "given" or baseline datum in research studies, rather than as phenomena that should *themselves* be open to challenge – and this is a fundamental difficulty that bedevils much of the research in this field (cf. House, 2004a, 2004b, 2009a, 2009b, 2010a).

My own approach to research is to adopt the stance of "ideology critique" (House, 2007). On this view, it is quite possible to retain the best aspects of rationality and coherence of argumentation, whilst taking up a committed, sometimes *political* position in relation to real-world phenomena. Such an engagement also entails a fearless exposing of the extent to which ICT commercial interests are profiting massively from the wholesale penetration of our nurseries and schools with all the paraphernalia of ICT (e.g. Sigman, 2005, 2011). On this view, perhaps the most effective way to reach a settled view on these issues is for everyone to make their most convincing case for their respective positions, drawing upon rhetoric, research, reason, passion, and the art of persuasion in whatever way they can – and then leave readers to choose whom they think has made the most convincing case.

Critical philosophical perspectives on ICT

Primary experience, gained through the senses, is our most basic way of understanding reality and learning for ourselves. For the philosopher Edward Reed (1996), it is direct contact with the world that most significantly influences our development, by helping us to develop and refine our interpersonal and physical skill. Our hyper-modern technological culture, it is argued, tends to favour *indirect*, mediated knowledge gained from secondary experience, in which information is selected, amended, packaged, and then presented to us by others, with everyday life thus becoming ever-more artificial – and with television-viewing perhaps being the paradigm case of such secondary experience (House, 2004a, 2004b).

Other cultural critics and researchers, like Postman (1992), Healy (1990, 1998), Elkind (2007) and Greenfield (2008), also maintain that unprecedented technological progress has led to a considerable regression in meaningful communication between people. They also caution that second-hand experience has become so dominant in our technology-dominated lives that primary experience, and all that goes with it, is under grave threat. They offer, instead, a vision of meaningful learning that places far greater emphasis on unmediated experience, and the *necessary* messiness of real-life experiential learning.

Reed's work is a development of the telling critiques of technology and the domination-driven technocratic mentality developed by philosophers like Rudolf Steiner (1914) and Martin Heidegger (1977). Although it is unavoidably difficult if not impossible to prove a direct causal relationship, it is difficult to imagine that the degradation of children's authentic play and imaginative thinking that are being increasingly observed in modern(ist) culture (e.g. Griffiths, 2006; Burkhead, 2009) are not, in some important sense, linked with the rampant "technologization" of early and middle childhood. This wider cultural perspective on ICT and associated technologies therefore demands our urgent attention – and some of these wider *Zeitgeist* questions are related to the evolution of human consciousness itself (Crook, 1980). As Bonnett (1998) has it, "an education that remained abstracted from this historical situation would be seriously lacking" (pp. 367–368), and I maintain that it is at least as important that we listen to the philosophers and the cultural critics on these questions, as it is to the empirical researchers.

Child development and the development of the senses

Educationalist Rudolf Steiner argued that human beings possess a *sense of movement*, which it is essential to develop in a healthy, relatively unhindered way in early childhood (cf. Goddard Blythe, 2005, 2011a, 2011b; Soesman, 2006). Young children's sense impressions have a crucial influence upon healthy physical development, and any unbalanced emphasis on intellectual-cognitive learning is argued to be developmentally inappropriate and potentially harmful in the early years (House, 2009b), diverting the growth forces needed for bodily and internal organ development (cf. Healy, 1998; Elkind, 2007; Steiner, 1988). Babies' sensory organs are not fully developed at birth, and first have to be fine-tuned and mastered. However, if they are over-loaded with sense impressions (and especially inhuman, machine-derived ones) before the senses are fully enough developed, their potential can be greatly curtailed, and the picture of the world that children can then mentally construct can be severely limited.

The implication is that we should therefore avoid as far as possible young children being exposed to essentially random, rapidly appearing and disappearing sensory impressions which are machine-originating, and which have little if any living human context; which young children cannot begin to comprehend; and which confer no human meaning – for the great danger is that such assaults on the senses will generate addiction, non-comprehension, alienation and/or anxiety. Put differently, young children need, above all, to experience the world in real human-relational terms (Reed, 1996) rather than according to incomprehensible "virtual" and "inhuman" ones (Lyotard, 1991; Sim, 2001).

The emphasis on the centrality of movement and the body in early childhood experience is one that resonates both with the arguments about *embodiment* developed by philosophers like George Lakoff (Lakoff and Boal, 1995; Lakoff and Johnson, 1999) and Maurice Merleau-Ponty (Cataldi, 1993), and also with the insights into children's developing senses articulated by Sardello and Sanders (1999). In the former case, Lakoff points out that "computers don't understand anything … they cannot experience things…. *We understand through the body.* Computers don't have bodies." (Lakoff and Boal, 1995: 122, my emphasis). Thus, the work of theorists like Damasio (e.g. 2006) have shown clearly that reason and logic are not disembodied, and that what Bonnett (1998) terms "the arrogance and poverty of pure reason" (p. 380) cannot be separated from the body and the brain. Yet this is precisely the illusion that the computer creates for the young child – and at the very time when her complex holistic development is rapidly underway, the influences on this may well have life-long consequences (Corrigan and Gordon, 1995). Thus, for Lakoff it is crucial that in face-to-face communication "there is a body present, where there is body language being shown, where there is emotion being shown" (Lakoff and Boal, 1995, p. 122). At least some educationalists recognize this issue only too well. Doddington and Hilton (2007), for example, have written that:

> [T]he body, not the mind, is the true organ of experience … [T]he sentient and sensuous body must be at the heart of even our most abstract thinking … If thought and feeling ultimately only make sense through our continued physical engagement and meaning-making with the world, then educationalists need to understand the nature of this engagement. Experience involving the emotions, physical engagement and meaning-making becomes the priority, and the form that education then takes must acknowledge and should reflect this.
>
> (Doddington and Hilton, 2007, pp. 77, 62)

What is crucial here is that the kind of binary mathematical logic that necessarily underpins computer language is not, for the most part, the kind of logic that is involved in human reasoning (Lakoff and Boal, 1995). Bonnett (1998) agrees: following Heidegger in advocating moving beyond the limiting "calculative thinking" of technocratic modernity, he echoes Rudolf Steiner (Bunzl, 2008) in arguing that we need to foster *a new kind of thinking* "which is precisely denied by much with which education conventionally concerns itself: the development of the intellect through the acquisition of an increasing range of categories for the operation of representational thought" (cf. Bonnett, 2002, pp. 233–234, cf. Lenz Taguchi, 2011). In contrast to the "soul emptiness" that accompanies machine-derived activity and the calculative thinking that accompanies it, for Bonnett, what Heidegger calls "poetic thinking generates its own intimately context-relative interpretations of criteria which express a receptive-responsive openness to things – constituting a whole-hearted engagement – such as vitality, perceptiveness, aptness, empathy with the subject" (p. 239). Perhaps Star Trek's beloved Mr Spock has something really important to teach us in this realm.

According to Sardello and Sanders (1999), we currently live in a world of sensory chaos – and we therefore live lives which are increasingly *sensorily disordered*. "Without a capacity to recognize the sensory world in which we are cast, we have no proper medium to develop thinking in healthy directions, *because the body is always disturbed*" (1999, p. 226, my italics). They write, further, that

> Our senses are very disordered in the present because the surrounding world has been largely replaced by a simulated world, a world of humanly constructed objects of every type imaginable, *which changes our experience from that of sensing the fullness of the world to being overwhelmed by sensory objects which capture our awareness.*
>
> (Sardello and Sanders, 1999, p. 226, my italics)

And if our senses do not give us access to the true, authentic qualities of the world, then we merely become surrounded by artificial, materialized representations. They further write, "We replace the inner movement of imagination and wonder with empty entertainment and stimulation to "hold" [children's] attention." (Sardello and Sanders, 1999, p. 228) Moreover, in relation to literacy learning,

> The conception of the human being as body, soul, and spirit intertwined with the world, differs from the thinking about the nature of the human being modeled on the computer, or the accumulation of information that dismembers perceptions into bits of data ... Today's children are learning to move in relation to the instantaneousness of the computer, and will be at even more of a disadvantage in relation to the movement of the written word, for *this new technology will most likely bring about deeper disruption to the sense of movement.* Watch for an increase in individuals with dyslexia of all kinds ... We move at computer time, and as such are always thrown off balance by the instantaneousness with which everything can happen, *with nothing touching us, nor we it.*
>
> (Sardello and Sanders, 1999, pp. 231–232 *passim*, my italics)

Research is increasingly showing that too much screen-based technology at an early age can interfere with at least some children's attentional skills and their ability to acquire literacy skills – and indeed with *all* children's capacity to read for pleasure (which ensures the practice necessary for true literacy) (for detailed reviews of the research evidence, see Sigman, 2011). This should be an argument for radically *reducing* these technologies in the schooling system (and especially in pre-school settings), and for giving children positive, empowering experiences of their world that are real and relational, rather than "virtual" and machine-generated.

Young children's phenomenological experience of time, and their learning about their relationship with "it" (or, better, their developing "temporal being-in-the-world") (e.g. Becker, 1992; Pollio *et al.*, 1997), is also important. Sardello and Sanders write, for example, that:

> The space in which life occurs is the time of duration. [But] duration has been lost for the sake of the tempo in which we think we are supposed to exist, but know to be hollow ... Computers, films, TV, etc. take the place of the warmth of human exchange and presence, and a capacity to give of one's self to another cannot develop.
>
> (Sardello and Sanders, 1999, p. 233)

Sardello and Sanders (1999) therefore show how the healthy development and maturing of the highest human senses that are centred in *human relationship* crucially depend upon the foundation laid early in life through bodily movement and physical development. Thus, "The greatest hindrance to [the developing higher senses] throughout life is … brought about by disturbances in the corporeal [bodily] senses, which occur very early in life. *If the corporeal senses are disordered, the [higher] relational senses cannot develop*" (p. 245, my italics; cf. Corrigan and Gordon, 1995; Goddard Blythe, 2011b). Healy (1998: 208) makes a similar point with regard to what she terms "intersensory integration", writing that young children need to develop the sensory areas of the brain in a way that is seamlessly automatic "so that around age seven, children can integrate them smoothly … [C]omputer use offers some combining of sensory abilities but differs qualitatively from nature's programming of whole-body, three-dimensional sensory experience".

In sum, then, with the sensual bombardment that typifies "modernist" culture, young children are in increasing danger of losing *the capacity to discriminate* subtle sense experience – with quite unknown and unpredictable consequences for their adult development.

Philosopher Martin Heidegger (1977) has written very penetratingly about the complexity and vicissitudes of technology, and the way in which human Being is being sacrificed to what he called "productionist metaphysics". For Heidegger, as for Steiner (1914), the antidote to an overdose of technology was the arts and artistic activity (cf. Bonnett, 2002); and on this view, it would be far more appropriate to make regular artistic activity and experiences of nature the bedrock of early childhood settings (cf. Doddington and Hilton, 2007).

There is an increasing cacophony of voices being raised challenging the prevailing conventional techno-"wisdom" that computers in early childhood necessarily improve the quality of learning. Thus, in 2000 the Alliance for Childhood published *Fool's Gold: A Critical Look at Computers in Childhood*, with a call for action endorsed by dozens of leading authorities on childhood, including many technology experts. They called for a moratorium on the further introduction of computers in early childhood and also in primary education. Then in 2004, the Alliance published *Tech Tonic: Towards a New Literacy of Technology*, in which it is argued that to define technological competency in terms of narrowly defined skills in operating computers is "dangerously outdated", with

> a new approach to technology literacy, calibrated for the 21st century, requir[ing] us to help children develop the habits of mind, heart, and action that can, over time, mature into adult capacities for moral reflection, ethical restraint, and compassionate service. (p. 7)

Imposing computer experience on to very young children cannot begin to meet these noble aspirations, and are very likely to militate against them.

In his celebrated book *The Hurried Child*, Elkind (2007) argues that young children obtain all the stimulation they need (and more!) by engaging with the real, everyday world through play; for children, he maintains, can learn to become self-motivated, confident learners without computers. Responding to the claim that most parents want ITC learning for their pre-schoolers, Elkind points out that the promoters of these products "play on our parental guilt and anxiety about our children's ability to compete in an increasingly technological and global economy" (2007, p. 104) – indicating that this alleged parental preference is motivated far more by fear and insecurity than by any informed understanding of the technology itself. Elkind also supports the concerns of holistic educators about the unknown effects on the visual system, and on sensory development and integration.

Discussions and conclusions

> The reliance on mind and the intellectual function at the expense of action and bodily experience can be a serious pathological factor in early development.
>
> (Edward G. Corrigan and Pearl-Ellen Gordon (psychoanalysts))

Across the globe, a veritable "paradigm war" is now unfolding, centred on childhood, with an ascendant technological "modernity" characterized by one-sided materialism, scientistic and commercial values, an unquestioned belief in technological "progress", and an inability to recognize that children are not "mini-adults" (House, 2009b), but human beings with a very distinct mode of consciousness and way of being. Others, like myself, believe that children's well-being is being fundamentally compromised by these seemingly inexorable cultural trends, and that there is an urgent need for us to reclaim our own conscious capacity *actively to create* human culture, rather being haplessly passive victims of its more noxious and child-unfriendly vicissitudes.

The advocacy of ICT and digital technologies for early childhood can be seen as another manifestation of the uncritical embracing of the view that young children need to be pro-actively prepared for formal schooling and learning, thus leading to an unthought-through rush to impose developmentally inappropriate learning experiences on them (House, 2009b). As Healy (1998) puts it, "The immature human brain neither needs not profits from attempts to "jump start" it" (p. 241), and such attempts (not least by the advocates of early ICT) betray a fundamental misunderstanding of early child development and "the minute we introduce an artificially engaging stimulus with fast-paced visuals [etc.], the brain is diverted away from its natural developmental tasks" (p. 241).

What commonly goes unquestioned, then, is the pernicious view that just because young children *can* be made to learn certain things at a young age, that the earlier this can be achieved, the better for the child (Moore and Moore, 1989; Katz, 2011). This is clearly a major logical non-sequitur, yet it illustrates again just how powerful is the modernist *Zeitgeist* and its accompanying shibboleths.

We urgently need an informed philosophical, psychoanalytic, and psychotherapeutic perspective on children's development, and on what is actually happening to children's brains, minds, senses, and delicate, nascent identity-formation through exposure to such computer technologies, the nature of which is quite new in human history. Naydler (2008) argues that "if the unconscious [to use a psychoanalytic term – RH] is more and more to be permeated by imagery of machine-derivation ... this constitutes a grave intrusion into the inner lives of human beings ... [M]achine-generated virtual worlds will ... *inhabit us*, by insinuating themselves into our unconscious" (p. 12, his italics). There are also implications in relation to burgeoning narcissistic tendencies present in modern culture resulting from importing these technologies into young children's worlds (Lasch, 1979), which Bonnett (1998, 2002) links to the issue of what is an increasingly nihilistic era (cf. Levin, 1987). Thus,

> Our view of the world becomes pre-formed, one track, closed off, and thinking becomes "constipated". Thus, as the technological way of relating to the world gains ascendancy ... so we move along a road whose ultimate destination is nihilism in the

sense of an empty meaninglessness resulting from an inability to receive meaning from outside ourselves, our "self"-centred plans, calculations and definitions.

(Bonnett, 2002, p. 235; cf. Bonnett, 1998, pp. 367, 381)

Moreover, the subtle balance between other-people relating and machine auto-relating may also be shifting significantly towards the latter, with quite unpredictable consequences for character and relational development at what is such a delicate and impressionable time in child development. We should certainly take notice of the arguments of philosophers like Levin (1987), that our technocratic nihilistic culture is responsible for generating a whole gamut of paradigm-specific "psychopathologies" in terms of narcissistic disorders, schizophrenia, and depression. With the narcissistic disorders being of especial concern, Levin quotes Jungian analyst Nathan Schwartz-Salant in a passage that might well have most of us wincing in recognition:

Incessant doing is a chronic condition of the narcissistic character. His basic belief that no center exists within [and that there is] no source of rest, results in seemingly endless activity, whether of an internal phantasy nature or an external rush to more and more achievements and tasks.

(Levin, 1987, p. 513)

And Levin further adds (ibid.), "Today, our technological economy is organized in attunement with the restless activity of the narcissistic character disorder".

We can only speculate as to the impact in terms of what Heidegger would call the *distraction from human Being* that these technologies enable (Lambeir, 2002), and for which they can so easily be used by children seeking distractions or escape from the "existential givens" and vicissitudes of human life and existence (Yalom, 1980). At a purely physiological level, moreover, these technologies may well be interfering with the child's developing brain (Greenfield, 2008; Jackson, 2005), with all manner of quite unpredictable consequences for children's identity development, and capacities for imagination and genuinely creative thinking (Griffiths, 2006; Burkhead, 2009).

Siraj-Blatchford and other supporters of early childhood ICT usage are keen to distract attention from the medium or process of computer use, and to confine the discussion purely to matters of (software) *content*. Yet it is the ICT process and medium that constitute the pivotal issue on which this debate turns (Sigman, 2011); and when taken together, philosophical, critical, holistic, and consciousness-evolutionary perspectives on technology do, at the very least, cast severe doubt on the appropriateness of these technologies for young children. Sigman (2011) has carefully reviewed the considerable research literature on the mal-effects of these technologies on young children, physiologically, psychologically, and socially – research studies that are strangely absent in the literature of ICT advocates – and the reader is referred to Sigman's 2011 chapter for a full review. In relation to screen technologies in early childhood, Sigman concludes his literature review thus:

There is ever-mounting evidence that:
(a) Exposure to screen technology during key stages of child development may have counterproductive effects on cognitive processes and learning.
(b) Learning through watching screens neither rivals nor exceeds early years learning through more traditional "non-virtual" means.

(c) These salient issues occur in the context of screen viewing in early life leading to higher levels of screen viewing later on.

(d) Even moderate levels of screen viewing are increasingly associated with a wide range of health risks.

In light of this accumulating evidence, there is an increasingly overwhelming case for education authorities explicitly reconsidering the role of screen technologies in schools.

(Sigman, 2011, p. 285)

I have written at length elsewhere on the issue of children growing up far too soon in the modern technological world (e.g. House, 2009b). The use of computers and ICT by young children is merely symptomatic of modern culture's uncritical (and often unaware) obsession with treating children as if they were "mini-adults". There are major forces of this kind throughout society, fed by all kinds of commercial vested interests that have a material stake in children growing up into savvy little "technophiles" (House, 2005), from whom money can then be made at ever-younger ages. These influences are now spreading into the nursery. Predictably, ICT advocates claim that there is no *necessary* connection between ICT technologies and the commercialization of early childhood experience, yet these technologies go hand-in-glove with aggressive commercial interests that will go to every length conceivable to colonize the developing minds of the very young; and the "schooling" of young children in these technologies prepares the ground very effectively for that capturing process.

There is also often a kind of unarticulated *fatalism* operating in these debates – implying that we are all somehow victims of modern technology, rather than having the will and the capacity to choose different kinds of values and lives for our children. Here is Yelland (2005), for example:

> It is impossible for any of us to avoid technologies since they are integral to everything we do. If schools ignore this, they cease to be relevant to life in the twenty-first century. Children need to be able to choose to use technologies for their activities in school when they need to. (p. 226)

It is yet another logical non-sequitur to leap from the fact of technology's ubiquity in modern culture to the view that we then might just as well introduce these ICTs to the youngest of children.

The strongest argument of all for keeping these technologies out of the nursery is surely this. If the critics of these technologies are right, then the implications for young children's healthy development may well be catastrophic; while if the ICT advocates are right, then perhaps the worst harm that can be done is that children will delay slightly the age at which they gain competence with these technologies. To this writer it seems like an incontestable "no-brainer" that the balance of risk comes out decisively in favour of a strict *precautionary principle*, whereby we acknowledge that the harm done by imposing ITC on children for whom it is developmentally inappropriate by far outweighs any harm that will be done to them by *not* introducing it when they could be developmentally ready for it.

Elkind (2007) concurs, arguing that many computer skills are learned more quickly, and more effectively, at a later age than at an early one – and also with less likelihood of developing bad habits or misunderstandings. Indeed, it might well be that "late techno-starters" will tend to be far *more* proficient and mature users than are those introduced to these technologies at a young age, because unlike so many other hapless children, they have not have their brains and souls subjected to these inhuman technologies before they have developed the quintessentially human virtue of discernment (Sardello, 2002) and the capacity informedly to choose – which are, I maintain, essential prerequisites to being able to create a healthy relationship with these technologies. For Elkind (2007), "All of the purported benefits of exposing infants and young children to computers can easily be acquired through other means and with less risk" (p. 108).

More generally, is ICT and our near obsession with it merely one instance of a wider, routinely uncritical "technology toxicity" that may well be having negative long-term learning effects on our children (cf. Burkhead, 2009)? As Naydler (2008, p.14) has recently written,

> The prevalent scientific view of the human being conceives of us in purely mechanistic terms (the spirit, of course, is denied) … If the human being is conceived as a machine, then the augmentation of human capacities by means of ever-deeper integration with machines seems an inevitable consequence.

If, finally, children *do* need to learn about what Sim (2001) following Lyotard (1991), calls "the inhuman", developmentally speaking they surely need to learn fully and uninterruptedly about *the human* first. And if the latter crucial learning is intruded upon and compromised (e.g. by having computers in the nursery), there is a danger that they may never fully learn about "the human" at all.

For this reason alone, then – let alone the other arguments in this chapter – we surely need to adopt an informed precautionary principle in this field, with the early years being a crucial developmental time when young children learn about being fully human, unintruded-upon by the virtual inhuman realities and the additive instantaneity of computer and information technologies. Contrary to the conventional "wisdom" found in some of the pro-ICT literature, those who advocate the kinds of views proposed here are very far from being reactionary "conservatives", or uncritical "moral panickers" (Buckingham, 2007), or nostalgic, over-sentimental "commentators romanticizing a non-technological past" (Plowman, Stephen and McPake, 2010, p.19) or "a golden age of childhood", or naive "technological determinists" (Plowman *et al.*, 2010, p. 22, 34); and we take great exception to being so condescendingly and dismissively labelled. What we *are* "guilty" of is bringing a radical, critically reflective capacity to the breathless momentum of modern technological developments, a concern with taking a paradigmatic, contextualizing meta-view of the place of technology in the evolution of human consciousness, and a passionate wish to protect what is fundamentally human from the march of "the inhuman". And there is surely no more important and emotionally charged place for the unfolding of this paradigmatic battleground than in the nursery.

Notes

1   There is also an inadequate discussion of Jane Healy's (1998) work, where it is misleadingly claimed that her view that using computers is damaging to pre-school children "because it undermines developmental tasks" rests on Piagetian theory (Plowman, Stephen and McPake, 2010).
2   A detailed response to Siraj-Blatchford's article can be found in House (2010b).

References

Alliance for Childhood (2000). *Fool's Gold: A Critical Look at Computers in Childhood*. MD: College Park.
——(2004). *Tech Tonic: Towards a New Literacy of Technology*. MD: College Park; available online at: www.allianceforchildhood.org/publications (accessed 25 January 2012).
Bauerlein, M. (2009). *The Dumbest Generation: How the Digital Age Stupefies Young Americans and Jeopardizes Our Future*. New York: Jeremy P. Tarcher/Penguin.
Bauman, Z. (2000). *Liquid Modernity*. Cambridge: Polity Press.
Becker, C. S. (1992). *Living and Relating: An Introduction to Phenomenology*. London: Sage.
Bonnett, M. (1998). 'Education in a destitute time: a Heideggerian approach to the problem of education in the age of modern technology', in P. H. Hirst and P. White (Eds.), *Philosophy of Education: Major Themes in the Analytic Tradition (volume 1)*. Florence, KY: Routledge, pp. 367–83.
——(2002). 'Education as a form of the poetic: a Heideggerian approach to learning and the teacher–pupil relationship', in M.A. Peters (Ed.), *Heidegger, Education and Modernity*. Lanham, MD: Rowman & Littlefield Publishers, pp. 229–243.
Buckingham, D (2007). *Beyond Technology: Children's Learning in the Age of Digital Culture*. Cambridge: Polity.
Bunzl, R. (2008). *In Search of Thinking: Reflective Encounters in Experiencing the World*. Forest Row: Sophia Books.
Burkhead, T. (2009). 'We've bred a generation unable to think', *Times Educational Supplement*, 6 February; available online: http://www.tes.co.uk/article.aspx?storycode=6008340 (accessed 25 January 2012).
Carr, N. (2010). *The Shallows: What the Internet is Doing to Our Brains*. New York: W.W. Norton.
Cataldi, S. L. (1993). *Emotion, Depth and Flesh: A Study of Sensitive Space: Reflections on Merleau-Ponty's Philosophy of Embodiment*. Albany: State University of New York Press.
Corrigan, E. G., and Gordon, P.-E. (Eds.) (1995). *The Mind Object: Precocity and Pathology of Self-Sufficiency*. Northvale, NJ: Jason Aronson.
Crook, J. H. (1980). *The Evolution of Human Consciousness*. Oxford: Oxford University Press.
Damasio, A. (2006). *Descartes' Error: Emotion, Reason and the Human Brain*. New York: Vintage Books.
Doddington, C. and Hinton, M. (2007). *Child-Centred Education: Reviving the Creative Tradition*. London: Sage.
Elkind, D. (2007). *The Hurried Child: Growing Up Too Fast Too Soon*, 3rd edn. Cambridge, MA: Da Capo Press.
Galloway, J. (2009). *Harnessing Technology for Every Child Matters and Personalised Learning*. London: Routledge/David Fulton.
Gleick, J. (1999). *Faster: The Acceleration of Just about Everything*. New York: Vintage Books.
Goddard Blythe, S. (2005). *The Well Balanced Child: Movement and Early Learning*, 2nd edn. Stroud: Hawthorn Press.
——(2011a). *The Genius of Natural Childhood*. Stroud: Hawthorn Press.
——(2011b.) 'Physical foundations for early learning', in R. House (Ed.), *Too Much Too Soon? Essays on Early Learning and the Erosion of Childhood*. Stroud: Hawthorn Press.
Greenfield, S. (2008). *ID: The Quest for Identity in the 21st Century*. London: Sceptre/Hodder and Stoughton.
Griffiths, S. (2006) 'Failing to teach them how to handle real life', *Sunday Times*, 29 January; available online: http://www.timesonline.co.uk/tol/news/article721863.ece (accessed 25 January 2012).
Habermas, J. (1971). 'Technology and science as "ideology"', in his *Toward a Rational Society*. London: Heinemann, pp. 81–122.
Hayes, M. and Whitebread, D. (Eds.) (2006). *ICT in the Early Years*. Maidenhead: Open University Press/McGraw Hill.
Healy, J. M. (1990). *Endangered Minds: Why Children Don't Think – And What We Can Do about It*. New York: Touchstone/Simon & Schuster.

——(1998). *Failure to Connect: How Computers Affect Our Children's Minds – for Better and Worse*. New York: Simon & Schuster.

Heaton, J. M. (2000). *Wittgenstein and Psychoanalysis*. Cambridge: Icon Books.

Heidegger, M. (1977). *The Question Concerning Technology and Other Essays*. New York: Harper Torchbooks.

Heim, M. (1994). *The Metaphysics of Virtual Reality*. New York: Oxford University Press.

Honoré, C. (2008). *Under Pressure: Rescuing Our Children from the Culture of Hyper-parenting*. London: Orion.

House, R. (2004a). 'Countering tele-visual assault: healthy sensory nourishment for a post-television age', *The Mother, 10,* 12–13.

——(2004b). 'Television and the growing child: a balanced view?', *New View, 32,* 21–25.

——(2005). 'Born to consume? – understanding and transcending the materialism rampaging through modern culture', *The Mother, 15,* 34–37.

——(2007). 'Schooling, the state and children's psychological well-being: a psychosocial critique' *Journal of Psychosocial Research, 2,* 49–62.

——(2009a). 'Television in/and the worlds of today's children: a mounting cultural controversy. *Research Bulletin, Research Institute for Waldorf Education, 14,* 2009: 43–46.

——(2009b). 'The mind object and "dream consciousness": a Winnicottian and a Steinerean rationale for challenging the premature "adultisation" of children', in R. House and Del Loewenthal (eds), *Childhood, Well-being and a Therapeutic Ethos*. London: Karnac Books, pp. 155–169.

——(2010a). 'Is technology harmful?' *Nursery Education PLUS*, August, 42–43.

——(2010b). 'Learning and development: ICT – byte back' (A 'precautionary principle' is essential), *Nursery World, 16,* 20–21.

House, R. (Ed.) (2011). *Too Much Too Soon? – Perspectives on Early Learning and the Erosion of Childhood*. Stroud: Hawthorn Press.

Idhe, D. (2010). *Heidegger's Technologies: Postphenomenological Perspectives*. Bronx, New York: Fordham University Press.

Jackson, G. (2005). 'Cybernetic children: how technologies change and constrain the developing mind' in C. Newnes and N. Radcliffe (eds), *Making and Breaking Children's Lives*. Ross-on-Wye: PCCS Books, pp. 90–104.

Jackson, M. (2009). *Distracted: The Erosion of Attention and the Coming Dark Age*. Amherst, NY: Prometheus Books.

Katz, L. G. (2011). 'Current perspectives on the early childhood curriculum', in R. House (ed.), *Too Much Too Soon? Perspectives on Early Learning and the Erosion of Childhood*. Stroud: Hawthorn Press.

Lakoff, G., with Boal, I. A. (1995). Interview: body, brain, and communication', in J. Brook and I.A. Boal (Eds.), *Resisting the Virtual Life: The Culture and Politics of Information*. San Francisco: City Lights, pp. 115–129.

Lakoff, G. and Johnson, M. (1999). *Philosophy in the Flesh: The Embodied Mind and Its Challenge to Western Thought*. New York: Basic Books.

Lambeir, B. (2002). 'Comfortably numb in the digital era: man's Being as standing-reserve or dwelling silently', in M. A. Peters (Ed.), *Heidegger, Education, and Modernity*. Lanham, MD: Rowman and Littlefield, pp. 103–122.

Lanier, J. (2010). *You Are Not a Gadget*. Harmondsworth: Penguin.

Large, M. (2003). *Set Free Childhood: Parents' Survival Guide to Coping with Computers and TV*. Stroud: Hawthorn Press.

Lasch, C. (1979). *The Culture of Narcissism: American Life in an Age of Diminishing Expectations*. New York: Norton.

Lenz Taguchi, H. (2011). 'Investigating learning, participation and becoming in early childhood practices with a relational materialist approach', *Global Studies of Childhood, 1* (1); available online: http://www.wwwords.co.uk/gsch/ (accessed 25 January 2012); abridged version in R. House (Ed.), *Too Much Too Soon?*. Stroud: Hawthorn Press.

Levin, D. M. (1987). 'Clinical stories: a modern self in the fury of being', in D. M. Levin (Ed.), *Pathologies of the Modern Self: Postmodern Studies on Narcissism, Schizophrenia and Depression*. New York: New York University Press, pp. 479–537.

Lyotard, J.-F. (1991). *The Inhuman*. Cambridge: Polity Press (orig. 1988).

Misa, T. J., Brey, P., and Feenberg, A. (Eds.) (2003). *Modernity and Technology*. Cambridge, MA: MIT Press.

Moore, R. S. and Moore, D. N., with Moore, D. R. (1989). *Better Late Than Early: A New Approach to Your Child's Education*. Camas, WA: Readers Digest Press/The Moore Foundation.

Naydler, J. (2008). 'Technology and the soul', *New View, 49*, 7–15.

——(2011). 'The unquenchable thirst to live in gratitude: digital technology and the afflicted soul of the earth', *New View, 60*, 37–41.

O'Hara, M. (2004). *ICT in the Early Years*. London: Continuum.

Oliver, D. W., Canniff, J., and Korhonen, J. (2002). *The Primal, the Modern, and the Vital Center: A Theory of Balanced Culture in a Living Place*. Brandon, VT: Foundation for Educational Review.

Palmer, S. (2006). *Toxic Childhood*. London: Orion.

Plowman, L, McPake, J. and Stephen, C. (2010). 'The technologisation of childhood? Young children and technology in the home', *Children and Society, 24*, 63–74.

Plowman, L., Stephen, C. and McPake, J. (2010). *Growing up with Technology: Young Children Learning in a Digital World*. London: Routledge.

Pollio, H. R., Henley, T. B. and Thompson, C. J. (1997). *The phenomenology of everyday life: Empirical investigations of human experience*. Cambridge, UK: Cambridge University Press.

Postman, N. (1992). *Technopoly: The Surrender of Culture to Technology*. New York: A.A. Knopf.

Poulter, T. and Basford, J. (2003). *Using ICT in Foundation Stage Teaching*. Exeter: Learning Matters.

Reed, E. S. (1996). *The Necessity of Experience*. New Haven: Yale University Press.

Sardello, R. (2002). *The Power of Soul: Living the Twelve Virtues*. Charlottesville, VA: Hampton Roads Publ. Co.

Sardello, R, and Sanders, C. (1999). 'Care of the senses: a neglected dimension of education', Chapter 12 in J. Kane (Ed.), *Education, Information, and Imagination: Essays on Learning and Thinking*. Columbus, Ohio: Prentice-Hall/Merril, pp. 223–247.

Schweizer, S. (2009). *Under the Sky: Playing, Working and Enjoying Adventures in the Open Air*. London: Rudolf Steiner Press.

Sigman, A. (2005). *Remotely Controlled: How Television is Damaging Our Lives*. London: Vermillion.

——(2011). 'Does not compute, revisited: screen technology in early years education', in R. House (Ed.), *Too Much Too Soon? Essays on Early Learning and the Erosion of Childhood*. Stroud: Hawthorn Press.

Sikorski, W. (1993). *Modernity and Technology: Harnessing the Earth to the Slavery of Man*. Tuscalousa: University of Alabama Press.

Sim, S. (2001). *Lyotard and the Inhuman*. Cambridge: Icon Books.

Siraj-Blatchford, J. (Ed.) (2010). 'Analysis: Computers benefit children', *Nursery World*, 7 October; available at: http://www.nurseryworld.co.uk/news/1033000/Analysis-Computers-benefit-children/?DCMP=ILC-SEARCH (accessed 25 January 2012).

Siraj-Blatchford, J. and Morgan, A. (2009). *Using ICT in the Early Years*. Salisbury: Practical Pre-School Books.

Siraj-Blatchford, J. and Whitebread, D. (Eds.) (2003). *Supporting Information and Communication Technology in the Early Years*. Maidenhead: Open University Press.

Soesman, A. (2006). *Our Twelve Senses: How Healthy Senses Refresh the Soul*. Stroud: Hawthorn Press.

Steiner, R. (1914). 'Technology and art: their bearing on modern culture', Lecture, 28 December 1914; available online at: http://wn.rsarchive.org/Lectures/Dates/19141228p01.html (accessed 25 January 2012).

——(1988). *The Child's Changing Consciousness and Waldorf Education*. London: Rudolf Steiner Press.

Tyler, L. (2010). '21st century digital technology and children's learning', in M. Reed and N. Canning (eds), *Reflective Practice in the Early Years*. London: Sage, pp. 38–51

Watson, R. (2010). *Future Minds: How the Digital Age is Changing Our Minds, Why This Matters and What We Can Do about It*. London: Nicholas Brealey Publishing.

Winner, L. (1977). *Autonomous Technology: Technics-out-of-control as a Theme for Political Thought*. Cambridge, MA: MIT Press.

Yalom, I. D. (1980). *Existential Psychotherapy*. New York: Basic Books.

Yelland, N. (2005). Curriculum, pedagogies and practice with ICT in the information age', in N. Yelland (Ed.), *Critical Issues in Early Childhood Education*. Maidenhead: Open University Press, pp. 224–42.

Part VI

How is school readiness best fostered?

In our view, asking schools to be ready for children, while defensible, ignores the enormous variability that characterizes the skill levels of America's preschool children. We must simultaneously strive to maximize the growth of important early skills while responding to the mosaic of strengths and weaknesses that each child brings to the first day of school.

Frederick Morrison and Annemarie Hindman

A common notion when discussing the issue of transition is children's "school readiness" (or lack thereof). This term suggests that children's success or difficulties in school is due to how well prepared they are, that is, that the solution to the problem (or the explanation to the success) lies with the child. However, if we intend to have "a school for all", as is an ideal in Sweden (Hjörne & Säljö, 2008), we could reverse the reasoning and demand of school to prepare itself for tending to the fact that children will enter this institution with a great variety of experience and expectations. Hence, what about "school's readiness"? How can school introduce children to and scaffold them in their entry into this institution with novel practices and rationale?

Niklas Pramling and Ingrid Samuelsson

Chapter 12

Promoting school readiness

An integrative framework

Frederick J. Morrison and Annemarie H. Hindman

Multiple sources raise mounting concerns about school readiness and how best to promote it. First, it has become clear that meaningful individual differences in children's cognitive, language, literacy, numeracy and executive function skills emerge well before children start school (Shonkoff and Phillips, 2000). Second, this variability does not, in most instances, resolve itself naturally, but persists and predicts children's functioning well into elementary school (McClelland *et al.*, 2006). Third, a host of environmental factors predict early childhood development, most notably parenting, early childhood education and larger sociocultural forces like socioeconomic status, ethnicity and culture (Morrison *et al.*, 2005). Finally, it is equally evident that these environmental influences are themselves complex and interact with each other and child factors to chart children's developmental pathways. These insights have heightened awareness of the critical importance of the early childhood years, while complicating the picture of how to nurture it in ways that ensure each child's readiness for school. In this chapter we will offer some evidence-based recommendations for fostering children's skills during the foundational preschool years leading up to school entry. We will limit ourselves to children in North America, recognizing that cultural factors moderate the influences of parenting and early education and temper any universal declarations of how to improve children's growth.

Orienting themes

What is school readiness?

In simple terms, most scientists and practitioners conceptualize school readiness as consisting of a level of functioning in children's cognitive, social and physical skills that permits them to benefit maximally from formal instruction and related classroom experiences. Unfortunately, at present there is insufficient evidence to precisely specify the skill levels that predict successful adaptation to formal schooling. Nor is it clear what mosaic of skill levels across language, social and physical domains constitute an absolute level of readiness. In addition, variability in children's rate of growth over the preschool period and sensitivity to appropriate instruction in school could render suspect the reliability of any assessment at one time point. Finally, given the important role of the environment in promoting early skill development, an exclusively child-centered definition of school readiness faces stiff resistance. For these reasons, some have argued that schools should be as ready for children as the reverse, and that strict guidelines about children's readiness are discriminatory and misguided. In our view, asking schools to be ready for children, while defensible, ignores the enormous variability that characterizes the skill levels of America's preschool children. We must simultaneously strive to maximize the growth of important early skills while responding to the mosaic of strengths and weaknesses that each child brings to the first day of school. In summary, a strict definition of the skill levels needed to be ready for school is not currently available and may not be realistically attainable. Hence, in our recommendations we will focus on ways to maximize each child's growth level, to minimize the degree of variability children present when they come to school, and to ease the school's burden in attempting to promote learning in each child they welcome.

The "braiding" of early skills

The attainment of sophisticated levels of cognitive, social, even physical skill requires many years of training, practice and maturation. Skilled reading, for example, involves gradual orchestration of many different component skills, including alphabet knowledge, phonological processing, word decoding, fluency and comprehension (listening and reading). Initially, during the preschool period, these skills follow rather independent developmental trajectories, with each skill requiring conscious mental effort to be learned. Further, the pattern of growth of these unique components can vary for different children, based on their own mix of strengths as well as on the unique environments they experience. Gradually these component skills become integrated into a hierarchically organized system capable of executing rapidly complex levels of cognitive, social and physical skill. This process has been referred to as "braiding" by Scarborough (2001), a term that reflects how individual strands of reading components are woven together to create a new, more unified and sophisticated level of functioning.

The implication of this metaphor for our discussion is that fostering early skill growth will require careful attention to nurturing all the essential components of early childhood development. Further, each child will likely manifest a unique pattern of early skill development and will therefore require a set of experiences tailored to her/his profile to optimize development. Finally, we need to be cognizant of the fact that there is specificity to the effect of early experiences. For example, Sénéchal and colleagues have demonstrated that shared book reading has a strong unique link to early language skill but no direct link to literacy skills, while the opposite is true of direct teaching of literacy (Sénéchal and LeFevre, 2001). Clearly these facts imply that one size does not fit all children, and that one activity will not enrich all skills.

Strive to individualize

Implicit in the foregoing discussion is the realization that each child presents a unique pattern or profile of strengths and weaknesses both within and across skill domains. Promoting strong skill development will require knowledge of these skill levels as well as a concerted effort to tailor the child's experiences to maximize their growth. Recent evidence regarding the impact of instruction on children's reading growth confirms that children starting the school year with different skill levels grow maximally with different patterns of instructional experiences (Morrison et al., 2005). These results have been found from preschool up to the end of elementary school. Again, the implications are clear that we need to strive as much as possible to know each child's skill levels and to tailor their experiences accordingly.

A complex, multi-level interactive view

On a broader scale, a major orienting theme of the present approach is that fuller understanding of human development in general and issues such as school readiness in particular will benefit from adopting a conceptualization of development as involving multiple forces from different levels of analysis interacting over time to produce unique trajectories of cognitive, social and physical growth. Factors in the child, home, school and larger sociocultural context all impinge on a child's life and interact in intricate ways to shape each child's pattern of change. Although it is common to focus on parenting when considering how best to foster school readiness, it is crucial to keep in mind that many other forces are at work independently and in combination over this early time period.

School readiness vs. life readiness

Finally, the recommendations we offer below are meant to apply to promoting skills most directly connected to school functioning and academic success. The totality of children's development encompasses a broader set of dimensions, including health, nutrition, personal care and habits, interpersonal skills and morality. Although learning in these other domains does occur to some extent in the school environment, we emphasize those cognitive, social and physical skills that play a central role in the core academic subjects emphasized in school.

School readiness skill sets

A constellation of skill sets falls beneath the umbrella of school readiness as we have defined it, including cognitive skills (e.g. language, literacy, mathematics, executive functions), social skills (e.g. approaches toward learning, interpersonal skills and behavior problems), and physical well-being (e.g. gross and fine motor skills) (NEGP, 1998). In this section, we briefly describe each of these areas of competence and note how families and teachers of young children can, independently and in partnership with one another, support development in these critical areas.

Cognitive skills

Language

Among the cognitive skills implicated in school readiness, one of the most fundamental is language. Knowing the meanings of words and understanding the syntax that governs how they fit together allows a young child to access the instruction provided by the teacher, to understand the feedback of a peer, and to discuss their own ideas with parents, teachers and friends (Barbarin et al., 2006; Gambrell, 2004). Language skills develop throughout a lifetime, but most typically developing children are relatively fluent users of language by the age of 6 years (Hoff, 2000). Language skills are particularly essential for academic success (Storch and Whitehurst, 2002). For example, these skills help children make sense of texts as they read them, decide how to express themselves as they write, and understand and reason about mathematical problems.

Substantial theory (e.g. Vygotsky, 1978) and research (Hart and Risley, 1995; Nagy and Scott, 2000) shows that language is built through rich experiences with others, particularly expert users of language including parents and teachers. In general, children learn language by hearing new words in meaningful contexts on multiple occasions. However, children also learn language by using it in conversation with experts and other children. Consequently, adults' expansions on children's language and requests for additional talk are key factors in building children's language skills.

Finally, beyond the language of communication, children also need opportunities to focus their attention on the individual sounds within words. Phonemic awareness, or recognizing and manipulating the sounds in words, begins with attention to syllables, followed by sensitivity to the onsets and rimes within words, and finally awareness of the individual phonemes within words (Muter et al., 2004). Phonemic awareness provides a key foundation for later information about sound–symbol correspondence and, thus, for word decoding.

Literacy

In order to take advantage of reading instruction in kindergarten or first grade, children need to build knowledge of the letters of the alphabet, the sounds in words and the processes involved in writing (Snow et al., 1998). Letter knowledge includes recognizing and differentiating all 52 upper- and lowercase forms of the letters, as well as forming those letters independently (Molfese et al., 2006). Together, awareness of the letters of the alphabet and the sounds in words prepare children to take advantage of phonics instruction (i.e. sound–symbol correspondence) once formal schooling begins. Early writing provides a forum for producing letters, with consideration for the sounds they represent increasing through the kindergarten and first grade years (Diamond et al., 2008). Finally, children need a rich understanding of the conventions that govern the workings of print (Clay, 1985). For example, children need to learn that print communicates a message; that individual letters comprise words, which in turn comprise sentences; and that print is read from left to right, with various punctuation marks and capital letters indicating where to start and stop. Together, these early print-related skills have strong connections to later reading (Storch and Whitehurst, 2002).

Building literacy skills is, for most children, a challenging endeavor that requires explicit instruction from parents, teachers, and peers over a period of several years (Foorman et al., 1998). Engaging opportunities to work with letters (e.g. identifying them on letter walks or in alphabet books, or constructing them out of component shapes or writing them using various media) help children learn and remember individual letter shapes. Playful activities such as rhyming games and books and alliterative texts (e.g. Peter Piper Picked a Peck of Pickled Peppers) help children examine the sounds in words. Meaningful opportunities for children to write, accepting that the product will likely deviate somewhat from conventional writing, further support learning of letters, sounds and conventions of print.

Mathematics

In recent years, several research groups have synthesized the available evidence and determined what young children can and should learn about mathematics before beginning formal schooling (Clements and Sarama, 2008; NRC, 2001). First, children need a sense of number and operations, including how numbers represent quantities, how numbers are sequenced, which numbers are larger than others and what kinds of arithmetic operations can be performed on these values. In preschool, counting is a central skill (Gelman and Gallistel, 1978) that provides a gateway to understanding in these areas. Second, young children can also build advanced understandings of space (e.g. finding hidden objects in an area, reading simple maps), shapes (e.g. circles, triangles), as well as measurement of space and objects (DeLoache and Pickard, 2010). Finally, children must be helped to organize these data (e.g. hash marks, charts, graphs) and discuss them using appropriate language (e.g. more, less, same, different, put together, take away, line, angle) (Clements and Sarama, 2009). Together, these early skills enable children to take advantage of instruction in geometry and arithmetic once schooling begins, and are strongly predictive of later math competence (Aunola *et al.*, 2004; Griffith, 2007).

As with literacy skills, mathematics skills are supported by parents' and teachers' explicit instruction in counting, identifying and drawing shapes, measuring the world and interpreting data; however, particularly for young children with limited attention spans, it is important that this instruction be engaging and relevant for their own lives (Clements and Sarama, 2007).

Executive functioning skills

This term refers to a constellation of related skills, managed in the prefrontal cortex, that underlie organized and goal-directed behavior (Best and Miller, 2010; Miyake *et al.*, 2000). Of the three primary strands of executive functioning skills, inhibition involves monitoring one's own behavior and emotion and then inhibiting inappropriate actions. For example, in a preschool classroom, children must inhibit the desire to call out the answer to a teacher's question during book reading, and instead quietly raise a hand. Second, attention shifting or switching involves monitoring one's own thinking and redirecting attention as necessary. Continuing with a preschool classroom example, when the book reading concludes and the teacher announces a transition into some follow-up activities, a child requires attention-switching skills to cease thinking about the story and to attend instead to the teacher's directions. Finally, working memory refers to holding information in one's mind for a brief period of time, even in the face of distraction, in order to process that information. Among preschoolers, working memory allows children to listen to a teacher's three-step direction and then remember and carry out each step.

Executive functioning skills develop over time, partly as a result of maturation in the prefrontal cortex and other areas of the brain, but partly as a result of experience, particularly around opportunities to practice and successfully implement these skills (Dowsett and Livesey, 2000). There is evidence that structures in the home and classroom that guide children's attention and behavior, such as providing clear and specific directions, can support these skills (Burrage *et al.*, 2008; Lan *et al.*, 2009).

Social skills

The umbrella of social skills is a broad one, encompassing behaviors and dispositions implicated in one's own relationship to others and to the surrounding environment. Certainly, many of these skills are intertwined with cognitive skills, including language and executive functions.

Motivation and approaches to learning

Approaches to learning include adaptive characteristics and behaviors that help young children succeed in the tasks of learning and schooling (Li-Grining et al., 2010; McClelland, et al., 2007; McWayne et al., 2004). Although definitions of approaches to learning vary somewhat in the literature, they generally include task focus and persistence, help-seeking, and emotion regulation (Li-Grining et al., 2010). For example, when a preschooler encounters a difficult puzzle, she needs to remain focused on her task and ignore the distractions of the classroom; persist in discovering a solution despite difficulties along the way; manage negative emotions such as frustration and disappointment as she works toward an elusive solution; and seek help from a peer, parent or teacher if necessary.

Although the component competencies within approaches to learning can develop with maturation, there is also evidence that these motivational dispositions are shaped by the learning context in which children are situated. Motivation is fostered when parents and teachers emphasize working hard and thinking of difficulties as an opportunity to learn (Murphy and Dweck, 2010).

Interpersonal skills

Interpersonal skills, sometimes referred to as social competence, help children form and maintain friendships with peers, comply with adult requests (or perhaps skillfully disagree), and express emotions and thoughts in socially acceptable ways (Reynolds et al., 2010). Children with powerful interpersonal skills have strong, positive bonds to one or more peers, are able to work in groups and manage disagreements, and can maintain positive relationships with teachers, even when accepting correction. As such, these interpersonal skills are essential for working productively in a classroom, because they allow children to engage appropriately with teachers and peers and, thus, to access explicit and implicit instruction (Izard et al., 2001; McClelland et al., 2007).

Children's expression of interpersonal skills is apparent in the toddler years, but increasing self-regulation allows children to demonstrate these skills more reliably during the preschool years and beyond (Zhai et al., 2011). Beyond maturation, however, opportunities to practice social competence, such as high-quality early schooling experiences, are positively associated with these skills (Joseph and Strain, 2003; Zhai et al., 2011). Conversely, environments with substantial disruptions and challenges can undermine children's positive interactions (Bulotsky-Shearer et al., 2010). Interestingly, there is some evidence that social competence declines for some children over the elementary grade years, perhaps indicating that although children might master these skills, they sometimes select less congenial social strategies such as confrontation and assertiveness to have their needs met (Reynolds et al., 2010).

Behavior problems

Problem behaviors are often separated into internalizing and externalizing categories. Internalizing problems involve unusual degrees of introversion, shyness, anxiety and depression. In contrast, externalizing problems involve noncompliance, aggression and confrontational behavior (Blandon et al., 2010). Although externalizing problems often receive more attention from teachers and parents, largely because they can disrupt the learning environment as a whole, internalizing behaviors can have pernicious effects on learning as they distract children and impede their productive interactions with peers; effects may operate at least partly through language (Spere and Evans, 2009; Spere et al., 2004). Not surprisingly, children with more behavior problems have weaker interpersonal skills (Reynolds et al., 2010). There is evidence that behavior problems are, for many children, relatively stable over time (Bilancia and Rescorla, 2010; Blandon et al., 2010; Slemming et al., 2010), although strategic interventions at home or school can reduce these challenges (Brotman et al., 2011; Morrison and Bratton, 2010).

In general, improvement of problem behaviors involves fostering a warm and structured environment in the classroom or home, as well as targeting individual students to receive guidance. Along these lines, several approaches have recently received a good deal of emphasis in school settings, including the Responsive Classroom social and emotional intervention (McTigue and Rimm-Kaufman, 2011), as well as the Positive Behavior Supports model (Blair et al., 2010).

Physical development

Although they are interrelated, gross and fine motor skills represent distinct aspects of physical development. Both are linked to later academic success, likely because motor development is the primary pathway through which children experience the world around them, and because difficulties in motor skills can distract children's attention from learning opportunities in school or at home (Son and Meisels, 2006).

Gross motor

Gross motor skills involve the control and coordination of large muscle groups in service of performing relatively large-scale, whole-body movements (Williams et al., 2009). Activities in which gross motor skills are implicated include walking, running, jumping, skipping or throwing a ball. For typically developing children, these skills develop as muscles mature, but practice in these areas is critical as well. Children's skills are best supported when opportunities are provided at home and school to engage in gross motor play that provides feedback on the accuracy of their execution (for example, when playing soccer, the player can determine for himself how close he came to the goal and make refinements, but as a child learns to skip, direct input from a peer or adult may be needed to shape behavior).

Fine motor

In contrast, fine motor skills involve using small muscle groups to perform relatively precise and nuanced actions (Darrah et al., 2009). Fine motor skills including holding and using a pencil or crayon (e.g. drawing, writing), cutting, pasting, pouring liquid from a pitcher into a glass, building with blocks, zipping or buttoning clothing, and working on a puzzle or with small toys or manipulatives. As with gross motor skills, fine motor skills develop both through maturation and through deliberate practice with careful feedback. Opportunities to play, build, write and draw support development in this area.

Overall health

On the whole, school readiness is a multifaceted and dynamic construct that includes factors inherent in children, as well as contributions by parents, teachers and the broader environment. Perhaps the most important implication of this work is that effective learning environments at home and school are those that provide children with multiple different opportunities to work on each aspect of this constellation of competencies, with attention to individual children's particular levels of skill in each area. Further, ideal learning environments intentionally track children's development and evolve with children over time. Thus, the task of preparing children for school is a complex and multifarious process that demands careful coordination among many stakeholders.

References

Aunola, K., Leskinen, E., Lerkkanen, M.-K. and Nurmi, J. E. (2004). Developmental dynamics of math performance from preschool to grade 2. *Journal of Educational Psychology, 96*, 699–713.

Barbarin, O., Bryant, D., McCandies, T., Burchinal, M., Early, D., Clifford, R. *et al.* (2006). Children enrolled in public pre-K: the relation of family life, neighborhood quality, and socioeconomic resources to early competence. *American Journal of Orthopsychiatry, 76*, 265–276.

Best, J. R. and Miller, P. H. (2010). A developmental perspective on executive function. *Child Development, 81*, 1641–1660.

Bilancia, S. D. and Rescorla, L. (2010). Stability of behavioral and emotional problems over 6 years in children ages 4 to 5 or 6 to 7 at Time 1. *Journal of Emotional and Behavioral Disorders, 18*, 149–161.

Blair, K. S. C., Fox, L. and Lentini, R. (2010). Use of positive behavior support to address the challenging behavior of young children within a community early childhood program. *Topics in Early Childhood Special Education, 30*, 68–79.

Blandon, A. Y., Calkins, S. D., Grimm, K. J., Keane, S. P. and O'Brien, M. (2010). Testing a developmental cascade model of emotional and social competence and early peer acceptance. *Development and Psychopathology, 22*, 737–748.

Brotman, L. M., Calzada, E., Huang, K.-Y., Kingston, S., Dawson-McClure, S., Kamboukos, D. *et al.* (2011). Promoting effective parenting practices and preventing child behavior problems in school among ethnically diverse families from underserved, urban communities. *Child Development, 82*, 258–276.

Bulotsky-Shearer, R. J., Domínguez, X., Bell, E. R., Rouse, H. L. and Fantuzzo, J. W. (2010). Relations between behavior problems in classroom social and learning situations and peer social competence in Head Start and kindergarten. *Journal of Emotional and Behavioral Disorders, 18*, 195–210.

Burrage, M. S., Ponitz, C. C., McCready, E. A., Shah, P., Sims, B. C., Jewkes, A. M. *et al.* (2008). Age- and schooling-related effects on executive functions in young children: a natural experiment. *Child Neuropsychology, 14*, 510–524.

Clay, M. E. (1985). *Concepts about Print.* Westport, CT: Greenwood Publishing.

Clements, D. H. and Sarama, J. (2007). Effects of a preschool mathematics curriculum: summative research on the Building Blocks project. *Journal for Research in Mathematics Education, 38*, 136–163.

——(2008). Experimental evaluation of the effects of a research-based preschool mathematics curriculum. *American Educational Research Journal, 45*, 443–494.

——(2009). *Learning and Teaching Early Math: The Learning Trajectories Approach.* New York: Routledge.

Darrah, J., Senthilselvan, A. and Magill-Evans, J. (2009). Trajectories of serial motor scores of typically developing children: implications for clinical decision making. *Infant Behavior & Development, 32*, 72–78.

DeLoache, J. S. and Pickard, M. B. (2010). Of chimps and children: use of spatial symbols by two species. In F. L. Dolins and R. W. Mitchell (Eds.), *Spatial Cognition, Spatial Perception: Mapping the Self and Space* (pp. 486–504). New York: Cambridge University Press.

Diamond, K. E., Gerde, H. K. and Powell, D. R. (2008). Development in early literacy skills during the pre-kindergarten year in Head Start: relations between growth in children's writing and understanding of letters. *Early Childhood Research Quarterly, 23*, 467–478.

Dowsett, S. M. and Livesey, D. J. (2000). The development of inhibitory control in preschool children: effects of 'executive skills' training. *Developmental Psychobiology, 36*, 161–174.

Foorman, B. R., Fletcher, J. M., Francis, D. J., Schatschneider, C. and Mehta, P. (1998). The role of instruction in learning to read: preventing reading failure in at-risk children. *Journal of Educational Psychology, 90*, 37–55.

Gambrell, L. (2004). Exploring the connection between oral language and early reading. *The Reading Teacher, 57*, 490–494.

Gelman, R. and Gallistel, C. R. (1978). *The Child's Understanding of Number.* Cambridge, MA: Harvard University Press.

Griffith, S. (2007). Early intervention for children at risk of developing mathematical learning difficulties. In D. B. Birch and M. M. Mazzocco (Eds.), *Why is Math so Hard for Some Children? The Nature and Origins of Mathematical Learning Difficulties And Disabilities* (pp. 373–396). Baltimore: Paul H. Brookes.

Hart, B. and Risley, T. R. (1995). *Meaningful Differences in the Everyday Experience of Young American Children.* Baltimore: Paul H. Brookes Publishing Co.

Hoff, E. (2000). *Language Development* (2nd edn). New York: Wadsworth.

Izard, C., Fine, S., Schultz, D., Mostow, A., Ackerman, B. and Youngstrom, E. (2001). Emotion knowledge as a predictor of social behavior and academic competence in children at risk. *Psychological Science, 12*, 18–23.

Joseph, G. E. and Strain, P. S. (2003). Comprehensive evidence-based social-emotional curricula for young children: an analysis of efficacious adoption potential. *Topics in Early Childhood Special Education, 23*, 65–76.

Lan, X., Ponitz, C. C., Miller, K. F., Li, S., Cortina, K. and Perry, M. (2009). Keeping their attention: classroom practices associated with behavioral engagement in first grade mathematics classes in China and the United States. *Early Childhood Research Quarterly, 24*, 198–211.

Li-Grining, C. P., Votruba-Drzal, E., Maldonado-Carreño, C. and Haas, K. (2010). Children's early approaches to learning and academic trajectories through fifth grade. *Developmental Psychology, 46*, 1062–1077.

McClelland, M. M., Acock, A. C. and Morrison, F. J. (2006). The impact of kindergarten learning-related skills on academic trajectories at the end of elementary school. *Early Childhood Research Quarterly, 21*, 471 Chi.

McClelland, M. M., Cameron, C. E., Connor, C. M., Farris, C. L., Jewkes, A. M. and Morrison, F. J. (2007). Links between behavioral regulation and preschoolers' literacy, vocabulary, and math skills. *Developmental Psychology, 43*, 947–959.

McTigue, E. M. and Rimm-Kaufman, S. E. (2011). The Responsive Classroom approach and its implications for improving reading and writing. *Reading & Writing Quarterly: Overcoming Learning Difficulties, 27*, 5–24.

McWayne, C. M., Fantuzzo, J. W. and McDermott, P. A. (2004). Preschool competency in context: an investigation of the unique contribution of child competencies to early academic success. *Developmental Psychology, 40*, 633–645.

Miyake, A., Friedman, N. P., Emerson, M. J., Witzki, A. H. and Howerter, A. (2000). The unity and diversity of executive functions and their contributions to complex "frontal lobe" tasks: a latent variable analysis. *Cognitive Psychology, 41*, 49–100.

Molfese, V. J., Beswick, J., Molnar, A. and Jacobi-Vessels, J. (2006). Alphabetic skills in preschool: a preliminary study of letter naming and letter writing. *Developmenal Neuropsychology, 29*, 5–19.

Morrison, F. J., Bachman, H. J. and Connor, C. M. (2005*). Improving Literacy in America: Guidelines from Research*. New Haven: Yale University Press.

Morrison, M. O. and Bratton, S. C. (2010). Preliminary investigation of an early mental health intervention for Head Start programs: effects of child teacher relationship training on children's behavior problems. *Psychology in the Schools, 47*, 1003–1017.

Murphy, M. C. and Dweck, C. S. (2010). A culture of genius: how an organization's lay theory shapes people's cognition, affect, and behavior. *Personality and Social Psychology Bulletin, 36*, 283–296.

Muter, V., Hulme, C., Snowling, M. J. and Stevenson, J. (2004). Phonemes, rimes, vocabulary, and grammatical skills as foundations of early reading development: evidence from a longitudinal study. *Developmental Psychology, 40*, 665–681.

Nagy, W. E. and Scott, J. A. (2000). Vocabulary processes. In M. J. Kamil, P. B. Mosenthal, P. D. Pearson and R. Barr (Eds.), *Handbook of Reading Research* (Vol. 3, pp. 269–284). Mahwah, NJ: Erlbaum.

National Education Goals Panel (NEGP) (1998). *Reconsidering Children's Early Development and Learning: Toward Common Views and Vocabulary*. Washington, DC: US Government Printing Office.

NRC (2001). *Adding It Up: Helping Children Learn Mathematics*. Washington, DC: National Academy Press.

Reynolds, M. R., Sander, J. B. and Irvin, M. J. (2010). Latent curve modeling of internalizing behaviors and interpersonal skills through elementary school. *School Psychology Quarterly, 25*, 189–201.

Scarborough, H. S. (2001). Connecting early language and literacy to later reading (dis)abilities: evidence, theory, and practice. In S. Neuman and D. Dickinson (Eds.), *Handbook for Research in Early Literacy*. New York: Guilford Press.

Sénéchal, M. and Lefevre, J. (2001) Storybook reading and parent teaching: links to language and literacy development. In P. R. Britto and J. Brroks-Gunn (Eds.), *New Directions in Child Development, no 92. The role of Family Literacy Environments In Promoting Young Children's Emerging Literacy*. San Francisco: Jossey-Boss, pp. 39–52.

Shonkoff, J. P. and Phillips, D. A., (2000) *From Neurons to Neighborhoods*. Washington, D.C.: National Research Council. Ch. 9 (Nurturing Relationships).

Slemming, K., Sørensen, M. J., Thomsen, P. H., Obel, C., Henriksen, T. B. and Linnet, K. M. (2010). The association between preschool behavioural problems and internalizing difficulties at age 10–12 years. *European Child & Adolescent Psychiatry, 19*, 787–795.

Snow, C. E., Burns, M. S. and Griffin, P. (1998). *Preventing Reading Difficulties in Young Children*. Washington, DC: National Academy Press.

Son, S.-H. and Meisels, S. J. (2006). The relationship of young children's motor skills to later reading and math achievement. *Merrill-Palmer Quarterly: Journal of Developmental Psychology, 52*, 755–778.

Spere, K. and Evans, M. A. (2009). Shyness as a continuous dimension and emergent literacy in young children: is there a relation? *Infant and Child Development, 18*, 216–237.

Spere, K. A., Schmidt, L. A., Theall-Honey, L. A. and Martin-Chang, S. (2004). Expressive and receptive language skills of temperamentally shy preschoolers. *Infant and Child Development, 13*, 123–133.

Storch, S. A. and Whitehurst, G. J. (2002). Oral language and code-related precursors to reading: evidence from a longitudinal structural model. *Developmental Psychology, 38*, 934–947.

Vygotsky, L. (1978). *Mind in Society: The Development of Higher Mental Processes*. Cambridge, MA: Harvard University Press.

Williams, H. G., Pfeiffer, K. A., Dowda, M., Jeter, C., Jones, S. and Pate, R. R. (2009). A field-based testing protocol for assessing gross motor skills in preschool children: the Children's Activity and Movement in Preschool Study Motor Skills Protocol. *Measurement in Physical Education and Exercise Science, 13*, 151–165.

Zhai, F., Brooks-Gunn, J. and Waldfogel, J. (2011). Head Start and urban children's school readiness: a birth cohort study in 18 cities. *Developmental Psychology, 47*, 134–152.

Chapter 13

School readiness and school's readiness

On the child's transition from preschool to school

Niklas Pramling and Ingrid Pramling Samuelsson

University of Gothenburg, Sweden

Introduction

The child's transition to school is much studied and discussed throughout the world today (e.g. Broström, 2005; Dockett and Perry, 2004; Davidsson, 2002; Einarsdottir *et al.*, 2008; Fisher, 2009; Fleer and Hedegaard, 2010; Hedegaard, 2009; Margetts, 2002, 2009; Thorsen *et al.*, 2006). Our intention with this chapter is not to review this literature. Instead, we will discuss the issue of how to make children's entry into school a positive experience, through the following steps. First, we will discuss some of the issues that tend to pose difficulties to children entering school, particularly in relation to their previous experience in preschool, and what this research implies for preparing children for school. Second, we will discuss some studies on what happens to some of the knowledge and experience children bring with them to the school. Third, and finally, we will reverse the very notion of "school readiness" and discuss the issue of "school's readiness", that is, how to prepare schools for responding to the fact that children enter school with a great variety of experience and expectations.

Transition from preschool to school: entering a novel logic regime

In order to introduce one of the foundational difficulties children face when entering the institution of school, we will return to one of the classic studies of developmental psychology, Alexander Luria's (1976) study on how novel institutional practices "inform" higher psychological processes such as reasoning, categorization and perception. In his pioneering research conducted in the 1920–1930s in the remote parts of what was then the Soviet Union, Luria investigated what happened to the cognitive and perceptual abilities of people (peasants who were illiterate) who were given the opportunity to attend newly opened schools. The study is highly complex and covers many areas. In this chapter we will only illustrate, discuss and draw some implications from some parts of his study, particularly the parts about reasoning and categorization. We argue that Luria's findings in these regards are highly relevant to discussing one of the major difficulties children face when entering school.

Studying the participants' categorization, Luria presented a number of abstract figures, figures that schooled subjects typically labeled with geometrical terms such as triangle, square and circle. The unschooled participants in contrast labeled these figures "coin", "moon", "window frame", "plate", "tent", "bracelet" etc., that is, as objects they were familiar with from their everyday life. Another task the participants were presented with consisted of four objects that they were being asked to categorize. The following is one example. Following Luria's own transcription, text in **bold** is the interviewer's words, text in "quotes" are the respondent's words, and words in *italics* and plain text are Luria's explanatory notes.

An unschooled participant (who was illiterate) was presented with the following four items: a hammer, a saw, a log, and a hatchet. The following conversation between the interviewer and the interviewee evolves:

Which of these things could you call by one word?
"How's that? If you call all three of them a 'hammer,' that won't be right either."
Rejects use of general term.
But one fellow picked three things – the hammer, saw, and hatchet – and said they were alike.
"A saw, a hammer, and a hatchet all have to work together. But the log has to be there too!"
Reverts to situational thinking.
Why do you think he picked these three things and not the log?
"Probably he's got a lot of firewood, but if we'll be left without firewood, we won't be able to do anything."
Explains selection in strictly practical terms.
True, but a hammer, a saw, and a hatchet are all tools.
"Yes, but even if we have tools, we still need wood – otherwise, we can't build anything."
Persists in situational thinking despite disclosure of categorical term.

(Luria, 1976, p. 56)

In terms of a more recent elaboration on various modes of reasoning, we could see the reasoning of the schooled participants as exemplifying a "paradigmatic" response, in contrast to the unschooled participants' "narrative" take (see Bruner, 1986, 1996, 2006, for extensive elaborations on this distinction). In a paradigmatic mode of reasoning, an abstract system forms the rationale, whereas in a narrative construal, parts are related as events in an evolving story.

In a somewhat similar way to the last example, the participants were also faced with a number of reasoning tasks in the form of syllogisms. This form of reasoning task from Antiquity consists of two premises. The task is then to formulate the conclusion. A classic example is: Socrates is a human being (premise 1), All humans are mortal (premise 2), Hence ... (conclusion). To schooled participants this kind of reasoning problem poses no problem. However, the following is an example of the reasoning of an unschooled (and illiterate) participant:

Cotton can grow only where it is hot and dry. In England it is cold and damp. Can cotton grow there?
"I don't know."
Think about it.
"I've only been in the Kashgar country; I don't know beyond that ..."

Refusal; reference to lack of personal experience.

But on the basis of what I said to you, can cotton grow there?

"If the land is good, cotton will grow there, but if it is damp and poor, it won't grow. If it's like the Kashgar country, it will grow there too. If the soil is loose, it can grow there too, of course."

[---]

The following syllogism is presented: **In the Far North, where there is snow, all bears are white. Novaya Zemlya is in the Far North and there is always snow there. What color are the bears there?**

"There are different sorts of bears."

Failure to infer from syllogism.

The syllogism is repeated.

"I don't know; I've seen a black bear, I've never seen any others ... Each locality has its own animals: if it's white, they will be white; if it's yellow, they will be yellow."

Appeals only to personal, graphic experience.

But what kind of bears are there in Novaya Zemlya?

"We always speak only of what we see; we don't talk about what we haven't seen."

The same.

But what do my words imply? The syllogism is repeated.

"Well, it's like this: our tsar isn't like yours, and yours isn't like ours. Your words can be answered only by someone who was there, and if a person wasn't there he can't say anything on the basis of your words."

(Luria, 1976, pp. 107, 108f.)

As is obvious to anyone who has gone to school and/or can read, being able to reason and learn about what one has not experienced oneself is of tremendous importance to our development as individuals and collectives. In fact, this could be seen as the very basis for the existence of the institution of school. Beginning school to many children will mean to learn new ways of learning, and hence develop as intellectual beings. Scaffolding children in this new way of thinking thus appears critical to teachers' task of introducing children to school.

Although Luria investigated the consequences of participating in novel institutional practices in the form of school among adults at the early part of the last century, more recent analogous examples can be found from children entering school. For example, Säljö (2000) writes that in school such problems (e.g. how many balloons will each of two children get if they have five balloons together) are typical. And, as he reasons,

In a sense, it is no more unreasonable – in a text-based reality – to imagine half a balloon than it is that Swedish women (according to statistical yearbooks) in a given year on average give birth to 1.9 children or that an American household has in average 1.6 cars. Half balloons, 1.9 children and 1.6 cars are functional and interesting descriptions for many purposes, despite being difficult to imagine in a physical reality.

(Säljö, 2000, p. 203f., our translation)

The institution of school, Säljö emphasizes, is based on the communicative technology of writing. Consequently, learning how to "take" meaning from texts is a basic characteristic of learning in that institution. Problems are expected to be "framed" (Goffman, 1974) in certain ways according to certain communicative genres (e.g. a paradigmatic as distinct to a narrative genre).

As cogently illustrated by Luria (1976), the institution of school builds upon a certain kind of logic. Whereas people outside this institution (such as the peasants in Luria's study or children in preschool) tend to and are even encouraged to reason on the basis of experience, familiar practices in their world, in school the learner is expected to reason in terms of a textual (discursive) document of the world (cf. Olson, 1994). Learning in school to a large extent could be characterized as being able to navigate in text-based realities (Säljö, 2000). This is a very important difference in how to make sense of and communicate about the world to what many children will be familiar with when entering school. Building upon the work of Luria's colleague and collaborator Vygotsky and writing on children's transition between institutions, Hedegaard (2009) points to the fact that "[t]hese forms of practice initiate but also restrict children's activities and thereby become conditions for their development" (p. 72). In the final section of this chapter, we will return to this issue and discuss the implications of this reasoning to the issue of how to facilitate children's entry into school and its logic.

What happens to the skills children have developed in preschool when they enter school?

In a longitudinal study, one of us (Pramling, 1994) traced the development of children's skills through certain pedagogical means and what became of these skills when the children entered school. The children in the experimental group had been in a preschool that worked with developing children's skills through the principles of developmental pedagogy. According to this theory, in a group of children there will be a variety of ways of experiencing and understanding something (e.g. the content thematized by the teacher). In all brevity, the approach to learning emanating from this perspective could be described in terms of: (i) the teacher choosing a learning object (what she or he wants children to learn about); (ii) creating situations and questions about which children are challenged and scaffolded in talking, thinking and reflecting; (iii) using meta-level talk intended to make children aware of their own ways of thinking and talking; and (iv) using variation of children's experience and ideas as a source for learning (for more developed presentations of this framework, see Pramling, 1996; Pramling Samuelsson and Asplund Carlsson, 2007).

In this particular study, I (Pramling, 1994) developed a curriculum based on earlier findings from research about children's understanding of aspects of natural and social phenomena as well as mathematics, literacy and of their own learning. I then implemented this new curriculum in six groups of children 5 and 6 years old (preschool classes). The children's development of skills and knowledge in the four areas of the curriculum were assessed. In the study's follow up, we investigated the participating children's ability to make sense of the subjects in school (Johansson et al., 1997). The children participating came from various socio-economic backgrounds. Still, in preschool they all developed their knowledge in the areas focused on at a level far above the children in the comparison group, including their understanding of their own learning. The children in the experimental group developed skills in thinking, talking and reflecting. In addition to the children participating in the preschool activities guided by the principles of developmental pedagogy, there were also comparison groups, where the teachers worked in a more traditional fashion, that is more based on activities as such and a belief that children's actions will result in their spontaneous knowledge development (e.g. making clocks in cardboard in order to develop children's understanding of time).

Hence, from the study (Pramling, 1994) it was clear that the children from the experimental and the comparison groups entered school with very different abilities. In the follow up, as we have already mentioned, we followed the children into school. What happened to the children and their skills as they entered the new institution? The children were followed both individually through case studies (Kullberg et al., 1996) and on a group level, looking at their answers to a number of tasks related to various school subjects (Pramling et al., 1995).

The first thing to notice is that teachers did not value children's reasoning (meta-cognitive) abilities. In fact, the children's inclination to engage in meta-issues was viewed by teachers as "disturbances". Hence, even though the children had developed such important reasoning skills as meta-cognition, which is known to benefit school learning (e.g. Brown, 1997; Sternberg, 1998; Olson, 2003), the teachers in these schools did not cater for and appreciate this skill in the children. Importantly, this also means that even if we prepare children for school through supporting their development of the important skills they will need in school, this preparation may be necessary but not sufficient for school success. Rather depressingly, and despite the favorable conditions with which these children met school, after only one semester in primary school the socio-economic background of different children came through in a way that had not been visible in preschool. The children from the experimental groups still did better than their classmates (the comparison children), but the comparison children from the higher socio-economic areas were already on the same level as the less advanced children from the experimental group. And in the longer run, after three years in primary school, there were only one noticeable difference between these children, and that was that the experimental group children still questioned and communicated more extensively than the other children. At an overarching level this research shows that even if we prepare children for school (support their school readiness), their schooling will be dependent upon how the school's representatives, that is the teachers, respond to the skills children bring with them to school (cf. Fast, 2007). On a personal note, one of the girls being interviewed about beginning primary school said that "At first it was fun, then it got dull, and then you got used to it" (Pramling et al., 1995).

From "school readiness" to "school's readiness" how to support children's transition

A common notion when discussing the issue of transition is children's "school readiness" (or lack thereof). This term suggests that children's success or difficulties in school is due to how well prepared they are, that is, that the solution to the problem (or the explanation to the success) lies with the child. However, if we intend to have "a school for all", as is an ideal in Sweden (Hjörne and Säljö, 2008), we could reverse the reasoning and demand of school to prepare itself for tending to the fact that children will enter this institution with a great variety of experience and expectations. Hence, what about "school's readiness"? How can school introduce children to and scaffold them in their entry into this institution with novel practices and rationale? Several observers writing on the practices of schooling have noted that the more basic something is, the less likely is it to be explicated (e.g. Bowden and Marton, 1998). In relation to Luria's (1976) study discussed above, one such basic feature of schooling is that students are expected to reason about the world on paper (Olson, 1994) as distinct from the world as experienced in everyday life. Making this clear to all children is one important part of making children familiar with this new institution, its rationale and expectation. Also other "ground rules" of this institution need to be communicated to the children in an explicit manner, as successfully introduced and studied by Mercer and colleagues in a number of studies (e.g. Mercer, 2008; Mercer and Littleton, 2007), even if the focus of these studies was not on transition issues. Different ground rules apply in preschool and school (or between the child's home and school). Whereas Mercer and colleagues have introduced and studied what they refer to as the "ground rules" of thinking together (e.g. in group work) in classrooms, the "ground rules" we emphasize in our account concerns features characteristic of the communicative premises of the institution more generally than how to collaborate in group tasks, hence, in a sense, what it means to be a pupil in school. Recently, in a framework (Vygotsky, 1998) harmonious with the present one (Luria, 1976), Fleer and Hedegaard have studied and theorized children's transition into school in terms of mundane activities, such as having a meal (Fleer and Hedegaard, 2010), and expectations by parents and children on school (Hedegaard, 2009). In contrast, our reasoning concerns the issue of transition in terms of the different modes of reasoning/logic inherent in the two institutions of preschool and school, as a key feature of the difficulties children face when they begin school. It should not be left to the children themselves to find this out. School has institutionalized certain forms of communication (Säljö, 2000). These tend to be what poses difficulties to children in that institution, as we have already mentioned. Hence, meta-communication, that is communicating about how one communicates in this setting, becomes a key task for teachers in scaffolding children's transition to school.

Another important feature of facilitating transition between preschool and school, as well as creating continuity in learning experiences between the child's life outside and inside school, is to support the child in relating his or her perspective to the perspective of the school (the school subject), instead of having the child leave his or her experience outside school (for such unfortunate examples in regards to literacy skills, see Fast, 2007). An example of how this could be done is the following from an age-integrated music class. The children in the arts group are 6–8 years old, which means that they are enrolled in two different institutional arrangements, the preschool class and primary school, respectively. What is in Sweden called the preschool class is an intermediate form of schooling for the six-year-olds between, and intended to bridge over, preschool and school. This one-year practice is in itself interesting as an attempt at facilitating children's transition to school (see Pramling Samuelsson, 2006, for an elaboration on this arrangement). The teacher and children have listened to music ("Die Moldau" by Smetana) and afterwards are discussing what they have heard and how it sounded. The following is one example of the nature of the educational conversations taking place:

MATILDA: Then the dolphin is in the sun, and then all the dolphins jump up.
TEACHER: Could one say that the dolphins are one of the instruments?
MATILDA: No.

TEACHER: One could not say that?

MATILDA: No, sorry.

BEATRICE: When I closed my eyes I saw what you said.

TEACHER: That shark, it came when …?

MATILDA: It came when they started to chase them.

TEACHER: Is that when the trumpet comes? When it became stronger?

MATILDA: Hm … then the shark is the trumpet!

MATILDA: I think that it is dolphins swimming in the water. And there is a shark behind. Then when it gets a bit louder, there's a trumpet, then the shark comes. Then the dolphins line up. Then they jump over a stone and when the shark tries to jump over it, then it cuts itself in the stomach. Then he is stuck there with the stone in its stomach and it comes out here …

(Wallerstedt, 2008, p. 141; our translation)

The child Matilda makes sense of what she has heard through a narrative construal. She has heard the music in terms of a story about dolphins and sharks. The teacher, in contrast, has an intention to develop children's knowledge of music. In this attempt she, among other things, introduces the children to instruments and sequential form, as two kinds of tools for understanding music. She does not, however, reject the child's sense of the music. Instead, in her response to Matilda's suggestion, she asks whether the dolphins could be one of the instruments. At first, the child rejects this idea. However, through her follow up in terms of sequence ("when") and instrumentation, the teacher supports the child into making such a connection between the story and these features of the music. This example is interesting in showing several things important to transition and how it can be supported. First, the child makes sense in terms of a narrative logic while the teacher's expectation is based on a paradigmatic construal (see Bruner, 1986, 1996, 2006, on this distinction) of, in this case, the music. The former rationale is characteristic of an everyday mode of reasoning and sense-making while the latter is typical of institutional practices such as schooling. Second, the teacher does not act to replace the child's understanding with the "correct" one. Instead, she supports the child into realizing that these two logics can be related. This means that the child's sense-making is allowed to become and is used as a resource in furthering her understanding. Additionally, the child starts appropriating a new set of tools for conceiving of music. Hence, her repertoire of cultural tools increases. Getting access to a new set of tools is one of the basic rationales of an institution such as school (Elkonin, 2005; Kozulin, 1998; Luria, 1976).

Coda

Although the transition into school poses difficulties for many children, it is also important to remember that the entry into a new institution and its practices affords new developmental possibilities for the child (Fleer and Hedegaard, 2010; Hedegaard, 2009; Luria, 1976; Vygotsky, 1987). For example, schooling may increase one's repertoire of ways of perceiving and reasoning about the world from what we know from lived experience to what we can find out about/from the world on paper, to use Olson's (1994) metaphor. Keeping this in mind, the fact that an institution like school differs could in itself be seen as one of the points of that institution. It affords the child/pupil to develop skills he or she would not have developed otherwise. Hence, transition difficulties are necessary for human development in so-called knowledge societies. Although we cannot do away with this transition difficulty due to its developmental necessity, supporting children in what this transition entails and how to respond to these challenges is a key task of schools. Being introduced into a novel institution that is in important ways discontinuous to the child's previous experience in itself provides an incentive for development. Scaffolding this development is a key task of the representatives of that institution, that is, the teachers. It is of pivotal importance for teachers to make explicit the logical framework and mode of reasoning expected of children in their role as pupils.

References

Bowden, J. and Marton, F. (1998). *The University of Learning: Beyond Quality and Competence in Higher Education*. London: Kogan Page.

Broström, S. (2005). Transition problems and play as transitory activity. *Australian Journal of Early Childhood*, *30*(3), 17–25.

Brown, A. L. (1997). Transforming schools into communities of thinking and learning about serious matters. *American Psychologist*, *52*, 399–413.

Bruner, J. S. (1986). *Actual Minds, Possible Worlds*. Cambridge, MA: Harvard University Press.

——(1996). *The Culture of Education*. Cambridge, MA: Harvard University Press.

——(2006). Narrative and paradigmatic modes of thought. In *In Search of Pedagogy, volume II: The Selected Works of Jerome S. Bruner* (pp. 116–128). New York: Routledge.

Davidsson, B. (2002). *Mellan soffan och katedern: En studie av hur förskollärare och grundskollärare utvecklar pedagogisk integration mellan förskola och skola* [Between the sofa and the teacher's desk: A study of how teachers in preschool and primary school develop pedagogic integration between preschool and school] (Göteborg Studies in Educational Sciences, 174). Göteborg, Sweden: Acta Universitatis Gothoburgensis.

Dockett, S. and Perry, B. (2004). What makes a successful transition to school? Views of Australian parents and teachers. *International Journal of Early Years Education*, *12*(3), 217–230.

Einarsdottir, J., Perry, B. and Dockett, S. (2008). Transition to school practices: comparisons from Iceland and Australia. *Early Years*, *28*(1), 47–60.

Elkonin, D. B. (2005). On the historical origin of role play. *Journal of Russian and East European Psychology*, *43*(1), 49–89.

Fast, C. (2007). *Seven Children Learn to Read and Write: Family Life and Popular Culture in Contact with Preschool and Primary School* [English summary] (Uppsala Studies in Education, no. 115). Uppsala, Sweden: Acta Universitatis Upsaliensis.

Fisher, J. A. (2009). 'We used to play in Foundation, it was more funner': investigating feelings about transition from Foundation Stage to Year 1. *Early Years*, *29*(2), 131–145.

Fleer, M. and Hedegaard, M. (2010). Children's development as participation in everyday practices across different institutions. *Mind, Culture, and Activity*, *17*(2), 149–168.

Goffman, E. (1974). *Frame Analysis: An Essay on the Organization of Experience*. New York: Harper & Row.

Hedegaard, M. (2009). Children's development from a cultural-historical approach: children's activity in everyday local settings as foundations for their development. *Mind, Culture, and Activity*, *16*(1), 64–81.

Hjörne, E. and Säljö, R. (2008). *Att platsa i en skola för alla: Elevhälsa och förhandling om normalitet i den svenska skolan* [To fit into a school for all: Pupil health and negotiating normality in the Swedish school]. Stockholm: Norstedts Akademiska.

Johansson, J.-E., Klerfelt, A. and Pramling, I. (1997). *Att skriva och lösa problem i grundskolans tre första årskurser: Uppföljning av en försöksverksamhet i förskolan* [Writing and solving problems in the three first years of primary school]. Paper presented at NERA's 25th Congress, Gothenburg, Sweden, March 6–9.

Kozulin, A. (1998). *Psychological Tools: A Sociocultural Approach to Education*. Cambridge, MA: Harvard University Press.

Kullberg, B., Pramling, I. and Williams-Graneld, P. (1996). *Möjligheter eller hinder till lärande: Fjorton nybörjarelevers erfarenheter* [Possibilities for or obstacles to learning]. University of Gothenburg: Department of Education.

Luria, A. R. (1976). *Cognitive Development: Its Cultural and Social Foundations* (M. Lopez-Morillas and L. Solotaroff, Trans.). Cambridge, MA: Harvard University Press.

Margetts, K. (2002). Transition to school – complexity and diversity. *European Early Childhood Education Research Journal, 10*(2), 103–114.

——(2009). Early transition and adjustment and children's adjustment after six years of schooling. *European Early Childhood Education Research Journal, 17*(3), 309–324.

Mercer, N. (2008). Talk and the development of reasoning and understanding. *Human Development, 51*(1), 90–100.

Mercer, N. and Littleton, K. (2007). *Dialogue and the Development of Children's Thinking: A Sociocultural Approach*. London: Routledge.

Olson, D. R. (1994). *The World on Paper: The Conceptual and Cognitive Implications of Writing and Reading*. Cambridge: Cambridge University Press.

——(2003). *Psychological Theory and Educational Reform: How School Remakes Mind and Society*. New York: Cambridge University Press.

Pramling, I. (1994). *Kunnandets grunder: Prövning av en fenomenografisk ansats till att utveckla barns sätt att uppfatta sin omvärld* [The foundations of knowing: Outlining a phenomenographic approach for developing children's ways of understanding their world] (Göteborg Studies in Educational Sciences, 94). Göteborg, Sweden: Acta Universitatis Gothoburgensis.

——(1996). Understanding and empowering the child as a learner. In D. R. Olson and N. Torrance (Eds.), *The Handbook of Education and Human Development: New Models of Learning, Teaching and Schooling* (pp. 565–592). Oxford: Blackwell.

Pramling, I., Klerfelt, A. and Williams-Graneld, P. (1995). *"Först var det roligt, sen blev det tråkigt och sen vande man sig": Barns möte med skolans värld* ["At first it was fun, then it got dull, and then you got used to it": Children's meetings with the world of school]. University of Gothenburg: Department of Education.

Pramling Samuelsson, I. (2006). Teaching and learning in preschool and the first years of elementary school in Sweden. In J. Einarsdottir and J. T. Wagner (Eds.), *Nordic Childhoods and Early Education: Philosophy, Research, Policy, and Practice in Denmark, Finland, Iceland, Norway, and Sweden* (pp. 101–131). Greenwich, CT: Information Age.

Pramling Samuelsson, I. and Asplund Carlsson, M. (2007). *Spielend lernen: Stärkung lernmethodischer kompetenzen* [Playful learning: Strengthening the learning-methodological competence] (S. Werner, Trans.). Troisdorf, Germany: Bildungsverlag Eins.

——(2008). The playing learning child: Towards a pedagogy of early childhood. *Scandinavian Journal of Educational Research, 52*(6), 623–641.

Säljö, R. (2000). *Lärande i praktiken: Ett sociokulturellt perspektiv* [Learning in practice: a sociocultural perspective]. Stockholm: Prisma.

Sternberg, R. J. (1998). Metacognition, abilities, and developing expertise: what makes an expert student? *Instructional Science, 26*(1), 127–140.

Thorsen, A. A., Bø, I., Løge, I. K. and Omdal, H. (2006). Transition from day-care centres to school: what kind of information do schools want from day-care centres and parents, and what kind of information do the two parties want to give schools? *European Early Childhood Education Research Journal, 14*(1), 77–90.

Vygotsky, L. S. (1987). *The Collected Works of L. S. Vygotsky, Volume 1: The Problems of General Psychology, including the volume Thinking and Speech* (N. Minick, Trans.; R. W. Rieber and A. S. Carton, Eds.). New York: Plenum.

——(1998). *The Collected Works of L. S. Vygotsky, Volume 5: Child Psychology* (M. J. Hall, Trans.; R. W. Rieber, Ed.). New York: Plenum.

Wallerstedt, C. (2008). Vad hörde du? Om musikalisk urskiljning. In I. Pramling Samuelsson and N. Pramling (Eds.), *Didaktiska studier från förskola och skola* [Didactic studies from preschool and school] (pp. 135–152). Malmö, Sweden: Gleerups.

Part VII

Is academic skill acquisition important during preschool and kindergarten?

Substantial evidence supports the importance of children's early development of foundational literacy, language, and math skills for their later success at acquiring conventional academic skills ... If the ultimate goal is to see all children – regardless of family background and earlier home and care environments – on a favorable learning trajectory, then the findings of developmental continuity of academic skills argue in favor of meeting children's early academic needs.

Christopher Lonigan and Beth Phillips

In preparing children to succeed in school, we need to remember that the whole child is our focus ... Context is also crucial as the teaching of skills that children need is more effective within a context of activities that children enjoy and through a medium, such as play, that reflects how children naturally learn.

Rebecca Marcon

Understanding the contributions of early academic skills to children's success in school

Christopher J. Lonigan

Department of Psychology and Florida Center for
Reading Research, Florida State University

Beth M. Phillips

Department of Educational Psychology and Learning
Systems, Florida State University

In this chapter we address whether academic skill acquisition is important during preschool and kindergarten. Our primary focus is on reading-related skills, given the scope of evidence in this area. The question and its answer are complicated by the fact that the question is, in reality, multi-faceted, with at least two main elements. The first element is whether the skills children develop early in their educational experiences are important for their later development. The second element is whether focused instruction or early intervention that targets these skills changes the developmental course of children's outcomes. Other aspects of this multi-faceted issue involve questions about the outcomes, the timing of those outcomes, and on what basis something is declared important. With these caveats in mind, the answer to the first main element of the question is a clear and unequivocal "yes." The answer to the second main element of the question is somewhat less clear but is most likely also "yes." As with many seemingly simple questions, the reality involves nuance, contextualization, and the fact that for some parts of the answer, there is simply too little evidence at present on which to base a strong conclusion. In the sections below, we summarize the evidence in support of these conclusions, provide some context for why stronger answers are not possible at this time, and outline how others might arrive – incorrectly, we believe – at different conclusions.

Defining reading and reading-related skills

There is perhaps no more important educational attainment than the acquisition of reading and writing skills. In a literate society, literacy skills form a foundation on which the acquisition of knowledge in multiple domains is built both in school and throughout life. As employment opportunities have shifted toward technology and information-oriented jobs, well-developed literacy skills have become even more important. Many children acquire these skills early in their school experiences and maintain them throughout school. The National Assessment of Education Progress (NAEP; National Center for Educational Statistics [NCES], 2009) revealed that 33 percent of 4th grade children and 32 percent of 8th grade children were reading at or above the proficient level. Conversely, a significant number of children struggle with literacy skills throughout their school experiences. According to the 2009 NAEP, 33 percent of 4th grade children and 25 percent of 8th grade children score below the basic level. Notably, a disproportionate number of early poor readers come from backgrounds associated with poverty (Hecht *et al.*, 2000; Kaplan and Walpole, 2005). Persistent poverty itself may contribute to the maintenance of this achievement gap in the absence of high-quality instruction (Aikens and Barbarin, 2008).

Several decades of studies of reading and reading-related skills have identified many of the core skills that underlie skilled reading. It is useful to divide reading skills into two domains when exploring the component skills that underlie skilled reading: code-related skills that represent the mechanics of "decoding" print into the language it represents and meaning-related skills that represent the myriad processes associated with understanding that language within a specific context. Both types of skills are required for skilled reading. This basic model describing reading is codified in the Simple View of Reading (SVR; Hoover and Gough, 1990; Joshi and Aaron, 2000), which states that skilled reading is the product of decoding skills and language skills (e.g. listening comprehension), both of which are necessary subcomponents. Aspects of these component processes can be further divided along additional dimensions, including accuracy versus fluency (Tilstra *et al.*, 2009), top-down versus bottom-up processes (Andrews and Bond, 2008), and what Whitehurst and Lonigan (1998) termed inside-out versus outside-in processes.

Accumulated research indicates that both phonological processing abilities (i.e. phonological awareness, lexical access, phonological memory; Wagner and Torgesen, 1987) and print knowledge are key components of code-related skills. The ability to rapidly access and manipulate units of sound within spoken words likely facilitates making connections between the sounds and the letters that represent them in print (i.e. the alphabetic code). According to the Phonological Core Deficit Model (e.g. Morris *et al.*, 1998; Stanovich and Siegel, 1994), reading difficulties are most often the result of a significant weakness in one or more of these phonological processing abilities, typically phonological awareness.

Multiple studies indicate that numerous subskills are related to the development of meaning-related reading skills. Many of these subskills leverage components of oral language skill as well as some conscious understanding of this system (i.e. metalinguistic skills). Consequently, meaning-related skills include semantic knowledge and vocabulary (Biemiller and Boote, 2006; Catts *et al.*, 1999), working memory, comprehension strategy use (National Reading Panel, 2000), awareness of text and story structure (i.e. the organizing features of written language and narrative; Cain and Oakhill, 2009; Williams *et al.*, 2009), inferencing, comprehension monitoring (Cain and Oakhill, 2009), and background knowledge (Rapp *et al.*, 2007).

Development of reading and reading-related skills

Empirical evidence for the development of reading provides clear and unequivocal support for our conclusion that skills children develop early in their educational experiences are important for their later reading development. Although most of this evidence concerns children learning to read in English, evidence indicates that the developmental precursors to reading skills are comparable across languages, including those that differ in how transparent the print-to-speech mapping is within the written language (e.g. Vaessen *et al.*, 2010). Studies also indicate, however, that learning to decode may be more difficult and time consuming in less transparent systems such as English (e.g. Aro and Wimmer, 2003), suggesting that early acquisition and the need for instructional focus of code-related skills may be particularly important for children learning to read English.

Continuity between early reading skills and later reading skills

The National Early Literacy Panel (NELP; Lonigan *et al.*, 2008a) conducted a meta-analysis of studies to identify the components of early literacy. Results from approximately 300 peer-reviewed, published studies that included an assessment of a potential early literacy skill from preschool or kindergarten and an assessment of a conventional reading skill from kindergarten age or older were included. Table 14.1 provides a summary of the results of this meta-analysis for the conventional literacy outcomes of word decoding, reading comprehension, and spelling, grouped by category of predictor variable.

Results for conventional literacy skills show the significant continuity of these reading and writing skills from an early age. Skills within the print-knowledge domain, particularly alphabet knowledge, were moderate to strong predictors of all conventional literacy skills. In this domain, the skill labeled "readiness" did not index maturational status but rather included elements from multiple domains (e.g. alphabet knowledge, phonological awareness, concepts of print, vocabulary). Within the phonological processing domain, phonological awareness and rapid-naming measures were moderate predictors of all conventional literacy outcomes. Measures of oral language were also moderate predictors of conventional literacy outcomes. Follow-up analyses of results for oral language revealed that measures of oral language beyond simple vocabulary (e.g. syntax, deep word knowledge) were stronger predictors of reading outcomes than were measures of vocabulary and that these skills were significantly stronger predictors of reading comprehension than of word decoding. Measures of children's general abilities, like IQ and arithmetic skills, were moderate to strong predictors of conventional literacy skills, and measures of visual-processing skills were weak predictors of conventional literacy skills.

Many of the studies summarized by the NELP were short-term prediction studies and studies of children already in kindergarten. To address questions concerning the timing of assessments and generality of predictive findings across time, the NELP reported two sets of follow-up analyses. First, results were compared for studies in which the initial assessment of children's skills was completed before kindergarten to studies in which the initial assessment of children's skills was completed in kindergarten. Age of initial assessment had little effect on the predictive relations, indicating that the results were not dependent on early schooling effects during kindergarten. Second, results were compared for studies in which the assessment of children's conventional literacy skills was completed in kindergarten versus first or second grade. In contrast to results for age of initial assessment, the strength of correlations in these analyses differed for about 50 percent of the skills depending on when the reading outcome was measured. In the majority of these cases, relations between predictors and reading were stronger when reading was measured in kindergarten than when it was measured in first or second grade; however, regardless of when reading outcomes were measured, those skills that were strong to moderate predictors of conventional literacy skills remained so. A simple explanation for these

Table 14.1 Summary of results from meta-analysis of national early literacy panel: average zero-order correlations between predictor variables and conventional literacy skill outcomes

Predictor Domain Specific Skill Used as Predictor	Conventional Literacy Skill Predicted Outcome		
	Word Decoding	Reading Comprehension	Spelling
Conventional Literacy Skills			
Decoding Real Words	.52	.41	.54
Decoding Non Words	.72	.40	.54
Spelling	.60	---[a]	.78
Print-Related Skills			
Alphabet Knowledge	.50	.48	.54
Concepts About Print	.34	.54	.43
Writing/Name Writing	.49	.33	.36
Print Awareness	.29	.48	---
Environmental Print	.28	---	.25
Readiness	.50	.59	---
Phonological Processing Abilities			
Phonological Awareness	.40	.44	.40
RAN Letters/Digits	.40	.43	---
RAN Objects/Colors	.32	.42	.31
Phonological Short-term Memory	.26	.39	.31
Oral Language	.33	.33	.36
General Abilities			
Full-Scale IQ	.45	---	.54
Arithmetic	.45	.35	.50
Performance IQ	.30	.34	.29
Visual Skills			
Visual-Motor Skills	.25	.22	.27
Visual-Memory Skills	.22	.17	---
Visual-Perceptual Skills	.22	.26	.44

Note. RAN = Rapid Automatized Naming; [a] No or insufficient studies with predictor variable.

differences in the strength of predictive relations is that, with more time between assessments, variation in intensity and quality of instruction across schools and classrooms exert larger effects on children's reading skills.

The majority of the studies included in the NELP meta-analysis were relatively short-term longitudinal studies with one to two years between assessments; however, Lonigan and Shanahan (2010) showed that the general pattern of findings held over longer periods of time. In a subset of studies from the NELP meta-analyses that represented intervals of between three and ten years between the initial assessment and the last assessment of reading outcomes, predictive relations remained moderate to strong and relatively equal for both code-related and meaning-related skills.

The meta-analysis conducted by the NELP utilized peer-reviewed studies to identify specific component early literacy skills predictive of conventional literacy outcomes. Findings for many of the predictive relations identified were based on sizable numbers of studies (i.e. > 50 for some skills) and included large numbers of children (i.e. 1,000–7,000 for many skills). Consequently, the findings are likely to be robust because they represent multiple replications over diverse sampling and measurement strategies.

Other studies, often not published in peer-reviewed journals, have been conducted that include very large samples and focus on more global sets of competencies than were the focus of the NELP's meta-analysis. Duncan *et al.* (2007) reported the results of longitudinal predictive analyses of data from six such studies. Each study included data on between 700 and 10,000 children who were enrolled as early as 3 years of age. Each of these six studies measured some combination of early reading, early math, and behavior skills at the initial assessment – typically kindergarten or preschool – and measures of reading skills, math skills, or both at some later grade (e.g. 3rd grade, 5th grade). Duncan *et al.* found significant longitudinal continuity between children's early reading and math skills measured in preschool or kindergarten and children's reading and math achievement at the later measurement periods. The average zero-order correlations between early and later abilities were .44 and .47 for reading and math, respectively. Measures of children's attention problems were negatively associated with later reading and math skills; however, measures of internalizing problems, externalizing problems, and social competence were unrelated to later achievement. All of these predictive relations held when measures of various child, family, and study variables were controlled in the analyses. Where possible, Duncan *et al.* also examined the relation between these early achievement and behavior variables and the broader academic outcome of grade retention, and the results of these analyses were similar to those for the achievement outcomes.

Taken together, results of the NELP's meta-analysis and Duncan *et al.*'s (2007) analysis of large-scale longitudinal studies provide compelling evidence for the developmental continuity from an early age of both the broad skill domain of reading and the contributory component skills. The results from Duncan *et al.* indicate that this developmental continuity exists for the broad skill domain of mathematics – perhaps to an even larger extent than for reading. Moreover, the results indicate that this developmental continuity exists primarily within domain. That is, academic skills predict academic skills over time, but behaviors within the socio-emotional domain – with the exception of attention – do not uniquely predict academic skills over time.

Attempts to marginalize strong evidence of developmental continuity for academic skills

It is not uncommon to read interpretations of findings of strong continuity between component early-literacy skills and later reading skills that argue that the findings are largely un-interpretable (or misinterpreted) or unimportant because of the nature of the predictor variables in the analyses. A common justification for these claims is that the predictor variables are "constrained skills," and such criticisms are typically grounded in Constrained Skills Theory (CST; e.g. Paris, 2005). The fundamental logic behind CST is that all readers ultimately master some reading-related skills completely, and because of this mastery, the period of time during which individuals differ on these skills is small and the distribution of skill level is sample dependent. That is, skills such as alphabet knowledge, phonological awareness, and print concepts are "constrained" because development progresses from a point where most children have no measurable skills in that area, to a period when children vary considerably on the skill, to a point where mastery of the skill is obtained by most children. CST argues that these skills' distributional properties render traditional parametric analyses (e.g. correlation, regression) inappropriate. Additionally, CST argues that the fact that all readers ultimately master these skills indicates that they are not causal factors in the development of reading, and, by extension, that these skills should not be instructional targets.

CST is based on several incorrect, idiosyncratic, and empirically unsupported assumptions (Schatschneider and Lonigan, 2010). Therefore, CST does not represent a serious challenge to the type of predictive relations between early reading-related or reading skills and later reading outcomes like those summarized by the NELP (Lonigan *et al.*, 2008a) or by Duncan *et al.* (2007), and arguments that dismiss or downplay such findings because the variables are "constrained" have no valid statistical, empirical, or logical basis. Analyses typically used to show relations between early literacy skills and later reading do not require assumptions of normally distributed variables either to describe the relations adequately (Hays, 1963) or to determine if the obtained relations were obtained by chance (i.e. statistical significance; Havlicek and Peterson, 1977). In fact, non-normal distributions of variables reduce, rather than inflate, relations between variables – exactly the opposite effect of claims by CST. Moreover, it is not clear that there are significant distributional problems for these skills when measured in the developmental period in which they are generally considered important indicators of literacy skill (i.e. most measures of skills like alphabet knowledge, phonological awareness, and word decoding yield normal distributions in preschool and kindergarten; Schatschneider and Lonigan, 2010).

CST argues that skills such as alphabet knowledge cannot be causes of reading because individual differences in reading skill exist even after individuals have completely mastered the earlier skill. CST implies that because many early literacy skills are acquired in a relatively brief period, they are only important predictors during their acquisition. Although it may be that a skill such as alphabet knowledge is not a good indicator of an adult's reading skill, the evidence summarized above indicates that it is a very good indicator of later reading skill for young children. Once measured, a child's ability to name letters of the alphabet at that time represents an enduring individual difference variable that predicts reading outcomes far into the future. Other supposedly constrained skills, like phonological awareness, are important indicators of reading even when measured further in development, given that many individuals with decoding difficulties also have phonological awareness weaknesses. CST includes an idiosyncratic notion of cause. In fact, some skills labeled constrained by CST meet relatively stringent definitions of cause.

Promoting the development of early literacy-related skills

Children from high-poverty homes have significantly less well-developed skills in oral language, phonological awareness, and print knowledge than do their peers from higher socioeconomic homes (e.g. Hart and Risley, 1995; Juel *et al.*, 1986; Lonigan *et al.*, 1998; Raz and Bryant, 1990). This slower development of key reading-related skills, coupled with the substantial continuity of these abilities, puts children from lower-SES backgrounds on a path toward early and enduring difficulties in school (NCES, 2009). Consequently, it makes sense that some form of early intervention, additional instruction, or specific forms of instruction could alter children's developmental trajectories and reduce the likelihood that children with weaker skills at school entry continue on a trajectory leading to poor long-term outcomes in school. In this section, we summarize the empirical evidence for the short- and long-term effectiveness of instructional activities designed to promote the development of early literacy skills.

Effective early literacy instructional interventions

In general, early childhood education has positive effects on children's early academic skills. For example, Wong *et al.* (2008), using a regression discontinuity design (RDD), demonstrated that the five state-funded preschool programs they examined had positive effects on children's skills, with larger and more consistent effects for print knowledge than for oral language and effects for mathematics falling in between. Similarly, the Head Start Impact Study (US Department of Health and Human Services [DHHS], 2010), a randomized evaluation of the effects of attending Head Start for 3- and 4-year-olds, found positive effects on 3-year-olds' alphabet knowledge, phonological awareness, and vocabulary skills and on 4-year-old's alphabet knowledge, spelling, and vocabulary skill following one year of participation.

These studies provide evidence for the short-term value of early childhood education or of particular funding streams used to provide those services; however, they do not identify which practices are important components of early childhood education or are more likely than other practices to produce positive outcomes. An increasing body of research, using rigorous evaluations, demonstrates that specific interventions and instructional practices have significant and positive impacts on children's early literacy, language, and math skills. The NELP summarized the research evidence for different types of literacy-related instructional practices for children between birth and kindergarten obtained from a comprehensive search of peer-reviewed articles. The Early Childhood Education Review of the What Works Clearinghouse (WWC; http://ies.ed.gov/ncee/ wwc/reports/topicarea.aspx?tid=13) examined center-based practices and curricula designed to enhance children's language, literacy, and math skills. The WWC review involved a comprehensive search of published and unpublished studies of instruction for preschool children produced between 1986 and 2010. Both reviews included studies that were group-design randomized experiments or well-conducted quasi-experiments with no confounding of the instructional practice with other factors.

Both the NELP (Lonigan *et al.*, 2008c) and the WWC reviews found that interventions making use of shared book reading yielded positive impacts on children's oral language skills, particularly vocabulary. In particular, a type of interactive shared book reading, called Dialogic Reading (e.g. Arnold *et al.*, 1994; Lonigan and Whitehurst, 1998), produces significant gains in children's vocabulary skills compared to a similar amount of non-interactive shared reading of books. Similarly, both the NELP (Lonigan *et al.*, 2008b) and the WWC reviews reported that instructional activities that involve teaching phonological awareness were effective in increasing children's phonological awareness skills. The NELP review, which included kindergarten children, found that such code-focused instruction that typically included phonological awareness instruction with or without teaching of aspects of print (e.g. letter knowledge, rudimentary decoding) had a sizable impact on children's reading and spelling skills. In fact, one study of a preschool phonological awareness intervention reported positive impacts of the intervention on children's reading skills through fifth grade (Byrne *et al.*, 2000).

Despite a wide variety of commercially available early childhood curricula, there are few studies of the impacts of specific preschool curricula on children's development (Molfese and Westberg, 2008). The WWC's review found that most early childhood curricula have no studies, or no studies allowing causal interpretations, concerning their effectiveness. For the 13 preschool literacy curricula with studies that allowed interpretation of effectiveness, only five yielded results indicating that the target curriculum resulted in better literacy-related outcomes for children than the comparison curriculum. Two early math curricula with interpretable studies showed positive effects on children's math skills. Similarly, the Preschool Curriculum Evaluation Research Consortium ([PCERC] 2008) reported that only two of 14 early childhood curricula or combinations of curricula included in its randomized evaluations showed clear evidence of positive effects at the end of preschool relative to the comparison curriculum. Thus, current evidence suggests that many commonly used curricula are not capitalizing on evidence-based instructional strategies to support children's development.

Long-term effects of early literacy interventions

Relatively few studies have examined the impacts of early interventions or early instructional practices over the longer term in a way that allows causal conclusions. Although numerous studies have examined longitudinal outcomes for children who participated in various intervention and education services (e.g. Camilli *et al.*, 2010), the majority of these were the type of quasi-experiments that cannot disentangle the effects of the intervention services from the effects of the reasons that some children received some types of intervention services whereas others did not. That is, in many studies, there were observed (and likely unobserved) differences between children who did and did not participate in various programs even before program participation. This makes it difficult to determine if any measured differences after program participation were due to the program or the initial differences. Only randomized experimental studies or some forms of quasi-experimental studies (e.g. RDD) that follow children longitudinally can provide unambiguous causally interpretable evidence for longer-term effects.

The few studies using rigorous evaluation designs that have examined longer-term impacts of early intervention or early childhood education have provided mixed results concerning whether effects are maintained across time. Early studies, such as the Abecedarian (e.g. Campbell *et al.*, 2002) and the Perry Preschool Projects (Schweinhart *et al.*, 1993), reported long-lasting, positive effects. In particular, the Abecedarian Project reported findings of sustained positive effects on children's cognitive and academic skills throughout school and into early adulthood. Most of these effects were attributable to the very intensive early childhood care received by the preschool intervention group from infancy through age five years rather than to the intervention received during the first three years of school. In contrast, the Head Start Impact Study (US DHHS, 2010) found that the positive effects of Head Start on children's academic and cognitive skills faded out one or two years after participation in Head Start. Studies of individual early childhood curricula also support enduring positive effects – at least in the short term. The PCERC (2008) followed children to the end of kindergarten and found that for curricula with evidence of positive impacts at the end of preschool, the effects were maintained, and there were positive kindergarten effects for two other curricula without evidence of positive impacts at the end of preschool.

In addition to these experimental studies of the effects of early childhood programs and curricula, non-experimental studies have examined the effect of different dosages of early schooling. For instance, DiCicca (2007) compared outcomes of children who attended full-day versus half-day kindergarten using data from the Early Childhood Longitudinal Study-Kindergarten Cohort (ECLS-K). In separate models computed for children of different ethnicities, DeCicca found substantial advantages of full-day kindergarten over half-day kindergarten on children's reading and math skills measured at the end of kindergarten; however, most of these advantages were no longer statistically significant by the end of first grade.

Teachers are often confronted with children whose background knowledge, prior-learning opportunities, and academic skills span a wide range (Bainbridge and Lasley, 2002; Xue and Meisels, 2004). Faced with this challenge, teachers may teach to the "middle" or employ the same instructional practices regardless of children's current skills (Al Otaiba *et al.*, 2008; Connor *et al.*, 2004). In these classrooms, children who experienced meaningful skill gains from earlier educational experiences may lose this advantage because the classroom's instructional focus is lower than their current skills. These classroom contexts present a challenge to answering questions regarding the long-term impacts of early childhood education; however, they speak to the need to better align early educational goals across grade levels rather than to the efficacy of early intervention and instruction.

Possible negative impacts of early intervention

Objections to providing young children more or more directed early-educational experiences are often rooted in concerns that such instruction will result in negative consequences, particularly in the domains of children's socio-emotional development and motivation. Different authors' views on this topic are often polarized around early childhood education that includes direct-instruction versus a child-centered approach, with the latter considered "developmentally appropriate practice" and the former considered "developmentally inappropriate practice." Indeed, some non-experimental evidence indicates that time spent in early childhood education is associated with less positive outcomes on socio-emotional indicators and lower levels of self-control (Belsky *et al.*, 2007; Magnuson, Ruhm and Waldfogel; 2007). For instance, Belsky (2001) reported that amount of out-of-home care was associated with higher levels of problem behaviors in school. Importantly, although these increases in externalizing behaviors were statistically significant, they were not in the range of clinical significance. Other non-experimental studies also suggest a link between an academic focus in preschool and worse socio-emotional outcomes for children. Stipek and colleagues (Stipek *et al.*, 1998; Stipek *et al.*, 1995) reported a variety of less positive motivational and behavioral outcomes for children who attended preschools with a more academic and didactic focus than children who attended more child-centered preschools.

As with any non-experimental (or non-RDD) study that cannot establish equivalency of groups before treatment exposure, these studies are open to many alternative and equally plausible explanations. For instance, factors associated with worse behavioral outcomes (e.g. poverty, less skilled parenting) may be the same factors that determine if, when, for how long, and in what type of child care a child is enrolled. Few experimental studies have investigated the impact of more versus less instructional focus within early childhood environments on children's socio-emotional development. However, the PCERC (2008) randomized evaluation did include measures of children's socio-emotional development at the end of preschool and in kindergarten. Across the 14 preschool curricula studied, there were no significant effects (negative or positive) on children's prosocial or problem behaviors in preschool, and only one curriculum yielded significant negative effects on children's prosocial and problem behaviors in kindergarten.

Interestingly, the comparison curriculum for this effect was a skills-based curriculum whereas the target curriculum was a more child-centered approach. The absence of socio-emotional impacts was observed for each of the curricula that produced positive impacts on children's academic skills, all of which had an academic-skills focus. Consequently, experimental evidence from the PCERC comparisons does not support non-experimental findings that preschool curricula with an academic-skills focus (or that use a more teacher-directed model of instruction) result in negative socio-emotional outcomes.

The view that intentional academic-skills instruction is developmentally inappropriate obscures many actual commonalities among the efficacious skills-focused curricula just discussed and generally accepted views of high-quality instruction (Burchinal et al., 2008; Pianta et al., 2005). We would argue, as have others (e.g. Burchinal et al., 2010; Graue et al., 2004), that this falsely dichotomized view represents a confounding of instructional content and method, raising the specter of whole-group, lengthy, drill or worksheet-based practices inconsistent with the reality of high-quality effective instruction. Virtually all of the evidence supporting explicit instruction has involved small-group, brief, hands-on activities that fit well with models of differentiated, scaffolded instruction (e.g. Lonigan et al., 2011; Phillips et al., 2008), with warm, sensitive interactions, and with the appropriateness of varying group sizes and modalities (Epstein, 2007). Moreover, recent findings suggest that attending to early academic needs within planned curricular models does not require trade-offs with attention to other aspects of children's development, including self-regulation and prosocial behavior (e.g. Bierman et al., 2008; Burchinal et al., 2008; Raver et al., 2008); rather both are supported when delivered by responsive teachers.

Conclusions

Substantial evidence supports the importance of children's early development of foundational literacy, language, and math skills for their later success at acquiring conventional academic skills. Convergent findings from both controlled experimental studies and community-based early childhood programs suggest that high-quality early childhood education can have a meaningful impact on early academic development, particularly for children from backgrounds placing them at risk for school failure. If the ultimate goal is to see all children – regardless of family background and earlier home and care environments – on a favorable learning trajectory, then the findings of developmental continuity of academic skills argue in favor of meeting children's early academic needs. Cautions against this approach are typically rooted either in untested assumptions about skills philosophically favored over early-academic skills or in results from a small set of studies – all using designs that cannot support strong causal conclusions – that are interpreted as providing evidence that early targeted instructional efforts have harmful effects on children over the long term. As noted above, results from high-quality experimental studies do not support these concerns. In fact, these studies provide preliminary evidence that both social-emotional and academic development can be enhanced within the same instructional model. We believe that the real question is not whether it is important to address key early academic and language skills but how to further the dissemination of efficacious instructional practices to classrooms serving those children most in need and how to structure and align children's later educational experiences to capitalize on the resultant gains.

Acknowledgements

Preparation of this work was supported by grants from the National Institute of Child Health and Human Development (HD052120, HD060292) and the Institute of Education Sciences (R305F100027, R305A090169). Views expressed herein are those of the authors and have not been reviewed or approved by the granting agencies.

References

Aikens, N. L. and Barbarin, O. (2008). Socioeconomic differences in reading trajectories: the contribution of family, neighborhood, and school contexts. *Journal of Educational Psychology, 100*, 235–251.

Al Otaiba, S., Connor, C., Lane, H., Kosanovich, M. L., Schatschneider, C., *et al.* (2008). Reading First kindergarten classroom instruction and students' growth in phonological awareness and letter naming-decoding fluency. *Journal of School Psychology, 46*, 281–314.

Andrews, S. and Bond, R. (2008). Lexical expertise and reading skill: bottom-up and top-down processing of lexical ambiguity. *Reading and Writing, 22*, 687–711.

Arnold, D. S., Lonigan, C. J., Whitehurst, G. J. and Epstein, J. N. (1994). Accelerating language development through picture-book reading: replication and extension to a videotape training format. *Journal of Educational Psychology, 86*, 235–243.

Aro, M. and Wimmer, H. (2003). Learning to read: English in comparison to six more regular orthographies. *Applied Psycholinguistics, 24*, 621–635.

Bainbridge, W. L. and Lasley, T. J. (2002). Demographics, diversity, and K-12 accountability: the challenge of closing the achievement gap. *Education and Urban Society, 34*, 422–437.

Bierman, K. L., Domitrovich, C. E., Nix, R. L., Gest, S. D., Welsh, J. A., *et al.* (2008). Promoting academic and social-emotional school readiness: The Head Start REDI Program. *Child Development, 79*, 1802–1817.

Belsky, J. (2001). Emanuel Miller lecture: developmental risks (still) associated with early child care. *Journal of Child Psychology & Psychiatry & Allied Disciplines, 42*, 845–859.

Belsky, J., Vandell, D. L., Burchinal, M., Clarke-Stewart, K. A., McCartney, K., *et al.* (2007). Are there long-term effects of early child care? *Child Development, 78*, 681–701.

Biemiller, A. and Boote, C. (2006). An effective method for building meaning vocabulary in primary grades. *Journal of Educational Psychology, 98*, 44–62.

Burchinal, M., Howes, C., Pianta, R., Bryant, D., Early, D., *et al.* (2008). Predicting child outcomes at the end of kindergarten from the quality of pre-kindergarten teacher-child interactions and instruction. *Applied Developmental* Science, *12*, 140–153.

Burchinal, M., Vandergrift, N., Pianta, R. and Mashburn, A. (2010). Threshold analysis of association between child care quality and child outcomes for low-income children in pre-kindergarten programs. *Early Childhood Research Quarterly, 25*, 166–176.

Byrne, B., Fielding-Barnsley, R. and Ashley, L. (2000). Effects of preschool phoneme identity training after six years: outcome level distinguished from rate of response. *Journal of Educational Psychology, 92*, 659–667.

Cain, K. and Oakhill, J. (2009). Reading comprehension development from 8 to 14 years: the contribution of component skills and processes. In R. K. Wagner, C. Schatscheider and C. Phythian-Sence (Eds.), *Beyond Decoding: The Behavioral and Biological Foundations of Reading Comprehension* (pp. 143–175). New York, NY: Guilford Press.

Camilli, G., Vargas, S., Ryan, S. and Barnett, W. S. (2010). Meta-analysis of the effects of early education interventions on cognitive and social development. *Teachers College Record, 112*, 151–179.

Campbell, F. A., Raimey, C. T., Pungello, E., Sparling, J. and Miller-Johnson, S. (2002). Early childhood education: young adult outcomes from the Abecedarian Project. *Applied Developmental Science, 6*, 42–57.

Catts, H. W., Fey, M., Zhang, X. and Tomblin, B. (1999). Language basis of reading and reading disabilities: evidence from a longitudinal investigation. *Scientific Studies of Reading, 3*, 331–361.

Connor, C. M., Morrison, F. J. and Katch, E. L. (2004). Beyond the reading wars: the effect of classroom instruction by child interactions on early reading. *Scientific Studies of Reading, 8*, 305–336.

DeCicca, P. (2007). Does full-day kindergarten matter? Evidence from the first two years of schooling. *Economics of Education Review, 26*, 67–82.

Duncan, G. J., Dowsett, C. J., Claessens, A., Magnuson, K., Huston, A. C., *et al.* (2007). School readiness and later achievement. *Developmental Psychology, 43*, 1428–1446.

Epstein, A. S. (2007). *The Intentional Teacher: Choosing the Best Strategies for Young Children's Learning*. Washington: DC: National Association for the Education of Young Children.

Graue, E., Clements M., A., Reynolds, A., J. and Niles, M., D. (2004). More than teacher directed or child initiated: preschool curriculum type, parent involvement, and children's outcomes in the child-parent centers. *Education Policy Analysis Archives, 12*, 1–38.

Hart, B. H. and Risley, T. R. (1995). *Meaningful Differences in the Everyday Experience of Young American Children*. Baltimore, MD: Brookes Publishers.

Havlicek, L. L. and Peterson, N. (1977). Effect of the violation of the assumptions upon significance levels of the Pearson *r*. *Psychological Bulletin, 84*, 373–377.

Hayes, W. L. (1963). *Statistics for Psychologists*. New York: Holt, Reinhart, and Winston.

Hecht, S. A., Burgess, S. R., Torgesen, J. K., Wagner, R. K. and Rashotte, C. A. (2000). Explaining social class differences in growth of reading skills from beginning kindergarten through fourth-grade: the role of phonological awareness, rate of access, and print knowledge. *Reading and Writing: An Interdisciplinary Journal, 12*, 99–127.

Hoover, W. A. and Gough P. B. (1990). The simple view of reading. *Reading and Writing: An Interdisciplinary Journal, 2*, 127–160.

Joshi, R. M. & Aaron, P. G. (2000). The component model of reading: simple view of reading made a little more complex. *Reading Psychology, 21*, 85–97.

Juel, C., Griffith, P. L. and Gough, P. B. (1986). Acquisition of literacy: a longitudinal study of children in first and second grade. *Journal of Educational Psychology, 78*, 243–255.

Kaplan, D. and Walpole, S. (2005). A stage-sequential model of reading transitions: evidence from the early childhood longitudinal study. *Journal of Educational Psychology, 97*, 551–563.

Lonigan, C. J. and Shanahan, T. (2010). Developing early literacy skills: things we know we know and things we know we don't know. *Educational Researcher, 39*, 340–346.

Lonigan, C. J. and Whitehurst, G. J. (1998). Relative efficacy of parent and teacher involvement in a shared-reading intervention for preschool children from low-income backgrounds. *Early Childhood Research Quarterly, 17*, 265–292.

Lonigan, C. J., Burgess, S. R., Anthony, J. L. and Barker, T. A. (1998). Development of phonological sensitivity in two- to five-year-old children. *Journal of Educational Psychology, 90*, 294–311.

Lonigan, C. J., Farver, J. M., Phillips, B. M. and Clancy-Menchetti, J. (2011). Promoting the development of preschool children's emergent literacy skills: A randomized evaluation of a literacy-focused curriculum and two professional development models. *Reading and Writing, 24*, 305–337.

Lonigan, C. J., Schatschneider, C. and Westberg, L. (2008a). Identification of children's skills and abilities linked to later outcomes in reading, writing, and spelling. In *Developing Early Literacy: Report of the National Early Literacy Panel* (pp. 55–106). Washington, DC: National Institute for Literacy.

——(2008b). Impact of code-focused interventions on young children's early literacy skills. In *Developing Early Literacy: Report of the National Early Literacy Panel* (pp. 107–151). Washington, DC: National Institute for Literacy.

Lonigan, C. J., Shanahan, T. and Cunningham, A. (2008c). Impact of shared-reading interventions on young children's early literacy skills. In *Developing Early Literacy: Report of the National Early Literacy Panel* (pp. 153–171). Washington, DC: National Institute for Literacy.

Magnuson, K. A., Ruhm, C. and Waldfogel, J. (2007). Does prekindergarten improve school preparation and performance? *Economics of Education Review, 26*, 33–51.

Molfese, V. and Westberg, L. (2008). Impact of preschool and kindergarten programs on young children's literacy skills. In *Developing Early Literacy: Report of the National Early Literacy Panel* (pp. 189–209). Washington, DC: National Institute for Literacy.

Morris, R. D., Stuebing, K. K., Fletcher, J. M., Shaywitz, S. E., Lyon, G. R., *et al.* (1998). Subtypes of reading disability: variability around a phonological core. *Journal of Educational Psychology*, *90*, 347–373.

National Center for Education Statistics (NCES) (2009). The nation's report card: Reading 2009. Retrieved March 1, 2010 from http://nces.ed.gov/nationsreportcard/pdf/main2009/2010458.pdf

National Reading Panel (2000). *Report of the National Reading Panel: Teaching Children to Read.* Washington, DC: US Department of Health and Human Services.

Paris, S. G. (2005). Reinterpreting the development of reading skills. *Reading Research Quarterly, 40*, 184–202.

Phillips, B. M., Clancy-Menchetti, J. and Lonigan, C. J. (2008). Successful phonological awareness instruction with preschool children: lessons from the classroom. *Topics in Early Childhood Special Education, 28*, 3–17.

Pianta, R., Howes, C., Burchinal, M., Bryant, D., Clifford, R. M., *et al.* (2005). Features of pre-kindergarten programs, classrooms, and teachers: prediction of observed classroom quality and teacher-child interactions. *Applied Developmental Science, 9*, 144–159.

Preschool Curriculum Evaluation Research Consortium (PCERC) (2008). *Effects of Preschool Curriculum Programs on School Readiness* (NCER 2008–2009). Washington, DC: US Government Printing Office, National Center for Education Research, Institute of Education Sciences, US Department of Education.

Rapp, D. N., van den Broek, P., McMaster, K., Kendeou, P. and Espin, C. A. (2007). Higher-order comprehension processes in struggling readers: a perspective for research and intervention. *Scientific Studies of Reading, 11*, 389–312.

Raver, C. C., Jones, S. M., Li-Grining, C. P., Metzger, M., Champione, K. M. and Latriese Sardin, L. (2008). Improving preschool classroom processes: preliminary findings from a randomized trial implemented in Head Start settings. *Early Childhood Research Quarterly, 23*, 10–26.

Raz, I. S. and Bryant, P. (1990). Social background, phonological awareness, and children's reading. *British Journal of Developmental Psychology, 8*, 209–225.

Schatschneider, C. and Lonigan, C. J. (2010). Misunderstood statistical assumptions undermine criticism of the National Early Literacy Panel's Report. *Educational Researcher, 39*, 347–351.

Schweinhart, L. J., Barnes, H. V. and Weikart, D. P. (1993). *Significant Benefits: The High/Scope Perry Preschool Study through Age 27.* Ypsilanti, MI: High/Scope Press.

Stanovich, K. E. and Siegel, L. S. (1994). Phenotypic performance profile of children with reading disabilities: a regression-based test of the phonological-core variable-difference model. *Journal of Educational Psychology, 86*, 24–53.

Stipek, D. J., Feiler, R., Byler, P., Ryan, R., Milbuiw, S. and Salmon, J. M. (1998). Good beginnings: what difference does the program make in preparing young children for school? *Journal of Applied Developmental Psychology, 19*, 41–66.

Stipek, D., Feiler, R., Daniels, D. and Milburn, S. (1995). Effects of different instructional approaches on young children's achievement and motivation. *Child Development, 66*, 209–223.

Tilstra, J., McMaster, K., Van den Broek, P., Kendeou, P. and Rapp, D. (2009). Simple but complex: components of the simple view of reading across grade levels. *Journal of Research in Reading, 32*, 383–401.

US Department of Health and Human Services (DHHS) (2010). *Head Start Impact Study: Final Report.* Washington, DC: Author.

Vaessen, A., Bertrand, D. Tóth, D., Csépe, V., Faésca, L., Reis, A. and Blomert, L. (2010). cognitive development of fluent word reading does not qualitatively differ between transparent and opaque orthographies. *Journal of Educational Psychology 102*, 827–842.

Wagner, R. K. and Torgesen, J. K. (1987). The nature of phonological processing and its causal role in the acquisition of reading skills. *Psychological Bulletin, 101*, 192–212.

Whitehurst, G. J. & Lonigan, C. J. (1998). Child development and emergent literacy. *Child Development,* *69,* 848–872.

Williams, J. P., Stafford, K. B., Lauer, K. D., Hall, K. M. and Pollini, S. (2009). Embedding reading comprehension training in content-area instruction. *Journal of Educational Psychology, 101,* 1–20.

Wong, V. C., Cook, T. D., Barnet, W. S. and Jung, K. (2008). An effectiveness-based evaluation of five state pre-kindergarten programs. *Journal of Policy Analysis and Management, 27,* 122–154.

Xue, Y. and Meisels, S. J. (2004). Early literacy instruction and learning in kindergarten: evidence from the Early Childhood Longitudinal Study kindergarten class of 1998–1999. *American Educational Research Journal, 41,* 191–229.

Chapter 15

The importance of balance in early childhood programs

Rebecca Marcon
University of North Florida

Is academic skill acquisition important during preschool and kindergarten? Yes, if in the proper balance and introduced in a manner consistent with young children's level of development, academic preparation can play an important role in preschool and kindergarten. The difficulty, however, occurs when the emphasis of preschool and kindergarten becomes overly academic at the expense of developing other domains. Maintaining an optimal balance across developmental domains that is appropriate for each age group as well as each individual child is the key. In the absence of balance, there is a potential to do more harm than good by emphasizing acquisition of academic skills during preschool and kindergarten. As an old English proverb warns us, "all work and no play makes Jack a dull boy." In the case of preschoolers and kindergartners, play remains an essential framework for learning and developing skills across cognitive, social, and physical domains.

Acquisition of academic skills is a primary goal of formal schooling where children learn to read and write, to gain mathematical knowledge and skills, and to acquire scientific understanding of the natural as well as the social world that surrounds them. Children's preparation for formal schooling begins long before they step foot into a school building. Each child brings with him or her a range of unique experiences garnered within their own familial and cultural context. To this is added each child's unique physical and mental health background which contributes to their preparation for formal learning.

How we can best add to what a child brings with him or her at the start of their formal schooling is a source of contention among parents, educators, researchers, and policymakers who all hold the same goal of wanting our children to succeed in school. Many children already bring with them all that they need to succeed. Many other children do not. Would it then be best to introduce academic skills earlier with the hopes that more children will have what it takes to succeed by the time they begin formal schooling? Are there any dangers in doing so? Are there any dangers in failing to do so?

The academization of kindergarten

Although kindergarten was once viewed as the transitional year between preschool and formal schooling, in the United States kindergarten now appears to have replaced first grade as the start of formal schooling (e.g. Miller and Almon, 2009). Kindergarten has changed, but Gullo and Hughes (2011, p. 324) note:

> the fundamental developmental characteristics of kindergarten children have not changed. The ways they construct knowledge and problem solve have not changed.

The ways they learn have not changed. The ways they socially interact have not changed.

Focusing on the academic skills to be attained without attending to the developmental abilities of the child and the way a young child learns is problematic (Elkind, 2001), especially when formal learning demands are placed on children at increasingly earlier ages. Neuman and Roskos' (2005) examination of state early learning standards for children ages three to five is a strong reminder that "we need to clearly differentiate between what children *can* do, and what they *should* do" (p. 142).

Looking closely at changes in kindergarten is important because preschool now faces a similar crossroad that kindergarten encountered two decades earlier. Russell (2011) traces the shift from more developmental kindergartens that provided balanced attention to social, emotional, and academic skills and behavior needed for future school success, to a rise in heavily academic kindergartens that emphasize mastery of basic skills in traditional academic subjects in order to ensure that benchmarks in later grades will be met. The shift in California kindergartens was not led by state policy, but rather by an upsurge of academic messages about kindergarten in the media. Once an academic logic of instruction for kindergarten was formalized in state policy with standards specifying 195 skills students were expected to master by the time they left kindergarten, teachers and professional organizations were "compelled to acknowledge a new vision of kindergarten, albeit reluctantly" (Russell, 2011, p. 21).

Although only 18 states and the District of Columbia require kindergarten attendance, nearly 92 percent of America's five-year-olds are enrolled in school: 73.4 percent in kindergarten, 12.8 percent in preschool, and 5.4 percent in elementary school (US Census Bureau, 2010). Interestingly, as kindergarten was subsidized by states and became part of the public K-12 educational system, not all groups of children benefitted equally. Dhuey (2011) found grade retention (below grade for age) dropped notably among Hispanics, children who did not speak English at home, and children of immigrant families. With increased availability of kindergarten, educational attainment increased significantly among Hispanics as did wages they earned as adults. Because Hispanics are less likely to enroll children in center-based preschool, Dhuey believed the introduction to formal schooling prior to first grade played a large role in positive outcomes for Hispanics when states subsidized kindergarten. At the same time, Dhuey (2011) noted educational attainment among African American males decreased significantly when kindergarten became a grade in public school. Cascio (2010) found evidence that state funding of kindergarten lowered high school dropout by 2.5 percent and institutionalization by 22 percent (proxy for incarceration) among whites but not African Americans. Both Dhuey and Cascio speculate that African Americans did not benefit from increased availability of kindergarten because state-funded kindergarten disproportionately pulled African Americans out of Head Start at age five. Head Start provides a more comprehensive program.

What will happen as states increasingly subsidize pre-kindergarten programs for four-year-olds? Nearly 65 percent of America's four-year-olds are enrolled in school: 57.9 percent in preschool and 6.7 percent in kindergarten (US Census Bureau, 2010). Three-fourths of the states now fund public pre-kindergarten programs and these programs enroll 25 percent of the nation's four-year-olds (Barnett *et al.*, 2009). If pre-kindergarten becomes a grade within elementary schools as part of a PK-12 system, will we see an increased shift toward academic pre-kindergarten as Russell (2011) noted for kindergarten? Will we see corresponding declines in educational attainment for African American males as Dhuey (2011) discovered when kindergarten became a grade in elementary school?

Some have proposed an integrated continuum of early education from pre-kindergarten through third grade (PK-3) that provides children with a seamless transition to formal schooling while taking into account the developmental characteristics and abilities of children in this age span (e.g. Bogard and Takanishi, 2005). Whitehurst (2001) underscored the importance of evidence-based practice in advancing the science of early education. He called for rigorous research to examine effects of content-centered preschool curricula using pedagogy that is appropriate for young children to prepare them for content-learning in kindergarten and elementary school. However, when a wide variety of published preschool curricula were evaluated using an experimental design, few differences in pre-kindergarten or kindergarten child outcomes were found between curricula targeting acquisition of academic skills and control conditions (Preschool Curriculum Evaluation Research Consortium, 2008). Decisions about the future direction of preschool and kindergarten programs will not be easy. Elkind (2001, p.20) cautiously advises us:

> The issues of directedness and content in teaching are very complex at all levels of education, and certainly at the early-childhood level ... early-childhood classrooms are not easily divided along the lines of content that is pre-academic versus content that is not. What really distinguishes them is whether or not the direction and the pre-academic content are developmentally appropriate.

What do preschoolers need?

If kindergarten is the beginning of formal schooling, what do preschoolers need in order to succeed in kindergarten and elementary school? Analyses of data from the Early Childhood Longitudinal Study-Kindergarten (ECLS-K) Class of 1998–1999 provide some helpful answers. ECLS-K reports of 3,305 kindergarten teachers indicated teachers from all regions of the United States placed a strong emphasis on school-related, social abilities that kindergartners need in order to engage in academic activities (Lin *et al.*, 2003). Social communication (e.g. tells needs/thoughts, is not disruptive, follows directions, takes turns/shares) was rated higher in importance than development of academic skills prior to kindergarten entry (e.g. knows most alphabet, counts to 20). The finding that younger teachers expressed higher expectations for academic preparedness than did older teachers, may have foreshadowed the heavily academic focus in US kindergartens more than a decade after these ECLS-K data were collected. Another interesting finding based on ECLS-K data is the different school-readiness profiles at kindergarten entry that predict academic performance and social adjustment in early elementary school (Hair *et al.*, 2006). Although physical well-being and motor development is one of the five dimensions of school readiness highlighted by the National Education Goals Panel (Kagan *et al.*, 1995), research often overlooks this area and focuses on the other four dimensions of readiness: social and emotional development, approaches to learning, language development, and cognitive development. Hair *et al.* (2006) identified approximately 30 percent of entering kindergartners as fitting a comprehensive positive development profile, 34 percent fit a social-emotional and health strengths profile, 13 percent fell into a social-emotional risk profile, and 22 percent had a health risk profile.

The 12 percent of children who had some form of limiting condition or disability at kindergarten entry were spread across profile groups. Disability was not the only major distinguishing characteristic of health risk as children in this profile were also less likely to be of normal weight and less likely to have adequately developed motor skills. After controlling for family, child, and classroom characteristics, researchers found having developmental strengths across the board at kindergarten entry was the best predictor of later school success in reading and math. Children who entered kindergarten with social-emotional or health risks performed poorly on first grade math and reading assessments. Hair *et al.* (2006) confirm that cognitive and language skills are clearly important components of readiness for formal schooling; they are just not the only crucial factors in predicting later school success. Fostering children's early health and physical development, along with social-emotional development, is also necessary.

Another non-academic dimension that contributes to young children's preparation for formal schooling is approaches to learning (ATL). Further examination of the ECLS-K data through fifth grade highlights the influence of young children's persistence, emotion regulation, and attentiveness on both reading and math achievement in elementary school (Li-Grining *et al.*, 2010). Children with better ATL at kindergarten entry experienced greater rates of academic growth than did children with less adaptive ATL, and these differences increased across the elementary years. Overall, children's early ATL was equally beneficial to future academic achievement regardless of race or ethnicity, SES, and parents' education or occupational status. It was especially important for children who entered kindergarten with lower academic skills as these children made greater academic progress when their ATL was more adaptive. The finding that better non-academic skills could compensate for initially lower academic skills led Li-Grining *et al.* (2010) to suggest improving ATL as a way to reduce achievement gaps related to differences in school readiness. Schooling alone is unlikely to increase preschoolers' self-regulation above and beyond general maturation and development (Skibbe *et al.*, 2011), but intentional classroom-based strategies can be implemented to improve young children's self-regulation (Raver *et al.*, 2011). Furthermore, Raver *et al.* (2011) demonstrated that increases in attention/impulse control and executive functioning significantly mediated Head Start children's gains in language development, letter naming, and early math skills. These findings highlight that "socio-emotional competence is key rather than peripheral to (children's) opportunities for learning in early childhood contexts" (Raver *et al.*, 2011, p. 374). Academic and non-academic dimensions come together to prepare young children for formal schooling.

Developmental approach to supporting young children's learning

A look at human development compared to that of other species might provide insight into optimal timing of academic skill acquisition. Bjorklund *et al.* (2009) examined the benefits of children's extended immaturity and high degree of plasticity that gives children time to master complex skills in preparation for adulthood as well as adapting to their immediate environment in a way that is unique to childhood and essential in the development of "humanness." This extended immaturity provides an opportunity for play as seen in children expending up to 40 percent of their time and energy in play. Although other mainly social species play, humans are the only one to do so throughout life, "showing a need for novelty that results in continued learning and behavioral flexibility" (Bjorklund *et al.*, 2009, p. 124). In the preschool and early school years human play becomes more complex with children engaging in more symbolic, make-believe play that fosters discovery and creative behaviors. Capitalizing on children's tendency for play, a skilled preschool teacher can promote higher-order play that enhances self-regulation, develops specific early literacy skills, and provides a foundation for higher-order thinking (e.g. Bodrova, 2008; Saifer, 2010). There is concern, however, that when formal learning experiences are introduced too early they may slow learning as Zimmerman found for receptive language (cited in Bjorklund *et al.*, 2009), and even hinder young children's subsequent achievement and motivation (e.g. Burts *et al.*, 1992, 1993; Stipek *et al.*, 1995). Focusing on acquisition of academic skills in preschool and kindergarten can reduce time for play (Winn, 1983) and other early experiences that are critical for human development. This does not mean we should never introduce academic skills before children begin formal schooling. Rather it is a caution to avoid overemphasis on academics at the expense of other developmental experiences preschoolers and kindergartners need. Play has a central role in achieving a balance among the physical, cognitive, and affective components of an early childhood curriculum (Isenberg and Quisenberry, 2002).

Benefits of developmental approach

Research on different preschool approaches supports the value of a developmental orientation in preschool and kindergarten and confirms cautions about using an overly academic approach in the early years. A developmental approach engages children in active learning by posing problems and asking questions that stimulate and extend learning, with teachers guiding and scaffolding children through skill acquisition activities while encouraging children to choose, plan, and reflect on their learning experiences. In this approach, the curriculum is integrated across subject areas and developmental domains.

Compared with an academically focused approach at the preschool level, positive short-term (e.g. Marcon, 1999) and long-term (e.g. Marcon, 2002; Miller and Bizzell, 1984) benefits of a developmental approach have been found for school achievement and social behavior (e.g. Marcon, 1999; Schweinhart and Weikart, 1997), as well as motivation (e.g. Stipek *et al.*, 1995). At the kindergarten level, some research finds no significant difference in end-of-kindergarten prereading skills between children whose teachers emphasized acquisition of literacy skills and teachers that emphasized self-esteem and social development (e.g. Massetti and Bracken, 2010). Other research reports academic advantages for children in kindergartens that emphasized developmental goals over academic skills acquisition (e.g. Burts *et al.*, 1993; Marcon, 1993). Young boys, in particular, appear to have difficulty with overly academic, highly didactic early learning approaches (e.g. Burts *et al.*, 1992; Marcon, 1993; Miller and Bizzell, 1984).

Providing instructional and emotional support

Research is equally convincing in showing that, for children who enter school without the pre-academic skills needed to succeed, more instructional and emotional support from teachers is needed. Hamre and Pianta (2005) found that demographically at-risk children in classrooms with high-to-moderate instructional support had similar levels of achievement at the end of first grade as low-risk peers with more educated mothers. High-quality instructional support included (a) focused literacy instruction; (b) verbal feedback on children's work, comments or ideas; (c) engagement of children in instructional conversations using open-ended questions to expand ideas and perceptions; and (d) encouragement of child responsibility. Academic achievement of children with high functional risks, however, was not moderated by instructional support. For children who displayed functional risks in kindergarten (e.g. difficulty sustaining attention; externalizing behaviors such as aggression or defiance; low levels of cooperation, assertion, and self-control; and poor learning-related behaviors), it was high emotional support (rather than instructional support) in the first-grade classroom that fostered academic achievement similar to low-risk peers who exhibited none or only one functional risk. High levels of emotional support included (a) teacher awareness of child's needs, interests, and capabilities which teachers used to guide their behavior with the child; (b) child-centered focus; (c) engagement in child's activities or conversations; (d) warm interactions with children; (e) clear yet flexible classroom rules and routines; and (f) options for activities within a responsive classroom structure. At-risk children in less supportive first-grade classrooms showed significantly lower achievement and more conflict with teachers.

The type of support children need to succeed in school depends a great deal on what skills children bring with them to school. For children having difficulty adjusting to a classroom setting, social and emotional support provided by a teacher may be as or even more important to academic progress than specific instructional practices (e.g. Hamre and Pianta, 2001; 2005). It is also wise to adjust amount and type of instructional practice to match children's entry level skills. Morrison and Connor (2002) found that first graders with low vocabulary and word decoding skills made the most progress when time devoted to teacher-managed explicit instruction was high, and when teachers began the year with relatively little child-managed implicit instruction but increased child-managed implicit instruction later in the school year. For children who arrived in first grade with strong vocabulary and decoding skills, the amount of time-managed explicit instructional support had little influence on acquisition of word decoding skills, although more independent child-managed implicit instruction throughout the year was associated with better outcomes for the more skilled children. A teacher's ability to provide appropriate instructional and emotional support based on children's individual needs is vital in preparing young children to succeed in school.

How much support a child needs will also depend upon the grade in which formal schooling and the expectation for acquisition of academic skills begins. The earlier this expectation begins, the more support a child will need to succeed and the more crucial it becomes that this support be individualized and appropriate for the child's level of development.

How appropriate are twenty-first-century pre-kindergartens?

In the first decade of the twenty-first century, pre-kindergarten programs for four-year-olds are increasingly assuming a transitional role between preschool and formal schooling in kindergarten. With increased state subsidization of pre-kindergarten it is important to examine current characteristics of these programs and monitor shifts in practices that may or may not help young children. According to reports from the research team involved in multi-state studies of established pre-kindergarten programs, the picture is somewhat dismal. In 2001–2002 when the National Center for Early Development and Learning

(NCEDL) study began, 79 percent of all US children participating in state-funded pre-kindergarten were in one of the 11 states included in the combined NCEDL Multi-State Study of Pre-Kindergarten and the State-Wide Early Education Programs (SWEEP) study that began in 2003–2004. Although states were fairly consistent in meeting regulatable aspects of programs that reflect structural quality (e.g. teacher qualifications, program location and length, adult: child ratio), researchers reported classroom process quality (e.g. provision of appropriate materials and activities, effective teaching, and teacher-child relationships) to be lower than anticipated (Clifford *et al.*, 2005). Howes *et al.* (2008) found structural quality was unrelated to academic outcomes in these state-funded pre-kindergarten programs. In contrast, children who experienced higher-quality instruction (i.e. frequent teacher-child interactions that scaffold skills through interactive feedback) or closer teacher-child relationships did show significant gains in language, literacy, and math skills.

Following the report that most state-funded pre-kindergartens failed to provide high-quality instructional support, Early *et al.* (2010) took a closer look at how children spend their time in pre-kindergarten. Although children spent 17 percent of their time in language and literacy activities, 19 percent in math and science activities, and another 20 percent in activities relevant to school readiness (e.g. art and music, gross and fine motor, social studies), a large proportion of the day (44 percent) was spent in no coded learning-activity. Scaffolded teaching interactions were infrequent and didactic, close-ended instruction was three times as likely to occur. The pedagogy of elementary school has arrived in the pre-kindergarten classroom. Early *et al.* (2010) expressed concern that "this strategy may be backfiring by giving children less time to explore materials on their own and fewer scaffolded teaching interactions, inadvertently exacerbating achievement gaps by reducing children's autonomy and minimizing the press for higher order thinking" (p. 190).

Conclusions

So where do we stand at this point in time? We are clearly at another crossroad in early childhood education and this time the direction preschools will take is of great concern. If formal schooling and the expectation for acquisition of academic skills is pushed down to age 4, there is a real danger that this push will backfire. Many children are already struggling to meet academic demands at age 6, let alone at age 5 or at age 4. The earlier formal schooling is introduced, the more support a child will need. At age 4, children will need exceptionally high quality instructional and emotional support from teachers if they are to have a chance at success. Furthermore, everything about these experiences will need to be developmentally appropriate for this age as well as for the individual needs of each child. Research shows us that state-funded pre-kindergarten in the United States is currently far from being able to provide that level of support. An overly didactic approach to teaching with an emphasis on rote memorization and correctness does little to develop children's higher order thinking. When it is embedded within a meaningful context and used judiciously, didactic teaching can help children acquire discrete skills. The difficulty arises, however, when didactic instruction focused primarily on the cognitive domain takes over and leaves little time for scaffolded teaching that begins with the child's interest and builds upon the child's understanding in order to expand ideas and perceptions. As we face this important crossroad it is wise to learn from lessons of the recent past. Will we see differential benefits of state-funded prekindergarten similar to what occurred with subsidization of kindergarten? If state-funded pre-kindergarten disproportionately pulls African Americans out of Head Start at age 4, as it did at age 5 when states subsidized kindergarten (Cascio, 2010), will we see further drops in educational attainment among African American males as Dhuey (2011) reported? This certainly is not what policymakers intended when they crafted legislation to fund pre-kindergarten.

Fortunately there is still time to turn things around by assuring that instructional practices, content, and curriculum materials take into account the developmental characteristics and abilities of children in this age span. Many skills that children need to succeed in school are both developmental and learned. In speaking about self-regulation, for example, Skibbe *et al.* (2011) state "at some point, children just cannot be more self-regulated than their age and maturity allow" (p. 47). In our effort to help children master complex skills they need not only in school but also in the years beyond, it is vitally important to avoid strategies that fail to consider the uniqueness of children. As Bjorklund *et al.* (2009) remind us, there is a benefit to our children's extended immaturity.

How then do we answer the question about importance of academic skill acquisition in preschool and kindergarten? Perhaps the best answer is just one word – balance. In preparing children to succeed in school, we need to remember that the whole child is our focus. Non-academic components are clearly important as we see in the readiness profiles of kindergartners with social-emotional or health risks who later do poorly in school, or in the struggles throughout elementary school of children who begin kindergarten with deficits in approaches to learning. Context is also crucial as the teaching of skills that children need is more effective within a context of activities that children enjoy and through a medium, such as play, that reflects how children naturally learn. There is a way to provide instructional support within activities that children have selected and to expand young children's understanding and higher-order thinking through teacher scaffolding. There is a way to provide emotional support through sensitive teacher-child interactions that enable young children to adjust to a classroom setting. Is acquisition of academic skills important in kindergarten and preschool? When acquired in a context using a medium that suits a child's development and when such skills are balanced with attention to all components that prepare a child for school, academics fit quite nicely into a young child's experiences; experiences that are among the many children bring with them to the first day of formal school.

References

Barnett, W. S., Epstein, D. J., Friedman, A. H., Sansanelli, R. A. and Hustedt, J. T. (2009). *The State of Preschool 2009.* New Brunswick, NJ: National Institute for Early Education Research.

Bjorklund, D. F., Periss, V. and Causey, K. (2009). The benefits of youth. *European Journal of Developmental Psychology, 6,* 120–137.

Bodrova, E. (2008). Make-believe play versus academic skills: a Vygotskian approach to today's dilemma of early childhood education. *European Early Childhood Education Research Journal, 16,* 357–369.

Bogard, K. and Takanishi, R. (2005). PK-3: An aligned and coordinated approach to education for children 3 to 8 years old. *SRCD Social Policy Report, 19*(3), 3–23.

Burts, D. C., Hart, C. H., Charlesworth, R., DeWolf, D. M., Ray, J., Manuel, K. and Fleege, P. O. (1993). Developmental appropriateness of kindergarten programs and academic outcomes in first grade. *Journal of Research in Childhood Education, 8,* 23–31.

Burts, D. C., Hart, C. H., Charlesworth, R., Fleege, P. O., Mosley, J. and Thomasson, R. H. (1992). Observed activities and stress behaviors of children in developmentally appropriate and inappropriate kindergarten classrooms. *Early Childhood Research Quarterly, 7*, 297–318.

Cascio, E. U. (2010). What happened when kindergarten went universal? *Education Next, 10*(2), 63–69.

Clifford, R. M., Barbarin, O., Change, F., Early, D., Bryant, D., Howes, C., *et al.* (2005). What is pre-kindergarten? Characteristics of public pre-kindergarten programs. *Applied Developmental Science, 9*, 126–143.

Dhuey, E. (2011). Who benefits from kindergarten? Evidence from the introduction of state subsidization. *Educational Evaluation and Policy Analysis, 33*, 3–22.

Early, D. M., Iruka, I. U., Ritchie, S., Barbarin, O. A., Winn, D-M. C., Crawford, G. M., *et al.* (2010). How do pre-kindergarteners spend their time? Gender, ethnicity, and income as predictors of experiences in pre-kindergarten classrooms. *Early Childhood Research Quarterly, 25*, 177–193.

Elkind, D. (2001). Young Einsteins: much too early. *Education Matters, 1*(2), 8–15, 20.

Gullo, D. F. and Hughes, K. (2011). Reclaiming kindergarten. Part I: Questions about theory and practice. *Early Childhood Education Journal, 38*, 323–328.

Hair, E., Halle, T., Terry-Humen, E., Lavelle, B. and Calkins, J. (2006). Children's school readiness in the ECLS-K: predictions to academic, health, and social outcomes in first grade. *Early Childhood Research Quarterly, 21*, 431–454.

Hamre, B. K. and Pianta, R. C. (2001). Early teacher-child relationships and the trajectory of children's school outcomes through eighth grade. *Child Development, 72*, 625–638.

——(2005). Can instructional and emotional support in the first-grade classroom make a difference for children at risk of school failure? *Child Development, 76*, 949–967.

Howes, C., Burchinal, M., Pianta, R., Bryant, D., Early, D., Clifford, R. and Barbarin, O. (2008). Ready to learn? Children's pre-academic achievement in pre-kindergarten programs. *Early Childhood Research Quarterly, 23*, 27–50.

Isenberg, J. P. and Quisenberry, N. (2002). Play: Essential for all children. A position paper of the Association for Childhood Education International. *Childhood Education, 79*, 33–39.

Kagan, S. L., Moore, E. and Bredenkamp, S. (1995). *Reconsidering Children's Early Development and Learning: Toward Common Views and Vocabulary*. Washington, DC: National Education Goals Panel Goal 1 Technical Planning Group.

Lin, H-L., Lawrence, F. R. and Gorrell, J. (2003). Kindergarten teachers' views of children's readiness for school. *Early Childhood Research Quarterly, 18*, 225–237.

Li-Grining, C. P., Votruba-Drzal, E., Maldonado-CarreZo, C. and Haas, K. (2010). Children's early approaches to learning and academic trajectories through fifth grade. *Developmental Psychology, 46*, 1062–1077.

Marcon, R. (1993). Socioemotional versus academic emphasis: impact on kindergartners' development and achievement. *Early Child Development and Care, 96*, 81–91.

——(2002). Moving up the grades: relationship between preschool model and later school success. *Early Childhood Research and Practice, 4*(1), 1–21.

Marcon, R. A. (1999). Differential impact of preschool models on development and early learning of inner-city children: a three cohort study. *Developmental Psychology, 35*, 358–375.

Massetti, G. M. and Bracken, S. S. (2010). Classroom academic and social context: relationships among emergent literacy, behavioural functioning and teacher curriculum goals in kindergarten. *Early Child Development and Care, 180*, 359–375.

Miller, E. and Almon, J. (2009). *Crisis in the Kindergarten: Why Children Need to Play in School*. College Park, MD: Alliance for Childhood.

Miller, L. B. and Bizzell, R. P. (1984). Long-term effects of four preschool programs: ninth- and tenth-grade results. *Child Development, 55*, 1570–1587.

Morrison, F. J. and Connor, C. M. (2002). Understanding schooling effects on early literacy: a working research strategy. *Journal of School Psychology, 40*, 493–500.

Neuman, S. B. and Roskos, K. (2005). The state of state pre-kindergarten standards. *Early Childhood Research Quarterly, 20,* 125–145.

Preschool Curriculum Evaluation Research Consortium. (2008). *Effects of Preschool Curriculum Programs on School Readiness: Report from the Preschool Curriculum Evaluation Research Initiative* (NCER 2008–2009). Washington, DC: US Government Printing Office.

Raver, C. C., Jones, S. M., Li-Grining, C., Zhai, F., Bub, K. and Pressler, E. (2011). CSRP's impact on low-income preschoolers' preacademic skills: self-regulation as a mediating mechanism. *Child Development, 82,* 362–378.

Russell, J. L. (2011). From children's garden to academic press: the role of shifting institutional logics in redefining kindergarten education. *American Educational Research Journal, 48,* 236–267.

Saifer, S. (2010). Higher order play and its role in development and education. *Psychological Science and Education, 3,* 38–50.

Schweinhart, L. J. and Weikart, D. P. (1997). The High/Scope preschool curriculum comparison study through age 23. *Early Childhood Research Quarterly, 12,* 117–143.

Skibbe, L. E., Connor, C. M., Morrison, F. J. and Jewkes, A. M. (2011). Schooling effects on preschoolers' self-regulation, early literacy, and language growth. *Early Childhood Research Quarterly, 26,* 42–49.

Stipek, D., Feiler, R., Daniels, D. and Milburn, S. (1995). Effects of different instructional approaches on young children's achievement and motivation. *Child Development, 66,* 209–223.

US Census Bureau. (2010). *School enrollment – Social and economic characteristics of students: October 2009.* Author.

Whitehurst, G. J. (2001). Young Einsteins: much too late. *Education Matters, 1*(2), 8–9, 16–21.

Winn, M. (1983). *Children without childhood.* New York, NY: Pantheon.

Part VIII

Is it important for children to acquire reading skills in preschool and kindergarten?

Even children who do not require an extra year or two to attain reading proficiency stand to benefit from earlier instruction. Reading skill gives them earlier access to more difficult reading materials and the possibility of building their vocabularies and world knowledge through reading at an earlier age. Earlier reading instruction and practice hold the potential for making all children smarter when they enter fourth grade.

Linnea Ehri

[I]nstead of acting like a snowball rolling down a mountain, the effects of early reading are more akin to watering the garden before a rainstorm; the earlier watering is rendered undetectable by the rainstorm, this watering wastes precious water, and the watering detracts the gardener from other important preparatory groundwork.

Sebastian Suggate

Is it important for children to acquire reading skills in preschool and kindergarten?

Why is it important for children to begin learning to read in kindergarten?

Linnea C. Ehri
Graduate Center, City University of New York

Presently there is great interest in teaching young children to read, even before they enter kindergarten (National Early Literacy Panel, 2008). Whereas formal reading instruction used to begin in first grade in the US, now it starts in kindergarten. Even preschool teachers may teach foundational skills in reading. Teaching reading early is viewed as the solution to reducing the high number of American children lacking reading proficiency (Snow *et al.*, 1998). The purpose of this chapter is to consider what learning to read involves and whether there are advantages in teaching children to read early.

Reading in young children

Various forms of reading have been observed in young children. *Pretend reading* occurs when children can recite verbatim the print in storybooks because they have heard them many times and memorized them. Pretend reading also applies when young children can read signs and labels in their environment by relying on logos and other salient visual cues. Reading is pretend rather than real because it is not governed by knowledge of the writing system. *Emergent reading* characterizes preschoolers who have interacted with adults in a print rich environment. They have listened to many stories, they have learned to identify letters, they have practiced rudimentary writing, and as a result they have acquired concepts about reading and writing. However, they have not yet learned to read print independently, that is, by decoding unfamiliar words in or out of text. *Precocious reading* characterizes preschoolers who *have* learned to read independently at an early age. They can decode words and read with comprehension typically at or above a second-grade level, and have achieved this capability apparently without formal reading instruction (Olson *et al.*, 2006). *Hyperlexic reading* is similar in that independent reading has emerged without formal instruction. However, it is distinguished from precocious reading in that children are able to decode words easily, sometimes obsessively, but they have lower-than-expected cognitive ability and hence lack much comprehension of the text they can decode. Many are diagnosed on the autism spectrum (Healy, 1982).

The focus of the present chapter is not upon teaching babies to read or upon nurturing reading in home environments but rather upon the acquisition of independent reading skill that results from formal instruction provided in kindergarten prior to age six. The question of interest is whether teaching children to read this early is feasible and beneficial.

Reading skill

Reading is complex, composed of many cognitive and linguistic processes and skills that enable readers to read text independently with comprehension. It rests on *foundational skills*, that is, capabilities that enable beginners to move into independent reading. These include knowledge of the spoken language, concepts about print such as reading left to right, familiarity with letter shapes, names, and sounds, and phonological awareness, that is, the ability to detect and manipulate sounds within words, for example, being able to produce rhyming words or to segment *ship* into its three smallest sounds called phonemes, /š/ /I/ /p/. These skills play a role in the development of *word reading skills*.

Words are read in various ways. To read words that are *unfamiliar* in print, readers may apply various strategies. They may apply a decoding strategy by sounding out letters and blending their sounds to form a recognizable word, for example, sounding out *RUME* or GOTE. They may read words by analogy to the spellings of other known words, for example, reading *throttle* by analogy to *bottle*. If the unfamiliar word appears in text, they may predict what the word is by using initial letters and context, for example, "Hospitals employ many doctors and n…" In contrast, *familiar* words that have been read before are recognized by matching their written forms on the page to their spellings stored in memory, also called sight word reading. Sight words are recognized quickly and automatically without conscious intent and without applying any strategy. Sight of the word just activates its pronunciation and meaning in memory. This facilitates text comprehension because it allows readers' attention to focus on the meaning without having to stop and figure out words.

Word reading skills combine with other skills to enable readers to *comprehend text*. Knowledge about how language is structured syntactically enables readers to convert strings of words into meaningful sentences in memory. Vocabulary knowledge combined with world knowledge and experiences are applied to interpret words, sentences, concepts, and ideas in order to construct text meanings in memory. Readers may also apply strategies to aid comprehension, for example, identifying the main ideas, monitoring their understanding of the text and initiating repairs when meaning goes awry, and constructing mental images of events described in the text. In comprehending the information, readers must not only retain the text's meaning in memory but also regularly update it by assimilating new information as reading proceeds. Thus, it is apparent that many processes, skills, and knowledge sources are involved in reading and comprehending text independently.

Development of reading skill

To explain how reading skill develops, two different types of underlying causes can be distinguished. One type involves *internal* mental processes that become established in memory and interconnected to enable reading. For example, input from the eyes becomes connected to speech areas in the brain. The other type of cause involves *external* experiences that occur outside readers' brains, principally, reading instruction and reading practice. The emergence of reading skill is explained by both types of causes.

Scarborough (2001) has used the analogy of rope construction to depict the operation of internal causes during acquisition. The various language and reading skills are conceptualized as separate strands that over time become more tightly intertwined to form one thick rope as children learn to read. These include readers' background world knowledge, vocabulary, and verbal reasoning as well as their letter knowledge, phonological awareness, decoding, and sight word memory. The ability to read independently emerges gradually as these skills become better integrated. Comprehension processes become increasingly strategic while word recognition skills become more automatic over time with instruction and practice.

Research on the brain provides support for this view. Findings have shown that learning to read involves establishing connections among different cortical systems associated with components of reading skill. These parts remain unconnected until children learn to read. They remain poorly connected in children with a reading disability, but when the disability is remediated by instruction, the connections become stronger (Frost *et al.*, 2009).

Internal causes involving age or maturation are much less important than external causes involving instruction. Morrison *et al.* (1997) compared two groups of children who were very similar in age as a result of their birth dates falling just before or just after the cut-off date for entering first grade. They found that the former group who had entered first grade and received formal reading instruction performed just like their older classmates on various measures of beginning reading skills and much better than their similar-age mates who had remained in kindergarten and had not been taught to read. Formal schooling was much more influential than age in learning to read.

Stages of development

Chall (1983) proposed a stage theory to provide a broad-brush view of reading development from birth through adulthood. She identified internal as well as external causes. Of interest here are Stages 0 through 3 that extend through the elementary grades. When Chall devised her theory, formal reading instruction began in first grade in the US, so the time periods for stages reflect this tradition.

During *Pre-reading Stage 0*, children develop spoken language through day-to-day verbal interactions with their social world. Listening comprehension that prepares children for text processing is fostered when adults read storybooks to children. Also, foundational knowledge for reading may be introduced informally by caretakers who teach letter names, phonological awareness, and concepts about print. This stage extends from birth through the end of kindergarten.

During *Decoding Stage 1*, children receive formal instruction in letter-sound relations, phonemic awareness, and the application of these foundational skills in learning to read words. Word reading and sentence processing skills are practiced and strengthened when children apply them to read simple text. Systematic phonics instruction is an important external cause that establishes foundational word and text reading skills so that children can read first-grade level text independently when Stage 1 is completed at the end of first grade.

During *Fluency Stage 2*, internal causes become more central. The various mental processes become more integrated and consolidated to produce greater reading fluency. Reading practice is an important external cause of growth. Children need to read a steady stream of texts that are appropriately leveled, engaging, and easy to comprehend. This stage runs through second and third grades.

By the end of Stage 2, children have mastered the mechanics of reading and are prepared to move into the *Reading to Learn Stage 3*. This happens in fourth grade when students are expected to be able to read, comprehend, and learn from more difficult texts in content areas such as social studies and science. Not only efficient word reading and fluent text processing skills but also a rich vocabulary and extensive world knowledge are important internal causes of growth in reading ability at this stage. Formal reading instruction is directed at enhancing students' vocabularies and world knowledge as well as their comprehension strategies and study skills.

Chall's (1983) theory makes it apparent that the major causes of reading development *differ* across the stages. This means that exceptional growth in reading at one stage as a result of especially favorable conditions may falter in the next stage if the causal events do not remain as favorable. In other words, whether or not children who learn to read early during the first stage maintain an advantage compared to children who learn to read later depends on the quality of the internal and external causes that operate at subsequent stages. Early success cannot inoculate readers against lack of progress later.

Juel and Minden-Cupp (2000) studied the relationship between various types of first grade instruction and student growth in reading during the school year. They found that the first graders who were least advanced in reading made the greatest reading progress in classrooms where explicit decoding instruction was provided and the least progress in classrooms where reading practice with trade books dominated instruction. In contrast, first graders who were most advanced in reading showed the opposite pattern. Their growth was enhanced the most by trade books and much reading practice. Connor *et al.* (2009) reported a similar interaction between type of first grade instruction and growth in reading.

These findings indicate that in order for external causes to promote growth in students' reading ability, the students' stage of development must be considered rather than their age or grade. If classroom instruction falls short during a grade, or if students lack sufficient reading practice when they need it, or if students have special difficulties achieving integration among the mental processes involved in reading, then it will take longer for them to become proficient readers. Receiving instruction a year or two earlier would make allowance for these setbacks by giving children more time to acquire the mechanics of reading before they reach fourth grade.

Studies of precocious readers (PR) have examined whether learning to read early gave these children a lasting advantage over children who learned to read later in school (NonPR). Results have been mixed. Whereas Stainthorp and Hughs (2004) found that PRs continued to outperform NonPRs at age 11 on several reading measures, lasting effects in fourth grade were not so evident in other studies (Durkin, 1974–75; Jackson, 1988; Tafa and Manolitsis, 2008). It may be that PRs' classroom instruction did not support their continued development. For example, when PRs were ready to build their Stage 2 fluency by reading many books independently in first grade, they received only Stage 1 decoding instruction and read too simple text (Durkin). This forestalled their reading growth, and allowed the non-precocious readers to catch up. Another possibility is that when the PR readers encountered more difficult texts in fourth grade, their reading comprehension was governed more by their vocabulary and knowledge of the subject than by superior decoding or fluency achieved in earlier grades (Jackson). In the study by Tafa and Manolitsis, PR fourth graders read text with greater fluency than their non-PR counterparts, but their reading comprehension was not superior.

Development of word reading skills

If children are taught to read early, it is important to examine the conditions that enable them to be successful. A central accomplishment during Stages 1 and 2 is attaining word reading accuracy and automaticity. This is not simply accomplished by teaching words on flash cards. The internal and external causes that govern the acquisition of word reading skills are more complex and interdependent.

I have conducted research and proposed a theory of phases to portray the emergence of word reading skills (Ehri, 2005a). Children might apply various strategies to read unfamiliar words: decoding letters to form recognizable words, analogizing from known words to new words, and predicting words based on partial letters and context. To read words that have been read before, sight of the written word activates its spelling, pronunciation, and meaning in memory. Its sequence of letters is recognized as a single unit, just as quickly as a single number is recognized (Ehri and Wilce, 1983). Sight word recognition happens much faster and consumes little if any attention during text reading compared to reading words by applying a decoding or analogizing or predicting strategy.

The process of establishing sight words in memory is not a matter of memorizing the shapes of words connected to their meanings, as was once thought. More recent evidence has shown that sight word learning requires foundational knowledge to support memory for the words (Ehri, 1998, 2005b). This foundation involves knowing the *structure of the writing system* and applying this knowledge to compute how letters or graphemes in *specific* words systematically represent sounds or phonemes their pronunciations. Readers must know letter shapes and their sounds, and they must be able to detect phonemes within pronunciations, because these are the sounds symbolized by graphemes. Written words are stored in memory when readers form connections between graphemes seen in spellings of words and phonemes detected in their pronunciations along with meanings. For example, when readers see the word *chain*, they connect the three graphemes, *ch, ai,* and *n,* to their respective phonemes, /ch/, /ā/ and /n/, and retain this information along with the word's meaning in memory. Next time they see the word *chain*, it activates the connections and the word is recognized.

In order to build a sight vocabulary, children's minds must be prepared to form connections. Systematic phonics instruction serves as an external cause to establish the various knowledge sources and skills in memory, and internal causes set up the connection-forming processes to build a sight vocabulary. This does not happen overnight. Learning takes time. My theory (Ehri, 2005a) distinguishes four phases of development to describe the course of sight word learning. In the *pre-alphabetic* phase, children lack the ability to process letter-sound relations to read or spell words. Their word recognition skills are limited or non-existent. Only pretend reading may be evident. They need to be taught letters to prepare for the next phase.

In the *partial alphabetic* phase, children can use partial letter-name or letter-sound relations to remember how to read words and to predict words in context. For example, they might connect the first and final letters, T and M, to the sounds "tee" and "m" in *team* to remember how to read the word. However, similarly spelled words that share partial letters are mistaken for each other, so word reading is not highly accurate. Although partial phase readers know the shapes and names of most letters and have some awareness of sounds in words, their knowledge is incomplete. For example, they have not learned the letters symbolizing short vowels, and they have trouble distinguishing all the phonemes in words. They have not yet acquired the strategy of decoding unfamiliar words. They can read simple text containing familiar sight words and words that can be predicted from context. When they spell words, they write letters for more salient sounds, for example, first and final sounds.

In the *full alphabetic* phase, children acquire sufficient knowledge of the writing system to form complete connections in memory between graphemes seen in spellings and phonemes detected in pronunciations to remember how to read specific words. This makes word reading more accurate. Also, they learn to decode unfamiliar words. This enables them to recognize the words on their own and store them as familiar words in memory for sight word reading, a process referred to as self-teaching (Share, 2004). Having more complete knowledge of the spelling system enables children to spell words correctly either by writing the sounds they hear or by remembering letters in words. The correlation between word reading and word spelling in beginners is very high, indicating that they are strongly related and should be taught together (Ehri, 1997). As children encounter new words in their reading and apply their decoding skill, their sight vocabularies and ability to read text independently grow. Word recognition becomes automatic (Guttentag and Haith, 1978).

The consolidated alphabetic phase emerges out of the previous phase as children learn spelling patterns in words, for example, spellings of syllables, prefixes, suffixes, and common endings of words such as *–ing, -ent, -ain, -ock*. Spelling units larger than grapheme-phonemes are learned and used for creating connections to store words in memory. They make it easier to remember longer multisyllabic words, for example, the four spelling units, *in ter est ing* connected to their syllables rather than the nine grapheme-phoneme units.

Learning larger letter units is facilitated by phonics instruction that involves teaching students to read words by analogy. For example, in a program developed by Gaskins *et al.* (1996–97), students are taught a set of 93 key words containing basic spelling patterns for example, ING in *king*, ACK in *black*, ENT in *tent*. Children are taught to use these key words to read unfamiliar words.

An important external cause of sight word learning during the full and consolidated phases is practice reading texts independently at increasingly higher levels. This enables beginners to store the spellings of specific words bonded to their pronunciations and meanings in memory. This is especially important as the number of words that children are expected to read when they reach fourth grade has grown over the years. Harris and Jacobson (1983) found a 62 percent increase from 1970 to 1980 in primary grade readers, and it is likely that this trend has continued. Teaching children to read early would increase the time available for independent reading practice and would enrich the semantic information in children's sight word vocabularies.

Vocabulary learning is not a simple matter of learning dictionary definitions (Nagy and Scott, 2000). The exposure required to learn the full and varied meanings of even basic vocabulary words is more extensive. Words may have multiple meanings, and these may be further nuanced by different contexts. The more frequent the word, the more meanings it is likely to have. Learning word meanings is an incremental process. Initial encounters with specific words establish partial representations of meaning in memory. With repeated exposure in varied contexts, knowledge is progressively refined. In addition, words are not isolated units of knowledge. Rather a person's understanding of words is dependent on their knowledge of other words. More extensive, independent reading of text expands readers' opportunity to acquire a vocabulary that is richer in these respects compared to exposure to spoken language in conversations and media (Cunningham, 2005). Teaching children to read early holds promise of increasing their vocabulary knowledge by extending the amount of time spent in independent reading prior to fourth grade.

Transparent versus opaque writing systems and early reading

Written languages differ in their transparency, that is, the regularity of the letter-sound mapping system (Seymour *et al.*, 2003). Writing systems like Spanish, Portuguese, and German are highly transparent and regular so that sounding out letters and blending them will almost always yield a recognizable spoken word. In contrast, English is highly variable and lacks this level of predictability. The same sound can be spelled in more than one way, the same letters can represent more than one sound, and plenty of exceptions to these regularities still remain. Seymour *et al.* compared first graders who were learning to read in different languages, all of which had alphabetic writing systems. English learners performed much worse than learners of all the other languages. In fact, the English rate of development in learning to read words and nonwords was twice as slow as in the more transparent writing systems. Greater decoding difficulty may be good reason to begin Stage 1 instruction earlier, especially for readers of English.

Contribution of early reading to special populations

Some groups of children may need more time to become proficient readers by fourth grade. Children who struggle in learning to read, that is, children with dyslexia, have special problems learning the alphabet, processing the phonological level of language, and forming fully bonded connections to remember how to read words so they may need extra time to read. Research has shown that they have greater difficulty learning to segment and blend words into phonemes and to decode words than typically developing readers. These difficulties impair their ability to learn to read words by sight and by analogy. They exhibit word reading skills characterizing partial alphabetic phase readers. Their reading is slower and less accurate. They rely more heavily on guessing words from partial letters and context than on fully analyzing letter-sounds in words. Remembering the spellings of words is especially difficult. Because they have not mastered Stage 1 reading skills, their reading fluency and comprehension are compromised as they struggle with reading demands in subsequent stages.

To treat these difficulties, reading instruction needs to be especially intense, explicit, and systematic (Gaskins *et al.*, 1996–97; Lovett *et al.*, 2003; Torgesen *et al.*, 1999). If begun earlier with children identified as at risk for dyslexia, this would lengthen the time for acquiring decoding skills and avert difficulties prior to Stage 2. If children have not mastered decoding, when they read text independently, they will acquire bad habits. They will skip words they cannot decode, and they will guess words based on partial letters and context. These practices in turn will limit growth of their sight vocabularies, and their comprehension of text will suffer.

It is possible to identify children who are at risk of dyslexia when they enter school. Children from families with a parent who struggled in learning to read are at higher risk because dyslexia is known to run in families. Children who are slow in learning letter names, who have difficulty distinguishing phonemes in words, and who are slower than peers in naming a randomly ordered sequence of familiar objects or numbers are at greater risk (Scarborough, 2001).

Children who are non-native speakers of English also should benefit from earlier reading instruction (Roberts, 2009). Their struggle in reading occurs not because they have more trouble learning to decode words but because they lack sufficient competence with the vocabulary and syntax of spoken English. They would benefit from extra learning time at Stage 2 to develop their knowledge of English through reading practice.

Pre-alphabetic readers who begin formal instruction with little knowledge of letters or experience with print may benefit from an extra year of instruction prior to fourth grade. They tend to be lower in socio-economic status (SES). They may come from homes where literacy is not valued, or families where parents have multiple jobs with little time to spare for informal emergent literacy activities, or day care centers where television and play occupy children's time. Studies indicate that children do not make much progress in reading until they have learned the majority of alphabet letters (Levin and Ehri, 2009; Seymour, 2005) and this learning takes time. There are 26 upper and 26 lower case forms whose arbitrary shapes, names, and sounds must be mastered. Beginning formal instruction earlier for them would extend the learning time needed to establish foundational knowledge for reading.

Summary: the case for early reading instruction

Learning to read takes time because there are many cognitive and linguistic processes for children's minds to acquire and integrate. Reading instruction and practice need to be tailored to children's stage and phase of reading development to facilitate growth because what is beneficial at one stage is not at another. Both internal and external causes and students' status as typically or atypically developing readers need to be considered. Reading proficiency must be accomplished by fourth grade when students are expected to use their reading skills to comprehend and learn from texts in academic subjects. Achieving proficiency is more difficult and may require longer learning time for atypical learners. Even children who do not require an extra year or two to attain reading proficiency stand to benefit from earlier instruction. Reading skill gives them earlier access to more difficult reading materials and the possibility of building their vocabularies and world knowledge through reading at an earlier age. Earlier reading instruction and practice hold the potential for making all children smarter when they enter fourth grade (Stanovich, 1993).

References

Chall, J. (1983). *Stages of Reading Development*. New York: McGraw Hill.

Connor, C. M., Piasta, S. B., Fishman, B., Glasney, S., Schnatscheider, C., Crowe, E., *et al.* (2009). Individualizing student instruction precisely: effects of child by instruction interaction on first graders' literacy development. *Child Development*, 801, 77–100.

Cunningham, A. (2005). Vocabulary growth through independent reading and reading aloud to children. In E. Hiebert and M. Kamil (Eds.), *Bringing Scientific Research to Practice: Vocabulary* (pp. 45–68). Mahwah, NJ: Erlbaum.

Durkin, D. (1974–75). A six-year study of children who learned to read in school at the age of four. *Reading Research Quarterly, 10*, 9–61.

Ehri, L. (1997). Learning to read and learning to spell are one and the same, almost. In C. Perfetti, L. Rieben and M. Fayol (Eds.), *Learning to Spell* (pp. 237–269). Hillsdale, NJ: Erlbaum.

——(1998). Grapheme-phoneme knowledge is essential for learning to read words in English. In J. Metsala and L. Ehri (Eds.), *Word Recognition in Beginning Literacy* (pp. 3–40). Mahwah, NJ: Erlbaum.

——(2005a) Development of sight word reading: phases and findings. In M. Snowling and C. Hulme (Ed.), *The Science of Reading, A Handbook* (pp. 135–154). Oxford, UK: Blackwell.

——(2005b). Learning to read words: theory, findings, and issues. *Scientific Studies of Reading, 9*, 167–188.

Ehri, L. and Wilce, L. (1983). Development of word identification speed in skilled and less skilled beginning readers. *Journal of Educational Psychology, 75*, 3–18.

Frost, S., *et al.*, (2009). Mapping the word reading circuitry in skilled and disabled readers. In P. McCardle and K. Pugh, (Eds.), *How Children Learn To Read: Current Issues and New Directions In The Integration of Cognition, Neurobiology and Genetics of Reading and Dyslexia Research and Practice* (pp. 3–19). Psychology Press.

Gaskins, I. W., Ehri, L. C., Cress, C., O'Hara, C. and Donnelly, K. (1996–97). Procedures for word learning: making discoveries about words. *The Reading Teacher, 50*, 312–328.

Guttentag, R. and Haith, M. (1978). Automatic processing as a function of age and reading ability. *Child Development, 49*, 707–716.

Harris, A. and Jacobson, M. (1983). *Basic Reading Vocabularies*. New York: MacMillan.

Healy, J. (1982). The enigma of hyperlexia. *Reading Research Quarterly, 17*, 319–338.

Jackson, N. (1988). Precocious reading ability: what does it mean? *Gifted Child Quarterly, 32*, 200–204.

Juel, C. and Minden-Cupp, C. (2000). Learning to read words: linguistic units and instructional strategies. *Reading Research Quarterly, 35*, 458–492.

Levin, I. and Ehri, L. (2009). Young children's ability to read and spell their own and classmates' names: the role of letter knowledge. *Scientific Studies of Reading, 13*, 249–273.

Lovett, M., Barron, R. and Benson, N. (2003). Effective remediation of word identification and decoding difficulties in school-age children with reading disabilities. In H. Swanson, K. Harris and S. Graham (Eds.), *Handbook of Learning Disabilities* (pp. 273–292). New York: Guilford.

Morrison, F., Alberts, D. and Griffith, E. (1997). *Developmental Psychology, 33*, 254–262.

Nagy, W. and Scott, J. (2000). Vocabulary processes. In M. Kamil, P. Mossenthal, P. Pearson and R. Barr (Eds.), *Handbook of Reading Research* (Vol. 3, pp. 269–284). Mahwah, NJ: Erlbaum.

National Early Literacy Panel (2008). *Developing Early Literacy: Report of the National Early Literacy Panel.* Jessup, MD: National Institute for Literacy.

Olson, L., Evans, J. and Keckler, W. (2006). Precocious readers: past, present, and future. *Journal for the Education of the Gifted, 30*, 205–235.

Roberts, T. (2009). *No Limits to Literacy: For Preschool English Learners.* Thousand Oaks, CA: Corwin.

Scarborough, H. (2001). Connecting early language and literacy to later reading (dis)abilities: evidence, theory, and practice. In S. Neuman and D. Dickinson (Eds.), *Handbook of early literacy research* (pp. 97–110). New York: Guilford.

Seymour, P. (2005). Early reading development in European orthographies. In M. Snowling and C. Hulme (Ed.), *The Science of Reading, A Handbook* (pp. 296–315). Oxford, UK: Blackwell.

Seymour, P., Aro, M. and Erskine, J. (2003). Foundation literacy acquisition in European orthographies. *British Journal of Psychology, 94*, 143–174.

Share, D. (2004). Orthographic learning at a glance: on the time course and developmental onset of self-teaching. *Journal of Experimental Child Psychology, 87*, 267–298.

Snow, C., Burns, M. and Griffin, P. (1998). *Preventing Reading Difficulties in Young Children.* Washington, DC: National Academic Press.

Stainthorp, R. and Hughes, D. (2004). What happens to precocious readers' performance by the age of eleven. *Journal of Research in Reading, 27*, 357–372.

Stanovich, K. (1993). Does reading make you smarter? Literacy and the development of verbal intelligence. In H. Reese (Ed.), *Advances in Child Development and Behavior, 24*, 133–180. San Diego, CA: Academic Press.

Tafa, E. and Manolitsis, G. (2008). A longitudinal literacy profile of Greek precocious readers. *Reading Research Quarterly, 43*, 165–185.

Torgesen, J. K., Wagner, R. K., Rashotte, C. A., Rose, E., Lindamood, P., Conway, T., *et al.* (1999). Preventing reading failure in young children with phonological processing disabilities: group and individual responses to instruction. *Journal of Educational Psychology, 91*, 579–593.

Chapter 17

Watering the garden before a rainstorm

The case of early reading instruction

Sebastian P. Suggate

Department of Education, Psychology, and
Sport Science, University of Regensburg

For many academics the question of when children need to begin to learn to read – particularly for disadvantaged children – is long settled, with any remaining disagreement confined to those on the fringes of science, with fuzzy "philosophical" research interests and questionable logical faculties of thought. Indeed, if truth were decided by ballot, the victory would be utterly resounding for those arguing for early reading instruction in kindergarten and preschool. Thus, the question is scarcely investigated in empirical reports, and governments the world over lower school entry ages and implement reading standards and instruction ever earlier.

Clearly, in a few pages of this book, my task to repeal this ingrained line of thinking is not slight and I will have to, therefore, centre on attacking the perceived benefits of early reading. Indeed, my own theory on this very question is forthcoming (Suggate, 2011a). The starting point of positivistic scientific research is the null hypothesis, framed as *treatment A has no effect*, or here *developing early reading skill has no (long-term) effect*, and should be accepted until there is sufficient reason to believe otherwise. Therefore, even without presenting a theory of why earlier reading creates no long-term advantage, it is an ideal first step to evaluate current evidence on this null hypothesis.

Key terms

For the sake of clarity, I consider learning to read *early* as during preschool and kindergarten, that is, before children are six years old. Reading skills, or better *decoding skills*, refer here to any skill directly involved in decoding text, such as learning the letters of the alphabet, letter-to-sound correspondences (e.g. that "d" is sounded as /dah/), and any other word reading strategies used to turn the code of text into language (e.g. word rhyming strategies). The term decoding skills usually refers to phonics-type sounding out, whereas here it is more broadly defined to include meaning-guided text decoding. Decoding skills are distinguished from *reading comprehension* skills (i.e. reading for meaning), which arise from a combination of decoding and *language comprehension skills* (LCS) (as in the Simple View of Reading; Gough and Tunmer, 1986). Here LCS refer to a broad array of cognitive and learning skills in addition to the many aspects of language. Finally, I define the importance of early decoding skills acquisition as resulting in long-term advantage in reading comprehension, decoding, or LCS skills, because short-term transitory gains that later wash out cannot easily be claimed to have educational significance.

The three pillars of early reading

The main scientific argument in favour of developing early reading skill comprises three strands. The first strand from longitudinal studies shows correlations in reading skills over time, such that struggling readers in kindergarten and first grade are likely to be the lowest performing later on. Second, many cite the positive effects that reading intervention programs for young children have, thereby proposing that these should play a vital role in preschool and kindergarten in reducing disadvantage. In the third strand, Matthew Effects in reading (Stanovich, 1986) are cited, whereby the achievement gap between the better and worse readers is thought to widen over time.

Pillar 1: correlational studies

Turning to the three arguments for early decoding development, strong methodological and logical objections can be raised against each. Beginning gently, one may gain the impression from some papers that children's failure to name letters or read in kindergarten locks them into later failure in school (e.g. Good et al., 1998; Lyon and Chhabra, 1996; Riley, 1996). To justify this position, authors often cite one famous paper published by Juel (1988) – in *google scholar* at the time of writing, this paper had been cited 1050 times – and the therein calculated probability of .88 that the lowest quartile readers in grade 1 will be in this low quartile in grade 4. This wide citation occurs despite this longitudinal study having only 54 participants at the end of grade 4. Indeed one might wonder how generalisable are findings from 21 children with initially lower reading trajectories. Since then, longer-term studies have suggested that correlations between early decoding skills decrease markedly over time (e.g. Blatchford and Plewis, 1990) and that reading trajectories are far from immutable (e.g. Phillips et al., 2002). But the greater question to ask is: What is the significance of stability in reading trajectory? As I discuss next, this evidence tells us nothing about the *causal influence* of early reading and instead only reassures us that school does not have the effect of taking the best readers and turning them into the worst!

Regardless of the perceived immutability of reading trajectories, determining the causal significance of relations between decoding and reading is another, more important, point. Specifically, correlational research predicting later reading from early decoding skills – even if this takes a broader perspective and includes home and school factors – cannot determine causation. Indeed there are likely a huge number of third variables that determine initial reading skills, and continue to drive the development of these factors (e.g. home environment, school, language, genetic, neighbourhood factors). Even if these factors are purportedly "controlled for", given the psychometric imperfection of psychological measures, this control can never be assured. In short, such longitudinal research simply demonstrates a degree of stability in individual performance over time, which is hardly surprising.

Pillar 2: early reading interventions

Unfortunately, due to inadequacies in designs, intervention research – the darling child of those advocating early reading – also cannot, in its current form, address the topic of this chapter. I acknowledge that early reading intervention research has the advantages of being experimental or quasi-experimental, existing in abundance, and of being conducted in preschool and kindergarten (e.g. Bus and van Ijzendoorn, 1999; Ehri *et al.*, 2001a; Ehri *et al.*, 2001b; Lonigan and Shanahan, 2008; Suggate, 2010). However, there are several features that prevent these studies from providing sound data on whether early decoding development benefits reading comprehension long-term.

For one, there are virtually no studies that look at the long-term effects of early decoding skills interventions. Most only report immediate post-intervention reading performance, with a proportion of around only 20 percent reporting data on average 13 months after post-test (Suggate, 2010). Not surprisingly, this small percentage of studies also exhibit publication bias (Suggate, 2011b). What this line of evidence actually tells us is that children who receive a reading intervention will, on average, have greater reading skill directly afterward, which has to some extent washed out 13 months later. After 13 months, we do not know what the effect is, and, as I demonstrate in this chapter, the longer term effect is likely to be zero.

Moreover, the vast majority of reading intervention studies compares a group of targeted children receiving special reading instruction with a group receiving more regular reading instruction. The problem with this design is that both groups of children receive reading instruction, precluding investigation of whether it is beneficial to receive reading instruction in the first place. Thus, we cannot know from these studies whether early reading instruction has unintended side-effects, such as demotivating children or taking them away from activities that could be more beneficial for their ultimate development, including their reading development (such as language, social interaction, imaginative development, or play). To clarify the point, I introduce the *suitcase problem*. When preparing for a holiday, one has a finite permissible capacity in one's suitcase, much like children's time in quality education is finite. If one adds an item to an already full suitcase or curriculum, then another has to be replaced. Yet, to the best of my knowledge, the suitcase problem in early intervention research has not yet been applied in the literature.

Finally, a related line of evidence from studies of preschool programmes for disadvantaged children is, with even less justification, often used to tout the benefits of early decoding skill development. In such programmes, children might participate in a preschool intervention that improves their later academic achievement. However, this line of reasoning is again weak because children in these programmes experience multifaceted and comprehensive early intervention in a number of domains, making it impossible to say that early decoding skill development *per se* had any specific effect. Some of these studies do report reading measures; I discuss these studies later in the chapter.

Pillar 3: Matthew Effects

The Matthew Effect has developed an almost cult following among researchers and forms the linchpin for advocating early reading programmes. The Matthew Effect proposes that initial differences in reading skill interact with subsequent reading experience, in a manner whereby the better readers read more and thereby improve more, and the poorer readers read less, falling further behind. Despite its eloquence and conceptual appeal, no study conducive to causal inference has demonstrated that early decoding acquisition causally relates to later reading. Specifically, research has explored Matthew Effects longitudinally by following groups of more and less able readers over time (Bast and Reitsma, 1998; Cunningham and Stanovich, 1997; Good, *et al.*, 1998; Shaywitz *et al.*, 1995; Tunmer *et al.*, 2003). Not only are the findings contradictory, with some showing Matthew Effects and others not, but this commonly used research paradigm is virtually useless in determining an *effect*, because it is highly likely that factors that lead to the initial differences in reading skill also drive later differences. The one study that tried to account for volume read and its interaction with reading skill over 10 years (i.e. Cunningham and Stanovich, 1997) is crippled by its small sample size of 27 students, which may well have lead to spurious relations in the complex multivariate regression analyses used to support their claims (Tabachnick and Fidell, 2007) and even if accurate, the design is still correlational, not causal.

Indeed, the likelihood that Matthew Effects in reading are instead caused by the operation of such third factors was demonstrated in the only controlled test of Matthew Effects, conducted using meta-analysis (Suggate, 2011b). In this study, I collected intervention studies from the literature that used effective short-term reading programs and then gathered data long-term. If initial differences in reading skill were causally related to later reading skill, then those receiving the reading intervention should improve more from post-intervention to follow-up compared to the control group, because they have better reading skill for a longer time and can profit more from their reading experiences. However, the opposite was the case; despite controlling for a range of sample, intervention, methodological, and outcome variable characteristics, those that had a disadvantage actually made comparative gains. Although age was a non-significant covariate, because most of the studies included older children, I could not test the existence of Matthew Effects for preschool and kindergarten readers. In summary, this third argument for learning to read early centred on Matthew Effects is, like the other two, also without compelling empirical support.

Additional arguments for early reading

In addition to these three "pillars" of early reading, there are more peripheral arguments, which I now consider.

The snowball effect

Cleary, the crux of the debate is that beginning reading early has a kind of snowball effect, becoming ever bigger and stronger as it rolls down a mountain. However, this analogy is inappropriate for the following reasons.

Most importantly, many decoding skills do not improve *ad infinitum* because they are highly constrained, finite skills that can be developed in a comparatively short amount of time (Paris, 2005). Consider learning the alphabet, learning the letter-sound correspondences (of which there are about 54 in English), and learning chunks of word stems for efficient word recognition. These are skills that can be perfected to a certain point, beyond which mastery thereof is futile for further improvements in reading comprehension. Accordingly, decoding development, under the right conditions, soon approaches an asymptote, effectively signifying that further improvements in these skills will not help reading comprehension. Thus, decoding skills are rather like a snowball that soon ceases rolling on a plateau.

Moreover, I agree that decoding skills could be taught to four- and five-year-old children; however, children aged six or seven could acquire these skills more readily, thus having fewer learning difficulties on the way and providing more value for money, so to speak. Specifically, language, memory, reasoning, concentration, learning, and meta-cognitive abilities are more developed in older children, as these are bound to maturational and developmental experiences (Suggate, 2009a, 2010, 2011b). These factors all play a role in reading comprehension and the development of competent reading skills. Accordingly, when older children are presented with letters, letter-sound correspondences, strategies for decoding unfamiliar words, and are required to decipher and read irregular words correctly (which depends on language, Nation *et al.*, 2007), they will be able to learn to do so more easily thanks to their greater pre-literacy foundation. In short, *older children acquire decoding skills more easily* so it is bound to be more efficient to begin this process later (Suggate, 2011a). Applying this logic to children who find learning to read difficult at older ages as well, I hypothesize that it would still be comparatively easier later, thanks to greater language, maturation, and development in general.

In contrast to decoding skills, LCS require ever improving finesse and subtlety with language, requiring decades, not months or years, to develop and only being mastered in exceptional cases (e.g. perhaps by William Shakespeare or Johann Wolfgang von Goethe, although even the latter struggled with spelling!). Concretely, there are 100,000 words in English, there is a similarly infinite distinction in grammar complexity and usage that conveys subtle nuances in meaning (e.g. the subjunctive, imperative, indicative, conditional tenses; word order effects; spatial, temporal, and verbal prepositions), and there are numerous styles and turns of phrase (e.g. consider the style of language used in the Bronx, at Oxford University, and by Australian cricketers). Developing this complicated foundation for achievement and integration into life, given the magnitude of the task, should be a priority over developing early, constrained decoding skills, unless the latter has a long-term effect.

Reading improves vocabulary

One commonly held belief is that reading improves aspects of children's language, with vocabulary being one candidate. However, this is highly unlikely for several reasons. First, there is meta-analytical evidence to suggest that children learn but few unknown words from text before age nine, with age, not reading skill, being the key predictor (Swanborn and de Glopper, 1999). Also, it has been estimated from a text complexity analysis that children would not begin to encounter words from reading that they would not encounter from oral language until around grade 3 or 4 (Nagy and Anderson, 1984). Furthermore, we studied the language development of children learning to read at different ages and did not find that children in kindergarten reading environments developed greater semantic and pragmatic language skills over those having no reading skills at this age, despite having initially superior decoding skills (Suggate *et al.*, 2011b). Even more recently, we collected experimental data showing that accomplished readers in grades 2 and 4 learned fewer words from reading text than from being read or told a story (Suggate *et al.*, 2012).

Two recent studies have been used to counter my contention that children are unlikely to acquire unique language skill from reading early. In these studies normal readers aged 8–9 (Ricketts *et al.*, 2009) and low SES readers aged 7 and 10 (Rosenthal and Ehri, 2008) learnt new words that were either accompanied or not by an orthographic representation. Results indicated greater word learning in the orthography-present condition. However, these studies compared word learning under formulaic vocabulary-instruction conditions, not during incidental word-learning from more naturalistic environments. Accordingly, the children's performance in these word-learning paradigms did not correlate with their vocabulary development, calling into question the generalisability of these experiments to real life learning. In short, they tested whether there was an advantage to having orthography in an abstract learning paradigm that bore no relation to how children had hitherto developed their vocabularies. Interestingly, consistent with my contention that only older children are likely to learn words from reading over language experiences (Suggate, 2011a), the orthography-present advantage in word learning was greater for grade 5 than grade 2 children (Rosenthal and Ehri, 2008).

Reading compensates for neglect

One key argument is that it is particularly necessary for children at-risk of dyslexia or living in impoverished conditions to learn to read early. It is wholeheartedly granted that it is important to direct well-informed efforts at helping such children, but is focusing on early decoding skills likely to bear any long-term fruit?

Unfortunately, as with the suitcase problem, research into whether early reading, in comparison to rich non-reading experiences, benefits disadvantaged children is lacking. I therefore will have to revert to logical considerations.

First, just because children hail from impoverished environments, it does not change that they need certain foundational levels of LCS and thinking skills to profit from reading. Thus, although well-intended, the idea that early reading will help close vocabulary or reading comprehension gaps seems flawed and, given the suitcase problem, may even have the opposite effect. Indeed, because disadvantaged children have less enriched language experiences at home (Dockrell *et al.*, 2010), remediation should first of all lie with these important unconstrained skills when children are primed for language learning (Lundberg, 2006).

Certainly, experimental and long-term evidence is lacking on whether having a preschool reading-specific programme provides any long-term benefit to disadvantaged children (especially in comparison to language or play programmes). With regards to children at risk of dyslexia, there is no study that compares such children's long-term development as a function of whether they received early reading instruction versus a similarly rich but non-reading environment.

My argument that early reading is unlikely to benefit even those at disadvantage may seem irresponsible, resting upon speculative reasoning when the stakes are indeed very high. However, evidence that early reading in the absence of special instruction helps these children is missing and until such evidence is forthcoming, early reading – regardless of its popularity – cannot be seen as key to combating complicated reading and social disadvantage.

Early reading leads to a life-long habit of reading

Some argue that it is important to learn to read early to establish habits of life-long learning. There is no compelling evidence for this claim and given the multifaceted and complex unfolding of the human being across the life course, this argument seems difficult to entertain – it is plausible that some find a passion for reading early and keep this, others lose it, and others find this later in life. Moreover, one has to ask what the active ingredient is – for example, would inspiring a love of learning or language early in children also inspire a later love of reading?

The evidence against learning to read early

Having examined arguments in favour of developing early reading skill in preschool and kindergarten, I now finish with evidence supporting the null hypothesis that early decoding skill acquisition has no long-term effect on later reading skill. Although this evidence is methodologically imperfect, it speaks more directly to the question at hand than the three pillars discussed earlier.

International studies

Two quantitative international analyses have investigated whether children attending schools in countries where reading begins earlier have a long-term advantage in reading. In the first study, after controlling for social and economic factors, Elley (1992) found that nine-year-olds in the top 10 countries in reading performance began school slightly earlier than nine-year-olds in the bottom 10 performing countries. However, he did not replicate this comparison with the 14-year-old children in the study to see whether any effects were enduring. To remedy this, I conducted a similar analysis on the 2007 PISA data, this time across 54 countries and controlling for social and economic indicators (Suggate, 2009b). I found no association between school entry age (a proxy for when children learn to read) and reading achievement at age 15.

Preschool studies

In a series of preschool studies (i.e. Evans, 1985; Magnusson *et al.*, 2007; Marcon, 2002; Reynolds, 1994; Schmerkotte, 1978; Schweinhart and Weikart, 1997) reviewed elsewhere (Suggate, 2011a), it was somewhat possible to look directly at outcome measures related to reading in broader preschool programmes, even though these programmes did not directly isolate early decoding-skill instruction. Almost universally, initial advantages in reading skill later disappeared.

Two of such preschool studies are of particular interest, because they more directly isolated reading skill. A government in Germany conducted a large-scale study in which 50 kindergartens (with children aged 5) were assigned to either an academically-focused or a play-arts focused year. After experiencing an initial advantage in reading skill, the groups soon became inseparable in academic performance (Schmerkotte, 1978). Similarly, Durkin (Durkin, 1974–1975) compared the reading development of children from age four in a two-year reading programme with those staying at home. After controlling for IQ, the initial advantage in reading skill for the early readers in grades 1 and 2 had disappeared by grades 3 and 4.

Studies from English-speaking school samples

A final set of studies comes from school-age children. Lillard and Else-Quest (2006) compared two cross-sectional cohorts of children enrolled to enter into a Montessori school "recognized for ... its good implementation of Montessori principles" (p. 1893) with those attending a normal school. Children applying for attendance at the Montessori school were selected into the schools by a district lottery. In Montessori schools, children often learn to read and write between ages three and six, perhaps due to the high individualisation of the curricula (Edwards, 2002). The younger Montessori school cohort (aged 5 to 6 years) had an advantage in reading but the older cohort (aged 12 years) did not, suggesting that reading advantages washed out. Importantly, because the design was cross-sectional, it could not be determined whether the 12-year-olds had an earlier advantage.

Steiner schools are based on a contrasting educational philosophy in which children do not begin learning to read until they are in their seventh year of life (Rose, 2007). In New Zealand, Steiner schools exist that receive equal funding from the government, such that comparisons can more readily be made with state schools, as socio-economic constraints preventing families from choosing one over the other schools do not exist. Accordingly, we studied the development of reading across the first six years of school in a cohort-sequential design, for children attending either state or Waldorf schools (Suggate et al., 2011a). No systematically significant differences for children attending different schools were found on a host of background variables (e.g. parental income and education, home literacy practices, child receptive vocabulary, school community affluence, ethnicity, and second language fluency) in favour of one over the other. The schools employed similar levels of teaching the relations between letters and sounds, and sounding-out-word strategies. As expected, the seven-year-old state school pupils had vastly superior reading skill compared to Steiner pupils at the same age; however, this advantage disappeared around the 10th to 11th year of life. A follow-up cross-sectional study employing similar controls was conducted with slightly older children (age 12); this analysis suggested again that there was no advantage for the children learning to read early and even a slight, statistically significant, edge in reading comprehension for the later readers (Suggate et al., 2011a).

Summary: the null hypothesis upheld

Positivistic scientific research of the kind used to argue for the necessity of children reading early is built around the notion of the null hypothesis, positing that *developing early reading skill has no long-term effect*. I have scrutinised evidence thought to reject this hypothesis and found it to be lacking for this purpose, due to failure to look both long-term and causally. Three lines of evidence from international, preschool, and school samples were examined, hailing from a rich range of experimental and quasi-experimental methodologies, often looking longer-term. Although this evidence lacks a definitive randomised-trial with struggling readers, there is still insufficient reason to maintain that the early and explicit development of decoding skills leads to unique long-term benefits for later reading. Therefore, instead of acting like a snowball rolling down a mountain, the effects of early reading are more akin to watering the garden before a rainstorm; the earlier watering is rendered undetectable by the rainstorm, this watering wastes precious water, and the watering detracts the gardener from other important preparatory groundwork.

References

Bast, J. and Reitsma, P. (1998). Analyzing the development of individual differences in terms of Matthew Effects in reading: results from a Dutch longitudinal study. *Developmental Psychology, 34*, 1373–1399.

Blatchford, P. and Plewis, I. (1990). Pre-school reading-related skills and later reading achievement: further evidence. *British Educational Research Journal, 16*, 425–428.

Bus, A. G. and van Ijzendoorn, M. H. (1999). Phonological awareness and early reading: a meta-analysis of experimental training studies. *Journal of Educational Psychology, 91*, 403–414.

Cunningham, A. E. and Stanovich, K. E. (1997). Early reading acquisition and its relation to reading experience and ability 10 years later. *Developmental Psychology, 33*, 934–945.

Dockrell, J. E., Stuart, M. and King, D. (2010). Supporting early oral language skils for English language learners in inner city preschool provision. *British Journal of Educational Psychology, 80*, 497–515. doi: 10.1348/000709910X493080

Durkin, D. (1974–1975). A six year study of children who learned to read in school at the age of four. *Reading Research Quarterly, 10*, 9–61.

Edwards, C. P. (2002). Three approaches from Europe: Waldorf, Montessori, and Reggio Emilia. *Early Childhood Research & Practice, 4*(1).

Ehri, L. C., Nunes, S. R., Stahl, S. A. and Willows, D. M. (2001a). Systematic phonics instruction helps students learn to read: evidence from the National Reading Panel's meta-analysis. *Review of Educational Research, 71*, 393–447.

Ehri, L. C., Nunes, S. R., Willows, D. M., Schuster, B. V., Yaghoub-Zadeh, Z. and Shanahan, T. (2001b). Phonemic awareness instruction helps children learn to read: evidence from the National Reading Panel's meta-analysis. *Reading Research Quarterly, 36*, 250–287.

Elley, W. B. (1992). *How in the World do Students Read? IEA Study of Reading Literacy.* The Hague: International Association for the Evaluation of Educational Achievement.

Evans, E. D. (1985). Longitudinal follow-up assessment of differential preschool experience for low income minority group children. *Journal of Educational Research, 78*, 197–202.

Good, R. H., Simmons, D. C. and Smith, S. B. (1998). Effective academic interventions in the United States: evaluating and enhancing the acquisition of early reading skills. *School Psychology Review, 27*, 45–56.

Gough, P. B. and Tunmer, W. E. (1986). Decoding, reading and reading disability. *Remedial & Special Education, 7*, 6–10.

Juel, C. (1988). Learning to reading and write: a longitudinal study of 54 children from first through fourth grades. *Journal of Educational Psychology, 80*, 437–447.

Lillard, A. and Else-Quest, N. (2006). Evaluating Montessori education. *Science, 313*, 1893–1894.

Lonigan, C. J. and Shanahan, T. (2008). Executive summary of the report of the National Early Literacy Panel. In National Early Literacy Panel (Ed.), *Developing Early Literacy: A Scientific Synthesis of Early Literacy Development and Implications for Intervention* (pp. v–xii): National Institute for Literacy & The Partnership for Reading.

Lundberg, I. (2006). Early language development as related to the acquisition of reading. *European Review*, 14, 65–79.

Lyon, G. R. and Chhabra, V. (1996). The current state of science and the future of reading disability. *Mental Retardation and Developmental Disabilities Research Reviews, 2*, 2–9.

Magnusson, K. A., Ruhm, C. and Waldfogel, J. (2007). Does kindergarten improve school preparation and performance? *Economics of Education Review, 26*, 33–51.

Marcon, R. A. (2002). Moving up the grades: relationship between preschool model and later school success. *Early Childhood Research & Practice, 4*(1).

Nagy, W. E. and Anderson, R. C. (1984). How many words are there in printed school English? *Reading Research Quarterly, 19*, 304–330.

Nation, K., Snowling, M. J. and Clarke, P. (2007). Dissecting the relationship between language skills and learning to read: semantic and phonological contributions to new vocabulary learning in children with poor reading comprehension. *Advances in Speech-Language Pathology, 9*, 131–139.

Paris, S. G. (2005). Reinterpreting the development of reading skills. *Reading Research Quarterly, 40*, 184–202.

Phillips, L. M., Norris, S. P., Osmond, W. C. and Maynard, A. M. (2002). Relative reading achievement: a longitudinal study of 187 children from first through sixth grades. *Journal of Educational Psychology, 94*, 3–13.

Reynolds, A. J. (1994). Effects of a preschool plus follow-on intervention for children at risk. *Developmental Psychology, 30*, 787–804.

Rickets, J., Bishop, D. V. M. and Nation, K. (2009). Orthographic facilitation in oral vocabulary acquisition. *The Quarterly Journal of Experimental Psychology, 62*, 1948–1966.

Riley, R. (1996). Improving the reading and writing skills of America's students. *Learning Disability Quarterly, 19*, 67–69.

Rose, M. (2007). *Living Literacy: The Human Foundations of Speaking, Writing and Reading*. Gloucestershire, UK: Hawthorn Press.

Rosenthal, J. and Ehri, L. C. (2008). The mnemonic value of orthography for vocabulary learning. *Journal of Educational Psychology, 100*, 175–191.

Schmerkotte, H. (1978). Ergebnisse eines Vergleichs von Modellkindergärten und Vorklassen in Nordrhein-Westfalen [Results from a comparison of typical kindergartens and preschools in Northrhein-Westphalia]. *Bildung und Erziehung, 31*, 401–411.

Schweinhart, L. J. and Weikart, D. P. (1997). The high/scope preschool curriculum comparison study through age 23. *Early Childhood Research Quarterly, 12*, 117–143.

Shaywitz, B. A., Holford, T. R., Holahan, J. M., Fletcher, J. M., Stuebing, K. K., Francis, D. J. and Shaywitz, S. E. (1995). A Matthew Effect for IQ but not for reading: results from a longitudinal study. *Reading Research Quarterly, 30*, 894–906.

Stanovich, K. E. (1986). Matthew effects in reading: some consequences of individual differences in the acquisition of literacy. *Reading Research Quarterly, 21*, 360–407.

Suggate, S. P. (2009a). *Response to Reading Instruction and Age-related Development: Do Later Starters Catch Up?* Doctor of Philosophy, University of Otago, Dunedin, NZ.

——(2009b). School entry age and reading achievement in the 2006 Programme for International Student Assessment (PISA). *International Journal of Educational Research, 48*, 151–161.

——(2010). Why "what" we teach depends on "when": grade and reading intervention modality moderate effect size. *Developmental Psychology, 46*, 1556–1579.

——(2011a). Matthew, Luke, and the Gospel of Early Literacy: A Model of what becomes of early reading. *Manuscript submitted for publication.*

——(2011b). Are Matthew Effects caused by initial differences in reading skill? *Manuscript submitted for publication.*

Suggate, S. P., Lenhard, W., Neudecker, E. and Schneider, W. (2012). Vocabulary acquisition from independent reading, shared reading and story telling. *Manuscript submitted for publication.*

Suggate, S. P., Schaughency, E., A. and Reese, E. (2011a). Children who learn to read later catch up to children who learn to read early. *Manuscript submitted for publication.*

——(2011b). The contribution of age and formal schooling to oral narrative and pre-reading skills. *First Language, 31,* 379–403. doi: 10.1177/0142723710395165

Swanborn, M. S. L. and de Glopper, K. (1999). Incidental word learning while reading: a meta-analysis. *Reviews of Educational Research, 69*, 261–285.

Tabachnick, B. C. and Fidell, L. S. (2007). *Using Multivariate Statistics* (5th edn). Boston: Allyn & Bacon.

Tunmer, W. E., Chapman, J. W. and Prochnow, J. E. (2003). Preventing negative Matthew Effects in at-risk readers: a retrospective study. In B. R. Foorman (Ed.), *Preventing and Remediating Reading Difficulties: Bringing Science to Scale*. Maryland: York Press.

Part IX

What are the best ways to develop primary school children's mathematical abilities?

Teachers need to know what children should be taught in their first mathematical lessons at school, which are currently mostly about counting and the number system, but if they turn to the psychological literature they will find two completely different kinds of information. What they find will depend on the radical split that we have described in this chapter. One group of studies will lead them to concentrate on teaching children to count single sets, the other to emphasising instead the relations between sets. Which is the right way to go?

Peter Bryant and Terezhina Nunes

Classroom instruction probably provides the most effective cultural source of synergy for the development of mathematics literacy and competence in children, defined as mathematics problem solving.

Yujing Ni

Chapter 18

The importance of reasoning and of knowing the number system when children begin to learn about mathematics

Peter Bryant and Terezinha Nunes

Department of Education, University of Oxford

In the search for new and effective ways of teaching children mathematics, the first important step must be to establish what they need to know about the subject. The question is an obvious one, but there is no universally accepted answer to it. In this chapter, we shall argue that from the beginning of their school learning about mathematics, children need to have, and to be able to use, two different types of knowledge. One is knowledge about quantitative relations and the other knowledge of the counting system. Our claim is that the distinction between the two should play a central role in plans for introducing children to arithmetic when they first go to school. We shall also argue that current theories about mathematical development tend to concentrate on one, and to ignore the other, of these two forms of mathematical knowledge.

Knowledge about quantities takes the form of understanding a set of relations. Suppose, for example, that you see two sets of objects, one of which is a set of eggs, the other a set of egg cups, and that for each eggcup in one set there is an egg in the other, and vice versa. In other words, the two sets are in one-to-one correspondence, which gives you enough information to judge that these two sets are equal in numerical quantity. If, however, each eggcup has its own egg, but there are still some eggs left over, you must conclude not just that the two sets are unequal, but also that there are more eggs than there are eggcups.

These are relational judgements. You can make them without counting and without knowing in any other way exactly how many objects there are in either set. Correspondence relations are just one example of a set of relations that underlie all understanding about quantity. Transitive relations are another. With three quantities, A, B, and C, A must be greater than C if A>B and B>C, or if A>B and B=C. In both cases, you do not have to make a direct comparison of A with C, or to count or measure either quantity, in order to know whether the two are equal or not, and it is easy to see the force of Piaget's claim that one has to understand relations to be able to deal with the fact that numbers are ordered from smaller to larger.

Quantitative relations are just as important for understanding changes in quantity. Conservation experiments, though still controversial, remind us that it is essential to know what changes a quantity and what does not. The importance of understanding that two sets, which are in one-to-one correspondence and therefore equal, will remain equal provided that nothing is added to or subtracted from either set, is undeniable, even though there is still a great deal of controversy about whether or not young children do understand this invariance. The inverse relation between addition and subtraction (and between multiplication and division) is also important in understanding quantitative changes. If I add a number of objects to an existing set, and then take the same number away, the final quantity of the set is the same as the initial quantity but, if I subtract more than I add, the set is diminished. Again, the fundamental importance of children being able to understand and use this principle of inversion is unquestionable, even though there is a lot of controversy about how well they grasp the opposite results of adding and subtracting. The concept of inversion must play an essential part in the understanding of another important quantitative relation which is the additive composition of number. This is the principle that all natural numbers above 1 are made up of other numbers: 8 is made up of 7 and 1 or 5 and 3 or 4 and 4 and 13 is made up of 10 and 3 or 9 and 4 and so on. Inversion is important here because if any number (x) is composed of two other numbers (y and z) so that $y+z=x$, then $x-y=z$ and $x-z=y$.

The second form of knowledge is about the number system. Practically every culture has devised ways of counting the absolute number of objects in a set of objects or events in a sequence of events, and of representing and thus communicating these numbers in speech and writing. Most counting systems are not just lists of numbers. Number words are usually organised into base systems, like the base-ten system which we know the best. These structures allow us to generate number words without having to remember them in long sequences. Base systems have varied over the years and between cultures, but nowadays many people learn a number system with a base ten structure. This aspect of counting gives us a first glimpse of one of the many reasons why children need to connect the two forms of knowledge that we have been outlining – a need that is the central point of this chapter. The foundation for counting in systems with a base is the additive composition of number: you cannot understand the system if you do not also understand that 24 is composed of two groups of 10 and 4 units, or that 35 consists of three 10s and a 5. Thus, this basic quantitative relation is also one essential basis for counting systems with a base, and at some level children eventually have to make a connection between relations between quantities, additive composition, and the counting system.

One reason why the distinction between these two kinds of mathematical knowledge is worth making is that most theories about children's mathematical development concentrate on one kind and ignore the other. The divergence between the two, therefore, is a neat way of categorising the relevant theories and the research that each has inspired, but it is also something of a blight, in our view, on the study of mathematical development.

Our main argument in this chapter will be that the way in which children connect the underlying relations in any arithmetical problem and the procedures needed to solve the problem should be a regarded as a crucial issue by researchers and teachers alike. To make this point in one chapter, we will have to concentrate on a single example only: this will be children's understanding of cardinality or cardinal number. We have chosen cardinality because it is an essential part of children's initial learning about number. How well they understand cardinality has a large impact on how effectively they can use the number system when they begin to count.

Piaget and Gelman

Two classic theories provide us with a clear example of the sometimes unfortunate theoretical division that we have mentioned already. One is Piaget's theory about the growth of mathematical knowledge. The other is the theory of Rochel Gelman, an American psychologist whose theory is largely based on children's counting and also on their judgements about how well other protagonists count.

Piaget's central argument (1952) was that we have to be able to reason logically about quantity in order to understand number (and, consequently, the number system, but Piaget was not interested in number systems). This view is almost certainly right, but it leaves out the possibility that learning to count eventually transforms children's reasoning by making it more powerful and more precise. In the opposite corner, Gelman's influential theory (Gelman and Gallistel, 1978) focuses on how children count single sets of objects. Their research by Gelman and her colleagues on the ease with which young children appear to grasp some aspects of the counting system remains a valuable and still quite surprising contribution to the debate on children's mathematical knowledge. However, the theory has the serious disadvantage that it by-passes children's reasoning about relations between quantities and ignores the possibility that numbers are important in children's learning only because they allow them to represent quantities and thus help them to make sense of quantitative relations.

The remarkable divergence between the two approaches is at its sharpest when they deal with the children's understanding of the properties of number and of the counting system. Numbers have both cardinal and ordinal properties. Cardinality refers to the apparently simple but profoundly important rule that sets with the same number are equivalent in quantity: a set which consists of 6 items is equivalent to any other set that contains just 6 items. Thus, two sets have the same cardinal value when the items in one set could be placed in one-to-one correspondence with those in the other: conversely if two sets are not in one-to-one correspondence they do not share the same cardinal number.

Numbers also have ordinal values, which is simply another way of saying that that they can be arranged in order of magnitude, going from smaller to larger or vice versa, and the relations between the different values in this ordered system are transitive: since 3 is more than 2, and 2 more than 1, 3 must be more numerous than 1. However, we do not have space to discuss children's learning about ordinality in this chapter. (For a discussion of this and other instances of the role of quantitative reasoning in children's mathematical learning, see Nunes *et al.*, 2009).

Notice that the cardinal and the ordinal properties both involve relations. Cardinality is defined by the one-to-one correspondence relations between sets of the same number, and ordinality by the transitive relations between different values. This will become an essential issue when we consider research on the two theories. Piaget's research on children's understanding of number deals entirely with comparisons between sets. In contrast, the research by Gelman and her followers is confined to the ways in which children work out the numerical quantity of single sets.

Cardinal number

Piaget argued that no one can understand the meaning of any number word unless he or she also understands the number's cardinal properties. He also claimed that children acquire this understanding slowly.

His initial evidence for this claim was the mistake that four- and five-year-old children often make when shown one set of items (e.g. a row of eggs) and asked to form another set (e.g. of eggcups) of the same number. They often match the new set with the old one on irrelevant criteria, such as the two rows' lengths, and make no effort to put the rows into one-to-one correspondence. Over time their ability to establish one-to-one correspondence between sets improves, but the initial difficulty shows that the understanding of the need to check whether two sets are in one-to-one correspondence cannot be taken for granted.

Even children who can establish one-to-one correspondence between two sets do not necessarily infer that counting the elements in one set tells them how many elements there are in the other. In one study, Piaget (1952) "bought" sweets from children, at the rate of one penny per sweet. After several of these swaps, Piaget asked the children how many pence the child had, and then how many sweets he had. Many of the children could not make the inference that the number of sweets that Piaget had was the same as the number of pence that they themselves had collected.

A remarkably similar pattern has been found when children share out sets of objects. Frydman and Bryant (1988) asked four-year-old children to share a set of bricks to two recipients. At this age, children often share things between themselves, and they typically do so on a one-for-A, one-for-B, one-for-A, one-for-B basis. When each child had done the sharing successfully, the experimenters counted out the number of items that had been given to one recipient, which was 6. Having done this, they asked the child how many items had been given to the other recipient. None of the children immediately made the inference that there was the same number of objects in one set as in the other, and therefore that there were also six items in the second set. Instead, all the children began to count the second set. In each case, the experimenter then interrupted the child's counting, asking him or her if there was any other way of working out the number of items in the second recipient's share. Only 40 percent of the group of four-year-olds made the correct inference that the second recipient had also been given 6 items. This is a striking result. All the children knew that the two recipients' shares were equal, and knew as well the number of items in one of the shares. Yet, many did not connect what they knew about the relative quantities to the number symbols. Other children, however, did make this connection, which we think is a significant step in understanding cardinality.

Piaget's theory of how children develop an understanding of cardinality was confronted by Gelman's nativist view of children's counting and its connection to cardinal number knowledge (Gelman and Gallistel, 1978). Gelman claimed that children are born with a genuine understanding of number and have no difficulty at all in grasping the principles of counting. She outlined five such principles. Anyone counting a set of objects should understand that:

1   you should count every object once and only once (*one-to-one correspondence principle*)
2   the order in which you count the actual objects (from left to right, from right to left or from the middle outwards) makes no difference (*order irrelevance principle*)
3   you should produce the number words in a constant order when counting: you cannot count 1-2-3 at one time and 1-3-2 at another (*fixed order principle*)
4   whether the objects in a set are all identical to each other or all quite different has no effect on their number (*the abstraction principle*)
5   the last number that you count is the number of items in the set (*cardinal principle*).

Each of these principles is valid in the sense that anyone who does not respect it will end up counting incorrectly. For example, a child who produces count words in different orders at different times is bound to make incorrect judgements about the number of items in a set. So will anyone who does not obey the one-to-one principle.

Gelman's original observations of children counting sets of objects, and the results of some subsequent experiments in which children had to spot errors in another protagonist's counting (e.g. Gelman and Meck, 1983), all supported her idea that children obey and apparently understand all five principles, at least with small sets of items, long before they go to school. The young children's success in counting smaller sets allowed her to dismiss their frequent mistakes with large sets of items as procedural errors rather than failures in understanding. She concluded that the children knew the principles of counting and therefore of number, but lacked some of the skills needed to carry them out. Her conclusion became known as the "principles-before-skills hypothesis".

Gelman's studies provoked a great deal of further research on children's counting, most of which has confirmed her original results, though with some modifications. For example, five-year-old children do generally count objects in a one-to-one fashion (one number word for each object) but not all of the time (Fuson, 1988). They often either miss objects or count some objects more than once, particularly in disorganised arrays. There is now evidence that gestures play an important part in helping children keep track during counting (Albilali and DiRusso, 1999), but sometimes they point at some of the objects in a target set without counting them.

The weakest part of Gelman's conclusions, however, is undoubtedly her claim about children's understanding of the "cardinal principle". Many people have objected to her criteria for cardinality. Fuson (Fuson and Hall, 1983; Fuson *et al.*, 1982) and Sophian (Sophian *et al.*, 1995) both made the reasonable argument that emphasising or repeating the last number word could just be part of an ill-understood procedure. This seems a reasonable objection. Another objection comes from Vergnaud (2009) who argued quite plausibly that any child who satisfies Gelman's cardinality criterion can be said to have some understanding of *ordinal*, not of cardinal, number: because the criterion is based on the *position* of the number word in the counting sequence.

Another objection is that many children respond in a way that satisfies Gelman's criterion for cardinality and yet do not seem to have a full grasp of when this principle should be applied. Fuson (1988) showed that many three-year-old children, who recognise that the last number word in the counting system represents the set's number when the counting is done correctly (Gelman's criterion), wrongly continue to use the last number word in the counting sequence to say how many items are in a set when the counting started from 2, rather than from 1. Counting in this unusual way should at least lead these children to reject the last word as the cardinal for the set, but it did not. Freeman *et al.* (2000) and Bermejo *et al.* (2004) reported highly similar results.

These are worrying criticisms, but there is in our view a much more serious objection to Gelman's test of cardinality. It is that her tasks were not relational ones. They were all about counting single sets, but cardinality, as we have seen, is about the relation between sets. Knowledge that the last number in a counting sequence is the crucial one does not in any way guarantee that the child understands that this set is in one-to-one correspondence with all other sets that have the same number. Gelman's five principles tell us nothing about children's understanding of numerical relations between sets.

Piaget's research on number, in contrast, was almost entirely concerned with comparisons between different quantities, and this has the confusing consequence that when Gelman and Piaget used the same term – cardinality – they gave it quite different meanings. In Piaget's view, understanding cardinality was about grasping that any two sets in one-to-one correspondence contain the same number of items and that any two sets with the same number of items are equivalent in quantity. When Piaget studied one-to-one correspondence, he looked at children's comparisons between two quantities (eggs and egg cups, for example): Gelman's concern with one-to-one correspondence was about children assigning one count word to each item in a set and taking the last one as the number in the set.

Counting and cardinal comparisons

Since two sets are equal in quantity if they contain the same number of items and unequal if they do not, one way to compare two sets quantitatively is by counting: count each of them and then compare the two numbers. How well do children realise that numbers are a measure by which they can compare the quantities of two or more different sets? Most of the relevant research on this topic suggests that many 4- to 6-year-old children seem not to have grasped the connection between counting and comparing even if they have been able to count proficiently.

Sophian (1988) asked children to judge whether someone else (a puppet) was counting the right way when asked to do two things. The puppet was given two sets of objects, and was asked in some trials to say whether the two sets were equal or not and in others to work out how many items there were on the table altogether. Sometimes the puppet did the right thing, which was to count the two sets separately when comparing them and to count all the items together when working out the grand total. At other times he got it wrong, e.g. counted all the objects as one set when asked to compare the two sets. The pre-school children found it very hard to make this judgement. Most of them could not reliably identify the right way to count as a function of the question they were asked.

There are other studies that seem to confirm Sophian's claim that many young children do not fully grasp the significance of numbers when they make quantitative comparisons. Gréco (1962), a colleague of Piaget's, demonstrated that children will count two rows of counters, one of which is more spread out and longer than the other, and correctly say that they both have the same number (this one has 6, and so does the other) but then will go on to say that there are more counters in the longer row than in the other. Sarnecka and Susan Gelman (2004) have replicated this hugely significant observation. A child who makes this mistake understands cardinality in Gelman's sense (i.e. can to say how many items in the set) but does not know what the word "six" means in Piaget's sense.

Children often fail to count the items in two sets that they have been asked to compare numerically even though they are able to count quite well (Cowan, 1987; Cowan and Daniels, 1989; Saxe et al., 1987); instead they rely on unreliable and inappropriate perceptual cues, like length. Children who understand the cardinality of number should realise that they can make the comparison only by counting or by using one-to-one correspondence, and yet at the age of five and six years most of them do neither, even when, as in the Cowan and Daniels study, the one-to-one cues are emphasised by lines drawn between items in the two sets that the children were asked to compare.

The evidence that we have presented so far suggests very strongly and remarkably consistently that *learning to count* and *understanding relations between quantities* are two different achievements. On the whole, children can use the procedures for counting long before they realise how counting allows them to measure and compare different quantities, and thus to work out the relations between them. We think that it is only when children establish a connection between what they know about relations between quantities and counting that they can be said to know the meaning of natural numbers.

Analogs and individuation in relation to number knowledge and cardinality

Several psychologists have proposed that young children have access to an inexact but powerful "analog" system, in which the magnitude of the signal produced by a set of items or events increases directly with the number of items in the set (Dehaene 1992; 1997; Gallistel and Gelman, 1992; Gelman and Butterworth, 2005; Xu and Spelke, 2000; Wynn, 1992; 1998; Carey, 2004). This gives them the ability to make approximate judgements about numerical quantities and they continue through life to use this capacity. The discriminations that this system allows us to make are much like our discriminations along other continua, such as loudness, brightness, and length. One feature of all these discriminations is that the greater the quantities (the louder, the brighter or the longer they are) the harder they are to discriminate (known, after the great nineteenth-century psycho-physicist who meticulously studied perceptual sensitivity, as the "Weber function"). To quote Carey (2004, p.63):

> Tap out as fast as you can without counting (you can prevent yourself from counting by thinking "the" with each tap) the following numbers of taps: 4, 15, 7, and 28. If you carried this out several times, you'd find the mean number of taps to be 4, 15, 7, and 28, with the range of variation very tight around 4 (usually 4, occasionally 3 or 5) and very great around 28 (from 14 to 40 taps, for example). Discriminability is a function of the absolute numerical value, as dictated by Weber's law.

The claim that this analog system is innate comes largely from studies of infants (Xu and Spelke, 2000; McCrink and Wynn, 2004) and the idea that it is important for learning about number and arithmetic is based on the difficulties shown in such tasks by adults with acquired dyscalculia (e.g. Butterworth *et al.*, 1996) or children who find it very difficult to learn mathematics in school (Landerl *et al.*, 2004). Although this basic system may indeed provide a neurological basis for number processing, it is not clear why there should be a strong link between an analog and imprecise system and a precise system based on counting: "ninety" does not mean "approximately ninety" any more than "six" could mean "approximately six".

The idea of an analog system is, nevertheless, part of Susan Carey's justly famous hypothesis (2004) about learning number. She argued that in the first three years of life, children represent number in different ways (Le Corre and Carey, 2007). One is through the analog system, but, although Carey thinks that this system plays a part in people's informal experiences of quantity, she does not seem to give it a role in children's learning about the counting system.

A second way in which very young children represent cardinal number, according to Carey, is though a "parallel individuation" system, which makes it possible for infants to recognise small numbers precisely (not approximately as with the analog system). The system only operates for sets of 1, 2, and 3 objects and there is a marked development in the system over children's first three years.

To begin with, the system makes it possible for very young children to recognise sets of 1 as having a distinct quantity. At this time, the child understands 1 as a quantity, not just as an object, though he or she does not at first know that there are special words to apply to quantities. Later on the child is able to discriminate and recognise – in Carey's words "to individuate" – sets of 1 and 2 objects, and still later, around the age of three to four years, sets of 1, 2, and 3 objects as distinct quantities. Young children progress, according to Carey, from being "one-knowers" to becoming "two-knowers", and then "three-knowers".

During the same period, these children also learn number words and, though their recognition of 1, 2, and 3 as distinct quantities does not in any way depend on their being able to count sets with these numbers of items, they do manage to associate the right count words ("one", "two", and "three") with the right quantities. This association between parallel individuation and the count list eventually leads to what Carey (2004) calls "bootstrapping" in the fourth or fifth year of young children's lives.

The bootstrapping takes two forms. First, with the help of the constant order of number words in the count list, the children begin to learn about the ordinal properties of numbers: 2 always comes after 1 in the count list and is always more numerous than 1, and 3 is more numerous than 2 and always follows 2. Second, since the fact that the count list that the children learn goes well beyond 3, they eventually infer that the number words represent a continuum of distinct quantities which also stretches beyond 3. They also begin to understand that the numbers above three are harder to discriminate from each other at a glance than sets of 1, 2, and 3 are, but that they can identify by counting. In Carey's words:

> The child ascertains the meaning of "two" from the resources that underlie natural language quantifiers, and from the system of parallel individuation, whereas she comes to know the meaning of "five" through the bootstrapping process – i.e., that "five" means one more than four, which is one more than three – by integrating representations of natural language quantifiers with the external serial ordered count list.

Carey called this new understanding "enriched parallel individuation (Carey, 2004, p. 65).

Carey's main evidence for parallel individuation and enriched parallel individuation came from studies in which she used a task, originally developed by Wynn, called "Give a number". In this, an experimenter asks the child to give her a certain number of objects from a set of objects in front of them: "Could you take two elephants out of the bowl and place them on the table?" Children sometimes put out the number asked for and sometimes just grab objects apparently randomly. Using this task Carey showed that different three-, four- and five-year-old children can be classified quite convincingly as "one-", "two-", or "three-knowers" or as "counting-principle-knowers". The one-knowers do well when asked to provide one object but not when asked the other numbers while the two-

and three-knowers can respectively provide up to two and three objects successfully as well. The "counting-principle-knowers" in contrast count quantities above three or four.

Note, however, that Wynn's "Give a number" task is not a satisfactory test of children's understanding of cardinality, for exactly the same reason that Gelman's cardinality criterion proved inadequate. Wynn's task involves counting out one set only, and no comparison between sets. Thus, we cannot be sure that a child, who succeeds in this task, understands that all sets with the same number are equal in quantity or even that a child who fails in the task does not understand this essential aspect of cardinality.

The evidence for the existence of these three groups certainly supports Carey's interesting idea of a radical developmental change from "knowing" some small quantities to understanding that the number system can be extended to other numbers in the count list. The value of her work is that it shows developmental changes in children's learning about the counting system. These had been by-passed both by Piaget and his colleagues because their theory was about the underlying logic needed for this learning and not about counting itself, and also by Gelman, because her theory about counting principles was about innate or rapidly acquired structures and not about development. However, Carey's explanation of children's counting in terms of enriched parallel individuation suffers the limitation that we have mentioned already: it has no proper measure of children's understanding of cardinality in its full sense. The prime measure of "knowing" a number is Wynn's give-a-number task which, as we have already remarked (but it deserves repeating), is, like Gelman's cardinality criterion and for exactly the same reason, a wholly inadequate test of cardinal knowledge. It is a counting task, not a comparison task, and cardinality is about comparisons between sets as well as about enumerating individual sets.

Conclusions

The issue of children's learning about cardinality is an important one for a number of reasons, but, for us, the most significant reason for studying it is its relevance to education. Teachers need to know what children should be taught in their first mathematical lessons at school, which are currently mostly about counting and the number system, but if they turn to the psychological literature they will find two completely different kinds of information. What they find will depend on the radical split that we have described in this chapter. One group of studies will lead them to concentrate on teaching children to count single sets, the other to emphasising instead the relations between sets. Which is the right way to go?

The research that we have reviewed suggests quite strongly that there are troubling weaknesses to conclusions based only on children's counting of single sets, even though research of this form continues unchecked in psychological research. For example, in a recent longitudinal study of the effect of parent-child interactions on children's understanding of cardinality (Gunderson and Levine, 2011), the only criterion for this understanding is a version of Wynn's task – a task that can be solved by knowing how to count single quantities. No valid conclusions, in our view, are to be drawn from this kind of study.

In the contrast between studies of counting single sets and research on reasoning about relational quantities, Piaget does come off much better because he is plainly right about the initial difficulties that children have with one-to-one correspondence, but the contrast itself reveals what we consider as a shortcoming in Piaget's approach to children's understanding of number. Unlike Carey, he ignores the possible input of counting and of knowing number names on children's learning about cardinality. Surely, it is possible that the links between equivalent sets are easier to recognise when a child sees that they share the same number word. Perhaps, children might also be helped by understanding that sets in one-to-one correspondence also always have the same number names. But we do not have good evidence on these possible and quite plausible developmental connections, and the reason for this glaring gap seems to be that researchers who, like Gelman, are primarily interested in counting are not so concerned with quantitative relations, while other researchers who, like Piaget, are mainly concerned with quantitative relations, pay little head to the counting system.

The most interesting exception to this double insularity, in our view, is Gréco's study, since he did look at children's counting and their comparisons of two sets. Gréco's demonstration that many children will say the two sets have the same number and yet judge one of them to be more numerous than the other suggests that they have not yet made an adequate connection between number words and numerical quantity. Nevertheless, we still need to know when and how children eventually do make this connection and how they manage to co-ordinate it with their understanding of one-to-one correspondence. It seems strange that there is no satisfactory answer to this question yet, but it shouldn't be too hard to find one.

References

Alibali, M. W. and DiRusso, A. A. (1999). The function of gesture in learning to count: more than keeping track. *Cognitive Development, 14,* 37–56.

Bermejo, V., Morales, S. and deOsuna, J. G. (2004). Supporting children's development of cardinality understanding. *Learning and Instruction, 14,* 381–398.

Butterworth, B., Cipolotti, L. and Warrington, E. K. (1996). Short-term memory impairments and arithmetical ability. *Quarterly Journal of Experimental Psychology, 49A,* 251–262.

Carey, S. (2004). Bootstrapping and the origin of concepts. *Daedalus, 133*(1), 59–69.

Cowan, R. (1987). When do children trust counting as a basis for relative number judgements? *Journal of Experimental Child Psychology, 43,* 328–345.

Cowan, R. and Daniels, H. (1989). Children's use of counting and guidelines in judging relative number. *British Journal of Educational Psychology, 59,* 200–210.

Dehaene, S. (1992). Varieties of numerical abilities. *Cognition, 44,* 1–42.

——(1997). *The Number Sense.* London: Penguin.

Freeman, N. H., Antonuccia, C. and Lewis, C. (2000). Representation of the cardinality principle: early conception of error in a counterfactual test. *Cognition, 74,* 71–89.

Frydman, O. and Bryant, P. E. (1988). Sharing and the understanding of number equivalence by young children. *Cognitive Development, 3,* 323–339.

Fuson, K. C. (1988). *Children's Counting and Concepts of Number.* New York: Springer Verlag.

Fuson, K. and Hall, J. W. (1983). The acquisition of early number word meanings: a conceptual analysis and review. In H. P. Ginsburg (Ed.), *The Development of Mathematical Thinking* (pp. 50–109). New York: Academic Press.

Fuson, K. C., Richards, J. and Briars, D. J. (1982). The acquisition and elaboration of the number word sequence. In C. J. Brainerd (Ed.), *Children's Logical and Mathematical Cognition* (pp. 33–92). New York: Springer Verlag.

Gallistel, C. R. and Gelman, R. (1992). Preverbal and verbal counting and computation. *Cognition, 44,* 43–74.

Gelman, R. and Butterworth, B. (2005). Number and language: how are they related? *Trends in Cognitive Sciences, 9*, 6–10.

Gelman, R. and Gallistel, C. R. (1978). *The Child's Understanding of Number.* Cambridge, MA: Harvard University Press.

Gelman, R. and Meck, E. (1983). Preschoolers' counting: principles before skill. *Cognition, 13*, 343–359.

Gréco, P. (1962). Quantité et quotité: nouvelles recherches sur la correspondance terme-a-terme et la conservation des ensembles. In P. Gréco and A. Morf (Eds.), *Structures numeriques elementaires: Etudes d'Epistemologie Genetique Vol 13* (pp. 35–52). Paris: Presses Universitaires de France.

Gunderson, E. A. and Levine, S. L. (2011). Some types of parent number talk count more than others: relation between parents' input and children's cardinal number knowledge. *Developmental Science, 14*(5), 1021–1032.

Landerl, K., Bevan, A. and Butterworth, B. (2004). Developmental dyscalculia and basic numerical capacities: a study of 8–9 year old students. *Cognition 93*, 99–125.

Le Corre, M. and Carey, S. (2007). One, two, three, nothing more: an investigation of the conceptual sources of verbal number principles. *Cognition, 105*, 395–438.

McCrink, K. and Wynn, K. (2004). Large number addition and subtraction by 9-month-old infants. *Psychological Science, 15*, 776–781.

Nunes, T., Bryant, P. and Watson, A. (2009) *Key understandings in Mathematics Learning. A Nuffield Foundation Report.* Available online: http://www.nuffieldfoundation.org/key-understandings-mathematics-learning (accessed 25 January 2012).

Piaget, J. (1952). *The Child's Conception of Number.* London: Routledge and Kegan Paul.

Sarnecka, B. W. and Gelman, S. A. (2004). Six does not just mean a lot: preschoolers see number words as specific. *Cognition, 92*, 329–352.

Saxe, G., Guberman, S. R. and Gearhart, M. (1987). Social and developmental processes in children's understanding of number. *Monographs of the Society for Research in Child Development, 52*, 100–200.

Sophian, C. (1988). Limitations on preschool children's knowledge about counting: using counting to compare two sets. *Developmental Psychology, 24*, 634–640.

Sophian, C., Wood, A. M. and Vong, C. I. (1995). Making numbers count: the early development of numerical inferences. *Developmental Psychology, 31*, 263–273.

Vergnaud, G. (2008). The theory of conceptual fields. *Human Development, 52*, 83–94.

Wynn, K. (1992). Children's acquisition of the number words and the counting system. *Cognitive Psychology, 24*, 220–251.

——(1998). Psychological foundations of number: numerical competence in human infants. *Trends in Cognitive Science, 2*, 296–303.

Xu, F. and Spelke, E. (2000). Large number discrimination in 6-month-old infants. *Cognition, 74*, B1–B11.

Chapter 19

Towards proficiency
The Chinese method of teaching mathematics to children

Yujing Ni

The Chinese University of Hong Kong, HKSAR, China

In October 2010, the Beijing Musical Festival presented only two performances featuring children. One was the Vienna Boys' Choir from Austria and the other was the Hulun Buir Fantasy Children's Choir from Inner Mongolia. Both choirs performed with distinction but were disparate in terms of contrasting songs and voices. The choirs were interviewed after the performance by a Hong Kong TV network. One notable difference was in history, with the Vienna Boys' Choir's 500 years of performing; in contrast, the Hulun Buir Children's Choir had only been established since 2007. It was also surprising to know from the interview that the 37 Mongolian boys and girls, from 5 to 13 years old, had learned the songs and their harmony by heart because they had not yet learnt to read the music scores in time for their brilliant performance on the stage of the National Opera Theatre. It would appear that Inner Mongolian children and Viennese children followed very different routes to achieve their respective excellence in singing. The point to be made from this example is that it is probably difficult to judge, without cultural context, which types of curriculum cum teaching methods are best suited for children to learn mathematics. This chapter will be developed around this position and will reflect on some Chinese methods of teaching children mathematics and as a consequence, the way that Chinese children learn mathematics.[1]

In his work, Geary (1995) has made the distinction between primary mathematical abilities and secondary mathematical abilities. The former refers to the abilities that may have some innate qualities or inherent elements. For example, in speech acquisition, an innate structural base is assumed that is language-specific and determines the way that language input is processed in a certain manner (Chomsky, 1986). In the domain of numerical cognition a similar innate cognitive mechanism is assumed, one that generates mental magnitudes to represent numerosities (Gelman and Gallistel, 1978). Subitizing (the competence to quickly enumerate small sets with one glance) and simple arithmetic are considered the instances of the primary mathematical abilities (Wynn, 1992). In contrast, the development of secondary mathematical abilities, such as composite units, base-10 concept and strategy, place value, rational numbers, equations and others, do not appear to have these biological advantages. In addition, the primary abilities may assist new learning, consistent with the early numerical representation, such as verbal counting and simple arithmetic. However, they may render the acquisition of knowledge more difficult when they do not fit the representation, such as fraction numbers (Ni and Zhou, 2005). As a result, the acquisition of secondary abilities is generally slow, laborious, and occurs only with sustained and deliberate instruction. Classroom instruction probably provides the most effective cultural source of synergy for the development of mathematics literacy and competence in children, defined as mathematics problem solving (Schoenfeld, 1992; Stigler and Hiebert, 1999; Vygotsky, 1997). In the sections that follow, the focus will be on the main features of mathematics education in China. Of particular importance will be curriculum objectives, textbooks, and classroom instruction that work as a social-cultural system, elements that are instrumental in shaping the achievement of mathematical learning in Chinese children.

School mathematics curriculum

China has had a nationally mandated school mathematics curriculum since 1949 (Ma, 1996; Ministry of Education, 2000; 2001). The Chinese mathematics curriculum has evolved from merely focusing on "the two basics" (basic mathematic concepts and basic mathematic skills) to emphasizing mathematic problem solving built on the two basics. However, the mathematics curriculum now places greater emphasis on the importance of mathematical problem solving as well as promoting a positive attitude towards mathematics along with the framework of the "two basics" emphasis (Liu and Sun, 2002; Ni *et al.*, 2011). Throughout the evolution of the curriculum, the *two-basics* have remained as the foundation of Chinese school mathematics (Zhang *et al.*, 2004). The two-basics view stresses the importance of acquisition of foundational knowledge, content and skills over the use of creative thinking. Consequently, Chinese mathematics curricula have four primary goals for students. They are as follows: 1) fast, accurate manipulation and computation of arithmetic and algebra involving integers, fractions, decimals, 2) accurate recall of memorized mathematics definitions, formulas, rules, and procedures, 3) understanding of logical categorizations and mathematics propositions, and 4) facile matching of solution patterns to types of problems via transfer (Zhang *et al.*, 2004).

There are several factors that may contribute to a greater understanding of the two-basics feature of the Chinese primary mathematic curriculum. First, mental arithmetic and problem solving are a significant part of the primary school mathematics curriculum. Chinese educators argue that repeated practice facilitates memorization. A greater exposure to these skills can encourage students to explore the underlying concepts with deeper knowledge (Dhlin and Watkins, 2000). Most urban Chinese children who attended regular preschool and kindergarten education showed proficiency in counting and calculating addition and subtraction within 20 before they entered first grade. First-grade students are required to mentally perform addition and subtraction using numbers up to and including one hundred (Ministry of Education, 2000). Chinese children were reported to perform better than their English-speaking counterparts on understanding of the base-ten system and using tens-complement strategy for addition and subtraction (Fuson and Li, 2009). The proficiency of Chinese children with mental arithmetic was also indicated in their early emergence of linear representation of number magnitude (Siegler and Mu, 2008).

The second factor relates to the way that the Chinese primary mathematic curriculum introduces the concepts of algebra for fourth grade students (Ministry of Education, 2000; 2001). Students in fourth grade learn to use letters that stand for numbers. In fifth and sixth grade, students learn the concepts of variables, equations, and equation solving. In contrast, US students generally do not learn these concepts until they are in the eighth grade (Mathematical Sciences Education Board, 1998). Chinese mathematic educators believe that algebraic thinking is a generalized way of thinking (Wu, 1993). It is important to teach these concepts and skills at the elementary school level because algebra not only lessens the burden of a learner struggling with unnecessary computational terms but more importantly assists the learner to explore the structure of mathematics and to view mathematics from a generative perspective. Cai (2004; 2005) conducted studies to document the effects of early algebra learning on teachers' expectation for students and on student performance. Chinese sixth grade students were more likely to use the algebraic approach to solve mathematics word problems, and so were more likely to reach correct answers than their US counterparts. On evaluating those student responses, Chinese teachers also expected their sixth grade students to use the generalized strategies to solve problems while US teachers did not have the same expectations of their students.

Third, the two-basics approach accents foundational mathematics. Ma (1999) did an analysis of mathematics knowledge for teaching in Chinese and US teachers in the key contents of primary mathematics: subtraction with regrouping, multi-digit number multiplication, and division by fractions. Discussion with Chinese teachers showed their emphasis on primary mathematics as a "knowledge package" (Ma, 1999, p.19). For example, according to the Chinese teachers, the concept and procedure of subtraction with regrouping develops step-by-step through the central sequence from addition and subtraction, beginning with the first 10 numerals and with addition and subtraction within the first 20 numerals, progressing to addition and subtraction with regrouping between numbers 20 and 100, and finally, being able to add and subtract with regrouping of even larger numbers. The Chinese teachers believed that addition and subtraction within the first 20 numerals was the key to mastery of this sequence. From these basic concepts, students would learn a process that would constitute the foundation for his/her later learning of more advanced forms of addition and subtraction with regrouping. Along the central sequence, the knowledge package also contains key concepts, such as "the composition of ten," "place value," and "composing and decomposing a higher value unit." These concepts are considered to be the basis of algorithm in subtraction with regrouping.

According to some scholars, Chinese school mathematics could be considered among the most demanding mathematics curricula in the world. All Chinese students are required to take mathematics each year when they are in the 9-year compulsory education program (Ma, 1996; Ministry of Education, 2000).

Textbooks and other curriculum materials

Consequently, curriculum materials, especially textbooks and the corresponding teaching manuals, are the most important vehicles used to implement the nationally mandated curriculum in China. The development and publishing of textbooks is closely regulated and monitored by the central government, the Ministry of Education. In the country, there are only a few officially designated publishers who are allowed to develop textbooks and teaching manuals. Only with the approval of a central government-appointed committee can developed textbooks and teaching manuals then be published and made available to public schools.

Comparative studies of mathematics textbooks indicated that there were high cognitive demands made of students using Chinese textbooks and that there was a link of the cognitive demands to the mathematics achievement of Chinese students (Ding and Li, 2010; Li et al., 2008). In Li et al. (2008) sixth grade students from American and Chinese elementary schools were asked to solve four questions in order to examine their conceptions of equality. The questions are similar to the following: $6 + 9 = a + 4$; $6 + 8 = 3 + 11$. It was found that 98 percent of the Chinese sample could answer all the questions correctly and provide an explanation using the concept of equality, whereas only 28 percent of the US sample could answer the questions at this level. The researchers then examined how the concept of the equal sign "=" was treated in Chinese curriculum materials and in the American equivalent, including teacher preparation materials, student textbooks, and teacher guides. The investigation indicated that the US teacher preparation textbooks treated the "=" sign and its implication for primary school students as cursory. Out of six US mathematics methods textbooks examined, only two directly addressed the use of the equal sign, and none included lesson examples or activities to help understand how use of the equal sign should be taught. In one text, it was just mentioned to use the equal sign "to tell how many blocks there are all together." In another text, it was suggested that the equal sign could be used interchangeably with words like "makes" (addition) and "leaves" (subtraction). The expressions do not focus on equality as symbolizing a relation, leading students to think about balance on both sides of the equal sign. On the contrary, Chinese mathematics method textbooks and student textbooks highlight equality as a relation by introducing the equal sign in a context of relationships and interpreting the sign as "balance," "sameness," or "equivalence." The equal sign often appears simultaneously with the sign ">" and "<" to highlight the equal sign representing a relation. The Chinese texts suggest teachers use the one-to-one correspondence concept and procedure to assist students in better understanding of the equal, greater, and less than symbols. The studies (Ding and Li, 2010; Li *et al.*, 2008) indicate that differences in the curricular and pedagogical treatments reflected in the curriculum materials can be a source of the disparity between the Chinese students and the US students' understanding of equality as a relation.

In addition to the textbooks, teaching manuals are also key tools for Chinese teachers, assisting them to learn about subject matter as well as ways of teaching. In fact, the Chinese teaching manuals are often very useful for teachers because they specify the objectives of teaching and explicitly identify what is "important" and "difficult" in each teaching unit. Specific teaching suggestions are provided for each lesson (J-H Li, 2004). The important points of curriculum content are not only significant for students to learn and master, but also important for teachers, enabling them to develop a profound understanding of mathematics for teaching (Ma, 1999). For example, for teaching first grade students about subtraction with word problems such as "There are 10 boys and 7 girls in a class. How many more boys are there than the number of girls?", the teacher manual advises the importance of teaching children to use the one-to-one correspondence principle to compare two quantities. The manual also stresses the importance of being able to address and overcome the possible misconception in students to think 10 minus 7 for the word problem as removing seven girls from the group of ten boys.

In addition, the organizational features of Chinese schools are an important factor. Teachers are organized into teaching research groups or lesson preparation groups by school subject and grade level. The groups meet regularly to study textbooks and teacher guides (Han and Paine, 2010). Chinese mathematics teachers rely on textbooks and teacher manuals for decision making with regards to content and ways of teaching (Fan *et al.*, 2004). Preparing and observing public lessons is a prime time to intensively study the curriculum materials in the lesson preparation/teaching research groups. Public lessons refers to the lessons that are conducted by the teachers whom are considered by respective school districts to be exemplary on teaching and are open to teachers in and outside of the schools. It is a regular part of teacher professional development activity in China, which helps to efficiently disseminate socially and culturally favored teaching methods. Han and Paine (2010) conducted a fine ethnographic documentation of the process required to prepare public lessons by a teaching research group of elementary mathematics teachers. The documentation led the researchers to conclude that the professional activities for lesson preparations provided the necessary orientation for teachers to design appropriate mathematics tasks for students, adopt methods for teaching the difficult mathematical ideas, and to use mathematical, pedagogically appropriate language. Chinese teachers were also found to be closely following the required textbooks and the teaching manuals (Cai, 2005). Chinese mathematics teachers' close adherence to the curriculum materials, a consequence of the centralized curriculum system, is a guarantee that teachers in most Chinese mathematics classrooms teach the subject according to the curriculum.

Mathematics teachers and classroom instruction

Chinese mathematics teachers specialize in teaching the subject at certain grade levels. Most elementary school mathematics teachers receive their training from normal schools or normal colleges. Secondary school mathematics teachers obtain their training from normal universities where they specialize in mathematics education. For most Chinese mathematics teachers, mathematics classes are the only subjects they teach in school because mathematics is one of the three major school subject matters (the other two are Chinese and English). Teaching assignments are usually made by grade-block. For example, a school district may allocate the teaching assignments so that one group of teachers would teach grades 1 and 2 mathematics, another group always taught grades 3 and 4, and another group would teach grades 5 and 6.

A typical urban Chinese elementary or secondary classroom usually has around 40–50 students, and some may even have as many as 60 or 70 students because of the rapid urbanization across the country in this century. Consequently, the lecture format still seems to be the most efficient way for teachers to conduct classes for large numbers of students. Also, as indicated in the previous section, the Chinese mathematics curriculum emphasizes the two basics: basic mathematics concepts and basic mathematical skills. Therefore, classroom instruction focuses on *refined lectures* and *repeated practice* (Zhang et al., 2004). A refined lecture is the result of taking the 8 steps to prepare lessons: knowing the curriculum materials, understanding the students, identifying objectives, selecting learning tasks, focusing on the content points that are "important" and "difficult", arranging an instruction sequence, designing methods to make the teaching content accessible to students, and putting the lesson plan on paper (Cao, 1991). To deliver such refined instruction, teachers in Beijing and Taipei spend more hours each day examining students' work and preparing lessons with colleagues than do their US counterparts (Stevenson and Stigler, 1992). Teachers present the well-prepared lessons that include strong teacher control, coherent instruction, and accurate and abstract mathematics. The last two factors will be discussed in the following section.

The refined lecture should unite teaching content and classroom discourse through coherent connections that guide students toward their learning goal for each lesson (Schleppenbach et al., 2007). As shown in the analysis of textbooks and teacher guides by Li et al. (2008) and Ding and Li (2010), the Chinese mathematics curriculum materials emphasize the conceptual connections between teaching contents. Following the curriculum materials, Chinese teachers enhance instructional coherence by emphasizing the relationships among mathematics concepts. Ma (1999) investigated the understanding of mathematics for teaching among 72 Chinese and 23 American elementary school teachers. The subjects chosen for comparison were three content cases, subtraction with regrouping, multi-digit multiplication, and division by fractions. The Chinese teachers demonstrated deep conceptual understanding of the teaching contents across the three content topics. Ma summarized her main findings by these contrasts:

> For the algorithm of subtraction with regrouping, while most U.S. teachers were satisfied with the pseudo-explanation of "borrowing," the Chinese teachers explained that the rationale of the computation is "decomposing a higher value unit." For the topic of multi-digit multiplication, while most of the U.S. teachers were content with the rule of "lining up with the number by which you multiplied," the Chinese teachers explored the concepts of place value and place value system to explain why the partial products aren't lined up in multiplication as addends are in addition. For the calculation of division by fractions for which the U.S. teachers used "invert and multiply," the Chinese teachers referred to "dividing by a number is equivalent to multiply by its reciprocal" as the rational for this seemingly arbitrary algorithm.
>
> (Ma, 1999, pp. 108–109)

Chinese mathematics teachers have a tendency to follow accurate mathematical expressions in classroom instruction based on their profound understanding of mathematics knowledge for teaching. In teaching subtraction with regrouping, the majority of the Chinese teachers interviewed in Ma's study (1999) described the borrowing step in the algorithm as "a process decomposing a unit of higher value instead of saying 'you borrow 1 ten from the tens place'" (p. 8), as advised by teacher guides on instruction. One third-grade teacher explained why she thought the expression of "decomposing a unit of higher value" was conceptually accurate: "'Borrowing' can't explain why you can take 10 to the ones place. But 'decomposing' can. When you say decomposing, it implies that the digits in higher places are actually composed of those at lower places. They are exchangeable. The term 'borrowing' does not mean the composing-decomposing process at all" (Ma, 1999, p. 9).

Chinese teachers pay close attention to details and expressions of students' responses to answering mathematics questions. Cai (2004) analyzed US and Chinese teachers' scoring of student responses. One set of student responses was to the following question: One step needs one block, two steps needs three blocks, three steps needs 6 blocks, four steps need 10 blocks ... How many blocks are needed to build a 20-step staircase? One student response was shown as this: $1 + 2 = 3 + 3 = 6 + 4 = 10 + 5 = 15 + 6 = 21 + 7 = 28 + 8 = 36 + 9 ... 190 + 20 = 210$. Over 60 percent of the US teachers gave the response 4 points (the highest point) and about 30 percent of them assigned it 3 points. In contrast, about a third of the Chinese teachers rated it 0 or 1 point and nearly half gave 2 or 3 points. Most of the Chinese teachers were intolerant of the errors. They commented that the answer was correct but two sides of an equal sign should be equal.

Classroom instruction and its effects on student learning outcomes are closely monitored at the school district level although China currently does not have a national-wide assessment system, such as NAEP (National Assessment of Educational Progress) in the US, to monitor educational progress of student learning in the compulsory education system. In informal conversations with elementary mathematical teachers from four different cities on different occasions, it was learned that student tests for mid-term and year-end examinations were set by the respective school districts and the test results were collected by the school districts. The close monitoring is another indication of strict adherence to the curriculum with regards to the teaching of mathematics in the Chinese classrooms.

Consequently, by aligning with the unified curriculum, well-designed and coherent mathematics lessons reduce ambiguity and confusion. The alignment and clarity assist Chinese students as they progress toward their challenging learning goals of memorization and understanding of mathematics concepts and skills.

Mathematics achievement of Chinese students and their costs

A national curriculum, unified textbooks, and teaching specialists in school mathematics have helped Chinese students to meet the challenging curriculum goals. However, more is required than the school mathematics curriculum system that has led Chinese students to prominence in international assessments of student mathematics achievements (Fan and Zhu, 2004; Stigler and Hilbert, 1999). Studies have shown that Chinese Americans outperformed other Asian-Americans and Caucasian-American students in mathematics (Huntsinger *et al.*, 2000), even when these Chinese-Americans were not exposed to formal Chinese schooling. Asian-Europeans also outperformed the native Europeans (Sirin, 2005). These results indicate that school factors alone do not fully explain achievement differences between Chinese and non-Chinese students. Specific social-cultural factors, uniquely Chinese, such as the strong belief in education as the driving force behind economic success (Reitz and Verma, 2004), effort that empowers ability (J. Li, 2004), and also academic achievement enhancing filial attachment (Hau and Salili, 1996) also explain these differences. These factors appear to facilitate the curricular and instructional influence on student mathematic achievement. Chinese parents spend more time than their American counterparts monitoring their children's homework or helping them directly (Stevenson *et al.*, 1990). Chinese students are much more likely to do their homework and they spend more time doing homework than either American or Japanese students (Chen and Stevenson, 1989; Stigler *et al.*, 1990).

Although Chinese students have high levels of accuracy and efficiency in dealing with school mathematics, these strengths are accompanied by two notable weaknesses, among others. Directive teaching and coherent instruction in Chinese mathematics classrooms potentially reduces ambiguity for students. However, there could also an inherent problem with the curriculum system in the basic approach to mathematic thinking. Factors such as trial and error, induction, imagination and hypothesis testing are not included in mathematics teaching (Ma, 1996; Wong *et al.*, 2002). This omission might prevent students from posing questions, taking risks and being creative. Chinese students appeared less willing to take risks when solving mathematic problems (Cai and Cifarelli, 2004).

Chinese students perform well in mathematics but feel worse than their Western counterparts about their self-concept of mathematics competence and attitude towards learning mathematics. For example, Chinese Hong Kong students were ranked first in the PISA assessment of mathematics literacy, but scored seventh lowest in mathematics self-concept among the 41 countries/regions (Ho, 2003/2004). The interest and confidence in learning mathematics of Mainland Chinese students deteriorated over the years as they moved up to higher grades (Liu and Sun, 2002). In a recent study to evaluate curricular influence on mathematics teaching and learning in the mainland China, students' interest in learning mathematics declined from the fifth grade to sixth grade over a period of 18 months. This decline was apparent regardless of whether the students received the more traditional curriculum or the reformed curriculum (Ni et al., 2011). Research has shown that attitudes and beliefs carry meaning for an individual and consequently, affect may empower or disempower students in relation to mathematics (Schoenfeld, 1992). Moreover, affective responses to mathematics are not only individual and internal; they also are shaped by social, institutional, and cultural contexts (DeBellis and Goldin, 2006). Therefore, it cannot be separated from the gains achieved as a result of the highly centralized curriculum system and the cultural beliefs associated with the mathematics achievement of Chinese students. As indicated in Bruner's (1996) analysis of education as acculturation, cultural learning takes place at two levels. At the macro level, participants learn to see the culture (or a school) as a system of values, rights, exchanges, obligations, opportunities, and power. On the micro level, participants learn to examine how the demands of a cultural system (or a school system) affect those who must operate within it. In that latter spirit, participants also learn how "individual human beings construct realities and meanings that adapt them to the system, but at what personal cost and with what expected outcomes" (Bruner, 1996, p. 12).

Notes

1   In this article, all instances of the word 'China' refer to the People's Republic of China, excluding Hong Kong, Macau, and Taiwan, unless when a reference is explicitly indicated.

References

Bruner, J. (1996). The Culture of Education. Harvard University Press.

Cai, J. (2004). Why do U.S. and Chinese students think differently in mathematical problem solving? Impact of early algebra learning and teachers' beliefs. Journal of Mathematical Behavior, 23, 135–167.

——(2005). U.S. and Chinese teachers' constructing, knowing, and evaluating representations to teach mathematics. Mathematical Thinking and Learning, 7, 136–169.

Cai, J. and Cifarelli, V. (2004). Thinking mathematically by Chinese learners. In L. Fan, N-Y, Wong, J. Cai and S. Li (Eds.), How Chinese Learn Mathematics: Perspectives from Insiders (pp. 71–106). River Edge, NJ: World Scientific.

Cao, C. H. (1991). Introduction to Teaching Secondary Mathematics. Beijing: Beijing Normal University Press. (in Chinese)

Chen, C. and Stevenson, H. W. (1989). Homework: a cross-cultural examination. Child Development, 60, 551–561.

Chomsky, N. (1986). Knowledge of Language. New York: Praeger.

DeBellis, V. and Goldin, G. (2006). Affect and meta-affect in mathematical problem solving: a representational perspective. Educational Studies in Mathematics, 63, 131–147.

Dhlin, B. and Watkins, D. A. (2000). The role of repetition in the processes of memorizing and understanding: a comparison of the views of Western and Chinese school students in Hong Kong. British Journal of Educational Psychology, 70, 65–84.

Ding, M. and Li, X. (2010). A comparative analysis of the distributive property in U.S. and Chinese elementary mathematics textbooks. Cognition and Instruction, 28(2), 146–180.

Fan, L. and Zhu, Y. (2004). How have Chinese students performed in mathematics? A perspective from large-scale international mathematics comparisons. In L. Fan, N.-Y., Wong, J. Cai and S. Li (Eds.), *How Chinese Learn Mathematics: Perspectives from Insiders* (pp. 3–26). River Edge, NJ: World Scientific.

Fan, L., Chen, J. A., Qiu, X. L. and Hu, J. Z. (2004). Textbook use within and beyond Chinese mathematics classrooms: a study of 12 secondary schools in Kunming and Fuzhou of China. In L. Fan, N-Y. Wong, J. Cai and S. Li (Eds.), *How Chinese Learn Mathematics: Perspectives from Insiders* (pp.186–212). River Edge, NJ: World Scientific Press.

Fuson, K. and Li, Y. (2009) Cross-cultural issues in linguistic, visual-quantitative, and written-numeric supports for mathematical thinking. *The International Journal on Mathematics Education, 41,* 793–808.

Geary, D. C. (1995). Reflections of evolution and culture in children's cognition: implications for mathematical development and instruction. *American Psychologist, 50*(1), 24–37.

Gelman, R. and Gallistel, C. R. (1978). *The Child's Understanding of Number.* Cambridge, MA: Harvard University Press.

Han, X. and Paine, L. (2010). Teaching mathematics as deliberate practice through public lessons. *The Elementary School Journal, 110,* 519–541.

Hau, K. T. and Salili, F. (1996). Achievement goals and causal attributions of Chinese students. In S. Lau (Ed.), *Growing Up the Chinese Way* (pp. 121–145). Hong Kong: The Chinese University Press.

Ho, E. S-C. (2003/2004). Accomplishment and challenges of Hong Kong education system: what we have learned from PISA. *Educational Journal, 31(2)/32(1),* 1–30.

Huntsinger, C. S., Jose, P. E., Larson, S. L., Balsink, K. D. and Shalingram, C. (2000). Mathematics, vocabulary, and reading development in Chinese American and European American children over the primary school years. *Journal of Educational Psychology, 92,* 745–760.

Li, J. (2004). Learning as a task or a virtue: U.S. and Chinese preschoolers explain learning. *Developmental Psychology, 40,* 595–605.

Li, J-H. (2004). Thorough understanding of the textbook – a significant feature of Chinese teacher manuals. In L. Fan, N.-Y., Wong, J. Cai and S. Li (Eds.), *How Chinese Learn Mathematics: Perspectives from Insiders* (pp. 262–279). River Edge, NJ: World Scientific.

Li, X., Ding M., Capraro, M. M. and Capraro, R. M. (2008). Sources of differences in children's understandings of mathematical equality: comparative analysis of teacher guides and student texts in China and in the United States. *Cognition and Instruction, 26,* 195–217.

Liu, J. and Sun, X. T. (2002). *Introducing the New Mathematics Curriculum Standards for the 9-year Compulsory Education.* Beijing: Beijing Normal University Press. (in Chinese)

Ma, L. (1999). *Knowing and Teaching Elementary Mathematics: Teachers' Understanding of Fundamental Mathematics in China and the United States.* Mahwah, NJ: Erlbaum.

Ma, X. (1996). Curriculum change in school mathematics. In X. Liu (Ed.) *Mathematics and Science Curriculum Change in the People's Republic of China* (pp.93–136). Ontario: Canada: The Edwin Mellen.

Mathematical Sciences Education Board. (1998). *The Nature and Role of Algebra in the K-14 Curriculum: Proceedings of a National Symposium.* Washington DC: National Research Council.

Ministry of Education (2000). *Syllabus for the Teaching of Primary Mathematics of the Nine-year Compulsory Education.* Beijing: People Education Press. (in Chinese)

——(2001). *Curriculum Standards for Mathematics Curriculum of the Nine-year Compulsory Education. Beijing: Ministry of Education.* Beijing: Beijing Normal University Press. (in Chinese)

Ni, Y. J. and Zhou, Y. D. (2005). Teaching and learning fraction and rational numbers: the origin and implications of whole number bias. *Educational Psychologist, 40,* 27–52.

Ni, Y. J., Li, Q., Li, X. and Zhang, Z. H. (2011). Impact of curriculum reform: evidence of change in classroom practice in mainland China. *International Journal of Educational Research, 50,* 71–86.

Reitz, J. G. and Verma, A. (2004). Immigration, race, and labor. *Industrial Relations, 43,* 835–854.

Schleppenbach, M., Perry, M., Miller, K. F., Sims, L. and Fang, G. (2007). The answer is only the beginning: extended discourse in Chinese and U.S. mathematics classrooms. *Journal of Educational Psychology. 99,* 380–396.

Schoenfeld, A. H. (1992). Learning to think mathematically: problem solving, metacognition, and sense making in mathematics. In D. A. Grouws (Ed.), *Handbook of Research on Mathematics Teaching and Learning* (pp. 334–371). New York: Macmillan.

Siegler, R. S. and Mu, Y. (2008). Chinese children excel on novel mathematics problems even before elementary school. *Psychological Science, 19*, 759.

Sirin, S. R. (2005). Socioeconomic status and academic achievement: a meta-analytic review of literature. *Review of Educational Research, 75*, 417–453.

Stevenson, H. W., Lee, S. Y., Chen, C., Lummis, M., Stigler, J. W., Liu, F. and Fang, G. (1990). Mathematics achievement of children in China and the United States. *Child Development, 61*, 1055–1066.

Stevenson, H. W. and Stigler, J. W. (1992). *The Learning Gap*. New York: Simon & Schuster.

Stigler, J. W. and Hiebert, J. (1999). *The Teaching Gap: Best Ideas from the World's Teachers for Improving Education in the Classroom*. New York: Free Press.

Stigler, J. W., Lee, S. Y. and Stevenson, H. W. (1990). *Mathematical Knowledge of Japanese, Chinese, and American Elementary School Children*. Reston, VA: National Council of Teachers of Mathematics.

Vygotsky, L. S. (1997). *Mind in Society: The Development of Higher Psychological Process*. Cambridge, MA: Harvard University Press.

Wong, N.-Y., Lam, C. C., Wong, K. M., Ma, Y. P. and Han, J. W. (2002). Conceptions of mathematics by middle school teachers in mainland China. *Curriculum, Teaching Materials and Methods, 1*, 68–73. (in Chinese)

Wu, W. J. (1993). Issues on modernization of mathematics education. In *Prospects for the Chinese mathematics education in the 21st century* (pp. 16–27). Beijing: Beijing Normal University Press (in Chinese).

Wynn, K. (1992). Addition and subtraction in human infants. *Nature, 358*, 749–750.

Zhang, D., Li, S. and Tang, R. (2004). The "two basics:" Mathematics teaching and learning in Mainland China. In L. Fan, N.-Y., Wong, J. Cai and S. Li (Eds.), *How Chinese Learn Mathematics: Perspectives from Insiders* (pp. 189–207). River Edge, NJ: World Scientific.

Part X

Is phonological awareness causally important in the acquisition of reading and spelling?

All of these [reviewed] studies showed that PA was significantly related to subsequent reading and spelling, and that a training of PA improved not only children's phonological skills but also – to a lesser extent – their reading and spelling competencies.

Wolfgang Schneider and Nicole Berger

It is not justified to subsume segmentation of utterances into words as an aspect of phonemic awareness in a broad sense. Insights into the concept of words as linguistic units and the conscious manipulation of phonemes are not prerequisites *per se*, but print-specific knowledge that is gradually acquired in the course of learning to read and spell.

Renate Valtin

Is phonological awareness crucially important in the acquisition of reading and spelling

Chapter 20

Re-impact of phonological awareness on the acquisition of literacy

Wolfgang Schneider and Nicole Berger

Universität Würzburg

A systematic treatment of the core issue emphasized in the title and content of this contribution requires a short clarification regarding the use of the term "causal" in our discussion. It seems important to differentiate its meaning in the philosophy of science from that typically implied in the social sciences, for instance, psychology and education. Whereas in the philosophy of science the term "causal" refers to deterministic relationships between variables ("whenever X, then Y"), the term "causal" as used in the social sciences refers to a probabilistic relationship between variables, indicating that individual differences in a specific variable X show a statistically significant impact on individual differences in another variable Y, which is typically assessed at some later time. Based on this definition, it is possible to talk about "multicausality", meaning that several variables significantly predict a given criterion variable, and also about "causal predominance" whenever it appears that one predictor variable has a substantially stronger impact on a specific criterion than other predictor variables. For instance, multivariate statistical tools such as structural equation modeling (causal modeling) represent tests of causality assumptions based on the probabilistic approach.

According to this, Stanovich (1986) refers to the link between phonological awareness (PA) and the acquisition of literacy. He postulates three different criteria which seem to be necessary for such an assumption: (a) correlational longitudinal studies should demonstrate a substantial link between early PA and subsequent reading and spelling, (b) intervention studies should demonstrate that training of PA not only increases the overall level of PA but also yields improvements in reading and spelling, and (c) comparisons of younger normal readers and older poor readers with equivalent levels of reading competence should yield significant group differences regarding PA, indicating higher levels of PA in the younger group. It is in this sense that we will subsequently use the term "causal" when discussing possible impacts of phonological awareness (PA) on the acquisition of literacy.

A brief historical sketch of the study of literacy acquisition and dyslexia

Research in reading and spelling has a long history. In the early twentieth century, assumptions about disabilities in reading and spelling were stated by Ranschburg (1916) who conceived of reading disorders as a type of "word-blindness". In other words, he postulated that dysfunctions of the visual system typically cause difficulties in learning how to read and/or to spell. Since the early 1960s, our views of the possible causes of reading and spelling problems have changed considerably. Several cross-sectional studies documented the importance of a functioning acoustic channel for the normal acquisition of reading and spelling, illustrating that the risk of being a dyslexic child was closely related to the inability to discover the sound structure of oral language. In several early studies, the importance of oral language development for subsequent literacy acquisition was also highlighted. But the question remained, which factors could be considered as important predictors? Although the literature on reading and spelling published through the mid-eighties of the last century identified various predictor variables for reading and spelling, findings from a number of early longitudinal studies were not consistent. According to a meta-analysis published in an inventory by Schneider and Edelstein (1990), a first generation of longitudinal studies on reading and spelling carried out before 1985 (about 30 studies), mostly conducted in Europe, suffered from the fact that the selection of predictor measures was not guided by theoretical considerations. Rather, a vast array of mostly psychometric measures were used that in most cases were not proximal to reading and spelling (e.g. motor skills, general cognitive ability, and behavioral-emotional functioning; for reviews, see Horn and Packard, 1985; Tramontana et al., 1988). Interestingly enough, many of these variables predicted later reading performance surprisingly well. However, their discriminative validity was rather low in that the precursor variables predicted developmental changes in math and other subject matters taught in school as well as literacy.

A second generation of longitudinal studies on the prediction of reading and spelling began to be published from the mid-eighties on. This second generation did base its selection of precursor variables on theoretical assumptions (e.g. Bradley and Bryant, 1985; Juel, 1988; Lundberg et al., 1988; Skowronek and Marx, 1989; Stanovich et al., 1984). The number of relevant studies increased rapidly during the 1990s and beyond. In an update of the 1990 inventory, Schneider and Stengard (2000) identified 144 longitudinal studies on reading and spelling in Europe, and estimated that the true number of relevant studies carried out on this issue internationally was considerably higher. One major common outcome of these studies was that early phonological skills seem important for subsequent success in reading and spelling. Several kindergarten indicators related to different aspects of phonological information processing were thought to be particularly influential, and will be discussed next.

The theoretical framework of phonolgical information processing

Overall, the second generation of longitudinal studies identified three relevant predictor domains within a broad theoretical framework labeled *phonological information processing* (cf. Wagner and Torgesen, 1987). A first predictor domain is phonological awareness (PA), that is, the ability to reflect on and to manipulate the phonemic segments of speech. PA is a very good predictor of children's later reading and spelling performance (see Tunmer and Nesdale, 1985; Wagner and Torgesen, 1987). According to Skowronek and Marx (1989), PA can be distinguished in a broad sense to refer to larger language units such as words, syllables, and rhymes, and in a more narrow sense that refers to small units such as phonemes and distinguishing sounds within words. Skowronek and Marx (1989) assumed that both components are relevant for subsequent reading and spelling performance in school. While PA in the broad sense is acquired naturally during the course of the kindergarten period, PA in the narrow sense usually develops at the beginning of first grade when children learn to read and write. One controversial issue discussed in the literature concerned whether PA in the narrow sense can be acquired without knowledge of the alphabetic code (e.g. Morais, 1991; Bradley and Bryant, 1985; Lundberg, 1991; Valtin, 1984).

A second relevant predictor domain is *phonological working memory* (cf. Brady, 1991; Gathercole and Baddeley, 1993; Wagner, 1988), which refers to children's ability to temporarily maintain phonological information in memory. Efficient recoding in working memory would aid beginning readers faced with a challenging task when encountering a new long word. They not only have to retrieve the sounds of the letters, but also have to store initial sounds while continuing the recoding process. Finally, the whole sequence of sounds has to be kept active in working memory when the decoding process starts, that is, when children try to make sense of the sound sequence, blend the sounds together, and identify the word.

A third relevant phonological information processing component is *verbal information processing speed*, in particular, the speed with which children can approach their semantic lexicon. It has been repeatedly shown that dyslexic children are slower than controls when asked to label picture items in confrontation naming tasks (cf. Wimmer *et al.*, 2000). Although all of these three components have been shown to predict individual differences in the acquisition of literacy, PA seems to be the most substantial and the only specific predictor. That is, whereas individual differences in working memory and information processing speed not only predict outcomes in reading and spelling but also math achievement and other school subjects, the predictive power of PA is specific in that it seems restricted to reading and spelling.

Evidence from prospective longitudinal studies

One large-scale longitudinal study that assessed developmental changes in many variables over time, including the development of reading and spelling and its relevant precursors, was the Munich Longitudinal Study on the Genesis of Individual Competencies (LOGIC; Weinert and Schneider, 1999). The LOGIC study was started in 1984 with about 200 kindergarten children (mean age: 3;6 years), and predictors of reading and spelling were assessed during the preschool period before children entered school. On the one hand, non-specific predictors of reading and spelling such as general cognitive ability, working memory, and information processing speed were included in the study. As demonstrated in earlier studies, these variables were not only predictive for reading and spelling but also for math development, thus indicating general predictor qualities (Tramontana *et al.*, 1988). On the other hand, specific precursors such as letter knowledge and PA were also used to predict the children's acquisition of literacy (see Schneider and Näslund, 1999).

The sample initially consisted of about 200 children. Due to drop-out and the fact that not all of the children entered first grade at the same time, complete data sets were available for 121 children. The design the authors used was a long-term follow-up study with annual assessment periods (waves) during middle and late childhood (Grades 2 to 6), followed by two further assessments when participants were 18 and 23 years old. Reading tests were given in Grade 2 when children were about 8 years old, and then again at the age of 23. Given that spelling is more important for German children's academic career than reading, spelling tests were provided more frequently, namely, in Grades 2, 3, 4, 5, and later again at the ages of 18 and 23.

Several important conclusions can be drawn from the findings (see Schneider and Näslund, 1999; Schneider, 2009). First of all, it was shown that PA, letter knowledge, and verbal information processing speed assessed during the last year of kindergarten all influenced subsequent reading and spelling in school. Interestingly, the impact of PA on spelling was stronger than its impact on reading. Hierarchical regression analyses using IQ as the first predictor variable (and thus overestimating the impact of this predictor) showed that PA in the broad sense (rhyming and syllable segmentation) predicted reading speed and reading comprehension and – together with listening span and letter knowledge – explained about 27 percent of the variance in both criterion variables. In comparison, PA in the narrow sense, along with letter knowledge and rapid naming, explained about 36 percent of spelling at the end of Grade 3. Please note that PA in the narrow sense explained considerably more variance in spelling than in reading, and that PA in the narrow sense was generally more predictive than PA in the broad sense. The predictive quality of these kindergarten measures even seemed to improve over time. When spelling at the end of Grade 3 was chosen as the dependent variable, almost 50 percent of the variance in spelling could be explained by PA, rapid naming, listening span, and letter knowledge (see Schneider and Näslund, 1999). However, the picture changed completely when spelling assessed at the end of Grade 2 was also included in the regression equation. Although the amount of variance explained in spelling at the end of Grade 3 remained about the same, now spelling at Grade 2 turned out to be the by far strongest predictor. Similar findings were reported by Wimmer et al. (1994), indicating that the pattern of results obtained in the LOGIC study seems robust, at least for German-speaking samples. The summary of European longitudinal studies provided by Schneider and Stengard (2000) indicates that this pattern of findings is also transferable to other orthographies.

Thus a second major outcome of this longitudinal study was that direct effects of PA and the other indicators of phonological information processing on reading and spelling are restricted to literacy development at the beginning of school. After that, individual differences in reading and spelling obtained at the first measurement in school proved to be by far the strongest predictors of subsequent literacy development. This conclusion is also supported by findings from structural equation modeling showing that IQ and PA exert direct effects on spelling only at the beginning of school, but not thereafter (cf. Figure 20.1). This indicates that individual differences in PA and other phonological information processing variables set the stage for further literacy development which is characterized by rather high stability over time. Thus early differences in literacy skills do matter and cannot be easily compensated for in subsequent school years.

Third, the findings of the LOGIC study seem to indicate that PA is a necessary but not sufficient cause of literacy development. Apparently, PA influences subsequent reading and (even more) spelling development, but only constitutes one out of several impact factors. They are in accord with the results of several other longitudinal studies carried out at that time (e.g. Juel, 1988; Skowronek and Marx, 1989). A more recent study on literacy development in German conducted by Landerl and Wimmer (2008) confirms these findings, showing that PA was the strongest predictor of spelling, whereas rapid naming was the best predictor of reading fluency at the end of school. Thus, there is multiple evidence in the literature that PA seems more important for the prediction of spelling than for the prediction of reading (see also de Jong and van der Leij, 2003). Taken together, the findings from correlational longitudinal studies provide evidence for a causal link between PA and later abilities in the written language.

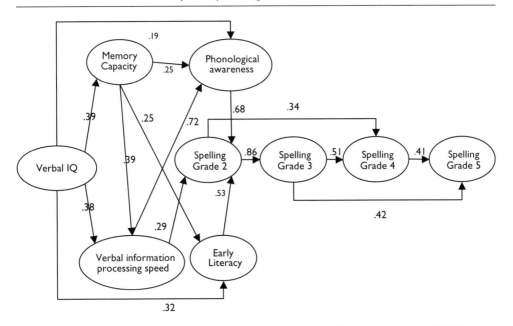

Figure 20.1 Causal model predicting spelling performance at different time points (LOGIC study, adopted from Schneider, 2009, Figure 9.2).

Evidence from experimental/intervention studies

Another way to establish the causality of PA is to conduct longitudinal intervention studies. Based on the findings of correlational longitudinal studies which confirmed the important role of PA as a predictor of later reading and spelling development, it was assumed that a systematic training of PA will yield positive effects on children's subsequent literacy development. To confirm the causal impact of phonological training in kindergarten on reading and spelling in school, it needs to be demonstrated that an improvement in phonological competencies after training can be systematically linked to better reading and spelling skills in elementary school. More specifically, PA training should facilitate the learning-to-read and -spell process if PA indeed is causally related to reading and spelling.

As shown by several statistical meta-analyses (e.g. Bus and van Ijzendoorn, 1999; Ehri *et al.*, 2001), there are now numerous training studies available which demonstrate that increases in PA are causally related to improved reading and spelling processes. One type of PA training program assumes that metalinguistic games developing children's sensitivity to phonemes in words enable them to understand the alphabetical principle more quickly as they learn to read and spell (e.g. Lundberg *et al.*, 1988; Schneider *et al.*, 1997). The classic study by Lundberg *et al.* was carried out in Denmark and built on strictly oral language activities. Their training program consisted of a system of games and was carried out during the last year of kindergarten, lasting about 8 months. A control group did not receive any instruction in PA but participated in the regular kindergarten program. Pre- and post-test measures taken immediately before and after training and tapping various metalinguistic abilities revealed significant treatment effects. Even more importantly, significant effects of the program on subsequent spelling skills were demonstrated for the first grades of elementary school. Please note that no explicit connection between phonemes and letters was provided in the training program. Thus this longitudinal intervention study showed that PA can be trained effectively in kindergarteners without any knowledge on letters or written language skills.

Given the success of Lundberg's program, we adapted this program and developed a German version. This program was labeled "Hören, Lauschen, Lernen" (HLL, "Hearing, Listening, Learning" in English) and became also known as the "Würzburg training program" (Küspert and Schneider, 2006). The training program consisted of 57 different "language games" in six consecutive training units to enhance PA in kindergarteners. Kindergarten teachers were carefully instructed in the program and asked to carry out the program within 20 weeks during the last year of kindergarten, spending about 10 to 15 minutes per day with the training units. Like Lundberg and colleagues, Schneider *et al.* (1997) were able to show that the training was successful. There were short- and long-term effects which lasted until the end of elementary school.

Later on, HLL was supplemented by a second program component "HLL2" (Plume and Schneider, 2004), which focused on knowledge about the relationship between sounds and letters. In a series of further evaluation projects, it was found that the combination of HLL and HLL2 was particularly effective in improving at-risk children's PA (e.g. Schneider *et al.*, 2000). This result is in accord with the "phonological linkage hypothesis" (Hatcher *et al.*, 1994), which assumes that a training approach systematically linking a PA training with a training component focusing on knowledge about letter-sound correspondences should yield larger effects than training these components in isolation. For further confirming results, see the two meta-analyses by Bus and van Ijzendoorn (1999) and Ehri *et al.* (2001).

A more recent study (Weber *et al.*, 2007) explored the effects of the combined training program for other groups with high risk. In this study, children with specific language impairment (SLI) as well as children with a migration background and suboptimal proficiency of the German language were compared with "normal" kindergarten children and a control group of SLI children. Although the "normal" group outperformed the three groups of children at risk in most aspects of language-related abilities at pretest, substantial training effects were found for all groups. Interestingly, trained SLI children clearly outperformed SLI control children at post-test (but not at pre-test) even though the SLI control children's teachers claimed that the content of our training program was part of their normal curriculum. Thus it could be shown that both SLI children and those with a migration background can substantially benefit from a combined training approach. A limitation of the study is that effects partly could be explained by the phenomenon of regression to the mean. This means that very low values in the beginning tend to improve on their own by time and "regress" to mean values, no matter if there is any training or not. To rule out this explanation completely, further studies will have to be conducted by using an equivalent control group, meaning another group of SLI children or children with a migration background.

Phonological awareness: a specific or non-specific precursor of literacy?

An interesting recent issue concerns whether the predictive relations of PA are restricted to reading and spelling, as assumed and found in earlier studies. For instance, Bradley and Bryant (1985) concluded from their training study that increases in PA had positive effects on subsequent reading and spelling but not on math performance. Similar findings were also reported by Durand *et al.* (2005) as well as by Fuchs *et al.* (2006). Given rather substantial correlations between literacy and maths competencies, ranging from between $r = .40$ and $.60$ (e.g. Berg, 2008; Koponen *et al.*, 2007), it does not come as a surprise that several studies also found significant relations between PA and math achievement (for a review, see Simmons and Singleton, 2008). For instance, Krajewski and Schneider (2009) carried out a long-term longitudinal study on mathematical competence development, starting with kindergarten children who were followed up until the end of elementary school. Preschool predictor variables not only included counting and estimation skills but also PA. Interestingly, PA predicted individual differences in number word knowledge, but did not directly contribute to the prediction of higher order math skills in school. The authors concluded that although PA facilitates the acquisition of basic numerical concepts such as number words and number word sequences, it seems less relevant for the formation of higher-order mathematical competencies.

Concluding remarks

Numerous studies demonstrate the importance of early PA for both reading and spelling in school. Overall, the evidence seems stronger for spelling than for reading; however, can we infer from this data that the impact of PA on the acquisition of literacy is causal?

In the beginning of this chapter, we considered Stanovich's three criteria for a causal link between PA and the acquisition of literacy. These were a) a substantial correlational link between the factors, b) training studies which take PA into account and show an substantial improvement of later reading and writing and c) comparisons of PA between younger normal readers and older poor readers with similar levels of reading competence.

Regarding these criteria, we have tried to show that PA is causally linked to the development of reading and spelling, focusing on supportive evidence from correlational longitudinal studies as well as intervention studies. All of these studies showed that PA is significantly related to subsequent reading and spelling, and that a training of PA improves not only children's phonological skills but also – to a lesser extent – their reading and spelling competencies (see Bus and van Ijzendoorn, 1999; Ehri *et al.*, 2001). Furthermore, there are also several experimental studies using matched designs and comparing children of different ages but equivalent reading competencies that confirmed the third assumption (cf. Stanovich, 1986; Wagner, 1988). Thus causality in the sense of a probabilistic concept outlined in the introduction to this chapter can be demonstrated for both reading and spelling. However, the findings indicate that PA represents only one of the observed causes of reading and spelling, and that "multicausality" should be assumed in this case. There are other predictors such as verbal IQ, working memory, information processing speed, and letter knowledge that are all influential in the initial stages of literacy acquisition. PA probably constitutes the strongest predictor, particularly in the case of spelling, and may exert "causal predominance". However, there is little doubt that the relation between phonological competencies and reading/spelling is reciprocal in the course of literacy development, with initial phonological competencies influencing subsequent literacy development, which in turn affects later phonological processing. The available longitudinal evidence clearly shows that the direct impact of kindergarten phonological competencies is restricted to the early period of literacy acquisition. Later on, developmental changes in reading and spelling skills are most strongly predicted by previous differences in these competencies.

References

Berg, D. H. (2008). Working memory and arithmetic calculation in children: the contributory roles of processing speed, short-term memory and reading. *Journal of Experimental Child Psychology*, *99*, 288–308.

Bradley, L. and Bryant, P. E. (1985). *Rhyme and Reason in Reading and Spelling*. Ann Arbor, MI: University of Michigan Press.

Brady, S. A. (1991). The role of working memory in language disability. In S. A. Brady and D. P. Shankweiler (Eds.), *Phonological Processes in Literacy – A Tribute to Isabelle Y. Liberman* (pp. 129–152). Hillsdale, NJ: Erlbaum.

Bus, A. G. and van Ijzendoorn, M. H. (1999). Phonological awareness and early reading: a meta-analysis of experimental training studies. *Journal of Educational Psychology*, *91*, 403–414.

de Jong, P. F. and van der Leij, A. (2003). Developmental changes in the manifestation of a phonological deficit in dyslexic children learning to read a regular orthography. *Journal of Educational Psychology*, *95*, 22–40.

Durant, M., Hulme, C., Larkin, R. and Snowling, M. (2005). The cognitive foundations of reading and arithmetic skills in 7- to 10-year-olds. *Journal of Experimental Child Psychology*, *91*, 113–136.

Ehri, L., Nunes, S., Willows, D., Schuster, B., Yaghoub-Zadeh, Z. and Shanahan, T. (2001). Phonemic awareness instruction helps children learn to read: evidence from the National Reading Panel's meta-analysis. *Reading Research Quarterly*, *36*, 250–287.

Fuchs, L. S., Fuchs, D., Compton, D. L., Powell, S. R., Seethaler, P. M., Capizzi, A. M., Schatschneider, C. and Fletcher, J. M. (2006). The cognitive correlates of third-grade skill in arithmetic, algorithmic computation, and arithmetic word problems. *Journal of Educational Psychology*, *98*, 29–43.

Gathercole, S. E. and Baddeley, A. D. (1993). *Working Memory and Language*. Hillsdale, NJ: Erlbaum.

Hatcher, P. J., Hulme, C. and Ellis, A. W. (1994). Ameliorating early reading failure by integrating the teaching of reading and phonological skills: the phonological linkage hypothesis. *Child Development*, *65*, 41–57.

Horn, W. F. and Packard, T. (1985). Early identification of learning problems: a meta-analysis. *Journal of Educational Psychology*, *77*, 597–607.

Juel, C. (1988). Learning to read and write: a longitudinal study of 54 children from first through fourth grades. *Journal of Educational Psychology*, *80*, 437–447.

Koponen, T., Aunola, K., Ahonen, T. and Nurmi, J.-E. (2007). Cognitive predictors of single-digit and procedural calculation skills and their covariation with reading skills. *Journal of Experimental Child Psychology*, *97*, 220–241.

Krajewski, K. and Schneider, W. (2009). Exploring the impact of phonological awareness, visual-spatial working memory and preschool quantity-number competencies on mathematics achievement in elementary school: findings from a 3-year-longitudinal study. *Journal of Experimental Child Psychology*, *103*, 516–531.

Küspert, P. and Schneider, W. (2006). *Hören, lauschen, lernen – Sprachspiele für Vorschulkinder (Hearing, Listening, Learning – language games for preschoolers*, 5th ed.). Göttingen: Vandenhoeck & Ruprecht.

Landerl, K. and Wimmer, H. (2008). Development of word fluency and spelling in a consistent orthography: an 8 year follow up. *Journal of Educational Psychology*, *100*, 150–161.

Lundberg, I. (1991). Phonemic awareness can be developed without reading instruction. In S. A. Brady and D. P. Shankweiler (Eds.), *Phonological Processes in Literacy. A Tribute to Isabelle Y. Liberman* (pp. 47–53). Hillsdale, NJ: Erlbaum.

Lundberg, I., Frost, J. and Petersen, O. P. (1988). Effects of an extensive program for stimulating phonological awareness in preschool children. *Reading Research Quarterly*, *23*, 263–284.

Morais, J. (1991). Constraints on the development of phonemic awareness. In S. A. Brady and D. P. Shankweiler (Eds.), *Phonological Processes in Literacy. A Tribute to Isabelle Y. Liberman* (pp. 5–27). Hillsdale, NJ: Erlbaum.

Plume, E. and Schneider, W. (2004). *Hören, Lauschen, Lernen 2 – Sprachspiele mit Buchstaben und Lauten für Kinder im Vorschulalter. (Hearing, Listening, Learning 2 – language games with letters and phonemes for preschoolers).* Göttingen: Vandenhoeck & Ruprecht.

Ranschburg, P. (1916). Die Leseschwäche und Rechenschwäche der Schulkinder im Lichte des Experiments. (Dyslexia and dyscalculia in school children. An experimental view.) Berlin: Springer.

Schneider, W. (2009). The development of reading and spelling: relevant precursors, developmental changes, and individual differences. In W. Schneider and M. Bullock (Eds.), *Human Development From Early Childhood to Early Adulthood. Findings from a 20 year Longitudinal Study* (pp. 199–220). New York: Psychology Press.

Schneider, W. and Edelstein, W. (1990). *Inventory of European Longitudinal Studies in the Behavioral and Medical Sciences.* Munich: Max-Planck-Institut für Bildungsforschung.

Schneider, W. and Näslund, J. C. (1999). The impact of early phonological processing skills on reading and spelling in school: evidence from the Munich Longitudinal Study. In F. E. Weinert and W. Schneider (Eds.), *Individual Development from 3 to 12: Findings from the Munich Longitudinal Study* (pp. 126–147). Cambridge: Cambridge University Press.

Schneider, W. and Stengard, C. (2000). *Inventory of European Longitudinal Studies of Reading and Spelling.* Brussels, Belgium: European Commission.

Schneider, W., Küspert, P., Roth, E., Visé, M. and Marx, H. (1997). Short- and long-term effects of training phonological awareness in kindergarten: evidence from two German studies. *Experimental Child Psychology, 66,* 311–340.

Schneider, W., Roth, E. and Ennemoser, M. (2000). Training phonological skills and letter knowledge in children at risk for dyslexia: a comparison of three kindergarten intervention programs. *Journal of Educational Psychology, 92,* 284–295.

Simmons, F. R. and Singleton, C. (2008). Do weak phonological representations impact on arithmetic development? A review of research into arithmetic and dyslexia. *Dyslexia, 14,* 77–94.

Skowronek, H. and Marx, H. (1989). The Bielefeld longitudinal study on early identification of risks in learning to write and read: theoretical background and first results. In M. Brambring, F. Lösel and H. Skowronek (Eds.), *Children at Risk: Assessment, Longitudinal Research and Intervention* (pp. 268–295). New York: De Gruyter.

Stanovich, K. E. (1986). Cognitive processes and the reading problems of learning disabled children: evaluating the assumption of specificity. In J. Torgesen and B. Wong (Eds.), *Psychological And Educational Perspectives on Learning Disabilities* (pp. 87–131). New York: Academic Press.

Stanovich, K. E., Cunningham, A. E. and Feeman, D. J. (1984). Intelligence, cognitive skills, and early reading progress. *Reading Research Quarterly, 19,* 278–303.

Tramontana, M. G., Hooper, S. R. and Selzer, S. C. (1988). Research on the preschool prediction of later academic achievement: a review. *Developmental Review, 8,* 89–146.

Tunmer, W. E. and Nesdale, A. R. (1985). Phonemic segmentation skill and beginning reading. *Journal of Educational Psychology, 77,* 417–427.

Valtin, R. (1984). The development of metalinguistic abilities in children learning to read and write. In J. Downing and R. Valtin (Eds.), *Language Awareness and Learning to Read* (pp. 227–260). New York: Springer.

Wagner, R. K. (1988). Causal relations between the development of phonological processing abilities and the acquisition of reading skills: a meta analysis. *Merill-Palmer-Quarterly, 34,* 261–279.

Wagner, R. and Torgesen, J. (1987). The nature of phonological processing and its causal role in the acquisition of reading skills. *Psychological Bulletin, 101,* 192–212.

Weber, J., Marx, P. and Schneider, W. (2007). Die Prävention von Lese-Rechtschreibschwierigkeiten bei Kindern mit nichtdeutscher Herkunftssprache durch ein Training der phonologischen Bewusstheit. (The prevention of reading and spelling difficulties in children with migration background through by training phonological awareness). *Zeitschrift für Pädagogische Psychologie (German Journal of Educational Psychology), 21* (1), 65–75.

Weinert, F. E. and Schneider, W. (1999). *Individual Development from 3 to 12: Findings from the Munich Longitudinal Study.* Cambridge, UK: Cambridge University Press.

Wimmer, H., Landerl, K. and Schneider, W. (1994). The role of rhyme awareness in learning to read a regular orthography. *British Journal of Developmental Psychology, 12,* 469–484.

Wimmer, H., Mayringer, H. and Landerl, K. (2000). The double-deficit hypothesis and difficulties in learning to read a regular orthography. *Journal of Educational Psychology, 92,* 668–680.

Chapter 21

Increasing awareness of phonological awareness – helpful or misleading?

Renate Valtin

Department of Education,
Humboldt-University of Berlin

In educational psychology, phonological awareness (PA) is supposed to be an important prerequisite skill for literacy learning; deficits are held to lead to difficulties in reading and spelling and should be compensated for, through specific training prior to the start of formal schooling. I present a critical analysis of the concept of PA and the empirical data used as evidence of its importance for the learning of reading and spelling, and then question the usefulness of phonemic training in kindergarten.

The concept of phonological awareness in educational psychology

Although there exist different definitions of this concept I will refer to the one that is most prominent in Germany, which comes from Schneider *et al.* (2000). PA is "the ability to explicitly reflect on the sound structure of spoken language" and has two components. In a broad sense PA refers to the "analysis of broader sound structures such as words and syllables", in a narrow sense it "concerns the ability to isolate phonemes within words and syllables" (Schneider *et al.*, 2000, p. 284).

PA is regarded as the strongest predictor of learning written language in alphabetic orthographies (e.g. Landerl and Wimmer, 1994). In this article I will mainly refer to German studies. This is justified by the fact that there are many similarities between English and German; aside from English having a deeper orthography, many of the same principles apply. In fact, if PA has no use as a precursor to reading and spelling in German, then how could it be important in an even less regular language such as English?

The empirical evidence in German studies is neither uniform nor convincing. Most of the research studies concerning PA are "theory free" and establish evidence by fact finding correlations between measures of PA and global measures of reading (reading fluency and accuracy) and spelling (number of spelling errors). The measures of reading and spelling are output-oriented and do not take into account the existing knowledge we have of strategies of learning to read and spell in the early phases of written language acquisition (see the developmental model below) and of qualitative analysis of spelling errors (Valtin and Hofmann, 2009). The correlational evidence comes from several studies (for an overview see Brügelmann, 2005). The relations between PA and later reading and spelling are low to medium (rs = .26 to .60), similar to those for letter knowledge, and are too low to alone be used for individual prognosis (Rackwitz, 2008).

Importantly, correlations refer to common variance between two measures and are not proof of a causal relationship. Observed common variance has many potential causes, such as general intelligence, vocabulary knowledge, or preschool reading competence. In a predictive study, Lundberg *et al.* (1980) concluded: "The most powerful determinant of reading achievement in grade one is the ability in kindergarten to analyze phonemes and reverse their order" (p. 166). However, my re-analysis of the data of this study suggested that those children successful in the PA tasks were already readers when entering school and that preschool reading ability correlated more highly with later reading achievement than the ability to reverse phonemes did (see Valtin, 1984b for greater detail). PA, therefore, is a product of reading, not a precursor.

In accordance with these relatively low correlations between measures of PA and later reading achievement, the positive correlations between reading and PA (as measured by the Bielefeld Screening, BISC) were not replicated (Brügelmann, 2005). The BISC includes PA tasks but could only correctly identify fewer than 20 percent of children with reading and spelling difficulties in first and second grade (Marx and Weber, 2006). Moreover, most of the "children at risk" developed normal reading and spelling competences (Brügelmann, 2005).

A critique of the concept of phonological awareness

PA, as the term is used by educational psychologists in Germany, does not refer to a unitary function (Andresen 2005, p. 232) but to an arbitrary conglomerate of heterogeneous linguistic units and operations. Thus, *words*, as parts of sentences, belong to a grammatical category, such that segmenting sentences into words is a grammatical operation that has nothing to do with the phonological level. *Syllables* are elementary, articulatory units of speech and thus easily perceptible. *Phonemes* belong to a linguistic model of language and are thus highly abstract units. Phonemes are not perceptual but conceptual categories.

From a psycholinguistic point of view, the components often subsumed under PA are components of language awareness, linguistic awareness or metalinguistics – terms that appeared with increasing frequency in reading theory in the 1970s and 1980s (Downing and Valtin, 1984). Over 30 years ago language awareness and its relationship to the acquisition of written language was investigated theoretically and empirically, both in Germany (Andresen, 1985) and internationally. Following an international research seminar on linguistic awareness and learning to read held at the University of Victoria, Canada in 1979, we collected articles, later compiled into a book, on linguistics, psycholinguistics, experimental and child psychology, and education (Downing and Valtin, 1984). This interdisciplinary body of research has been ignored in educational psychology in Germany. Various studies from that time showed that the skills of perception and understanding of syllables, words, and phonemes developed independently of one another and in different phases in children's development (e.g. Clark, 1978; Hakes, 1980; Valtin, 1984a; Andresen, 1985).

Early in the preschool years, children are able to segment speech into *syllables*. They are able to use rhymes either spontaneously or after brief instruction. However, sometimes they confuse the phonological and the semantic level, as exemplified by my niece, aged 4 years: "House and mouse are rhymes – and apples and pears too".

The development of the concept of a *word* and the ability of children to segment utterances into words has been intensely investigated in developmental psychology and psycholinguistics, using different procedures (e.g. counting words in sentences, interviews about the meaning of a word, giving examples of long and short words). These studies (Januschek *et al.*, 1979; Valtin *et al.*, 1986/1994; Kirschhock, 2004) show that children at the same time have quite different and multiple concepts of a "word" which are narrowed under the influence of school and the learning of reading and writing. For preschool children, words and language in general are embedded in the context of action and they have difficulty in differentiating between words and their referents (Homer and Olson, 1999). For example, they might think that "cow" is a longer word than "butterfly" (Bosch, 1937; Valtin *et al.*, 1986/1994; Kirschhock, 2004), and that "leaves" are many words (Januschek *et al.*, 1979). Because of this embeddedness in context children have difficulties when prompted to segment utterances into words (Ferreiro, 1978; Valtin *et al.*, 1986/1994; Valtin, 1989).

The task of segmenting words into sounds or phonemes is very difficult. Training studies with preschool children demonstrate that children at best are able to identify the first phoneme of a word if it is a syllable (a-pron) or when it is a continuant (/s/, /f/, /m/). Preschool children fail with stop consonants (/t/, /p/) (Bryant, 1993). Since the ability to segment words into phonemes and to combine phonemes into a word is only relevant when learning an alphabetic script it is useful to look at this skill within a framework of written language acquisition.

Phonological awareness and written language acquisition

A theoretical model on the acquisition of reading and spelling was outlined by Downing (1984) in his theory of cognitive clarity: the learner must reconstruct the linguistic insights possessed by the inventors of the alphabetic script, and rediscover for themselves the rules by which it is coded. During this process the learner has to gain cognitive clarity or insight into the function of print (that the squiggles on the page are a visual representation of language and not merely a set of symbols whose content is arbitrary), and the structure of our alphabetic system, that is the recognition of certain linguistic units represented in print.

Our longitudinal pilot study (Valtin *et al.*, 1986/1994; Valtin, 1989) and the intervention study by Kirschhock (2004) demonstrated that children entering school have vague concepts about both the function of reading and writing and the concepts of print (what is a letter, a word, a sentence?). In both studies, average readers and spellers gained this cognitive clarity during the first year in school while slower readers still had difficulties at the end of first grade (Valtin, 1989). Kirschhock (2004) showed that the development of these concepts varies with the reading instruction methods used by the teacher.

In the process of learning to read and spell, learners have to acquire certain cognitive and linguistic abilities and insights that may be differentiated into the following elements.

Element I The ability to objectify language and to reflect on formal properties of language

This is a real "prerequisite" for learning to read and write in an alphabetic code. Only when children are able to shift from content to form and to concentrate on the acoustic features of a word, they are able to "hear" sounds as the following example illustrates: When a teacher asked "Listen, what does >car< begin with?" the child replied: "with a bumper."

This ability may be measured by syllable and rhyming tasks as well as comparison of long and short words and requires a certain level of cognitive decentration in the Piagetian sense (Lundberg, 1982; Watson, 1984; Van Leent 1983). PA in a broad sense covers this ability. It is not justifiable, however, to also subsume the analysis of words under this category.

Element 2 The concept of a word and the ability to segment sentences into words

When learning print the child has to grasp the concepts of the word as a linguistic unit and of word boundaries, that a written sentence contains all parts of speech, and that gaps are left between the words. Such insights develop only gradually and reflect experience with print (Ehri, 1984; Valtin, 1989; Kirschhock, 2004). In their invented spellings, preschool children and first graders leave no gaps between words and segment sentences into semantic units, often leaving out function words. Interviews with children about "What is written in a written sentence?" show that children believe that only content words such as nouns or verbs are visually represented in print, but not articles and other function words (Ferreiro, 1978; Valtin, 1989). This is reflected in their dictations and their invented spellings (examples from Valtin, 1989: *"OPAOMALESN"* for "Oma und Opa lesen", meaning "grandma and grandpa are reading").

Element 3 Phonemic awareness and analysis and synthesis

In addition to gaining an awareness of phonemes, the learner must be able to analyze and to synthesize phonemes. In fact, this is an artificial operation, only needed when learning an alphabetic code. Consequently, illiterate adults and people who can read a non-alphabetic script like traditional Chinese orthography have the same difficulties in dealing with phonemes as beginning readers when confronted with alphabetic scripts (for a review see Bryant, 1993).

Beginning learners have great difficulty in analyzing spoken words because of the nature of the acoustic signal. In pronunciation, the speech sounds are not discrete units, but overlap and are also co-articulated such that the phonetic properties of sounds may be altered by adjacent sounds (Ehri, 1984, p. 120). Since phonemes are abstract units, phonemic segmentation and synthesis are thus not simple associative memory tasks but highly demanding conceptual tasks (Andresen, 1985; Valtin, 1984b). Even when children have learned to match sounds with letters they need many months of schooling to cope with phonemic segmentation of difficult words, especially those with consonant clusters.

Observation of children's spellings of unknown words demonstrates these difficulties and points to characteristic developmental stages:

- Recognition and representation of prominent speech sounds ("L" for elephant).
- Rudimentary or skeleton writing: Some phonetic elements are represented, e.g. "GBSA" for Geburtstag (birthday).
- Phonetic-articulatory strategy: When discovering the alphabetic principle children develop the rule: "Spell as you speak", and start with an analysis of their articulatory cues, often affected by local accents. Children may omit sounds within clusters, or may detect extra segments not symbolized in print. Similar phenomena have been

observed by Ehri (1984) with spellings as "FEREND" for "friend" and "BALAOSIS" for "blouses".

- Phonemic strategy with first use of orthographic patterns: At this phase children begin to segment phonemically. Experience with conventional spellings helps children to learn which phones to ignore (Ehri, 1984). Mainly under the influence of print children develop the phonemic classification system and detect also inconsistencies between the sounds and orthographic patterns of words. In their spellings they now begin to use orthographic regularities.

The problem with German and English orthography is that correct phonemic segmentation alone does not guarantee correct spelling. In a study by Löffler (personal communication), German children who were able to correctly segment the word "Elefant" phonemically produced 106 variants of this word by assigning incorrect graphemes to the phonemes (e.g. Älefant, Ellefant, Elefannt, Ehlefant, Elevant, Ellefant). These examples demonstrate that the main difficulty in spelling is not phonemic analysis but the complexity of phoneme-grapheme correspondences.

Element 4 Learning the phoneme-grapheme-correspondence rules and principles of orthography

Competence models of orthography include two dimensions: *phonographic abilities* (phoneme analysis and assigning of graphemes) and *grammatical* operations, including word and sentence levels (Löffler and Meyer-Schepers, 2005). In German orthography, about 40 phonemes (including 16 vowels and 3 diphthongs) are represented by 85 graphemes, each consisting of one, two, or three letters. So the phoneme-grapheme-correspondence rules are complex. Additionally, the principles of German orthography reflect phonemic, orthographic, morphemic, and grammatical information.

Children acquire the insights outlined above only gradually. Observations of children (Dehn, 1987) as well as case studies (Scheerer-Neumann, 2001) and our pilot longitudinal study (Valtin *et al.*, 1986/1994; 1989; 1997) demonstrate the existence of a developmental sequence (see Table 21.1), which is the result of an interaction between the child's emerging insights, the structure of orthography and the teaching method. Only at stage 3 and 4 is phonemic awareness relevant.

Table 21.1 Developmental model of reading and spelling

Level	Skills and insights	Reading	Spelling
1	Imitation of behaviour	Pretend reading	Scribbling
2	Knowledge of single letters in a figurative sense, but no insight into the relationship between letters and sounds	"Naive-holistic" reading. Children guess at words, orienting themselves to context and figurative cues	Logographic strategy: drawing arbitrary sequences of letters or letterlike forms, ("pseudo-words")
3	Beginning insight into the function of letters. Knowledge of some letters/sounds	Beginning alphabetic strategy (phonetic cue reading)	Rudimentary or skeleton writings

Level	Skills and insights	Reading	Spelling
4	Insight into the alphabetic principle, ability to segment words into speech sounds and phonemes	Sounding-out strategy (reading letter by letter), sometimes without understanding	Phonetic-articulatory strategy (I spell as I speak)
5	Knowledge and use of orthographic patterns	Alphabetic reading with use of chunks	Phonemic strategy with first use of orthographic patterns
6	Automatized processes	Automatized word recognition	Correct spelling

Phonological training as preparation for learning to read and write?

In Germany there are many large-scale and smaller studies investigating the transfer effects of a phonological training in kindergarten to later reading and spelling development. Not all studies have shown effects from such phonological training (Rothe, 2008; Wolf *et al.*, 2010) or even from training of PA combined with letter training (Hartmann, 2002). Marx *et al.* (2005) reported that the preventive effects of training existed for decoding only (which is in line with the interpretation given above) and not to reading comprehension. Roos and Schöler (2007) reported effects only for girls, not for boys. Other studies that compared different approaches in kindergarten did not succeed in demonstrating that isolated phonological training had an advantage over more comprehensive methods where children were confronted with a book-rich environment and had many opportunities to gather experiences with written language (Lenel, 2005; Rackwitz, 2008; Franzkowiak, 2008).

I have argued (Valtin, 2003), along with other experts in first grade reading instruction (e.g. Bosch, 1937) that an isolated training of letters and sounds outside the context of reading and writing does not lead children to grasp the *function* of letters and sounds (let alone phonemes).

I wish, therefore, to examine how Schneider *et al.* (2000) proceeded in their training study. Twelve letters were chosen because of their frequency in written texts (A, E, M, I, O, R, U, S, L, B, T, N). Each letter was introduced in the context of a sound story, e.g. "a" (like in f**a**ther) with a child visiting a dentist (!) and saying "/aaa/". Children had to buzz like a bee ("zzz") for the letter "S". This so-called "interjection" method is a variety of the synthetic approaches to teaching reading that are no longer in use in German schools. Seventy years ago, these methods were criticized by Bosch (1937). He observed that children who had learned to associate letters with natural sounds when reading a word like "in" muttered: "Eeee cries the rooster, mmm mumbles the bear". Children of low intelligence, in particular, were unable to "forget" the associations they had learned earlier. Bosch's main argument against all sorts of synthetic approaches is that children learn meaningless units (letters) and have difficulty in grasping the *function* of letters in words. These synthetic methods have been abandoned in primary schools in Germany, since at least the 1980s. For many years now the so-called "analytic-synthetic method" has been prescribed in most of the German states (Valtin, 2003). It starts with meaningful words and each word is analyzed into its graphemic and phonemic elements so that children grasp the function of letters and the alphabetic code (Valtin, 2003). Also children are encouraged to invent spellings and to learn phonetic analysis, and to experience the communicative function of writing. Newer studies show that these instructional methods also lead to phonemic awareness (Kirschhock, 2004; Marx and Weber, 2006). This seems to be a rather trivial insight because the alphabetic principle consists in the representation of phonemes by graphemes. Even if children start with "deficits" in phonological tasks, teachers are able to compensate for these (Brügelmann, 2005; Kirschhock, 2004; Rackwitz, 2008). If the synthetic approach (teaching isolated letters in combination with natural sounds) was abandoned in first grade for good reasons more than 30 years ago, why should we use this questionable approach in kindergarten? It is of interest that in the Schneider *et al.* intervention study (2000) some kindergarten teachers eventually refused to participate in the letter-sound training.

Another negative example of a phonological training task stems from the multimedia games of the "Würzburger Trainingsprogramm" (available online at http://www. phonologische-bewusstheit.de). In the part "Funny stories" twelve sentences are orally presented (e.g. "Ohrwurm Olli organisiert originelle Opern") and children are told that all the words begin with the same sound. Unfortunately the authors of this task confuse letters and phonemes – and thus ignore the fact that the letter "O" in these words represents two different phonemes: a long vowel and a short vowel. From an educational point of view these kinds of tasks produce a cognitive confusion for children who may well hear the difference in the vowel sounds but are told that they have to hear the same sound. It is also doubtful whether children understand the complicated vocabulary of foreign loan words and thus the meaning of this sentence. This may be especially true for children at risk of failing to learn to read successfully: The majority of these children are from low socio-cultural backgrounds and their home language is frequently not German (Valtin *et al.*, 2010). Furthermore, preschool children are not familiar with the concept of word as it is used in this task.

The relevance of preschool education for the foundation of literacy

In Germany there is a strong correlation between success in school and pupils' social background, with a high proportion of pupils failing in school coming from lower sociocultural and migrant backgrounds. Educational policy aims at improving both family literacy (Hornberg and Valtin, 2011) and the quality of early childhood education and care. As the international study *PIRLS* demonstrates, children who have spent at least two years in kindergarten have an advantage in reading and mathematic in grade 4 over children with less or no participation in kindergarten (Bos *et al.*, 2007).

Competence in the German language is the key to learning to read and spell, and therefore children need a comprehensive programme to develop their oral language before entering school. Instead, however, of learning meaningless elements of written language such as letter-sound-associations in didactically questionable formats, the time in kindergarten should be used for a comprehensive approach, with the aim of broadening children's vocabulary and grammatical knowledge as well as their communicative abilities. Kindergarten teachers should use or provide situations where children can learn and experience different functions of language: in social play and role play, in conflict situations, and for problem solving. The ability to shift the attention from content to form may be fostered in language games, using rhymes, tongue-twisters, and poems. Kindergarten teachers should provide a literacy environment where children learn and engage in communicative functions of reading and writing with the aim of developing curiosity and motivation to learn to read and write in school. Reading aloud books, telling stories, presenting picture books, using writing in communicative contexts (e.g. the teacher writes down words or sentences from the child's dictation) – these are all well-known methods.

Conclusions: is phonemic awareness causally important in reading and spelling?

The vague concept of PA and also the differentiation into a broad and a narrow sense need to be embedded into a psycholinguistic theory dealing with the development of language awareness and with literacy acquisition, as developed last century in Germany (Andresen, 1985) and in international research (Downing and Valtin, 1984). A necessary prerequisite for learning an alphabetic script is the ability to objectify language (Bosch, 1937) and to focus the attention on the formal structure of speech. In order to perform this shift from content to form, the child needs to have achieved a certain degree of cognitive decentration in the Piagetian sense (Lundberg, 1982; Watson, 1984). It is not justified to subsume segmentation of utterances into words as an aspect of PA in a broad sense. Insights into the concept of words as linguistic units and the conscious manipulations of phonemes are print-specific knowledge, gradually acquired in the course of learning to read and spell.

Phonemic awareness may be seen as an indicator of children's insight into the structuring of the flow of speech upon which our alphabetic script is based. Phonemic synthesis is an essential *component* of the recoding process (which is only one aspect of the word-decoding sub-skill). Phonemic analysis is likewise an essential component of the *spell-as-you-speak* strategy in spelling. Both components refer to stage 4 of the developmental model, but they are only necessary and not sufficient components when later stages of written language acquisition are considered. For example, for reading comprehension, the knowledge of orthographic structures is needed as well as vocabulary knowledge and various reading strategies. In spelling children have to master difficult orthographic rules. However, for further development in reading and spelling, it is essential that all children gain mastery in these components, be it by the analytic-synthetic teaching method, where these tasks are embedded (Valtin, 2003) or by specific training in addition to normal classroom reading instruction (Kirschhock, 2004).

I would like to close with some speculative remarks. Why has phonological awareness received so much attention? In the United States and in England the whole-language approach is very popular. Children learn to read and write, being confronted with whole words, sentences or texts. No explicit training of phonics is given. In such a context those children who are aware of phonemes and are able to segment and blend speech sounds have a clear advantage and are better able to grasp the alphabetic code than children without these insights. The importance of explicit and structured phonics instruction – embedded in the reading of words and in meaningful reading tasks so that children gain cognitive clarity – has been recognized only lately, together with the insight that not the method but the individual learner with his/her learning needs must be the focus of attention.

References

Andresen, H. (1985). *Schriftspracherwerb und die Entstehung von Sprachbewußtheit*. Opladen: Westdeutscher Verlag.

——(2005). *Vom Sprechen zum Schreiben*. Stuttgart: Klett.

Bos, W., Hornberg, S., Arnold, K.-H., Faust, G., Fried, L., Lankes, E.-M., Schwippert, K. and Valtin, R. (2007) (Eds.), *IGLU 2006. Lesekompetenzen von Grundschulkindern in Deutschland im internationalen Vergleich*. Münster: Waxmann.

Bosch, B. (1937). *Grundlagen des Erstleseunterrichts*. Korrigierte Reprintausgabe. Frankfurt: Arbeitskreis Grundschule 1984.

Bryant, P. (1993). Phonological aspects of learning to read. In R. Beard (Ed.), *Teaching Literacy Balancing Perspectives*. London: Hodder & Stoughton.

Brügelmann, H. (2005). Das Prognoserisiko von Risikoprognosen – eine Chance für „Risikokinder"? In B. Hofmann and A. Sasse (Eds.), *Übergänge. Kinder und Schrift zwischen Kindergarten und Schule* (pp. 146–172). Berlin: Deutsche Gesellschaft für Lesen und Schreiben.

Clark, E. V. (1978). Awareness of language: some evidence from what children say and do. In A. Sinclair, R. J. Jarvella and W. J. M. Levelt (Eds.), *The Child's Conception of Language*. New York, N.Y.: Springer.

Dehn, M. (1987). Wie Kinder Schriftsprache erlernen. In I. Naegele and R. Valtin (Eds.), *Rechtschreibunterricht in den Klassen 1–6* (pp. 28–37). Frankfurt: Arbeitskreis Grundschule (3rd edn 1994).

Downing, J. (1984). Task awareness in the development of reading skill. In J. Downing and R. Valtin (Eds.), *Language Awareness and Learning to Read* (pp. 27–56). New York: Springer.

Downing, J. and Valtin R. (1984). (Eds.). *Language Awareness and Learning to Read*. New York: Springer.

Ehri, L. C. (1984). How orthography alters spoken language competencies in children learning to read and spell. In J. Downing and R. Valtin (Eds.), *Language Awareness and Learning to Read* (pp. 119–148). New York: Springer.

Ferreiro, E. (1978). What is written in a written sentence: a developmental answer. *Journal of Education, 160*, 25–39.

Franzkowiak, T. (2008). Vom BLISS-Symbol zur alphabetischen Schrift. Entwicklung und Erprobung eines vorschulischen Förderansatzes zur Prävention von Lernschwierigkeiten beim Schriftspracherwerb. Dissertation im FB 2. Universität: Siegen. http://dokumentix.ub.uni-siegen.de/opus/volltexte/2008/351/index.html [Accessed 3 February 2010].

Hakes, D. T. (1980). *The Development of Metalinguistic Abilities in Children*. New York, N.Y.: Springer.

Hartmann, E. (2002). *Möglichkeiten und Grenzen einer präventiven Intervention zur phonologischen Bewusstheit von lautsprachgestörten Kindergartenkindern*. Fribourg: Sprachimpuls.

Homer, B. D. and Olson, D. R. (1999). The role of literacy in children's concept of word. *Written Language and Literacy, 2*, 113–140.

Hornberg, S. and Valtin, R. (2011) (Eds.), *Mehrsprachigkeit: Chance oder Hürde beim Schriftspracherwerb?* Berlin: Deutsche Gesellschaft für Lesen und Schreiben

Januschek, F., Paprotté, W. and Rohde, W. (1979). The growth of metalinguistic knowlegde in children. In M. Van de Vlede and W. Vandeweghe (Eds.), *Sprachstruktur, Individuum und Gesellschaft. Akten des 13. Linguistischen Kolloquiums, Gent 1978*. Vol. 1. Tübingen: Niemeyer, 243–254.

Kirschhock, E.-M. (2004). *Entwicklung schriftsprachlicher Kompetenzen im Anfangsunterricht*. Bad Heilbrunn: Klinkhardt.

Landerl, K. and Wimmer, H. (1994). Phonologische Bewusstheit als Prädiktor für Lese-Rechtschreibfertigkeiten in der Grundschule. *Zeitschrift für Pädagogische Psychologie, 8*, 153–164.

Lenel, A. (2005). *Schrifterwerb vor der Schule. Eine entwicklungspsychologische Längsschnittstudie*. Weinheim: Beltz PVU.

Löffler, I. and Meyer-Schepers, U. (2005). Orthographische Kompetenzen: Ergebnisse qualitativer Fehleranalysen, insbesondere bei schwachen Rechtschreibern. In W. Bos, E.-M. Lankes, M. Prenzel, K. Schwippert, R. Valtin and G. Walther (Eds.), *IGLU. Vertiefende Analysen zu Leseverständnis, Rahmenbedingungen und Zusatzstudien.* (pp. 81–108). Münster: Waxmann.

Lundberg, I. (1982). *Longitudinal Studies of Reading and its Difficulties in Sweden.* Unpublished manuscript. University of Umea, Sweden

Lundberg, I., Wall, S. and Oloffson, A. (1980). Reading and spelling skills in the first school years predicted from phonemic awareness skills in kindergarten. *Scandinavian Journal of Psychology, 21,* 159–173.

Marx, P. and Weber, J. (2006). Vorschulische Vorhersage von Lese- und Rechtschreibschwierigkeiten. Neue Befunde zur prognostischen Validität des Bielefelder Screenings (BISC). *Zeitschrift für Pädagogische Psychologie, 20,* 251–259.

Marx, P., Weber, J. and Schneider, W. (2005). Langfristige Auswirkungen einer Förderung der phonologischen Bewusstheit bei Kindern mit Defiziten in der Sprachentwicklung. *Die Sprachheilarbeit, 50*(6), 280–285.

Rackwitz, R.-P. (2008). Ist die phonologische Bewusstheit wirklich Voraussetzung für einen erfolgreichen Schriftspracherwerb? In *Erziehungswissenschaft und Bildungsforschung kontrovers* http://nbn-resolving.de/urn:nbn:de:bsz:752-opus-12 [Accessed 13 April 2011].

Roos, J. and Schöler, H. (2007). *Zur Wirkung des Trainings der phonologischen Bewusstheit im Vorschulalter auf den Schriftspracherwerb: Abschlussbericht des Projektes EVES* http://www.ph-heidelberg.de/wp/Schoeler/Datein/Abschlussbericht-Stadt-%20Heidelberg_Januar%202007.pdf. [Accessed 13 July 2011].

Rothe, E. (2008). Effekte vorschulischen und schulischen Trainings der phonologischen Bewusstheit auf den Schriftspracherwerb. *Wortspiegel, Fachzeitschrift von LOS, 1/2,* 3–5.

Scheerer-Neumann, G. (2001). Förderdiagnostik beim Lesenlernen. In I. M. Naegele and R. Valtin (Eds.), *LRS – Legasthenie in den Klassen 1–10. Handbuch der Lese-Rechtschreib-Schwierigkeiten. Band 2.* (pp. 70–86). Weinheim: Beltz.

Schneider, W., Roth, E. and Ennemoser, M. (2000). Training phonological skills and letter knowledge in children at risk for dyslexia: a comparison of three kindergarten intervention programs. *Journal of Educational Pychology, 92,* 284–295.

Wolf, K., Stanat, P. and Wendt, W. (2010). Evaluation der kompensatorischen Sprachförderung. Zweiter Zwischenbericht. http://www.isq-bb.de/uploads/media/ekos-bericht-2-endfassung.pdf [Accessed 13 April 2011]

Valtin, R. (1984a). The development of metalinguistic abilities in children learning to read and write. In J. Downing and R. Valtin (Eds.), *Language Awareness and Learning to Read* (pp. 207–226). New York: Springer.

——(1984b). Awareness of features and functions of language. In J. Downing and R. Valtin (Eds.), *Language Awareness and Learning to Read* (pp. 227–260). New York: Springer.

——(1989). Prediction of writing and reading achievement – some findings from a pilot study. In M. Brambring, F. Lösel and H. Skowronek (Eds.), *Children at Risk: Assessment, Longitudinal Research, and Intervention* (pp. 245–267). Berlin, New York: Walter de Gruyter.

——(1997). Strategies of spelling and reading of young children learning German orthography. In: C. K. Leong and M. Joshi (Eds.), *Cross-Language Studies of Learning to Read and Spell* (pp. 175–194). Series D: Behavioural and Social Sciences, Vol. 87, Dordrecht/Boston/London: Kluwer Academic Publishers.

——(2003). Methoden des basalen Lese- und Schreibunterrichts. In U. Bredel, H. Günther, P. Klotz, J. Ossner and G. Siebert-Ott (Eds.), *Didaktik der deutschen Sprache. Ein Handbuch.* Vol 2, (pp. 760–771). Paderborn: Schöningh.

Valtin, R., Bemmerer, A. and Nehring, G. (1986/1994). Kinder lernen schreiben und über Sprache nachzudenken – Eine empirische Untersuchung zur Entwicklung schriftsprachlicher Fähigkeiten. In R. Valtin and I. Naegele (Eds.), *„Schreiben ist wichtig!" Grundlagen und Beispiele für kommunikatives Schreiben(lernen)* 4th edn. (pp. 23–53). Frankfurt: Arbeitskreis Grundschule.

Valtin, R. and Hofmann, B. (2009). *Kompetenzmodelle der Orthographie. Empirische Befunde und förderdiagnostische Möglichkeiten*. Berlin: Deutsche Gesellschaft für Lesen und Schreiben.

Valtin, R., Hornberg, S., Voss, A., Kowoll, M. E. and Potthoff, B. (2010). Schülerinnen und Schüler mit Leseproblemen – eine ökosystemische Betrachtungsweise. In W. Bos, K. H. Arnold, S. Hornberg, G. Faust, L. Fried, E.-M. Lankes, K. Schwippert, I.Tarelli and R. Valtin (2010) (Eds.), *IGLU 2006 – die Grundschule auf dem Prüfstand* (pp. 43–90). Münster: Waxmann-Verlag.

Van Leent, H. (1983). Auditieve analyse en leren lezen. *Pegogische Studien, 60*, 13–27.

Watson, A. J. (1978). Cognitive development and units of print in early reading. In J. Downing and R. Valtin (Eds.). (1984). *Language Awareness and Learning to Read* (pp. 93–118). New York: Springer.

Part XI

What form should reading instruction in kindergarten and elementary school take?

To mark the end of the "great debate" we argue that reading instruction must make use of differentiated instruction which begins with effective assessment of cognitive entry skills such as alphabet knowledge, phonological awareness, and vocabulary ... It will not disadvantage children to receive a greater amount of phonics if they do not need it, but it will hurt children to miss out on the phonics instruction if they do need it.

Alison Arrow and William Tunmer

If explicit phonics is taught, the questions sometimes asked are: How much should be taught? At what levels of reading development should it be taught? These questions, however, should be secondary to the question, what is the purpose of such phonics?

Brian Thompson and Claire Fletcher-Flinn

Chapter 22

Contemporary reading acquisition theory

The conceptual basis for differentiated reading instruction

Alison W. Arrow and William E. Tunmer
Massey University

Reading instruction in the classroom has been at the mercy of the "Reading Wars" for much of the last century. This "great debate" has been focused on the best way to teach children how to read. The debate revolves around whether words should be broken down into component parts when teaching children to read them, usually known as phonics, or whether they should be left intact, which includes approaches such as "look-say", "whole-word", and more recently, "whole-language". One of the main reasons for the perversity of this debate is that this argument has focused on the right method, or approach, to teach children how to read. Liberman and Liberman (1990) argued that up to 75 percent of children will learn to read, regardless of the method of instruction. It cannot follow that children learn to read by way of the theory underpinning an approach to teaching reading, rather there must be something in what children bring to the task that enables them to learn to read regardless of approach. What is needed is knowledge of how children acquire reading skills, and the cognitive developmental processes needed for learning to read (Tunmer and Nicholson, 2011). We will argue that the most effective form of reading instruction starts with the reading-related knowledge, skills, and experiences that each child brings to the process of learning to read, and that attention needs to be focused on the specific literacy-related learning needs required by each child.

A framework for learning to read

Byrne (2005) provides a framework for considering a theory of learning to read that makes use of the differences in learners, and what they bring to the process of learning to read. The notion of *division of labor* assumes that any act of learning is a product of both the environment and of the learner. Regarding school learning, the environment differs in the amount of contribution by way of explicit, teacher-directed instruction provided for each act of learning. The learner also contributes, which is dependent on his or her known skills and strategies necessary for each act of learning. If a learner brings little known skills and strategies to the act of learning to read, then the environment must provide structured, explicit instruction. If a learner brings a great deal of known skills and strategies to the act of learning, then the environment can provide less explicit and structured instruction. In terms of real-world practice, if what the learner knows is already assessed, the instruction required can be readily identified.

This framework also requires a theory of learning to read that can be applied, so that what is required for each learning act – from the teacher and the learner – can be identified. Learning to read requires the child to learn a range of skills and strategies that are, in turn, dependent on a number of forms of knowledge and skills, or *cognitive entry skills*, that are acquired prior to conventional literacy learning (Tunmer and Nicholson, 2011). At school entry, the range of variability in students in cognitive entry skills is the first place in which individual differences in literacy learning become apparent (Tunmer *et al.*, 2003, 2006; Whitehurst and Lonigan, 2001). The cognitive entry skills identified by Tunmer and Nicholson include alphabet knowledge, primarily knowledge of the names of letters of the alphabet (Foulin, 2005); oral language, particularly children's vocabularies which are facilitated through talk in the home (Lonigan, 2007; Snow and Beals, 2006); phonological awareness, whereby children are aware of rhyming words and words that share the same onset (Arrow, 2009); print knowledge, such as directionality of print and the differences between letters and words (Justice *et al.*, 2002); and emergent writing, such as using letters in invented spelling (Richgels, 1995).

Phonological decoding and word recognition

Word recognition and decoding are taken as the goal of early reading instruction, enabling efficient reading comprehension as a result of the automaticity of word reading. As word reading becomes more efficient, more cognitive effort can be applied to the general comprehension of text (Pressley, 2006), as well as to the application of effective comprehension strategies and analysis of text. In support of this claim, Connelly *et al.* (2001) found that children who had been taught to read through phonics read slowly but more accurately than a group of non-phonics taught children. Additionally, they had greater comprehension, indicating that taught strategies for reading enabled words to be read accurately through using both explicit strategies and contextual cues which further enabled the comprehension of text. The relationship between reading comprehension and word recognition and decoding is also mediated by oral vocabulary knowledge. The depth and breadth of vocabulary contributes to reading comprehension (Tannenbaum *et al.*, 2006), while vocabulary also aids in decoding and word recognition (Tunmer and Chapman, 2011).

Vocabulary assists in decoding and word recognition indirectly through *set for variability*, which is the ability to generate the correct pronunciation of attempted approximations of spoken words (Venezky, 1999). Children learn to use their knowledge of spelling-to-sound relationships acquired through phonics instruction to produce approximate phonological representations, or partial decodings, for unknown words, especially those containing irregular, polyphonic (e.g. *ear* as in *bear* and *hear*), or orthographically complex spelling patterns. The phonological representations provide the basis for generating alternative pronunciations of target words until one is produced that matches a word in the child's lexical memory and makes sense in the context in which it appears. Additional spelling-sound relationships, especially context-sensitive patterns, can then be induced from the stored orthographic representations of words that have been correctly identified (Tunmer and Chapman, 2011). Arguments against phonics instruction that are based on the notion that English language is too irregular are not justified when it can provide the initial mechanism for induced sublexical relationships.

Phonological decoding is the cognitive ability to translate letters and letter patterns into phonological forms (Tunmer and Arrow, in press). It requires that the reader have a stored set of sublexical relations (Thompson and Fletcher-Flinn, 2007; Thompson *et al.*, 2004) to enable the implicit decoding to occur. Most sublexical relationships are induced from the current body of stored sight-words in the readers' lexicon. The relationships typically apply conditionally according to the position of the grapheme-phoneme correspondence in a word. A reader who has had little experience in reading the grapheme *th* at the ends of words, but has had a great deal of experience with the grapheme at the beginnings of words, such as *the, this*, will be able to read nonwords that start with *th*, but be less able to accurately read nonwords that end with *th* (Thompson *et al.*, 1996).

Learning to read starts with cognitive entry skills

The application of phonological decoding is dependent on the development of the necessary cognitive entry skills (Tunmer and Nicholson, 2011). Thus, children who begin school with relatively high levels of literacy skills and knowledge will be able to apply phonological decoding almost from the beginning. Juel and Minden-Cupp (2000) found that children with high levels needed less phonics, and did well in learning environments that were less structured with more reading and writing of text. Such children, therefore, are *learner-dependent* in the division of labour continuum suggested by Byrne (2005). They bring knowledge and skills to the learning act of learning to read.

Many of these cognitive entry skills are those that facilitate the alphabetic principle to enable children to explicitly decode print, such as phonological awareness of onset-rime, at least, and alphabetic knowledge. Many of these children also begin school with the ability to recognise some words through paired, selective, association. Gough (1993), for example, found that children would quickly learn to associate a salient feature with a spoken word. He taught children to read a number of words using flashcards. One printed word was on a card that also had a large fingerprint in the corner. When tested after the flashcard intervention, the children were unable to read the sight-word that had been matched with the fingerprint, but did say the matched word when provided with a different word that was presented with the fingerprint. Ehri and Wilce (1985) found that once children were beginning readers, the salient features of printed words were those that represented phonetic elements of the words they were learning. More recently, Share and Gur (1999) found that children who were not yet receiving conventional literacy instruction attended to the initial letters in the printed names of their friends. These studies all provide evidence of beginning readers pairing of salient features with the spoken word, whether the salient feature is a fingerprint or a letter.

Beyond this use of salient features of print words, beginning readers must become consciously aware that speech maps onto print through graphemes and phonemes, called *the alphabetic principle*. Byrne and Fielding-Barnsley (1989, 1990) found that pre-readers can be taught to discriminate between the words FAT and BAT, but are unable to generalise this knowledge to discriminating between FUN and BUN. The pre-readers were unable to induce the relationship between /f/ and the letter "F" or /b/ and "B", and are focused on the meaning rather than individual print items (Byrne and Fielding-Barnsley, 1989). Similarly, research on environmental print indicates that children are attending to meaning and salient features of environmental print, such as logos, rather than attending to print features (Blair and Savage, 2006), although children did attend to print features in their own names. This indicates that the induction of sublexical relationships is environment-dependent. Some children may begin taking advantage of sublexical connections, if they have sufficient cognitive entry skills, particularly alphabet knowledge and phonological awareness.

Once children begin to read only making use of paired-association cues, they begin to run into problems. The first problem is that they will reach saturation point; new words can no longer be learned as there are fewer and fewer salient cues that can be attended to. The second problem is that, unlike the use of phonological decoding induction, the application of paired-association for remembering new words does not allow the reader to work out new words; it is not generative. Seymour and Elder (1986), for example, found that although Scottish Grade 1 children knew a large number of sight words, they had great difficulty reading untaught words. Similarly, Connelly *et al.* (2001) found that non-phonics taught children were unable to read nonwords as well as phonics taught children, even though their reading ages were matched. Being able to recognise some words through selective paired-association does not enable the beginning reader to induce new words, when the storage mechanism in place is to recall the words by means of partial cues.

As part of this inefficient method of storing words, and the process of remembering them, children are more likely to make use of contextual guessing for unknown words, as the skills for phonological decoding are not in place. In a study that supports this claim, Tunmer *et al.* (2003) asked children what strategies they used when they came to an unknown word. Responses were classified as either text-based strategies (e.g. "guess," "read it over again," "have a look at the picture," "miss it out and go to the end and go back and guess a word that makes sense") or word-based strategies (e.g. "sound it out," "hear all the letters," "think of the sounds"). The children with the poorer outcomes (a reading age nine months below the chronological age) after two years of school had the greater number of children who said they used text-based strategies compared to those who said they used word based strategies (50.0 percent and 20.8 percent respectively). In contrast, the children with the greater abilities (a reading age two months above chronological reading age) after two years at school had fewer children who used text-based strategies, and more who used word-based strategies (29.1 percent and 61.8 percent respectively). The process of learning to read must be environment-dependent at this point to enable the learning to become learner-dependent. Learners who do not have an explicit awareness of the alphabetic principle will need explicit instruction, that is, environment dependent instruction, to enable them to acquire this explicit understanding of the alphabetic principle. One of the key ways to do this is to provide phonics instruction.

The role of phonics

Scarborough and Brady (2002) define phonics as "an approach to, or type of, reading instruction that is intended to promote the discovery of the alphabetic principle, the correspondences between phonemes and graphemes, and phonological decoding" (p. 326). Scarborough and Brady's definition highlights the purpose of phonics – to teach the alphabetic principle to enable children to learn to read words in a learner dependent fashion, through induced phonological decoding. Instruction that provides the learner with a firm grasp of the alphabetic principle allows children to come to the explicit realisation that speech maps onto print, and that looking more closely at the spellings of words enables them to find out how this mapping occurs (Snow and Juel, 2005).

Phonics instruction also provides a "kick-start" to phonological decoding to children who come to reading with little cognitive entry skills, and rely mostly on picture cues, partial visual cues, and sentence-context cues, with little interaction between the graphemes of printed words, and phonemes of spoken words (Tunmer and Greaney, 2010). For these children the word recognition skills remain weak because they are unable to develop a rich network of sublexical connections between the orthographic and phonological representations in lexical memory. The use of inefficient word recognition processes make the reading of text capacity draining, with less capacity for comprehending the text being read.

Venezky (1999) argues that phonics instruction provides the learner with the processes by which they can make estimates of the phonological representation of an unknown word. Explicit phonics instruction enables the learner to explicitly produce approximate phonological representations (i.e. partial decodings) of unknown printed words (Tunmer and Arrow, in press). These partial decodings are then used to generate alternative pronunciations of the words until one is found that matches a word in lexical memory and fits the context as well (Tunmer and Chapman, 2011). The size of the reader's vocabulary is a critical component of the generation of alternative pronunciations. If a reader does not have the attempted word in their vocabulary they will not be able to come up with it as an alternative, and will be unable to induce the patterns from that word. As the spelling-sound relationships are correctly identified they are stored with the accurate orthographic representation of words which provide the data base from which further letter-sound patterns can be induced. Once children reach this point of development, reading instruction takes the form of reading practice, where the learner contributes the most to decoding, and explicit instruction is not needed for word recognition and decoding. De Jong and Share (2007) found, for example, that Dutch third graders were able to recall the orthographic patterns of nonwords after between two and six presentations in text.

There are a number of approaches to teaching phonics instruction which vary along the dimensions of explicitness, systematicity, analysis, or synthesis practices, and the level of focus (Brady, 2011). A range of research studies have found that explicit, systematic phonics at the grapheme-phoneme level makes a greater contribution to students' reading growth than other forms of phonics instruction (that differ, for example, across the dimensions of level of focus and the level of systematicity), and other, non-phonics, forms of instruction such as whole language (Adams, 1990; Brady, 2011; de Graaff et al., 2009; Ehri et al., 2001; Hattie, 2009; Snow and Juel, 2005).

Large scale meta-analyses, such as the one conducted by the National Reading Panel (Ehri, et al., 2001; National Reading Panel, 2000), have indicated that systematic, explicit, phonics instruction is best with readers who are considered at-risk than those who are normally achieving. This effect is most evident when at-risk Grade 1 students (Cohen's $d = 0.74$) are compared to normally achieving Grade 1 students ($d = 0.48$). In this younger age group the effect of instruction is also stronger for synthetic phonics ($d = 0.58$) where letter-sounds are taught and then blended, than for instruction where instruction included larger phonic units such as rimes or word families ($d = 0.46$), or mixed forms of instruction ($d = 0.27$).

Systematic phonics instruction that teaches letter-sound or grapheme-phoneme correspondences is a more effective approach to early reading instruction for students who do not have all cognitive entry skills available to them at school entry. The contrast to these approaches are whole-language approaches that have, at their core, an emphasis on the "natural learning" of reading, which is based on the assumption that learning to read is similar to learning to speak (Goodman and Goodman, 1979; Smith, 1999). The approaches advocate that the teaching of reading requires little or no direct instruction in the code. To do so would detract from the main purpose of reading; that is, to take meaning from what is read. The reading of unfamiliar words is thought to make use of multiple cues in text; text meaning, sentence structure, visual, and phonological (Clay and Cazden, 1990; see also Stuart *et al.*, 2008). Children are expected to use these cues from the start of learning to read, and to build the use of multiple cues into a "*self-improving system*" (Clay and Cazden, 1990, p. 207). That is, the more children read, the better they are at making use of the four cues. However, the cues are not all equal, according to this view, as text meaning is paramount, and teachers should not dwell on the detail of print (Clay and Cazden, 1990). In short, such approaches assume that learning to read is largely *learner-dependent*, and that very little contribution from the environment, by way of explicit instruction, is required.

Goodman (1970) claims that during reading children sample text and make predictions based on textual cues, such as meaning and syntax. In this way, the reader makes guesses at what the unfamiliar word will be. If the guess fits the context, it will be enough, as textual accuracy is not necessary (Goodman and Goodman, 1990). Contextual guessing, however, does not appear to contribute to a *self-improving system*, as research indicates that, although context aids younger, weaker readers, it does not assist older, better readers (Nicholson, 1991). That is, the younger, weaker, readers continue to use context in reading text to compensate for their poor decoding skills, but older, better, readers are using word-level decoding strategies.

Focusing on the specific literacy needs of each child

We have argued that better readers are able to make use of implicit phonological decoding, and are acquiring through self-teaching an increasing number of sight words as they do so. Weaker readers use strategies for decoding that include making guesses based on context; the use of such a strategy does not enable them to make inductions about print in any accurate way. Lower levels of vocabulary in the weaker readers are also implicated as they are less able to make use of semantic knowledge to arrive at correct identifications of words based on close approximations to the target word. Consistent with this view, Connor *et al.* (2004) found that children with the lowest vocabulary scores at the start of the school year achieved greater decoding growth in classrooms with greater teacher-managed explicit decoding than those with less explicit instruction. Children with higher vocabulary scores made greater improvements in classrooms with greater amounts of child-managed implicit instruction. Connor *et al.* did find, however, that it was changing instruction that made a difference. When classrooms increased the amount of child-managed implicit instruction over the school year, and decreased teacher-managed explicit instruction, children with the low vocabulary scores continued to make good growth in decoding. These results indicate that children who have lower vocabularies achieve better when instruction is explicit and environment-dependent, but as they make decoding progress their learning can become more learner-dependent through increasing induction of sublexical relationships.

Children who arrive at school with fewer cognitive entry skills are dependent on the environment to provide instruction that makes explicit the connections between print and speech. Environment-dependent learners require greater, higher-dose, systematic phonics instruction to enable them to close the gap between them and the children who started school with greater skills. Tunmer *et al.* (2003) found that when they provided children with instruction that was designed to develop awareness of sounds in words and to make use of letter-sounds in decoding the at-risk group of children – who had significantly less cognitive entry skills at school entry – were not performing significantly different from the normally achieving children after six months, and there continued to be no differences on reading measures after two years of school. In contrast, children who arrive at school with more cognitive entry skills are more learner-dependent. Such children may require less explicit instruction in letter-sound instruction beyond the initial instruction directing them to the alphabetic principle. These children already have the cognitive skills that enable them to begin the induction of sublexical relationships, and to identify unknown words through phonological decoding.

Concluding remarks

To summarise, beginning reading instruction does not work as a one-size-fits all approach of either phonics or whole-language. To mark the end of the "great debate" we argue that reading instruction must make use of differentiated instruction which begins with effective assessment of cognitive entry skills such as alphabet knowledge, phonological awareness, and vocabulary. Assessment of these skills enables the selection of instructional approaches and content that varies along the division of labour; child-managed, implicit instruction for learner-dependent children (those with more cognitive entry skills), and more teacher-managed, explicit instruction for environment-dependent children (those with less cognitive entry skills). The implications for educational practice are that reading instruction requires early assessment of the critical cognitive entry skills, and that beginning literacy instruction should be differentiated to meet the learning needs of the children. It will not disadvantage children to receive a greater amount of phonics if they do not need it, but it will hurt children to miss out on the phonics instruction if they do need it (see, for example, Tunmer *et al.*, 2003).

References

Adams, M. J. (1990). *Beginning to Read: Thinking and Learning about Print.* Cambridge, MA: MIT Press.

Arrow, A. W. (2009). Emergent literacy skills in New Zealand kindergarten children: implications for teaching and learning in ECE settings. *He Kupu, 2,* 57–69.

Blair, R. and Savage, R. (2006). Name writing but not environmental print recognition is related to letter-sound knowledge and phonological awareness in pre-readers. *Reading & Writing, 19,* 991–1016.

Brady, S. (2011). Efficacy of phonics teaching for reading outcomes: indications from post NRP research. In S. Brady, D. Braze and C. A. Fowler (Eds.), *Explaining Individual Differences in Reading: Theory and Evidence* (pp. 69–96). New York, NY: Psychology Press.

Byrne, B. (2005). Theories of learning to read. In M. J. Snowling and C. Hulme (Eds.), *The Science of Reading: A Handbook* (pp. 104–119). Malden, MA: Blackwell.

Byrne, B. and Fielding-Barnsley, R. (1989). Phonemic awareness and letter knowledge in the child's acquisition of the alphabetic principle. *Journal of Educational Psychology, 81,* 313–321.

——(1990). Acquiring the alphabetic principle: a case for teaching recognition of phonemic identity. *Journal of Educational Psychology, 82,* 805–812.

Clay, M. M. and Cazden, C. B. (1990). A Vygotskian interpretation of Reading Recovery. In L. C. Moll (Ed.), *Vygotsky and Education: Instructional Implications and Applications of Sociohistorical Psychology* (pp. 206–222). Cambridge, UK: Cambridge University Press.

Connelly, V., Johnston, R. and Thompson, G. B. (2001). The effect of phonics instruction on the reading comprehension of beginning readers. *Reading & Writing, 14,* 423–457.

Connor, C. M., Morrison, F. J. and Katch, L. E. (2004). Beyond the reading wars: exploring the effect of child-instruction interactions on growth in early reading. *Scientific Studies of Reading* (Vol. 8, pp. 305–336): Lawrence Erlbaum Associates.

de Graaff, S., Bosman, A. M. T., Hasselman, F. and Verhoeven, L. (2009). Benefits of systematic phonics instruction. *Scientific Studies of Reading, 13,* 318–333.

de Jong, P. F. and Share, D. L. (2007). Orthographic learning during oral and silent reading. *Scientific Studies of Reading, 11,* 55–71.

Ehri, L. C. and Wilce, L. S. (1985). Movement into reading: is the first stage of printed word learning visual or phonetic? *Reading Research Quarterly, 20,* 163–177.

Ehri, L. C., Nunes, S. R., Stahl, S. A. and Willows, D. M. (2001). Systematic phonics instruction helps students learn to read: evidence from the National Reading Panel's meta-analysis. *Review of Educational Research, 71,* 393–447.

Foulin, J. N. (2005). Why is letter-name knowledge such a good predictor of learning to read? *Reading & Writing, 18,* 129–155.

Goodman, K. S. (1970). Reading: a psycholinguistic guessing game. In H. Singer and R. B. Ruddell (Eds.), *Theoretical Models and Processes of Reading* (Vol. 1, pp. 259–272). Newark, DE: International Reading Association.

Goodman, K. S. and Goodman, Y. M. (1979). Learning to read is natural. In L. B. Resnick and P. A. Weaver (Eds.), *Theory and Practice of Early Reading* (Vol. 1, pp. 137–154). Hillsdale, NJ: Erlbaum.

——(1990). Vygotsky in a whole-language perspective. In L. C. Moll (Ed.), *Vygotsky and Education: Instructional Implications and Applications of Sociohistorical Psychology* (pp. 223–250). Cambridge, UK: Cambridge University Press.

Gough, P. B. (1993). The beginning of decoding. *Reading & Writing, 5,* 181–192.

Hattie, J. (2009). *Visible Learning: A Synthesis of Over 800 Meta-analyses Relating to Achievment.* London: Routledge.

Juel, C. and Minden-Cupp, C. (2000). Learning to read words: linguistic units and instructional strategies. *Reading Research Quarterly, 35,* 458–504.

Justice, L. M., Weber, S. E., Ezell, H. K. and Bakeman, R. (2002). A sequential analysis of children's responsiveness to parental print references during shared book-reading interactions. *American Journal of Speech Language Pathology, 11,* 30–40.

Liberman, I. Y. and Liberman, A. M. (1990). Whole language vs. code emphasis: underlying assumptions and their implications for reading instruction. *Annals of Dyslexia, 40,* 51–76.

Lonigan, C. J. (2007). Vocabulary development and the development of phonological awareness skills in preschool children. In R. K. Wagner, A. Muse and K. R. Tannenbaum (Eds.), *Vocabulary Acquisition: Implications for Reading Comprehension* (pp. 15–31). New York, NY: Guilford Press.

National Reading Panel (2000). *Teaching Children to Read: An Evidence-based Assessment of the Scientific Research Literature on Reading and Its Implications for Reading Instruction Reports of the Subgroups* (No. BBB35631). Bethesda, MD: National Institute of Child Health and Human Development.

Nicholson, T. (1991). Do children read words better in context or in lists? A classic study revisited. *Journal of Educational Psychology, 83,* 444–450.

Pressley, M. (2006). *Reading Instruction that works: The Case for Balanced Literacy Instruction* (3rd edn). New York: Guilford Press.

Richgels, D. J. (1995). Invented spelling ability and printed word learning in kindergarten. *Reading Research Quarterly, 30,* 96–109.

Scarborough, H. S. and Brady, S. A. (2002). Toward a common terminology for talking about speech and reading: A glossary of the "phon" words and some related terms. *Journal of Literacy Research, 34*, 299–336.

Seymour, P. H. and Elder, L. (1986). Beginning reading without phonology. *Cognitive Neuropsychology, 3*, 1–36.

Share, D. L. and Gur, T. (1999). How reading begins: a study of preschoolers' print identification strategies. *Cognition and Instruction, 17*, 177–213.

Smith, F. (1999). Why systematic phonics and phonemic awareness instruction consistute an educational hazard. *Language Arts, 77*, 150–155.

Snow, C. E. and Beals, D. E. (2006). Mealtime talk that supports literacy development. *New Directions for Child and Adolescent Development, 111*, 51–66.

Snow, C. E. and Juel, C. (2005). Teaching children to read: what do we know about how to do it? In M. J. Snowling and C. Hulme (Eds.), *The Science of Reading: A Handbook* (pp. 501–520). Malden, MA: Blackwell.

Stuart, M., Stainthorp, R. and Snowling, M. J. (2008). Literacy as a complex activity: deconstructing the simple view of reading. *Literacy, 42*, 59–66.

Tannenbaum, K. R., Torgesen, J. K. and Wagner, R. K. (2006). Relationships between word knowledge and reading comprehension in third-grade children. *Scientific Studies of Reading, 10*, 381–398.

Thompson, G. B. and Fletcher-Flinn, C. M. (2007). Lexicalised implicit learning in reading acquisition: the knowledge sources theory. In C. M. Fletcher-Flinn and G. M. Haberman (Eds.), *Cognition and language: Perspectives from New Zealand*. Bowen Hills, QLD: Australian Academic Press.

Thompson, G. B., Cottrell, D. S. and Fletcher-Flinn, C. M. (1996). Sublexical orthographic-phonological relations early in the acquisition of reading: the knowledge sources account. *Journal of Experimental Child Psychology, 62*, 190–222.

Thompson, G. B., McKay, M. F. and Fletcher-Flinn, C. M. (2004). New theory for understanding reading and reading disability. *Australian Journal of Learning Disabilities, 9*, 1–5.

Tunmer, W. E. and Arrow, A. W. (in press). Reading: phonics instruction. In J. Hattie and E. Anderman (Eds.), *Handbook of Student Achievement*. London: Routledge.

Tunmer, W. E. and Chapman, J. W. (2011). Does set for variability mediate the influence of vocabulary knowledge on the development of word recognition skills? *Scientific Studies of Reading*. doi: 10.1080/10888438.2010.542527

Tunmer, W. E. and Greaney, K. T. (2010). Defining dyslexia. *Journal of Learning Disabilities, 43*, 229–243.

Tunmer, W. E. and Nicholson, T. (2011). The development and teaching of word recognition skill. In M. L. Kamil, P. D. Pearson and P. P. Afflerbach (Eds.), *Handbook of Reading Research* (Vol. 4, pp. 405–431). New York: Routledge.

Tunmer, W. E., Chapman, J. W. and Prochnow, J. E. (2003). Preventing negative Matthew effects in at-risk readers: a retrospective study. In B. R. Foorman (Ed.), *Ingredients of Effective Preventions and Interventions for Children at Risk of Reading Difficulties or with Identified Reading Disabilities* (pp. 121–163). Baltimore, MD: York Press.

——(2006). Literate cultural capital at school entry predicts later reading achievement: a seven year longitudinal study. *New Zealand Journal of Educational Studies, 41*, 183–204.

Venezky, R. L. (1999). *The American Way of Spelling: The Structure and Origins of American English Orthography*. New York: Guilford Press.

Whitehurst, G. J. and Lonigan, C. J. (2001). Emergent literacy: development from prereaders to readers. In S. B. Neuman and D. K. Dickinson (Eds.), *Handbook of early literacy research* (pp. 11–29). New York: Guilford Press.

Chapter 23

Toward better teaching
Revising the fundamentals of learning to read

G. Brian Thompson
Victoria University of Wellington

Claire M. Fletcher-Flinn
University of Otago

Conflict over the "better" approach for teaching beginner readers persists. Two approaches that are often contrasted are those that include *explicit phonics* and those that are *text-centred*, without explicit phonics. In explicit phonics approaches, the common sound for each alphabet letter is taught, and how to use these to attempt pronunciation of unfamiliar words. The successive sounds of the letters making up a word can be uttered, and then blended together to attempt the pronunciation of an unfamiliar word (as in "kuh" – "o" – "tah" for "cot"). This taught "sounding-out" procedure is called *explicit phonological recoding*, the purpose of which is to assist the children in reading texts without the teacher providing the word responses. The children may also be taught *phoneme awareness*, which is the skill to reflect on and break up spoken words into their smallest segments of sound. This skill is claimed to be necessary in explicit phonological recoding.

In the text-centred approach, story texts are the basis of nearly all instruction. A distinctive feature of the New Zealand text-centred approach has been the teacher's careful matching of many story reading books at finely graded levels to the individual child's reading level. At the earliest level, teacher guidance included showing the children how to listen to sounds in words that correspond to letters of the words, especially the initial letter (e.g. the matching initial sound of print words *big*, *bus*, *book*). At all levels there has been guidance for obtaining meaning, using context cues, and letter cues of the words (including initial letter or letter cluster, rhyme analogies, spelling patterns). Most of this guidance arises during text reading. For these teaching approaches there are published observations from classrooms (Connelly *et al.*, 2001; Thompson *et al.*, 2008) and descriptions (Fletcher-Flinn and Thompson, 2010).

We introduce some theories for what they offer as fundamentals of learning to read, particularly for beginner readers, and describe facts that test these claimed fundamentals in the contrasting teaching approaches.

Fundamentals in theories of learning to read

The influential theory of Ehri (1999, 2005) postulates learning to read as a linear process of advancement through several successive developmental phases. Critical factors in progress are the child's explicit knowledge of the sounds of the alphabet letters (1999, pp. 90–92), and phoneme awareness (1999, p. 87). Sufficient levels of such knowledge must be acquired before beginner readers can learn to read familiar words from their letter-based word storage. Share's (1995) developmental theory is similar in its emphasis on these explicit skills for beginners, although there is not a sequence of developmental phases. In beginners, phonological recoding is explicit, and not influenced by the child's letter-based storage of familiar words (pp. 160, 197). Nevertheless, such influence of "lexicalised" phonological recoding is postulated beyond the beginner levels of progress (pp. 155–156).

There have been a few attempts to apply a computational model of adult word reading (Plaut et al., 1996) in simulations of trends in mean word reading accuracy for successive school grade levels. These were not successful unless major theoretical modifications of the model were made, including those assumed to represent the effects of teaching with explicit phonics (Hutzler et al., 2004; Powell et al., 2006).

The child's initial learning of letter-based storage of (English) words during the first few months of reading instruction was the subject of theory construction and computational modelling by Cassidy (1992). The model involved the letter components of words stored in a partial ordering with reference to word boundaries. Depending upon the level of learning of each print word, this storage may include only some letters of the word, and the extent of letter ordering stored may range from none to complete left-to-right ordering. Using the words of initial-level school reading books for input into the model, Cassidy conducted a series of detailed simulations. As well as simulating accuracy of word identification, these included results consistent with the extensive data (Stuart and Coltheart, 1988) on the word substitution errors in children's word reading attempts. However, significant new data on the acquisition of letter-based storage of words has recently appeared (Thompson, 2009).

In a current theoretical article, Grainger and Ziegler (2011) put forward a theoretical proposal for modelling orthographic (letter-based) processing, not only for skilled adult readers, but also for children's acquisition of word reading. This is a proposal for two routes for orthographic processing, one a self-generated and implicit coarse-grained route, of the type modelled by Dufau et al. (2010), or Glotin et al. (2010), and the other a fine-grained route for orthographic processing that provides more precise information on the order of letters within the word. As in the "self-teaching hypothesis" of Share's (1995) theory, this orthographic information about a word is acquired by the child in unassisted reading only if the child has been successful in phonological recoding of the word. For the beginner, this is nonlexical phonological recoding. It is "nonlexical" in so far as the letter-sound relations the child uses in the recoding are acquired as taught items of knowledge (phonic sounds), and do not have their source in the child's experience of print words with the associated sounds and meanings of the words.

Fundamentals that do not fit the facts

Does this "self-teaching hypothesis" fit the facts? The hypothesis would predict, for the child's unassisted reading, a significant positive association between phonological recoding accuracy for unfamiliar words and the child's success in acquiring orthographic storage of these words (Share, 2008). Although several studies (Bowey and Muller, 2005; Cunningham, 2006; Share, 2004) claimed to test this association, only that by Nation et al. (2007) provided this for young children for a word-by-word association, which is that predicted by the theory. In this study of 7- and 8-year-olds learning to read, the association was not statistically significant, which is contrary to the predicted result. As a claimed fundamental the self-teaching hypothesis has a poor fit to the facts.

Nonlexical phonological recoding

Accuracy in oral reading of pseudowords (e.g. *lom*, *teep*, *yaik*) is a commonly accepted measure indicating the reader's proficiency in nonlexical phonological recoding. (It was used as the measure of phonological recoding in the studies on the self-teaching hypothesis.) But how do we know whether accuracy of pseudoword reading is a valid indicator of phonological recoding that is nonlexical? The phonological recoding procedure expected for beginner readers in the theories of Ehri (1999, pp. 90–92) and Share (1995, pp. 160, 197) is the taught explicit phonological recoding that involves the child responding to letters of the pseudoword with pronunciation of the taught phonic sounds ("sounding out"), with the intention of assembling them into a word-like pronunciation. However, among the hundreds of published studies using pseudoword reading measures from beginner readers, it is rare to find any which include observations that determine whether such sounding out ever in fact takes place. There seems to be only one study (Thompson *et al.*, 2008, Study 1) that does this, and at the same time cross-classifies the incidence of that sounding out with accuracy of the outcomes for reading the pseudowords. Results were obtained for samples of children receiving from nil to high levels of school instruction in explicit phonics. These results are shown in Table 23.1 for 110 6-year-olds who were making slower than average (but within normal range) progress in learning to read English. The samples were matched on normative scores for text word reading accuracy (and comprehension of the texts did not vary between samples). The two samples with nil explicit phonics received text-centered instruction in which story texts were the basis of nearly all teaching of reading, as previously described.

The results for pseudoword reading (Table 23.1) show that only a minority of the accurate responses followed from the sounding of letters that was taught to the samples with high and moderate levels of explicit phonics. Accuracy without such sounding was predominant. In fact, for this the mean levels of the samples did not differ significantly in

Table 23.1 Mean percentage accuracy for reading isolated pseudowords and words of text by level of explicit phonics instruction in samples of 6-year-olds of below average reading progress

Measure	Level of explicit phonics instruction			
	High (Scotland)	Moderate (Australia)	Nil A (Australia)	Nil B (New Zealand)
Reading isolated pseudowords				
Accurate following sounding beyond first phoneme	20	10	3	2
Accurate without this sounding	43	43	32	33
Total accuracy	63	53	35	35
Reading words of text				
Accurate following sounding beyond first phoneme	4	2	1	1
Accurate without this sounding	73	77	83	79
Total accuracy	77	79	84	80

a standard statistical test (Thompson *et al.*, 2008, Study 1). Although all samples of children were at an early reading level, it is possible that a portion of this accuracy for the high and moderate samples had been achieved by what had previously been explicit phonological recoding but had since been internalised and hence no longer observable. Nonetheless, such cannot be of significance for the two nil phonics samples, as they had almost no explicit recoding to internalise. Although phonological recoding, in the explicit form, was rare among the children of the two nil samples, they had reached the same level of text word reading accuracy as the two phonics samples. This fact does not fit with the proposition that such phonological recoding is fundamental to the beginner's reading. It is also worth noting that in reading words of text, explicit phonological recoding makes only a very small contribution to word accuracy among those instructed in the procedure (Table 23.1).

Explicit knowledge of sounds for letters

It is accepted as a fundamental, without question by most researchers, that the child's explicit knowledge of the most common sound for each of the alphabet letters is required for the acquisition of reading. But does this fit the facts? Results on accuracy in responding with the sound, and the name, for each of the isolated 26 (lower-case) letters are available (Table 23.2) for three English-speaking age groups from New Zealand who, as 5- and 6-year-olds, had been taught to read by a text-centred approach without either explicit phonics or teaching of explicit letter sounds (Fletcher-Flinn and Thompson, 2004; Thompson *et al.*, 2009; Thompson *et al.*, 1999). All three samples had high accuracy in giving names for the 26 letters but much lower accuracy with sounds for the letters. All had normal attainment in reading. These facts do not fit the claimed fundamental proposition that the child's explicit knowledge of the sounds for letters is required for learning to read.

Moreover, despite their deficiency in explicit knowledge of the letter sounds, both the 11-year-old and the university samples responded well to a large set of pseudowords designed for administration to university students. The 11-year-olds scored 63 percent accuracy (Fletcher-Flinn and Thompson, 2004), while the university students, for whom the pseudowords were designed, scored 74 percent accuracy (Andrews and Scarratt, 1998, Experiment 2). A large subset of the same pseudowords was administered to the university sample reported in Table 23.2 who as children were taught without explicit phonics. They scored at the same overall accuracy level as a matched university sample who, as 5- and 6-year-olds, had been taught with a high level of explicit phonics (Thompson *et al.*, 2009). Phonological recoding of whatever form that is involved in accurate reading of pseudowords was available to these 11-year-olds and adults, despite their low levels of explicit letter-sound knowledge.

To summarise, we have cited five research publications that yield facts that do not fit one or other of these claimed fundamentals of learning to read. Four of these have included results from New Zealand with samples taught by the text-centred approach without explicit phonics. In response to these findings, a comment we have received is that with such an anomalous teaching approach in New Zealand only anomalous results can be expected. As "anomalous facts," they fail to form a valid test of the fundamentals. This argument is troublesome. To rule out results from children who are taught to read without this phonics teaching is to rule out a valid test of predictions from the fundamentals, putting them beyond empirical test.

Table 23.2 Mean percentage of correct sounds and names given for the 26 isolated alphabet letters among normal New Zealand samples taught reading without explicit phonics or letter sounds

Measure	Sample		
	5-year-olds[1]	*11-year-olds*	*University students*
Sounds	59	65	75
Names	83	92	100

[1] Mean age 5 years 9 months. Children commence first year of school instruction at approximately their fifth birthday.

Revised fundamentals: the Knowledge Sources theory

The Knowledge Sources theory of reading acquisition is an alternative but can it account for these facts that do not fit the claimed fundamentals? In this chapter the focus is on what the theory says about phonological recoding. For other aspects of the theory the reader should refer to Thompson and Fletcher-Flinn (2006). In the theory there are two potential forms of phonological recoding for beginner readers: lexicalised phonological recoding and nonlexical phonological recoding.

Lexicalised phonological recoding

When children have acquired (usually with teacher assistance) (i) correct reading responses to a few words, and (ii) attention to the relationship in which letters of words often match sound units of the spoken word, they implicitly learn patterns of letter–sound relations from their lexical storage (reading vocabulary). This is the stored knowledge of letters of print words, along with the knowledge of meanings of the words and of the aural (sound) information of the words. Letter-based storage of words is learnt from the beginning, as the child becomes familiar enough with component letters of a few print words to distinguish between them, and distinguish them from other words not known. Without conscious intention or awareness that it is taking place, the children acquire patterns of letter–sound relations that are common across subsets of their reading vocabularies. For example, they implicitly learn from their lexical knowledge of *see, so, said* ... a common letter–sound relation for initial position *s* of words; and from knowledge of *got, cat, went* ... a common letter–sound relation for final-position *t* of words. These letter–sound patterns that are derived from the child's lexical experience are used in the child's lexicalised phonological recoding, which facilitates a reading response to new or unfamiliar print words (see Figure 23.1). The patterns of letter–sound relations that the child learns will depend on what the child's current reading vocabulary can yield. (The learning and processing of the multiplicity of letter–sound relations across the child's reading vocabulary is mainly implicit, as conscious explicit processing is too limited in the quantity and speed with which such information can be handled.)

As words become familiar, they become part of the updated accumulated reading vocabulary of the child, which in turn enables implicit learning that updates patterns of letter–sound relations common to subsets of this reading vocabulary (see Figure 23.1). This implicit letter–sound knowledge enables lexicalised phonological recoding, which,

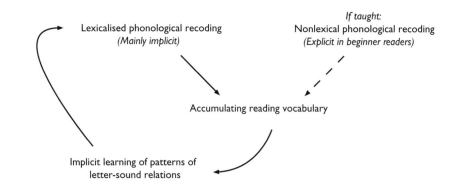

Lexicalised phonological recoding
(Mainly implicit)

If taught:
Nonlexical phonological recoding
(Explicit in beginner readers)

Accumulating reading vocabulary

Implicit learning of patterns of
letter-sound relations

Figure 23.1 Two types of phonological recoding according to the Knowledge Sources theory for both beginner and more advanced readers.

in turn, facilitates learning of further new reading vocabulary. This is a continuing recursive relationship between the child's accumulating reading vocabulary, and the updated patterns of letter-sound relations, which are used in the child's lexicalised phonological recoding that facilitates the acquisition of further reading vocabulary. In the theory, lexicalised phonological recoding is normally involved in learning to read from the beginner level and beyond, whether or not teaching of explicit phonics is provided.

Nonlexical phonological recoding

As already described, in this taught procedure the child responds to letters of a word with taught letter-sound correspondences, with the intention of assembling them into a word pronunciation. In beginner readers this procedure is usually explicit but later in development it becomes internalised and hence not directly observable. In the theory, nonlexical phonological recoding is optional for learning to read. Children may learn to read effectively without it.

Lexicalised phonological recoding cannot be directly observed at any reading level. It can only be inferred from factual tests of the implications of its postulated characteristics. This, however, is not a reason to dismiss it in favour of that which is directly observable. To do so may neglect a powerful aspect of learning to read. There is such in the recursive relationship between the child's accumulating reading vocabulary and implicit learning of letter-sound relations derived from that vocabulary for use in lexicalised phonological recoding (see Figure 23.1). Nonlexical phonological recoding is not involved in any such recursive relationship, only a one-way relationship. Nonlexical phonological recoding can only facilitate, and is not facilitated by, the child's gains in reading vocabulary.

Does the theory fit the facts?

Are there published facts that fit the postulated lexicalised phonological recoding of the Knowledge Sources theory? If only the nonlexical form of phonological recoding existed in beginner readers, then their learning of reading vocabulary would have no influence on their phonological recoding. However, they would show an influence from reading vocabulary if they possessed the lexicalised form of phonological recoding. We tested these predictions in a series of studies (Thompson *et al.*, 1996) conducted with 5- and 6-year-old children receiving text-centred teaching without instruction on explicit phonics or the sound for each alphabet letter. With information on the frequency of letter-sound relations available from the vocabulary of their reading books, the researchers successfully predicted, from lexicalised phonological recoding of Knowledge Sources theory, which letter-sound relations the children would know within pseudowords. No such prediction is possible if the children were exclusively using the nonlexical form of phonological recoding in responding to the pseudowords. In the final study of this series, the successful prediction was made on the basis of new reading vocabulary taught to the children over several weeks.

The limited explicit knowledge of sounds for isolated letters that was achieved by the 5-year-olds without teaching of letter sounds, as reported in Table 23.2, was partly accounted for (Thompson *et al.*, 1999) by the children's derivation of the sound from the initial pronunciation element of the name of the letter, which was known to them. For the letter sounds that did not provide this relation to the letter name, the researchers successfully predicted the children's level of accuracy for letter sounds from the frequency of the letter sound as the initial component of words in their reading books. This prediction indicates that the children, in their responses to the isolated letters, were making use of knowledge from their implicit learning of letter-sound relations in their accumulating reading vocabulary. (The converse direction of influence, from the children's knowledge of the sound of the isolated letter to the frequency of the words in their reading books, is implausible. The plausible common influence of a third factor, the children's knowledge of spelling of the letter sounds was tested by the researchers and not supported.)

Lexicalised phonological recoding also explains results for 6-year-olds' successes in responding with sounds for digraphs (e.g. *ee*, *ea*) that they had not been taught (Stuart *et al.*, 1999). It also explains 6-year-olds' successes (Treiman *et al.*, 2006) in responding to context-dependent letter-sound relations in pseudowords in the same way as in print words they had experienced (e.g. pseudoword *prook* with *oo* pronounced as in "look"), instead of responding with the taught phonic sound (e.g. with *oo* pronounced as in "zoo").

Moreover, between samples of beginning readers of equal word reading accuracy, there was large variation in pseudoword reading accuracy that was associated positively with the extent of their instruction in explicit phonics (Thompson and Johnston, 2000; Thompson *et al.*, 2008, Study 1). The use of implicit lexicalised phonological recoding, by children without explicit phonics, accounts for the findings that they reached the same level of word reading accuracy with low levels of pseudoword reading accuracy. Implicit lexicalised phonological recoding also accounts for the otherwise inexplicable results from an intensive study of a precocious reader (Fletcher-Flinn and Thompson, 2000, 2004), and a case study of a child with a divergent pattern of reading development (Fletcher-Flinn and Thompson, 2007).

Toward better teaching

The comparison of the outcomes of a current teaching programme with a selected modification (e.g. the introduction of more explicit phonics instruction) has been an influential type of research (Ehri *et al.*, 2001; National Reading Panel, 2000). However, this type of research is of more limited value than is often apparent. While the modification may be superior in some outcomes (e.g. accuracy in reading isolated words and pseudowords), both teaching programmes may be unsatisfactory in another aspect of learning (e.g. speed and accuracy of text reading), which has not been considered. To avoid troublesome exclusions, alternative theories should be considered and the facts to test them ought to come from a wide range of theoretically relevant teaching traditions and approaches (see also Ramus, 2004, and Thompson and Johnston, 1993.)

Does Knowledge Sources theory offer anything that can guide parents and teachers toward a better way for children learning to read? In Knowledge Sources theory there is the proposition that there are two types of phonological recoding that can function from near the beginning of learning to read. This explains why children in the text-centred approach, despite almost no use of explicit phonological recoding in text reading (see Table 23.1), do learn to read (Thompson *et al.*, 2008); and are superior in the speed of text reading to those receiving a high level of explicit phonics instruction (Table 23.3). The implicit lexicalised form of phonological recoding would provide these beginners with the necessary phonological recoding while having almost no use of the explicit form.

The Nil phonics samples who reached the same level of word reading accuracy as the phonics samples read 46 percent more words of text (for both total and accurate words) in the same period of time as those with a high level of phonics instruction (Table 23.3). The source of their faster reading speed was considered to be the greater classroom time available to them for text reading as a consequence of the zero time devoted to explicit phonics instruction. Children who use lexicalised phonological recoding exclusively may require more exposures to a word to reach the same level of word accuracy as those children using some explicit phonological recoding. This is not a disadvantage for those using lexicalised phonological recoding if they receive the greater text reading practice that enables their faster reading speed, which in turn provides the extra word exposures within the same unit of time. It is noted that in the frequently cited review of research on the effects of explicit phonics instruction (Ehri *et al.*, 2001; National Reading Panel, 2000), no study of beginner readers was reported that had outcome measures of both speed and accuracy for reading text.

According to Knowledge Sources theory, from the beginner level a fundamental that is underlying all implicit learning of letter-sound patterns is the child's letter-based storage of words. As a fundamental, it is appropriate for the teacher to strongly support the child's learning of this letter-based storage. Leaving the support until the child has learnt most or all of the explicit sounds for the alphabet letters is not appropriate. It also follows that in assessing the child's learning progress reading vocabulary is of critical importance. In contrast, as shown here, the child's pseudoword reading is clearly misleading as a generally applicable measure of learning progress. This is explained by the two types of phonological recoding postulated in the Knowledge Sources theory of learning to read, and the effects on them of different types of teaching.

It follows from the Knowledge Sources theory that lexicalised phonological recoding can take place as an implicit process without teaching the child the nonlexical phonological recoding procedures of explicit phonics. If explicit phonics is taught, the questions sometimes asked are: How much should be taught? At what levels of reading development should it be taught? These questions, however, should be secondary to the question, what is the purpose of such phonics? From the point of view of Knowledge Sources theory, explicit phonics may have a significant purpose if it effectively supplements or replaces teacher guidance on listening to sounds corresponding to letters in words that we have

Table 23.3 Mean speed of reading text by level of explicit phonics instruction in samples of 6-year-olds of below average reading progress

Level of explicit phonics instruction of sample	Mean number of words read accurately per minute[1]	
Nil (A and B)	26.8	
Moderate		22.4
High	18.4	18.4
Difference between levels	+ 8.4	+ 4.0
Percentage advantage above the High level for		
Nil (A and B)	46%	
Moderate		22%

[1] The mean word reading accuracy across the samples was 80 percent of the total words read. Accuracy did not vary significantly between samples.

described in the text-centred approach (Connelly *et al.*, 2001; Thompson, 2002; Thompson *et al.*, 2008). This purpose would be assisting the child to attend to a critical source of knowledge for learning to read in the initial weeks of instruction. From this source the child learns the implicit principle that letters of words have quasi-regular relations with sound units within the spoken form of the word. Such learning from explicit phonics would not involve instruction in a large set of explicit letter–sound relationships. It would involve learning the implicit principle from exemplars provided by the teacher, from which children as soon as practicable can acquire their own large set of instances of the principle. According to the Knowledge Sources theory, they can do this by implicit learning of patterns of letter–sound relations from their reading vocabulary, rather than continuing to receive more taught explicit letter–sound relationships.

If, as children's beginning reading develops, they continue using explicit nonlexical phonological recoding, the question arises, how will that facilitate, or interfere, with the optimal development of lexicalised phonological recoding? For example, beginners taught explicit phonics will learn to pronounce the "short sound" for the letter *e*, which will directly assist their nonlexical phonological recoding of words such as *went* but not those such as *be*. However, implicit learning of patterns of letter–sound relations from across the whole of the beginner's small reading vocabulary would have a different effect. If this small reading vocabulary included the words *bed*, *get*, *red*, *he*, *me*, *we*, then the child could implicitly form two distinct patterns of sounds that relate to the letter *e*, depending upon the position of that letter in the word. The children's implicitly learnt letter–sound patterns would be attuned to their current reading vocabularies in a way not possible with a prescribed set of taught explicit sounds for letters. For teachers choosing to use explicit phonics, more evidence on these aspects is urgently needed to avoid either teaching, or interfering with, what the child has already learnt implicitly (and therefore may not be directly observable by the teacher). Some initial results are available from beginner readers (Fletcher-Flinn *et al.*, 2004).

Other important results for optimal development of reading come from adults, in a comparison of long-lasting effects from the type of teaching of reading received in their initial school years. These results were from the first study of this kind (Thompson *et al.*, 2009). There was a bias toward regular pronunciations of new words, which is inherent in explicit phonics teaching. This bias remained strong into adulthood. For example, new words such as *thild* were pronounced with the *i* as in "it". In contrast, with text-centred teaching in their initial school years, adults made more use of lexicalised phonological recoding. For example, among such adults, *thild* was pronounced to match the pattern as in "child", "wild", "mild". Similar effects also occurred for low frequency real words. Consistent with the Knowledge Sources theory, these adults were making use of a wider range of stored information about letter-sound relations from their reading vocabularies than those who had initially learnt to read with explicit phonics.

References

Andrews, S. and Scarratt, D. R. (1998). Rule and analogy mechanisms in reading nonwords: Hough dou peapel rede gnew wirds? *Journal of Experimental Psychology: Human Perception & Performance, 24,* 1052–1086.

Bowey, J. A. and Muller, D. (2005). Phonological recoding and rapid orthographic learning in third-graders' silent reading: a critical test of the self-teaching hypothesis. *Journal of Experimental Child Psychology, 92,* 203–219.

Cassidy, S. (1992). *A Computer Model of Reading Development*. Unpublished doctoral dissertation, Victoria University of Wellington.

Connelly, V., Johnston, R. and Thompson, G. B. (2001). The effect of phonics instruction on the reading comprehension of beginning readers. *Reading and Writing, 14,* 423–457.

Cunningham, A. E. (2006). Accounting for children's orthographic learning while reading text: do children self-teach? *Journal of Experimental Child Psychology, 95,* 56–77.

Dufau, S., Lété, B., Touzet, C., Glotin, H., Ziegler, J. C. and Grainger, J. (2010). A developmental perspective on visual word recognition: new evidence and a self-organising model. *European Journal of Cognitive Psychology, 22,* 669–694.

Ehri, L. C. (1999). Phases of development in learning to read words. In J. Oakhill and R. Beard (Eds.), *Reading Development and the Teaching of Reading* (pp. 79–108). Oxford, UK: Blackwell.

——(2005). Development of sight word reading: phases and findings. In M. J. Snowling and C. Hulme (Eds.), *The Science of Reading: A Handbook* (pp. 135–154). Oxford, UK: Blackwell.

Ehri, L. C., Nunes, S. R., Stahl, S. A. and Willows, D. M. (2001). Systematic phonics instruction helps students learn to read: evidence from the National Reading Panel's meta-analysis. *Review of Educational Research, 71,* 393–447.

Fletcher-Flinn, C. M., Shankweiler, D. and Frost, S. J. (2004). Coordination of reading and spelling in early literacy development: an examination of the discrepancy hypothesis. *Reading and Writing, 17,* 617–644.

Fletcher-Flinn, C. M. and Thompson, G. B. (2000). Learning to read with underdeveloped phonemic awareness but lexicalized recoding: a case study of a three-year-old. *Cognition, 74,* 177–208.

——(2004). A mechanism of implicit lexicalized phonological recoding used concurrently with underdeveloped explicit letter-sound skills in both precocious and normal reading development. *Cognition, 90,* 303–335.

——(2007). Dissociation between deficits in explicit procedures and implicit processes in the visual-spatial and the phonological systems during reading acquisition. *Cognitive Neuropsychology, 24,* 471–484.

——(2010). Learning to read: teaching approaches and theories of word recognition. In J. Low and P. Jose (Eds.) *Lifespan Development: New Zealand Perspectives* (2nd edn). North Shore, New Zealand: Pearson.

Glotin, H., Warnier, P., Dandurand, F., Dufau, S., Lété, B., Touzet, C., Ziegler, J. C. and Grainger, J. (2010). An Adaptive Resonance Theory account of the implicit learning of orthographic word forms. *Journal of Physiology – Paris, 104,* 19–26.

Grainger, J. and Ziegler, J. C. (2011). A dual-route approach to orthographic processing. *Frontiers in Psychology, 2,* 1–13.

Hutzler, F., Ziegler, J. C., Perry, C., Wimmer, H. and Zorzi, M. (2004). Do current connectionist learning models account for reading development in different languages? *Cognition*, *91*, 273–296.

Nation, K., Angell, P. and Castles, A. (2007). Orthographic learning via self-teaching in children learning to read English: effects of exposure, durability, and context. *Journal of Experimental Child Psychology*, *96*, 71–84.

National Reading Panel (2000). *Teaching children to read*. Reports of the subgroups. Washington, DC: National Institute of Child Health and Human Development.

Plaut, D. C., McClelland, J. L., Seidenberg, M. S. and Patterson, K. (1996). Understanding normal and impaired word reading: computational principles in quasi-regular domains. *Psychological Review*, *103*, 56–115.

Powell, D., Plaut, D. and Funnell, E. (2006). Does the PMSP connectionist model of single word reading learn to read in the same way as a child? *Journal of Research in Reading*, *29*, 299–250.

Ramus, F. (2004). The neural basis of reading acquisition. In M. S. Gazzaniga (Ed.), *The Cognitive Neurosciences* (3rd edn, pp. 815–824). Cambridge, MA: MIT Press.

Share, D. L. (1995). Phonological recoding and self-teaching: *sine qua non* of reading acquisition. *Cognition*, *55*, 151–218.

——(2004). Orthographic learning at a glance: on the time course and developmental onset of self-teaching. *Journal of Experimental Child Psychology*, *87*, 267–298.

——(2008). Orthographic learning, phonological recoding, and self-teaching. In R. V. Kail (Ed.), *Advances in Child Development and Behaviour*, *Vol. 36* (pp. 31–82). Amsterdam, The Netherlands: Elsevier.

Stuart, M. and Coltheart, M. (1988). Does reading develop in a sequence of stages? *Cognition*, *30*, 139–181.

Stuart, M., Masterson, J., Dixon, M. and Quinlan, P. (1999). In T. Nunes (Ed.), *Learning to Read: An Integrated View from Research and Practice* (pp. 105–120). Dordrecht, The Netherlands: Kluwer.

Thompson, G. B. (2002). Teaching and the phonics debate: what can we learn? *New Zealand Annual Review of Education*, *11*, 161–178.

——(2009). The long learning route to abstract letter units. *Cognitive Neuropsychology*, *26*, 50–69.

Thompson, G. B., Connelly, V., Fletcher-Flinn, C. M. and Hodson, S. J. (2009). The nature of skilled adult reading varies with type of instruction in childhood. *Memory & Cognition*, *37*, 223–234.

Thompson, G. B. and Fletcher-Flinn, C. M. (2006). Lexicalised implicit learning in reading acquisition: The Knowledge Sources theory. In C. M. Fletcher-Flinn and G. M. Haberman (Eds.), *Cognition and language: Perspectives from New Zealand* (pp. 141–156). Bowen Hills, Queensland: Australian Academic Press.

Thompson, G. B., Fletcher-Flinn, C. M. and Cottrell, D. S. (1999). Learning correspondences between letters and phonemes without explicit instruction. *Applied Psycholinguistics*, *20*, 21–50.

Thompson, G. B. and Johnston, R. S. (1993). The effects of type of instruction on processes of reading acquisition. In G. B. Thompson, W. E. Tunmer and T. Nicholson (Eds.), *Reading acquisition processes* (pp. 74–90). Clevedon, UK: Multilingual Matters.

——(2000). Are nonword and other phonological deficits indicative of a failed reading process? *Reading and Writing*, *12*, 63–97.

Thompson, G. B., Cottrell, D. S. and Fletcher-Flinn, C. M. (1996). Sublexical orthographic-phonological relations early in the acquisition of reading: the Knowledge Sources account. *Journal of Experimental Child Psychology*, *62*, 190–222.

Thompson, G. B., McKay, M. F., Fletcher-Flinn, C. M., Connelly, V., Kaa, R. T. and Ewing, J. (2008). Do children who acquire word reading without explicit phonics employ compensatory learning? Issues of phonological recoding, lexical orthography, and fluency. *Reading and Writing*, *21*, 505–537.

Treiman, R., Kessler, B., Zevin, J. D., Bick, S. and Davis, M. (2006). Influence of consonantal context on the reading of vowels: evidence from children. *Journal of Experimental Child Psychology*, *93*, 1–24.

Part XII

What is the pedagogical value of homework?

We assert that homework is important for students' success in school, but the design and quality of homework must be improved to help more students succeed.

Joyce Epstein and Frances Van Voorhis

The belief that homework from a young age leads to sound patterns of working that will help them in later years persists despite the limited research evidence on this issue.

Julian Elliott and Peter Tymms

Chapter 24

The changing debate

From assigning homework to designing homework

Joyce L. Epstein and Frances L. Van Voorhis

Center on School, Family, and Community Partnerships,
Johns Hopkins University

Are you buying a car? A home? A computer? Friends will ask: *Have you done your homework?* Homework helps you make good decisions and smart investments. Do you want to play the guitar or shoot basketball hoops? To do anything well, you have to practice. A lot. You must do your homework.

Worldwide, there is pressure to improve education, increase the number of graduates from high school, and ensure that students will succeed in the competitive international economy (Duncan, 2011). Policy leaders know that the most successful students in every nation will be those who attend school regularly, take school seriously, and do their homework.

Reflecting earlier studies, a recent report noted that about 80 percent of students, teachers, and parents said that homework was important or very important for increasing learning and success in school (Markow *et al.*, 2007). The same survey reported that up to one third of students, teachers, and parents rated the quality of some homework assignments as fair, poor, uninteresting, or just busy work. These contrasting realities frame our argument in the debate on homework.

Overview of this chapter

This chapter joins the debate *for* homework. We assert that homework is important for students' success in school, but the design and quality of homework must be improved to help more students succeed. First, we summarize research on the results of homework for student learning. Then, we discuss how the quality of homework can be improved and report results of an intervention to improve the homework process. Finally, we draw conclusions to redirect the debate from the settled topic of homework versus none to more interesting questions of the effects of high-quality homework on the number of students who do their homework and succeed in school.

Homework and the homework process

Most agree that homework is an assignment from a teacher for a student to complete during non-instructional time (Bembenutty, 2011; Cooper, 1989). Behind the simple definition, however, is a complex set of variables that defines the homework process. This includes the work that teachers do to develop, assign, and follow up on homework; work that students do on common tasks, creative activities, and special projects; and work that parents do to support and guide their children. Homework affects all partners. Students' investments in homework affect their attitudes, behaviors, and achievements. Teachers' decisions about assignments affect their next lessons and tests. Parents' efforts affect their understanding of the curriculum, attitudes about school and homework, and their interactions with their children.

The full model of the homework process includes over 100 variables concerning the characteristics and conditions of schools, teachers, parents, and students (Epstein, 2011, pp. 277–280). To date, most research on homework and resulting policies and practices have focused on *time*. The model shows that there is a broad agenda for new research on the nature and effects of homework – an agenda that could produce results that inform policy and improve school practice.

Research on time on homework and achievement

Researchers have used two main designs – cross-sectional and longitudinal – to understand the homework process. There are lessons to learn from both kinds of studies.

Cross-sectional studies on homework reveal provocative patterns of null and negative correlations of time on homework and student achievement in the elementary grades (Epstein, 1990) and at the high school level (Kitsantas *et al.*, 2011). Two factors contribute to *negative* correlations of time on homework and student achievement at one time point. First, students who learn more slowly or deliberately take more time to complete their work. Second, some parents are informed about and active in monitoring their children's homework completion and keep struggling students on task, especially in the elementary grades.

Other factors may produce a *null* relationship of time on homework and student achievement. For example, some advanced students take extra time on homework to perfect their products, whereas others speed through to completion. If advanced and remedial students in a study sample vary in how quickly or slowly they complete their assignments, there may be no significant association of homework time and level of achievement at that time point.

The null and negative correlations are not causal patterns. That is, spending more minutes on homework does not cause lower achievement. Rather, the cross-sectional correlations tell us that students vary in the time they need to complete their homework and provide useful clues about other important variables (e.g. family resources and support, student attitudes and beliefs of their own math abilities) that are associated with homework completion.

School factors also affect students' time on homework. In the younger grades, all students in a class may be given a common assignment (e.g. complete 10 math examples or write 10 sentences for spelling or vocabulary words). Students who think or write at slow and fast speeds will differ in time spent on the same assignment. In the older grades and in advanced or honors classes, teachers expect students to do more homework (Warkentien *et al.*, 2008), but not all students take the time they need to do the work.

On most assignments and at all grade levels, then, some students take longer than others to complete an assignment, due to starting skills, distractions at home, quests for perfection, parental prodding, or other conditions or constraints. In cross-sectional studies, variations in time on homework for students within and across ability levels result in a provocative mix of positive, null, and negative associations of time on homework and students' achievement. Although informative, cross-sectional studies point to the need for longitudinal studies to identify the effects of homework on student achievement over time.

Longitudinal studies explore the effects of homework on achievement and on other attitudes and behaviors, after accounting for students' initial achievement. Countless studies and meta-analyses of these studies conducted over thirty years confirm that, regardless of starting ability, students who did their homework increased their scores on reading and math achievement tests and report card grades, compared to similar students who did no homework or spent less time on homework (Cooper, 1989, 2007; Gorges and Elliott, 1995; Keith *et al.*, 2004; Zimmerman and Kitsantas, 2005).

Some have reported different effects by grade level, with larger positive effects of homework on achievement at the high school level and smaller effects for students in the elementary grades. Meta-analyses of longitudinal studies of the effects of homework on student achievement conducted between 1983 and 2007 revealed effect sizes of $d=.21$ to $d=.97$, which translated to 8 percent to 31 percent percentile gains on students' achievement test scores (Cooper *et al.*, 2006; Marzano and Pickering, 2007). Although the differences in effect sizes are interesting, the consistency of positive effects on achievement at all grade levels is striking and important.

Homework and other outcomes

Some studies explored whether doing homework contributed to other school outcomes, including student attitudes and behaviors. Overall, when they did their homework, students strengthened personal attitudes about learning and work habits that contribute to success in school. Compared to students who did no homework or spent less time on homework, students who did their homework were more likely to manage tasks and time well, meet due dates and deadlines, limit distractions, delay gratification, and increase their motivation to learn (Deslandes and Rousseau, 2008, Trautwein *et al.*, 2006).

Motivation to learn

Research on the connections of homework and students' motivation is particularly interesting. Across studies conducted from 1986 to 2010, doing homework contributed to students' self-direction, self-regulation, feelings of efficacy, academic interest, and other school-linked attitudes and behaviors from elementary school through high school and at the college level (Bembenutty, 2011, Bempechat *et al.*, 2011; Corno, 2000; Ramdass and Zimmerman, 2011; Xu *et al.*, 2010). There seems to be a self-fulfilling process of completing assignments, strengthening skills, and feeling motivated to learn more. Indeed, Bempechat (2004) argued that without homework, students miss important opportunities to develop beliefs and confidence in their own abilities to learn school subjects.

One study reported that students recognized and responded to the quality of homework assignments. High school students who rated their homework as high in quality were more motivated to do their assignments, and if they did, increased their math achievement (Dettmers *et al.*, 2010). Also, students given a choice of assignments selected activities that were meaningful to them and were motivated to complete more assignments (Patall *et al.*, 2010).

Executive function

Studies of cognitive development indicate that when students put their minds to work, they, literally, build brain power. Executive function – developed, strengthened, and controlled in the prefrontal cortex of the brain – helps students think, learn, reflect on choices, and make decisions (Diamond, 2009). High-quality classwork and homework provide students with many opportunities for active and reflective learning, which, in turn, strengthen the executive function and enable students to make better decisions as they mature.

Brain-building exercises are not busywork. Rather, classroom lessons and homework assignments engage and challenge all students – not only the top students – to continually stretch their thinking and talents. Regardless of their starting abilities, devoted students use their executive function to think, learn, and continue in the role of student.

Role of student

At first, students may do homework because they are told to do it by a teacher and parent. Later, as they see the results of their efforts, they may be self-motivated to do their work. The combination of external press and internal motivation is common, expected, and important as most students develop the joy of learning when they are guided by wise and creative teachers and parents (Warton, 1997).

In short, regardless of ability level, students who do their homework are conducting the "job of childhood" (Corno and Xu, 2004). We argue that these youngsters accept the role of student and are more likely to develop and strengthen skills and attitudes that help them succeed and stay in school.

Parental involvement in the homework process

Another line of research focuses on whether and how parental involvement influences students to do their homework. Because parents vary in education and experiences, some feel comfortable about helping their children on homework at each grade level, whereas other parents feel uncomfortable or confused (Epstein and Van Voorhis, 2001; Hoover-Dempsey *et al.*, 2001)

Some parents may disrupt the homework process if, for example, they help on tasks that students are supposed to do independently (Cooper *et al.*, 2000). Parents may observe or contribute to tensions on homework if they become frustrated or embarrassed because they cannot answer their children's questions or if they learned skills in different ways from the student (Balli *et al.*, 1998; Xu and Corno, 2003).

By contrast, researchers also report positive effects of parental involvement on students' attitudes and behaviors on homework. Most parents (87 percent) view helping with homework as a chance to talk and spend time with their child in the elementary and secondary levels (Markow *et al.*, 2007). Many parents send clear messages about their expectations for students' success in school; motivate children to learn; influence students' attitudes about school, and reinforce the need to do their homework. They may give advice about organizing homework time; help children reduce distractions; monitor students' completion of assignments; and interact with students in helpful ways (Corno and Xu, 2004; Patall *et al.*, 2008).

When parents were present, students were more positive about doing their work, had higher attention levels, and were more likely to complete their homework (Leone and Richards, 1989). Students were more satisfied with homework that guided parent-child interactions, and parents in low- and high-income communities responded well to guided interactions with their children (Epstein, Simon, and Salinas, 1997; Van Voorhis, 2003). Across many studies, parent involvement helped increase student achievement (Patall *et al.*, 2008; Sheldon, 2009).

Taken together, studies indicate that parent-child interactions around homework will vary – some positive, some negative. This is due, in part, to the fact that educators vary in whether and how well they share information with parents or guide them in how to help their children with homework. Most surveys indicate that most parents want and need more and better guidance from teachers in how to help their children on homework (Dauber and Epstein, 1993; Walker *et al.*, 2009).

Summary

Extant studies not only confirm that time on homework contributes to student achievement and positive attitudes about school, but also reveal critical inequities that must be resolved for more students to succeed:

- Some students do their homework; others do not.
- In the younger grades, more struggling students take the time they need to complete their assignments. In the older grades, some students do little or no homework, and some drop out of school.
- Some parents are informed about and monitor the homework process, while other parents disengage with their students on homework, especially in the older grades.

These issues raise important new questions for research and for practice on the quality of homework:

- IF homework improves student achievement over time, THEN how can teachers design homework that motivates students at all grade and ability levels – including struggling students in secondary schools – to take the time they need to complete their assignments?
- IF parental involvement contributes to students' homework completion and success in school, THEN how can more teachers guide parents of students at all grade levels to remain engaged and influence their children to do their assignments and stay in school?

The new questions open a broad and important agenda for research, practice, and on-going professional development on homework. It is clear that more homework is not necessarily better homework. Students who presently do little or no homework will not work harder or longer if more homework is assigned. Students who already do their homework do not need more of the same. It is necessary to step back from the prominent research on homework *time* and redirect attention to issues of equity to learn whether improving the quality of homework – specifically the purposes and designs of assignments – results in more student success in school.

Functions, purposes, and designs of homework

In the US and many other countries, educators are being pressed to use research-based curricula and instructional approaches to help students reach important learning goals. This means that class lessons and homework must be designed to serve specific purposes that support students' progress toward set goals. Based on an extensive literature review, we identified ten purposes of homework, nine of which are valid (Epstein, 2011; Epstein and Van Voorhis, 2009). The purposes of homework serve three functions: instructional, communicative, and political (Van Voorhis, 2004).

Instructional function and purposes

Homework increases instruction with designs for *practice, preparation, participation* as active learners, and *personal development* of skills and talents. The most common purpose for homework is for students to practice skills and study for quizzes or class tests (Markow *et al.*, 2007). For example, math homework (the most common subject for homework at every grade level) typically guides students to practice skills that were taught in class, master them, and be prepared for the next lesson. Also, learning to study for a test is a difficult skill that must be practiced, but will be useful in many subjects and at all grade levels (Bempechat, 2004).

Communicative function and purposes

Homework improves communications among key partners in students' education by organizing and increasing *parent-teacher, parent-child,* and *peer-peer* interactions. Homework is a natural connector between home and school and may activate social learning opportunities in which students learn by talking and working with others (Corno, 2000; Good and Brophy, 2003; Van Voorhis, 2003). For example, homework may be designed to increase parent-child conversations by guiding students to interview a parent, read an original story aloud, write about a family experience, meet with a parent or other family or community member for advice, or gather examples of how a parents uses math or reading in everyday activities.

If homework is well-designed to improve communications, then students benefit by interacting with parents, other adults, or peers in positive ways to activate the power of learning from and with others. In addition, innovative approaches to the communicative function help parents feel connected to teachers, to the curriculum, and to their children as students.

Political function and purposes

Districts and schools often are rated by the public and press on their rigor and requirements, including whether or not homework is assigned regularly (Van Voorhis, 2011c). Teachers, too, are known to be tough or easy in their expectations for students and their assignments for homework. Homework may be assigned to fulfill *policies* and to improve *public relations*, but not as *punishment* for students.

Some districts set policies for the number of minutes for daily homework assignments in specific subjects and at different grade levels (Cooper, 2007; Henderson, 1996). These guidelines should not be prescriptive, as some students need more time to complete an activity. Homework policies need to be flexible enough for good teachers to design purposeful assignments that help more students meet important learning goals within reasonable time periods.

It is common for principals and teachers to communicate homework policies to parents each year so that they know what to expect and how to monitor or supervise their children in age- and grade-appropriate ways. Yet, some educators communicate well and others communicate poorly.

In sum, the purposes of homework serve different functions (instructional, communicative, and political) and require high-quality designs that meet specific purposes and that should increase the number of students who take the time to do their work. Without attention by teachers to the purposes and designs of homework, some students will opt out of homework and may, ultimately, drop out of school.

Teachers Involve Parents in Schoolwork (TIPS): interactive homework

Some researchers have been studying new questions on the effects of contrasting homework designs to fulfill specific purposes. For example, the *Teachers Involve Parents in Schoolwork (TIPS)* process guides teachers to design homework that requires students to engage parents or other family members in purposeful conversations and activities in different subjects (Epstein and Van Voorhis, 2009). Without such guidance, schools leave parents on their own to figure out how to help their children on homework.

TIPS activities are designed to serve more than one purpose. Each assignment guides students to demonstrate and discuss a particular skill with a parent or family partner. This relieves parents from thinking they are supposed to know how to teach school subjects.

Homework always is the students' responsibility, but students may tap parents' life experiences – known as "funds of knowledge" (Moll *et al.*, 1992). TIPS activities are designed to improve parent-child conversations so that homework time is purposeful and positive, rather than confusing and conflict-producing. The assignments in different subjects always include an instructional function for students to practice math skills, conduct science experiments at home, or develop personal art, music, or writing talents. All TIPS activities include real-world applications to show students that adults use school skills in every-day life, and a section for home-to-school communications where parents may send teachers comments or questions about the homework assignments and their children's work.

Three longitudinal studies were conducted to evaluate the effects of TIPS vs. homework-as-usual on students' attitudes and achievement and on parents' attitudes and actions in math in elementary grades 3 and 4, in language arts in middle grades 6 and 7, and in science in grades 7 and 8 (Van Voorhis, 2009, 2011a, 2011b). The studies were conducted in racially diverse communities where about 60 percent of students received free or reduced-price meals.

Teachers were randomly assigned to TIPS or control homework conditions. Students, then, were in TIPS classes for one year, two years, or neither year. Analyses of the data indicated that large percentages of students in all grades completed the TIPS activities and that parents were involved and signed the home-to-school communications. With grade level, students' prior achievement, and other background variables statistically controlled, TIPS students had higher standardized test scores in the TIPS subjects than did control students. Effect sizes of these and other TIPS studies ranged from $d=.23$ to $d=.49$, indicating small to medium effects of TIPS on student achievement, with stronger effects for students who were in TIPS classes for two years (Van Voorhis, 2011b).

The three studies also measured students' and families' attitudes and emotions. Results showed that students and families rated their emotions about homework significantly more positively in the TIPS than in the control condition. Compared to controls, TIPS students reported more positive interactions with a family partner (66 percent to 51 percent) and TIPS families reported more positive exchanges with their children on homework (50 percent to 32 percent). More than 80 percent of students and families evaluated TIPS as more enjoyable than "regular" homework and recommended using TIPS in the next school year (Van Voorhis, 2009).

In sum, TIPS studies suggest that if teachers and administrators *designed* homework as seriously as they *assigned* homework, more students at all ability levels would be engaged in and complete their assignments, more parents would be involved with their children on homework in positive ways, and more students would improve their achievement and other school-linked behaviors.

Conclusion and recommendations

"Homework wars" have been fought every decade since the 1890s (Gill and Schlossman, 2004). There is, then, no shortage of opinions about homework – pro and con, but facts must trump opinions. In the great homework debate, four things now are clear. First, homework helps students increase achievement and other measures of success in school. Second, homework is part of almost all school programs and students' experiences. Third, it is time to close the narrow debate on the benefits of homework versus none. It will not be productive to continue to confirm the same effects with more of the same studies.

The fourth conclusion is that extant studies of homework versus no homework will *not* end the great homework debate. Only some students do their homework, only some parents continue to interact with their children on homework, and, in the secondary grades, more students opt out of homework. These inequities require researchers and educators to find new approaches to improve the design and quality of homework and to increase the number of students who do their assignments and succeed in school.

To frame the new debate on the quality of homework, we make the following recommendations.

1   *Teachers and researchers should accept the confirmed finding that doing homework benefits students and move on to other important questions.* Scores of studies show that, on average, whatever their starting abilities, students at all grade levels increased their achievement and improved other attitudes and behaviors if they did their homework. Researchers should move from studies of homework versus none or more versus less time on homework to more difficult questions on the effects of contrasting purposes, designs, and qualities of homework on academic and behavioral results for students. Rigorous studies are needed on the nature and effects of contrasting homework designs.

New cross-sectional and longitudinal studies using quantitative and qualitative methods might start by examining the effects of new homework designs versus homework-as-usual in specific subjects. The studies not only should measure the time students spend on homework, but also students' reactions to and attitudes about the assignments, rate of homework completion, accuracy of work, and resulting achievements.

Such studies would help educators and policy leaders learn how to solve the documented inequities in students' homework behaviors by identifying which homework designs are more positively associated with students' motivation to learn and homework completion through the secondary grades.

2 *Teachers and administrators should view the design of new and better homework as part of curriculum and instruction – part of lesson plans – not an afterthought.* This means that teachers should identify the purpose(s) of each homework assignment and design the activity to meet the purpose(s). If, for example, an assignment is instructional and aims to help students practice and master a math skill, then traditional math homework still is a good idea. If a teacher wants students to see that a particular math skill is used by a parent in every-day life, then new and different designs – such as interactive homework – will be needed to match that purpose.

Teachers and administrators must communicate and discuss their homework policies with students and families. This includes the educators' strategies to provide clear and timely information so that more parents will feel comfortable about supporting their children's homework behaviors.

School principals and district subject matter coordinators should guide teachers to improve their homework designs to support, enrich, and extend their lessons. Presently, it is rare for districts to offer professional development or technical assistance to teachers on designing more interesting, active, and interactive assignments. With informed administrators and subject-matter coaches, teams of teachers could work together to develop high-quality homework assignments that may be shared with other teachers.

3 *Higher education programs that prepare future teachers and administrators should include research on homework and information on exemplary and innovative homework practices in courses on teaching methods and educational administration.* College courses that prepare future teachers and administrators for their professional work need to include research on homework and opportunities to design and test homework for specific purposes. Future administrators also should learn how to guide and evaluate teachers on the quality of their homework assignments, just as they assess and work to improve the quality of lesson plans.

These recommendations change the focus of research on homework, teaching practice, and the debate on homework from the narrow topic of time on homework to broader questions of the purposes, design, and quality of assignments. If these recommendations were enacted, educators would gain knowledge and skills to improve homework in order to change the distribution of students who take time to complete their assignments and succeed in school.

Acknowledgements

This chapter is based on work supported by MetLife Foundation and NICHD grant 5R01HD47101. Our conclusions do not necessarily reflect positions of the funding agencies.

References

Balli, S. J., Demo, D. H. and Wedman, J. F. (1998). Family involvement with children's homework: an intervention in the middle grades. *Family Relations, 47*, 149–157.

Bembenutty, H. (2011). The first word: a letter from the special issue editor. *Journal of Advanced Academics, 22*, 185–193.

Bempechat, J. (2004). The motivational benefits of homework: a social-cognitive perspective. *Theory Into Practice, 43,* 189–196.

Bempechat, J., Li, J., Neier, S. M., Gillis, C. A. and Holloway, S. D. (2011). The homework experience: perceptions of low-income youth. *Journal of Advanced Academics, 22,* 250–278.

Cooper, H. (1989). *Homework.* White Plains, NY: Longman.

——(2007). *The Battle over Homework. Common Ground for Administrators, Teachers, and Parents,* 3rd edn. Thousand Oaks, CA: Corwin Press.

Cooper, H., Lindsay, J. J. and Nye, B. (2000). Homework in the home: how student, family, and parenting-style differences relate to the homework process. *Contemporary Educational Psychology, 25,* 464–487.

Cooper, H., Robinson, J. C. and Patall, E. A. (2006). Does homework improve academic achievement? A synthesis of research, 1987–2003. *Review of Educational Research, 76,* 1–62.

Corno, L. (2000). Looking at homework differently. *The Elementary School Journal, 100,* 529–548.

Corno, L. and Xu, J. (2004). Homework as the job of childhood. *Theory Into Practice, 43,* 227–233.

Dauber, S. L. and Epstein, J. L. (1993). Parents' attitudes and practices of involvement in inner-city elementary and middle schools. In N. Chavkin (Ed.), *Families and Schools in a Pluralistic Society* (pp. 53–71). Albany, NY: SUNY Press.

Deslandes, R. and Rousseau, M. R., (2008). Long-term students' management strategies and parental involvement in homework at the elementary level. *International Journal of Parents in Education, 2,* 13–24.

Dettmers, S, Trautwein, U., Ludtke, O, Kunter, M and Baumert, J. (2010). Homework works if homework quality is high: using multilevel modeling to predict the development of achievement in mathematics. *Journal of Educational Psychology, 102,* 467–482.

Diamond, A. (2009). Learning, doing, being: a new science of education. Interview on *Speaking of Faith,* National Public Radio, November 19, 2009.

Duncan, A. (2011*). Lessons from High-performing Countries.* National Center on Education and the Economy National Symposium, May 24, 2011. Retrieved from www.ed.gov (accessed 28 May 2011).

Epstein, J. L. (1990). Homework practices, achievements, and behaviors of elementary school students. *ERS Information Folio: Homework.* Arlington, VA, Educational Research Service.

——(2011). *School, Family, and Community Partnerships: Preparing Educators and Improving Schools* (2nd edn). Boulder, CO: Westview Press.

Epstein, J. L. and Van Voorhis, F. L. (2001). More than minutes: teachers' roles in designing homework. *Educational Psychologist, 36,* 181–193.

——(2009). Implement Teachers Involve Parents in Schoolwork (TIPS), 275–297 in J. Epstein, M. G. Sanders and B. S. Simon, *School, Family, and Community Partnerships: Your Handbook for Action* (3rd edn). Thousand Oaks, CA: Corwin Press.

Epstein, J. L., Simon, B. S. and Salinas, K. C. (1997). Effects of Teachers Involve Parents in Schoolwork (TIPS) language arts interactive homework in the middle grades. *Research Bulletin, 18,* (September), Bloomington, IN: Phi Delta Kappa, CEDR.

Gill, B. P. and Schlossman, S. L. (2004). Villain or savior? The American discourse on homework, 1850–2003. *Theory Into Practice, 43,* 174–181.

Good, T. L. and Brophy, J. E. (2003). *Looking in Classrooms* (9th edn). Boston: Allyn & Bacon.

Gorges, T. C. and Elliott, S. N. (1995). Homework: parent and student involvement and their effects on academic performance. *Canadian Journal of School Psychology, 11,* 18–31.

Henderson, M. (1996). *Helping Your Student Get the Most Out of Homework.* Chicago: National Parent Teacher Association and the National Education Association.

Hoover-Dempsey, K. V., Battiato, A. B., Walker, J. M. T., Reed, R. P., DeJong, J. M. and Jones, K. P. (2001). Parental involvement in homework. *Educational Psychologist, 36,* 195–210.

Keith, T. Z., Diamond-Hallam, C. and Fine, J. G. (2004). Longitudinal effects of in-school and out-of-school homework on high school grades. *School Psychology Quarterly, 19,* 187–211.

Kitsantas, A., Cheema, J. and Ware, H. W. (2011). Mathematics achievement: the role of homework and self-efficacy beliefs. *Journal of Advanced Academics, 22,* 185–193.

Leone, C. M. and Richards, M. H. (1989). Classwork and homework in early adolescence: the ecology of achievement. *Journal of Youth and Adolescence, 18,* 531–548.

Markow, D., Kim, A. and Liebman, M. (2007). *The MetLife Survey of the American Teacher: The Homework Experience.* New York: Metropolitan Life Insurance Company (MetLife, Inc.).

Marzano, R. J. and Pickering, D. J. (2007). Special topic/The case for and against homework. *Educational Leadership, 64,* 74–79.

Moll, L. C., Amanti, C., Neff, D. and Gonzalez, N. (1992). Funds of knowledge for teaching: using a qualitative approach to connect homes and classrooms. *Theory Into Practice, 31,* 132–141.

Patall, E. A., Cooper, H. and Robinson, J. C. (2008). Parent involvement in homework: a research synthesis. *Review of Educational Research, 78,* 1039–1101.

Patall, E. A., Cooper, H. and Wynn, S. R. (2010). The effectiveness and relative importance of choice in the classroom. *Journal of Educational Psychology, 102,* 896–915.

Ramdass, D. and Zimmerman, B. J. (2011). Developing self-regulation skills: the important role of homework. *Journal of Advanced Academics, 22,* 194–218.

Sheldon, S. B. (2009). Improving student outcomes with school, family, and community partnerships. In J. Epstein, M. G. Sanders and B. S. Simon, *School, Family, and Community Partnerships: Your Handbook for Action,* 3rd edn (pp. 40–56). Thousand Oaks: Corwin Press.

Trautwein, U., Ludtke, O., Kastens, C. and Koller, O. (2006). Effort on homework in grades 5–9: development, motivational antecedents, and the association with effort on classwork. *Child Development, 77,* 1094–1111.

Van Voorhis, F. L. (2003). Interactive homework in middle school: effects on family involvement and science achievement. *Journal of Educational Research, 96,* 323–338.

——(2004). Reflecting on the homework ritual: assignments and designs. *Theory Into Practice, 43,* 205–211.

——(2009). Does family involvement in homework make a difference? Investigating the longitudinal effects of math and language arts interventions. In R. Deslandes (Ed.), *International Perspectives on Student Outcomes and Homework: Family-school-community Partnerships* (pp. 141–156). London, England: Taylor and Francis.

——(2011a). Adding families to the homework equation: a longitudinal study of family involvement and mathematics achievement. *Education and Urban Society, 43,* 313–338.

——(2011b). Costs and benefits of family involvement in homework. *Journal of Advanced Academics, 22,* 220–249.

——(2011c). Engaging families in student homework: action steps for educators. In H. Kreider and H. Westmoreland (Eds.), *Promising Practices for Family Engagement in Out-of-school Time* (pp. 71–84). Charlotte, NC: Information Age Publishing.

Walker, J. M., Hoover-Dempsey, K., Ice, C. L. and Whitaker, M. C. (2009). Parental involvement supports better student learning. In R. Deslandes (Ed.), *International Perspectives on Student Outcomes and Homework* (pp. 25–38). New York: Taylor and Francis.

Warkentien, S., Fenster, M., Hampden-Thompson, G., and Walston, J. (2008). *Issue Brief: Expectations and Reports of Homework for Public School Students in the First, Third, and Fifth Grades.* Washington DC: US Department of Education.

Warton, P. M. (1997). Learning about responsibility: lessons from homework. *British Journal of Educational Psychology, 67,* 213–221.

Xu, J. and Corno, L. (2003). Family help and homework management reported by middle school students. *The Elementary School Journal, 103,* 503–517.

Xu, M., Benson, S. N. K., Mudrey-Camino, R. and Steiner, R. P. (2010). The relationship between parental involvement, self-regulated learning, and reading achievement of fifth graders: a path analysis using the ECLS-K database. *Social Psychological Education, 13,* 237–269.

Zimmerman, B. J. and Kitsantas, A. (2005). Homework practices and academic achievement: the mediating role of self-efficacy and perceived responsibility beliefs. *Contemporary Educational Psychology, 30,* 397–417.

Chapter 25

What the evidence says and what we need to investigate

Julian Elliott and Peter Tymms

School of Education, Durham University, UK

Introduction

That homework will have a valuable impact upon academic achievement might seem obvious. It surely provides valuable opportunities to reinforce, sustain, and extend classroom learning. It should encourage complementary activities, such as project work, and could involve student creativity whilst drawing on the home environment. Removed from the direct presence of the teacher, the student is encouraged to take responsibility for, and self-regulate, their study patterns, work independently, operate to tight deadlines, and resist alternative leisure attractions. If started at a young age this should establish patterns of work that could last a lifetime. Given such potential benefits, it is surely surprising that the arguments for assigning academic work to children outside of school remain controversial. Many of the hypotheses outlined in the "obvious" claims above are not strongly supported by the research to date. Some remain unanswered.

Much of the early research into homework was conducted in the United States, a country where a traditional separation of home and school has resulted in a degree of ambivalence about schooling "intruding" into other aspects of children's lives (Steinberg, 1996; Bennett and Kalish, 2006). Kralovec and Buell (2002), for example, refer to the campaign against homework in the US in the first half of the twentieth century, citing a 1901 Californian law that no child under the age of fifteen should be required to undertake homework. In the immediate post-war years, few high school students were required to study for more than an hour or two per week outside of school hours (Hollingshead, 1949).

Demands in the US for an increase in homework time were periodically fuelled by anxieties about the nation's competitiveness with others. Thus, homework time increased following *Sputnik* in 1957, and students at this time were exhorted to match their Soviet counterparts. Such a trend was short-lived only to be reignited by the publication of *A Nation at Risk* (National Commission on Excellence in Education) in 1983. This report suggested that homework demands for high school seniors had decreased and that two-thirds of students were studying for less than one hour a night.

In other societies, the importance of homework is less controversial. In the Soviet Union, for example, homework demands were heavy and might average as many as 20 hours a week (Zhurkina, 1973). Such trends have persisted and it would appear that Russian children continue to spend many more hours on homework than children in the US and England (Elliott *et al.*, 2005). In many South East Asian countries, learning in class and associated homework activities are supplemented by various forms of additional schooling in cram institutions such as *Buxiban* in Taiwan, *Juku* in Japan, and *Hagwon* in

Korea. While these institutions often provide instruction geared to preparing students for high-stakes examinations, and appear to make a difference to academic performance (Liu, 2011) with critical periods when this may be more effective (Lin and Lue, 2010), many forms of shadow education in countries across the world also exist to provide additional tuition for those who struggle with school-based instruction (Baker *et al.*, 2001).

Despite this variation across cultures, the value of homework for academic achievement appears to have been generally accepted by parents, teachers, and social commentators (Cooper *et al.*, 1998; Xu, 2005). Much of the debate about homework in countries as diverse as the US (Kralovec and Buell, 2002) and Russia (Filippov, 2001) has been primarily concerned with the tensions that are placed upon family wellbeing (Burnett and Fanshawe, 1997; Hoover-Dempsey *et al.*, 2001) and achieving a desirable balance between academic and other pursuits. But is the assumption that homework will necessarily enhance academic achievement for schoolchildren of all ages wholly valid?

Does more time on homework lead to greater academic gains?

It would appear that for secondary school students, homework does impact positively upon achievement. Although there have been conflicting findings (Epstein, 1988; Tymms and Fitz-Gibbon, 1992; Olympia *et al.*, 1994; Cooper *et al.*, 1998; Farrow *et al.*, 1999; De Jong *et al.*, 2000), what is widely considered to be a sound, up-to-date, meta-analytic review (Cooper *et al.*, 2006) concluded that, despite the design flaws in most of the studies, homework did appear to offer a positive contribution to academic achievement in secondary schools. However, there appeared to be no relation between this association and the type of outcome measure (e.g. grades versus standardized tests) or subject discipline (e.g. maths versus reading). For primary school students, the link to homework was unclear, a finding that is in line with Cooper *et al.*'s (1998) earlier review of empirical studies in which he similarly concluded that the effect of homework upon achievement in the elementary grades was negligible.

Although the review was restricted to studies in the US, an association between homework and academic achievement has been found in many other countries for older students, although the academic gains are modest. For example, Tymms and Fitz-Gibbon (1992) reported that students who worked on an A level (pre-university) subject for more than seven hours a week over two years tended to get a third of a grade better than students of the same ability and gender who worked for just two hours a week. Findings from the Programme for International Student Achievement (PISA; OECD, 2001) showed a relationship between homework and reading achievement for almost all of the 31 countries studied, with homework explaining 4.5 percent of the variation of student performance in reading across the OECD countries. Trautwein (2007) rightly questions how homework in the domains of mathematics and science would lead to gains in reading, although it could be that a general tendency to do homework could be important.

Although Cooper *et al.*'s (2006) review was careful and extensive, it has been criticised on the grounds that other variables that might influence outcomes were not appropriately considered in most of the studies examined (Trautwein *et al.*, 2009). In addition, while there was some evidence of a causal effect of homework upon achievement, this tended to be found when the outcome was the relatively immediate unit test. It was not possible to offer causal claims in relation to class grades or standardized tests. Cooper *et al.* (2006, pp. 53–55) highlight this point and other weaknesses in the literature and provide some helpful pointers for future research.

Farrow *et al.* (1999) reported a similar lack of impact of homework in primary school students. Their investigation involved a large dataset of nearly 20,000 primary school students from 492 schools across 33 Local Education Authorities in England and the Isle of Man. Students in their final year of primary education (aged 11) were asked to indicate whether they received homework in each of science, maths, and reading on the basis of one of four categories: never, once a month, once a week, or more often. The amount of homework reported by the children fluctuated by subject area, with reading proving to be more regularly undertaken than mathematics, and with rather less frequency for science. For all three subjects, it was found that the group reporting "once a month" tended to achieve the highest "value added" test scores, with the overall relationship between reported homework and academic achievement in all three subjects appearing to be very limited (effect size: $d < 0.2$). The paper by Tymms and Fitz-Gibbon (1992) found fairly consistent relationships across A-level subjects with one exception. That exception was General Studies, which does not have a clear syllabus and is designed to test students' ability to respond during the examination time. For General Studies, the more time that students reported spending on homework the lower their grades. Perhaps the amount of time spent on homework in General Studies was an indication of a worried state of mind.

Researchers have put forward a number of reasons to explain the weak link between homework and attainment for younger students (e.g. Cooper *et al.*, 2006; Rønning, 2011). Firstly, it is possible that younger children have poorer study habits (Dufresne and Kobasigawa, 1989) and are more prone to be distracted by other factors in the home environment. Secondly, academically weaker students may require more time to complete their assignments, thus confounding the time by achievement association (Muhlenbruck *et al.*, 1999). Trautwein *et al.* (2009) noted that the time spent on homework may not all be "active time", with poorer performers being more likely to have problems of concentration and engagement. However, it should be noted that Farrow *et al.*'s findings showing minimal homework effects examined the frequency that homework was undertaken, rather than the amount of time on task. Furthermore, it is not clear why the ability by time factor would not play out similarly for high school students. Another factor might be that teachers set more homework for those who are struggling. However, Farrow *et al.* found no relationship between frequency of homework and non-verbal intelligence test scores. Furthermore, at the class, rather than the individual level, Muhlenbruck *et al.* (1999) found no evidence that teachers in elementary schools provided more homework to those classes that were achieving poorer academic standards.

But the finding that homework does not lead to greater attainment in primary schools may have a more fundamental explanation. Consider the learning of languages. Young children acquire their first languages effortlessly and certainly without homework. Later in life, competence in a new language requires effort and conscious study. These differences correspond to different modes of learning for the young child and the teenager. In developmental terms the natural disposition of the youngster is to absorb what is in the environment, be that language, social customs, behaviour, or mathematics. Societies may coerce the youngsters to conform but their natural curiosity and inclination to copy, play, and learn are strong and major features of their activities. In the secondary school and beyond, the curriculum becomes more removed from the environment whilst play becomes less important. More conscious effort is needed to acquire knowledge and understanding. In short, homework becomes more salient.

The need for multilevel analysis

Since the publication of Cooper *et al.*'s (2006) meta-analysis, and their calls for more complex analyses, researchers have endeavoured to move beyond the rather simplistic analysis of the relationship of homework time and academic achievement. Trautwein (2007; Trautwein *et al.*, 2009) highlights the importance of multilevel analyses, which were almost completely absent from the studies Cooper *et al.* (2006) reviewed, although Tymms and Fitz-Gibbon (1992) carried out such work. Trautwein (2007; Trautwein and Köller, 2003) differentiates between effects that operate at the level of the class and those at the level of the student. At the class level, a homework assignment effect would be found where students in classes with higher amounts of homework perform better than those where homework is more rarely allocated as opposed to the relationship at the student level where students who do more work within a given class than some of their classmates may gain greater benefit from homework as a result of their extra effort. To compare the effects of homework on achievement at the student level (described by Trautwein *et al.*, 2009, p. 78, as the "homework completion effect") one may examine the extent to which academic achievement varies for students in the same class who engage in differing amounts of homework. At the student level, one could examine whether students who engage fully and purposively have a greater grasp of relevant academic material in comparison with their own baseline. The Tymms and Fitz-Gibbon (1992) study did this with A-level results as the outcome in England. As noted earlier there was, for almost all subjects, an advantage to the individual student of doing more homework, but there was no class effect. That is to say, there was no evidence that being in a class where a lot of homework was reported benefited the individual student beyond the amount reported by that individual. In primary schools, Farrow *et al.* (1999) found no class effect for reading and weak class effects for maths and science.

At this point, as a methodological aside, it is worth noting a complication in multi-level modelling when searching for class or school level effects. This is that when a predictor, such as homework, is measured with error at the student level, a positive class (or school) effect is likely to be observed; the greater the error the greater the phantom compositional effect (Harker and Tymms, 2004). Thus, a class level effect may be seen in the multi-level models that is an artefact of the data collected and thus, this should not be interpreted as a meaningful class level effect.

Trautwein (2007) undertook a reanalysis using data from a German extension of the PISA study. He found that homework was moderately positively related to achievement at the school level but was negatively related at the individual level. In the same paper, Trautwein analysed data from a German extension of the Third International Mathematics and Science Study (TIMSS) (Beaton *et al.*, 1996). This analysis permitted an opportunity to consider homework frequency separate from homework time. It was found that frequency, but not time, was a significant predictor at the class level. At the student level, homework time was negatively related to academic achievement and gains in academic achievement. Trautwein suggested that longer duration of student homework may not reflect greater engagement or effort, but instead might reflect student difficulties in undertaking the tasks.

In recognising that the TIMSS analysis did not permit consideration of the differing influence of *time on homework* and *effort on homework,* Trautwein (2007) reported a third study involving 8th grade German students at schools for high-achieving students (*Gymnasia).* Here the focus was on homework completion rather than homework assignment. There was no correlation between effort and time and it was only the former that was related to achievement or achievement gains.

In the light of these findings, Trautwein *et al.* (2009) carried out a study of Swiss eighth grade students learning French as a second language. Analysis was undertaken at the class and student levels; self-reported student emotions were also included. At the class level, more frequent homework assignments were associated with higher achievement. In examining between-student relationships, it was found that effort positively predicted achievement while the relationship between time and achievement were negative. When examining students' subjective reports of their homework using diaries, considerable day-to-day variation was reported. As the authors predicted, effort positively predicted students' subjective evaluations of their homework although, less expectedly, and in contrast to the class and between level findings, time spent on homework also predicted student reported positive outcomes. Of course, given the subjective nature of the student evaluations, it is possible that these estimates are influenced by various forms of bias.

Using PISA 2003 data, Dettmers *et al.* (2009) examined the relationship between homework time and mathematics achievement for 231,759 students from 40 countries. A multilevel analysis was undertaken which permitted examination at country, school and student level. Data were also collected about students' socioeconomic backgrounds.

At the school level a positive relationship between homework time and mathematics achievement was found for most countries. That is, students attending schools that allocated more frequent or lengthier homework tasks tended to outperform those attending institutions which made fewer homework demands. At the student level, however, the picture was more mixed with positive, negative or nonsignificant associations found for different countries. Socioeconomic status (considered by the authors to be a form of implicit tracking) was found to be a confounding variable, with teachers in schools attended by high-achieving or economically advantaged students tending to provide greater amounts of homework than those in less privileged school settings. The authors concluded that the association found between homework time and achievement may be partly attributable, therefore, to selection processes associated with socioeconomic status.

Dettmers *et al.* (2009) built on this analysis by examining PISA 2003 results for grade 9 or 10 students in six school systems (Austria, Flanders, Germany, Japan, Korea, and the US) where more explicit details about academic grouping were available. Five of these countries used between school tracking; the US was the only one of these countries to use within-school differential grouping. As anticipated, while homework was found at the school level to be positively associated with mathematics achievement, the relationship decreased substantially once track and socioeconomic status were controlled.

Who benefits from homework?

Although for older students, homework is held to be a means of individual study, for the younger child, parental input will often be important. This input may involve both assistance with content and supervision and guidance in task engagement and completion.

However, the extent of parent support appears to vary according to level of parental education and socioeconomic status (Guryan *et al.*, 2008; Rønning, 2011). In order to examine whether homework effects differed for children from more and less advantaged backgrounds, as he anticipated, Rønning (2011) conducted a large-scale analysis of data obtained from a Dutch survey of elementary schoolchildren. To counter the confounding factors of unobserved teacher and student effects, he examined only those classes where either all or none of the children were assigned homework. If there were a socioeconomic factor in relation to the influence of homework, one would expect that the differences between such groupings would be greater where homework is given than where it is not. Specifically, if Rønning's hypothesis is valid, those at the higher end of the socioeconomic scale should gain from homework, whereas those at the lower end are unlikely to benefit. Such a possibility is supported by a study of Norwegian students using data obtained from TIMSS 2007 (Rønning, 2010). In this study, it appeared that students from lower socioeconomic backgrounds (measured on the basis of the presence of books in the home) achieved higher scores in mathematics when less homework was assigned. In seeking to explain this rather puzzling finding, Rønning speculates that homework may impact negatively upon student motivation, not only in the home but also in class. However, it is noted that further investigation is needed to gain greater understanding of this phenomenon.

The overall effect of homework upon student achievement in this study did not prove to be statistically significant. However, when comparison is made between advantaged and disadvantaged students, a rather more nuanced picture emerges. It appears that students from more advantaged backgrounds demonstrate higher academic performance when given homework but, in contrast, such benefits do not accrue to those from disadvantaged backgrounds. The test score gap proved to be significantly larger in classes that received homework than those that did not. This finding was, in part, explained by data obtained on the involvement in homework on the part of these children's parents. Here, the study found a significant difference in help across socioeconomic backgrounds with parents from more disadvantaged groups providing less assistance. As Rønning notes, it is likely that parents of disadvantaged children will have difficulty in following up on instructions from school, and the quality of that support that is offered to children may vary in line with the degree of the family's cultural capital. This work is important in explaining the weak or non-existent effects of homework for younger children. It would be valuable to see it replicated and extended to children of different ages in different countries.

The future of homework research

In most studies that have examined the value of homework, the nature of the activity itself has tended to be considered as something of a "black box". However, it would seem likely that the effects of homework would be influenced by its nature, role, quality and relevance to classroom learning (Dettmers *et al.*, 2009). Given the low association often found between homework time and academic achievement, it might be tempting for teachers to conclude that, given the amount of tension and stress that can result from attempts to ensure completion of homework (Ratnesar, 1999; Xu and Corno, 1998; Burnett and Fanshawe, 1997), the evidence for continuing the practice is insufficient. However, this would be to ignore not only the likelihood that the positive effects of homework vary for individuals on the basis of such factors as age, socioeconomic status, and academic ability, but are also dependent upon the nature and meaningfulness of the activities involved. Where homework activities are bolt-on (that is, when they are not closely matched to ongoing activities) or inconsequential, and thus poorly integrated with classroom learning, it is unlikely that they will contribute greatly to academic achievement (Baker and LeTendre, 2005). Where they are a core component of a learning cycle, their contribution may be significant.

This distinction can be observed by comparing differences in practices across cultures. Thus, in their comparative studies of education in Russia, England and the US, Elliott and colleagues (Elliott *et al.*, 2005; Hufton and Elliott, 2000) have illustrated the very different ways in which homework tasks were integrated into the totality of student learning. Hufton and Elliott (2000) wrote of the pedagogical nexus in Russian classrooms (reflecting longstanding Soviet practices) in which intimate links existed between the use of textbooks, lessons, homework, and assessment. Compared with lessons in the US or England, lessons typically contained a significant number of demanding activities – almost all teacher-led or directed (see Alexander, 2000, for detailed discussion). Underpinning these activities was a deeper three-part lesson structure. The initial phase would typically involve the rehearsal of previous learning, with much of this drawn from the immediately preceding homework tasks. The second phase usually involved the introduction and consideration of new material. Finally, this new material would be examined in detail, related to previous learning, and then rehearsed in order to achieve a sound level of maintenance. Homework activities would then be allocated with the express function of consolidating this new learning. Often the time that students were required to spend upon their homework was dependent upon their grasp and understanding of the lesson content. Thus, those who struggled academically were often required to spend many hours studying at home in order to keep up with classmates. Such a picture differs greatly from countries such as England, where secondary school students who are perceived as more able are likely to be given high levels of homework in order to achieve the highest examination scores, while those considered less able will often have fewer homework demands made of them (Hallam and Ireson, 2003).

Elliott *et al.* (2005) found a very different picture in their study of practices in Kentucky in the US. Here homework often competed with sporting and social activities, longstanding priorities for many US adolescents (Coleman, 1961). To further complicate matters, homework was often undertaken during school hours, either in the latter part of lessons or during periods designated for independent study (sometimes known as "study hall" or "home room"). In some cases, it appeared that classwork was being redesignated as homework principally to serve as a motivational tool to ensure classroom engagement. The tendency for American students to undertake homework in class was also a feature of the TIMSS study (TIMSS-R) (Mullis *et al.*, 2000) where US students reported the highest levels of such practice. In self-reports, 79 percent of American children stated that they "almost always" or "pretty often" were given time to do homework in class, compared with the international average of 55 percent. This may explain why, despite the apparently high levels of homework reported in the US (Baker and LeTendre, 2005) many children in the US do not appear to find it necessary to spend lengthy periods in the evenings and weekends on homework activities (Stevenson and Nerison-Low, 1998).

Given the very different functions and understandings about the role of homework as part of the learning process, it is highly unlikely that treating homework as a black box variable will provide meaningful findings across diverse contexts.

The belief that homework from a young age leads to sound patterns of working that will help them in later years persists despite the limited research evidence on this issue. Although the sophistication and diversity of research into homework has increased over time, there is a clear need for more incisive methodologically sound research studies which are theoretically based. Educational research owes this to education; we should be able to advise teachers and give them models that can be used in planning their work. Calls for more incisive work are not original; in their review of homework research up to 2003, Cooper *et al.* (2006) reflected upon the benefits that could be derived from experimental studies yet acknowledged the difficulties that these studies typically present. They also highlighted the relative dearth of longitudinal studies that could follow cohorts of students and offer insights into the cumulative effects over time of homework activity. Despite such calls, studies providing rich accounts of this kind have yet to be reported and are long overdue.

References

Alexander, R. (2000). *Culture and Pedagogy: International Comparisons in Primary Education.* Oxford: Blackwell.

Baker, D. P. and LeTendre, G. K. (2005). *National Differences, Global Similarities: World Culture and the Future of Schooling.* Stanford, CA: Stanford University Press.

Baker, D. P., Akiba, M., LeTendre, G. K. and Wiseman, A.W. (2001). Worldwide shadow education: outside-school learning, institutional quality of schooling, and cross-national mathematics achievement. *Educational Evaluation and Policy Analysis, 23*(1), 1–17.

Beaton, A. E., Mullis, I. V. S., Martin, M. O., Gonzalez, E. J., Kelly, D. L. and Smith, T. A. (1996). *Mathematics Achievement in the Middle School Years: IEA's Third International Mathematics and Science Study.* Chestnut Hill, MA: Boston College.

Bennett, S. and Kalish, N. (2006). *The Case Against Homework.* New York: Crown.

Burnett, P. C. and Fanshawe, J.P. (1997). Measuring school-related stressors in adolescents. *Journal of Youth and Adolescence, 26,* 415–428.

Coleman, J. (1961) *Adolescent Society: The Social Life of the Teenager and its Impact on Education.* New York: Free Press.

Cooper, H., Lindsey, J. J., Nye, B. and Greathouse, S. (1998). Relationships among attitudes about homework, amount of homework assigned and completed, and student achievement. *Journal of Educational Psychology, 90,* 70–83.

Cooper, H., Robinson, J. C. and Patall, E. A. (2006). Does homework improve academic achievement? A synthesis of research, 1987–2003. *Review of Educational Research, 76,* 1–62.

De Jong, R., Westerhof, K. J. and Creemers, B. P. M. (2000). Homework and student math achievement in junior high schools. *Educational Research and Evaluation, 6,* 130–157.

Dettmers, S., Trautwein, U. and Ludtke, O. (2009). The relationship between homework time and achievement is not universal: evidence from multilevel analyses in 40 countries. *School Effectiveness and School Improvement, 20*(4), 375–405.

Dufresne, A. and Kobasigawa, A. (1989). Children's spontaneous allocation of study time: differential and sufficient aspects. *Journal of Experimental Child Psychology, 42,* 274–296.

Elliott, J. G., Hufton, N., Illushin, L. and Willis, W. (2005). *Motivation, Engagement and Educational Performance.* London: Palgrave Press.

Epstein, J. L. (1988). *Homework Practices, Achievements and Behaviors of Elementary School Students.* Baltimore, MD: Center for Research on Elementary and Middle Schools.

Farrow, S., Tymms, P. and Henderson, B. (1999). Homework and attainment in primary schools, *British Educational Research Journal, 25*(3), 323–341.

Filippov, V. C. (2001). Education in Russia: current state, problems and prospects. *Russian Education and Society, 43,* 5–27.

Guryan, J., Hurst, E. and Kearney, M. (2008). Parental education and parental time with children. *Journal of Economic Perspectives, 22*(3), 23–46

Hollingshead, A. (1949). *Elmstown's Youth; The Impact of Social Classes on Adolescents.* Oxford: Wiley.

Hallam, S. and Ireson, J. (2003). Secondary school teachers' attitudes to and beliefs about ability grouping. *British Journal of Educational Psychology, 73,* 343–356.

Harker, R. and Tymms, P. (2004). The effects of student composition on school outcomes. *School Effectiveness and School Improvement, 15*(2): 177–199.

Hoover-Dempsey, K. V., Battiato, A. C., Walker, J. M., Reed, R. P., DeJong, J. M. and Jones, K. P. (2001). Parental involvement in homework. *Educational Psychologist, 36,* 195–209.

Hufton, N. and Elliott, J. (2000). Motivation to learn: the pedagogical nexus in the Russian school: some implications for transnational research and policy borrowing, *Educational Studies, 26,* 115–136

Kralovec, E. and Buell, J. (2002). *The End of Homework: How Homework Disrupts Families, Overburdens Children and Limits Learning.* Boston, MA: Beacon Press.

Lin, E. S. and Lue, Y. (2010). The causal effect of the cram schooling timing decision on maths scores. *Economics Bulletin, 30*(3), 2330–2345.

Liu, J. (2011). Does cram schooling matter? Who goes to cram schools? Evidence from Taiwan. *International Journal of Educational Development, 32,* 46–52. doi: 10.1016/j.ijedudev.2011.01.014

Muhlenbruck, L., Cooper, H., Nye, B. and Lindsay, J. J. (1999). Homework and achievement: explaining the different strengths of relation at the elementary and secondary school levels. *Social Psychology of Education, 3,* 295–317.

Mullis, I. V., Martin, M. O., Gonzalez, E. J., Gregory, K. D., Garden, R. A., O'Connor, K. M., Chrostowski, S. J. and Smith, T. A. (2000). *TIMSS 1999: International Mathematics Report.* Boston, MA: Boston College.

National Commission on Excellence in Education (1983). *A Nation at Risk: The Imperative for Educational Reform.* Washington,DC: NCEE.

Olympia, D. E., Sheridan, S. M. and Jenson, W. (1994). Homework: a natural means of home-school collaboration. *School Psychology Quarterly, 9*(1), 60–80.

Organisation for Economic Co-operation and Development (OECD) (2001). *Knowledge and Skills for Life: First Results for PISA 2000.* Paris: OECD.

Ratnesar, R. (1999). The homework ate my family. *Time,* January 25, 55–63

Rønning, S. (2010). *Homework and Pupil Achievement in Norway: Evidence from TIMSS.* Oslo: Statistics Norway.

Rønning, M. (2011). Who benefits from homework assignments? *Economics of Education Review, 30,* 55–64.

Steinberg, L. (1996). *Beyond the Classroom: Why School Reform Has Failed and What Parents Need to Do.* New York: Touchstone Books

Stevenson, H. W. and Nerison-Low, R. (1998). *To Sum It Up: Case Studies of Education in Germany, Japan, and the United States.* Washington: National Institute on Student Achievement, Curriculum and Assessment: US Department of Education.

Trautwein, U. (2007). The homework-achievement relation reconsidered: differentiating homework time, homework frequency, and homework effort. *Learning and Instruction, 17,* 372–388.

Trautwein, U. and Köller, O. (2003). The relationship between homework and achievement: still much of a mystery. *Educational Psychology Review, 15,* 115–145.

Trautwein, U., Schnyder, I., Niggli, A., Neumann, M. and Lüdtke, O. (2009). Chameleon effects in homework research: the homework-achievement association depends on the measures used and the level of analysis chosen. *Contemporary Educational Psychology, 34,* 77–88.

Tymms, P. B. and Fitz-Gibbon, C. T. (1992). The relationship of homework to A-level results. *Educational Research, 34*(1): 3–19.

Xu, J. (2005). Purposes for doing homework reported by middle and high school students. *The Journal of Educational Research, 99*, 46–55.

Xu, J. and Corno, L. (1998). Case studies of families doing homework. *Teachers College Record, 100*, 402–436.

Zhurkina, A.Y. (1973). *Time-budgets of High-school Students: Sociological Problems of Education*. Moscow: Pedagogika.

Part XIII

Is regular standardized assessment important for childhood education?

Hence we need standardized tests because they can provide evidence of reliability, calibration, and validity, and can provide information and interpretations to teachers and students. Of course there can be misuse, misunderstanding, and incorrect interpretations from using any test, but these can be reduced if the quality of the test has the required and desired attributes that are associated with standardized assessments.

Gavin T. Brown and John Hattie

There are issues with how standardized assessments are conducted and despite the concerns expressed about observation methods, teachers do need a full picture of a child if they are going to cater for all their needs and this picture cannot realistically be achieved through objective assessments alone. A balance of assessment methods is required and there will always be a particular aspect of a child's behaviour or development elicited through a non-standardized method which is useful and important within the context of that individual.

Christine Merrell

Chapter 26

The benefits of regular standardized assessment in childhood education

Guiding improved instruction and learning

Gavin T. L. Brown

The University of Auckland

John Hattie

University of Melbourne

We consider that regular standardized testing does help in childhood education, provided certain conditions are met. In this chapter we will discuss the conditions that lead to the worthwhile use of standardized assessments with children. First, though, we wish to clearly identify what does not work and thus what we believe is not good standardized assessment. Then we will review and exemplify standardized assessments that have been shown to be useful and important for children's education. We presume standardized assessment pertains to any assessment that has gone through a systematic set of analyses and refinements that provide high levels of comfort to the user in their development, reference points for making interpretations (e.g. age, grade, or other norms), and can be used in many different situations by appropriately trained assessors.

Ideally, standardized assessments help inform students how good they are (i.e. their strengths and gaps), what they may still need to learn, and such tests should aim to motivate students to greater effort. However, student self-reported grades obtained before assessments are highly correlated with actual achievement; in other words, when a child is asked to predict their own performance before sitting a test they are often very accurate ($r = .58$ or *effect-size* = 1.44, Hattie, 2009, pp. 43–44). So the question of why we would need to bother administering such tests is worth asking. One problem is that this high relationship applies less to minority students, who tend to be more inaccurate in their estimates of ability. For example, Maori and Pasifika students in New Zealand are generally two years behind majority ethnicity students; however, in a national survey of academic achievement the correlation of their self-rated ability and their performance in writing and mathematics was statistically non-significant while it was statistically significant for the majority students ('Otunuku and Brown, 2007). Thus, if we are to take advantage of student self-awareness, it is vital that students gain an accurate understanding of their ability. Here is where teachers with standardized assessments can make a difference.

Another implication of the often high predictability of the results of testing by students is that we may need to raise their expectations. Students so often predict a "safe target", that is, they predict an outcome that they can have some assurance of obtaining. Maybe what is needed is confidence and skill to exceed their expectations. One of the valuable purposes of using standardized tests is that they can assist teachers to then help students "raise the bar" as to what students can attain. Further, they can assist in providing "surprises" to both teachers and students (Hattie and Brown, 2008, 2010) – merely giving a test to confirm prior expectations is not as informative as learning new and often surprising information about what a student can or cannot do.

Tests must go beyond simply reporting a total score or rank order score; tests need to give rich diagnostic information to the teacher, so that the teacher can clearly identify a student's strengths and gaps, and who needs to be taught what next. With such information, it is possible for a teacher to provide accurate feedback to students; and feedback is a teaching strategy that has a large positive effect on performance ($d = .73$) (Hattie, 2009, pp. 173–178). When the goal of assessment is to inform teachers so that they can take appropriate decisions and actions, then regular standardized assessments are helpful to children's development.

For a standardized test to achieve this goal, the information flow has to be under the control of the school and/or teacher so that: (a) the content of the test is defensible given the teaching context, (b) the analysis of the data is prompt enough to make a difference to the teaching context, and (c) the consequences are low enough so that neither teachers or students are motivated to cheat or game the test. Furthermore, the tests must be well-aligned to all the key aspects of the taught curriculum; that means covering not just surface processing (i.e. recall of material in isolation or lists) but also deep processing (e.g. relational or abstract processing) (Hattie and Brown, 2004). Indeed, there is evidence that teachers believe that schools can be evaluated accurately only through assessments that require deep processing (Brown, 2009a).

Another reason to make use of standardized tests over less formal assessments is the quality assurance processes used to develop standardized tests. High-quality standardized tests typically are developed in such a way that the users can have confidence that the tasks are well written, the answers are correct, the tasks cover the learning objectives of the domain in a valid and balanced fashion, the appropriateness of the material has been trialled on representative samples of children, the relative difficulty of tasks has been established through sophisticated statistical modelling, the possibility of bias or insensitivity in the tasks has been addressed, and the degree of accuracy or reliability in awarding scores has been estimated (see Hattie et al., 2004, chapter 4 for a description of the development processes for the New Zealand standardized test system called Assessment Tools for Teaching and Learning or 'asTTle'). In other words, while there is no perfectly accurate test score, teachers, students, and parents can have confidence in the quality and accuracy of a standardized test. There has been a large corpus of studies, manuals, standards, and other resources dedicated to these processes for developing and defending standardized tests.

This stands in stark contrast to what we know about the accuracy of teacher or marker judgements based on informal or non-standardized tests. For example, when scoring essays, markers are notoriously unreliable in their judgements (Brennan, 1996; Brown, 2009b) and thus systematic and often standardized processes are needed to calibrate and control teacher judgments (e.g. the development of standardized essay scoring rubrics). While we cannot estimate readily the amount of error in a teacher's "on-the-fly" or "in-the-moment" evaluations, we know that there is inaccuracy in every judgement (Haertel, 2006). Humans can introduce error into scores of performances (e.g. essays, portfolios, and dramatic or spoken performance) through a number of biases, including a tendency to inflate scores for a number of reasons, such as believing moderate grades do not reflect the quality of the instruction or students, a tendency to be a harsh or tough marker (or conversely to be a lenient or soft marker), a tendency to be inconsistent, perhaps through inattention or fatigue, and a tendency to judge the learner rather than the performance itself (Hoyt, 2000; Lane and Stone, 2006). Indeed, careful study of rater inaccuracy or disagreement is undertaken in large-scale standardized testing of performance assessments in order to establish the limits of validity and credibility of assessment decisions (Haertel, 2006; Lane and Stone, 2006). This is why rubrics, marker panels, and multiple tasks are among the tools needed to ensure that there is quality in teacher assessment. Indeed, given the potential for inaccuracy in human estimation of performance, it is no wonder that the effect of non-test formative assessment practices is relatively low.

Another important aspect of the classroom environment is that it is a social space; assessment is often carried out in a public way that may have ramifications for the individuals involved. For example, student self- and/or peer-assessment, recommended alternatives to standardized testing (e.g. Harlen, 2007), require significant levels of psychological safety and trust in the social space of the classroom. Students need to trust that the teacher will not be offended if the student self-assesses and communicates persistent lack of understanding, students need to know that their classmates will not use self-admitted failure to learn as a means to then provide derision or exclusion, and students need to believe that their classmates are giving valued, accurate, and constructive feedback (Cowie, 2009; Harris and Brown, 2010; Peterson and Irving, 2008). Indeed, survey studies with New Zealand secondary students have shown that they do not associate non-test practices as being assessment at all (Brown et al., 2009a), and that defining assessment in terms of tests (e.g. essays, 1–3 hour examinations, and teacher marking of tests) led to higher academic performance in mathematics (Brown et al., 2009b). In a testimony to the power of active student involvement in responding to standardized tests, Archer (2009) reported that in one Auckland school using the asTTle reading and writing tests, students were confidently aware that they were learning, knew why they were in different groups for different aspects of literacy learning, and were happy in their learning. Confidence in teachers' use of standardized tests appears to characterize student understanding of assessment and is associated with better academic outcomes. Hence, the challenge becomes relatively simple; students trust information based on standardized tests, so should we not use them?

Another key aspect in our research into effective use of standardized tests has to do with the more egregious responses teachers and schools have been known to make to high-stakes standardized accountability tests. For example, much cheating and gaming of standardized tests has been recorded in contexts where high stakes can lead to negative consequences (e.g. Cannell, 1989; Phelps, 2009). Indeed, just as students need an environment of psychological safety to make effective use of assessment, so too do teachers and school leaders need protection from negative consequences. Good standardized tests can show educators some very discomforting news; for example, your class or your school is well below expectations and averages. This clearly could be made into bad news by some and many will seek to avoid this message by blaming the test or doing whatever is necessary to increase scores. We have argued (Hattie and Brown, 2008) that schools need safety from punishment if they are to discover and respond to the bad news about what is not going so well in their context. Hence, comparative information is valuable, but it must be put in the hands of educators in a timely and safe fashion, so as to allow them time to understand the issues and put into action appropriate responses.

This is exactly what has been done in New Zealand, where comparative data from standardized tests is owned and controlled by schools who can evaluate, implement, monitor, and demonstrate their effectiveness in making a difference to identified learning needs in light of this dependable assessment information. As reported elsewhere (Brown and Hattie, 2009), there is much evidence of New Zealand high schools using standardized asTTle tests to design cohort wide department teaching plans and monitoring the effect of those instructional responses. More systematically, Parr *et al.* (2007) showed that teachers who were taught how to use the asTTle standardized tests for reading and writing had considerable gains in writing (d = 1.28) and moderate gains in reading (d = .48). McDowall *et al.* (2007) found that the gains in student learning outcomes were associated with teachers who believed they had strong abilities to use and interpret assessment tools, specifically asTTle, and greater knowledge of literacy. Thus, use of the asTTle standardized test system led to improved pedagogical content knowledge, especially in writing, which in turn led to greater student learning gains. It is worth noting that this type of formative evaluation of programs by teachers using assessment data to inform them about their impact on student learning is very educationally effective (d = .90, Hattie, 2009).

The belief systems of teachers are a significant factor in whether standardized tests can be educationally useful. Clearly, pre-existing beliefs that standardized tests are irrelevant can and will influence how teachers respond to the possibility of using tests educationally. But there are other options for understanding the purpose and nature of assessment; assessment can evaluate schools, it can evaluate or certify students, and it can be for improvement (Brown, 2008). For example, in the development of the asTTle standardized tests system, it was found that teachers who endorsed the conception of assessment related to "assessment is powerful for improving teaching" had higher interpretation scores on a test about the meaning of the asTTle test score reports (r = .34). In contrast, teachers who endorsed more strongly the conception of assessment as a means of evaluating or holding schools accountable had the lowest interpretation scores (r = -.21) (Hattie *et al.* 2006). Thus, successful use of standardized tests requires believing that they can contribute to improved teaching and student learning for the individuals in a teacher's class. This belief leads to more accurate interpretation to the educationally useful information communicated in standardized test reports.

Of course, standardized tests can serve more than one purpose – they can be for improved teaching and to demonstrate the quality of schools. Brown and Harris (2009) showed that, while most teachers in a study of Auckland schools perceived assessment as a means of fulfilling school quality improvement purposes, there were individual teachers who saw the legitimacy of both school accountability and improvement purposes. Keeping both purposes in balance may be one of the key capabilities of highly accomplished teachers and school administrators.

Hence we need standardized tests because they can provide evidence of reliability, calibration, and validity, and can provide information and interpretations to teachers and students. Of course there can be misuse, misunderstanding, and incorrect interpretations from using any test, but these can be reduced if the quality of the test has the required and desired attributes that are associated with standardized assessments.

References

Archer, E. (2009). *Beyond the Rhetoric of Formative Assessment: Seeking Solutions for South Africa in New Zealand's Assessment Tools for Teaching and Learning.* Unpublished manuscript. University of Pretoria. Pretoria, South Africa. .

Brennan, R. L. (1996). Generalizability of performance assessments. In G. W. Phillips (Ed.), *Technical Issues in Large-scale Performance Assessment (NCES 96–802)* (pp. 19–58). Washington, DC: National Center for Education Statistics.

Brown, G. T. L. (2008). *Conceptions of Assessment: Understanding What Assessment Means to Teachers and Students.* New York: Nova Science Publishers.

——(2009a). Teachers' self-reported assessment practices and conceptions: using structural equation modelling to examine measurement and structural models. In T. Teo and M. S. Khine (Eds.), *Structural Equation Modeling in Educational Research: Concepts and Applications* (pp. 243–266). Rotterdam, NL: Sense Publishers.

——(2009b). The reliability of essay scores: the necessity of rubrics and moderation. In L. H. Meyer, S. Davidson, H. Anderson, R. Fletcher, P. M. Johnston and M. Rees (Eds.), *Tertiary Assessment and Higher Education Student Outcomes: Policy, Practice and Research* (pp. 40–48). Wellington, NZ: Ako Aotearoa.

Brown, G. T. L. and Harris, L. R. (2009). Unintended consequences of using tests to improve learning: How improvement-oriented resources heighten conceptions of assessment as school accountability. *Journal of MultiDisciplinary Evaluation, 6*(12), 68–91.

Brown, G. T. L. and Hattie, J. A. (2009). *Understanding Teachers' Thinking About Assessment: Insights for Developing Better Educational Assessments.* Paper presented at annual conference of the National Council for Measurement in Education, San Diego, CA.

Brown, G. T. L., Irving, S. E., Peterson, E. R. and Hirschfeld, G. H. F. (2009a). Use of interactive-informal assessment practices: New Zealand secondary students' conceptions of assessment. *Learning and Instruction, 19*(2), 97–111. doi: 10.1016/j.learninstruc.2008.02.003

Brown, G. T. L., Peterson, E. R. and Irving, S. E. (2009b). Self-regulatory beliefs about assessment predict mathematics achievement. In D. M. McInerney, G. T. L. Brown and G. A. D. Liem (Eds.), *Student Perspectives on Assessment: What Students Can Tell Us About Assessment For Learning* (pp. 159–186). Charlotte, NC: Information Age Publishing.

Cannell, J. J. (1989). *How Public Educators Cheat on Standardized Achievement Tests.* Albuquerque, NM: Friends for Education.

Cowie, B. (2009). My teacher and my friends helped me learn: student perceptions and experiences of classroom assessment. In D. M. McInerney, G. T. L. Brown and G. A. D. Liem (Eds.), *Student Perspectives on Assessment: What Students Can Tell Us About Assessment For Learning* (pp. 85–105). Charlotte, NC: Information Age Publishing.

Haertel, E. H. (2006). Reliability. In R. L. Brennan (Ed.), *Educational Measurement* (4th edn, pp. 65–110). Westport, CT: Praeger.

Harlen, W. (2007). *Assessment of Learning.* Los Angeles: Sage.

Harris, L. R. and Brown, G. T. L. (2010). *"My teacher's judgement matters more than mine": Comparing Teacher and Student Perspectives on Self-assessment Practices in the Classroom.* Paper presented at the Annual Meeting of the American Educational Research Association, Denver, CO.

Hattie, J. (2009). *Visible Learning: A Synthesis of Meta-analyses in Education.* London: Routledge.

Hattie, J. A. C. and Brown, G. T. L. (2004). *Cognitive processes in asTTle: The SOLO Taxonomy* (asTTle Tech. Rep. #43). University of Auckland/Ministry of Education.

Hattie, J. A. and Brown, G. T. L. (2008). Technology for school-based assessment and assessment for learning: development principles from New Zealand. *Journal of Educational Technology Systems, 36*(2), 189–201.

——(2010). Assessment and evaluation. In C. Rubie-Davies (Ed.), *Educational Psychology: Concepts, Research and Challenges* (pp. 102–117). Abingdon, UK Routledge.

Hattie, J. A. C., Brown, G. T. L., Keegan, P. J., MacKay, A. J., Irving, S. E., Cutforth, S., Campbell, A., Patel, P., Sussex, K., Sutherland, T., McCall, S., Mooyman, D. and Yu, J. (2004). *Assessment Tools for Teaching and Learning asTTle Manual* (Version 4, 2005). Wellington, NZ: University of Auckland/ Ministry of Education/ Learning Media.

Hattie, J. A., Brown, G. T. L., Ward, L., Irving, S. E. and Keegan, P. J. (2006). Formative evaluation of an educational assessment technology innovation: developers' insights into Assessment Tools for Teaching and Learning (asTTle). *Journal of MultiDisciplinary Evaluation, 5*(3), 1–54.

Hoyt, W. T. (2000). Rater bias in psychological research: when is it a problem and what can we do about it? *Psychological Methods, 5*, 64–86.

Lane, S. and Stone, C. A. (2006). Performance assessment. In R. L. Brennan (Ed.), *Educational Measurement* (4th edn, pp. 387–431). Westport, CT: Praeger.

McDowall, S., Cameron, M., Dingle, R., Gilmore, A. and MacGibbon, L. (2007). *Evaluation of the Literacy Professional Development Project*. Wellington, NZ: Ministry of Education, Research Division.

'Otunuku, M. and Brown, G. T. L. (2007). Tongan students' attitudes towards their subjects in New Zealand relative to their academic achievement. *Asia Pacific Education Review, 8*(1), 117–128. doi: 10.1007/BF03025838

Parr, J. M., Timperley, H., Reddish, P., Jesson, R. and Adams, R. (2007). *Literacy Professional Development Project: Identifying Effective Teaching and Professional Development Practices for Enhanced Student Learning*. Wellington, NZ: Ministry of Education, Research Division.

Peterson, E. R. and Irving, S. E. (2008). Secondary school students' conceptions of assessment and feedback. *Learning and Instruction, 18*, 238–250.

Phelps, R. P. (2009). Educational achievement testing: critiques and rebuttals. In R. P. Phelps (Ed.), *Correcting Fallacies about Educational and Psychological Testing* (pp. 89–146). Washington, DC: American Psychological Association.

Chapter 27

Developments in standardized assessment

A perspective from the UK

Christine Merrell

Centre for Evaluation and Monitoring (CEM), Durham University

I begin this chapter by considering the purposes of assessment in childhood. I then focus on reasons for standardized assessment. Within the definition of standardized assessment, I include the way that assessments are conducted and aspects of the standardization of outcomes in terms of norm referencing. Examples of standardized assessments and their use are considered, ranging from the more traditional approach of pencil and paper group assessments to recent developments in personalized computer-delivered assessments. I then discuss the merits and disadvantages of different methods and reach the conclusion that it is not only the type of assessment that matters but how it is used.

Purposes of assessment in childhood

We are assessed before we are even born. Expectant mothers in many countries are given ultrasound scans at various stages of pregnancy to check that the foetus is developing normally and to estimate when the baby is likely to be born. Immediately after birth, a baby is weighed and his or her condition and reactions are scored against standardized scales to decide whether specialist care is required. The assessments continue as the baby grows with, for example, the Newborn Hearing Screening Programme which measures the hearing of 99 percent of all babies born in England during the first few weeks of their lives so that early intervention can be offered where needed. Assessments continue through childhood and into adulthood.

In terms of educational assessment, there are many different reasons for collecting information. Newton (2007) presented a list of eighteen purposes for which educational judgements may be used. He acknowledged that the list was not exhaustive and that the purposes for which information derived from assessments is used are expanding all the time.

If individuals or groups are going to be compared to each other, we need to be sure that they have all been assessed in the same way; namely, the content of the assessment, the way that is scored and the interpretation of those scores should be the same for all individuals. In other words, the assessment is standardized.

Different users of assessment data require different levels of detail. From the beginning of kindergarten, a child's teacher needs to have high-quality information about what children can do and understand, including their cognitive development, personal, social and emotional development, motor development, dispositions and attitudes, in order to plan and support appropriate learning experiences. At this early stage, potential special educational needs may be identified. This information is useful to be able to appropriately target resources, although a formal diagnosis of a specific difficulty should be made with caution, bearing in mind that children develop at different rates and difficulties may simply be due to immaturity. An example of problems which may be a consequence of immaturity rather than a chronic disorder is the behaviour of young children. Many young children have a limited span of attention, are very active and impulsive. These behaviours, however also characterize the diagnostic criteria for Attention Deficit Hyperactivity Disorder (ADHD), thought to be a consequence of impaired behavioural inhibition and executive functions (Barkley, 1997). Importantly, very few children with such "symptoms" are eventually diagnosed with ADHD because behavioural inhibition and executive functions continue to develop throughout childhood. Therefore even accurate assessment does not necessarily reflect accurate diagnosis.

Assessments conducted in a variety of ways and from different sources, including a child's teacher and parents, can build up a comprehensive profile which can be shared between them to provide complementary care, education and support for personal development. At an individual level, assessments administered at regular intervals throughout kindergarten and school can monitor the amount of progress that children are making in their development, knowledge and skills.

Aggregated assessment scores provide information about groups of children from which comparisons can be made. Aggregated information can be useful to a number of stakeholders; a teacher who wishes to obtain a broad picture of the strengths and weaknesses of the class as a whole, school managers who might wish to compare classes and cohorts, district officers who are making comparisons between schools, or by policy-makers at national level. These comparisons, from an individual to population level, are all valid and important uses of assessments and require information that is collected using reliable standardized assessments of individual children at regular intervals.

Comparisons of standards within a single cohort may be made from assessments administered to groups at a particular time in their education. For example, an assessment administered to all pupils in a country at the end of a stage of learning or upon completion of compulsory education can be used to compare the performance of students in different schools or districts across a country. Large-scale, international studies compare educational standards across the world.

Assessments which remain comparable in their content from one year to the next can be used to monitor changes in standards over time. For this type of comparison, not only is it necessary to have an assessment whose *content* is comparable over time, it is also necessary to conduct the assessment with *groups* that are comparable over time, such as students who took an assessment at the same age or time of year. For example, we investigated changes in children's cognitive development on entry to school in England over a period of nine years from 2001 to 2008 (Merrell and Tymms, 2010). We collected data from every child starting school, each year, in the same sample of 470 schools. The children were assessed by their class teachers within the first six weeks of the academic year using a computer-delivered assessment of early reading, vocabulary and mathematics, which remained the same over the period. Studies such as these reflect the impact of government policies and contribute a perspective to inform future direction. The period covered by the Merrell and Tymms' study was a time of significant investment (tens of billions of GBP) by the English government into pre-school facilities to improve the educational outcomes of children in the early years, particularly those children from deprived backgrounds. If the interventions had been effective, it would have been expected that children's early vocabulary, reading and mathematics development at the start of school would have improved. The study showed that there was no difference in children's vocabulary and reading standards and very little improvement in mathematics. Interestingly, although the government commissioned a national evaluation of those policies, it had not implemented the necessary standardized assessments to assess their impact on a national scale.

Standardized *assessments* enable comparisons between individuals and groups to be made. If they are administered to a representative sample or full population, standardized *scores* can be calculated.

So far, some of the purposes of assessment and uses of information from standardized assessments have been discussed in general terms and examples given. The next section of the chapter explores different stages of schooling and why it is useful to measure their impact in a standardized way.

Baseline assessment on entry to school

There is a long tradition of conducting a baseline assessment of children's development on entry to school. Within England, back in the 1960s, the main purpose of a baseline assessment at the start of school, reflected by the popular instruments of the time, was to identify children's special educational needs at an early stage rather than establishing a baseline from which progress in schooling could be measured.

In 1998, there was a change in focus as on-entry baseline assessment of children within the first few weeks of starting school became a statutory requirement for all English schools which received any state funding (Blatchford and Cline, 1992; Wolfendale and Lindsay, 1999). Establishing a reliable baseline at the start of formal education from which progress can be monitored has the potential to identify individuals, classes, schools and districts where progress is lower than expected and thus remedial actions can be taken. Over ninety baseline assessment schemes were accredited and schools were able to select the scheme of their preference.

One such accredited scheme, which had the biggest market share, was the Performance Indicators in Primary Schools On-entry Baseline Assessment (PIPS-BLA), was published by the Centre for Evaluation and Monitoring (CEM) at Durham University, UK (Tymms, 1999). The content of the PIPS BLA was underpinned by research (Tymms, 1999) and it was used on a large scale with mainstream children to provide reliable information for teaching and learning. It includes measures of vocabulary acquisition, concepts about print, phonological awareness, letter and word recognition, reading and comprehension, concepts about maths, digit identification and simple number problems. These were all areas of development which were identified from published research as being strongly related to later educational outcomes. The PIPS BLA is a computer-adaptive assessment which is administered by an adult working with one child at a time. The software tailors the assessment to the ability of a child on the basis of his or her answers and the whole assessment takes between fifteen and twenty minutes per child. The method of administration, which combines the presentation of items by the computer with teachers' decisions on whether children answer correctly or incorrectly, is standardized to such a degree that the re-test reliability has been found to be 0.98 and the internal reliability, measured by Cronbach's alpha, is 0.94 (Tymms *et al.*, 2004; Tymms, 1999). The assessment was originally developed for use by schools in the United Kingdom from which progress in the elementary years could be measured. In recent years, it has been adapted and, where necessary, translated for use in many other countries including Abu Dhabi, Australia, Germany, Hong Kong, the Netherlands, New Zealand and South Africa. After analysing the data for cultural bias, international comparisons of children starting school in different countries have been published (Tymms et al., 2004). The large-scale international studies of student attainment (e.g. TIMSS) compare the effect of education across different countries but that information is limited without knowing the knowledge and skills which children started school with and thus the progress that they have made between that point and the later assessment. The study by Tymms et al. demonstrates that it is realistic to compare children's development at the start of school in different countries. Such a comparison reflects each country's policy on pre-school care and education as well as offering a context for the interpretation of the data collected in later years by the international studies. The authors compared children starting school in Australia, England, the Netherlands, New Zealand and Scotland. Although the study included several thousand children, not all countries' samples were nationally representative; therefore it was proposed as a pilot study which demonstrated a model for a much larger, systematic study. A linear relationship between age and reading/maths development was found at the start of school and countries largely fitted on that line. Deviations were found for sub-groups; for example the scores of the indigenous children in Australia were consistently lower for their age compared with other children.

A reliable assessment of children's development at the start of school is crucial for teachers to plan appropriate learning experiences, but standardized scores which compare children's development against population norms are, for that purpose, less important. However, when it comes to identifying learning difficulties or gifted children for, perhaps, the allocation of scarce resources or specialist help, standardized assessments provide an extremely useful reference point. Although some teachers will have extensive experience working with a wide range of children in different situations and can spot deviations from the norm that warrant specialist intervention, many do not. Without the reference to population norms, how would those teachers with less experience of a wide range of children know whether or not a child's development was significantly different to the average?

Monitoring progress in school

Moving on from an initial assessment of children at the start of school, teachers need feedback about how pupils are progressing. In her book titled *Monitoring Education: Indicators, Monitoring and Effectiveness* (1996), Carol Taylor Fitz-Gibbon described the work of a number of statisticians and researchers, for example W. Edwards Deming, who followed the principle of identifying a problem, proposing and implementing a solution, monitoring the impact of that solution and adjusting as necessary. Although these methods had been applied to processes such as engineering and production, and while acknowledging the complexity of education, she nevertheless suggested that they were applicable to educating children.

Of course the processes can be applied to the growth and development of individual children using assessments which are not standardized, and in this way teachers would be able to see the value that education has added. However, although teachers can see their pupils learning new things and developing, without standardized assessments at regular points throughout their education it is difficult to estimate whether a child is making good progress compared with others of the same age, ability and time in school, that is, whether their methods are as effective as those of other teachers. This method of feedback, where a baseline measure is used to predict an outcome measure for a group, and then individuals' performance is measured against the group's regression line can be described as "relative value-added", that is, a comparison of how well individual children, classes, schools or districts are progressing in comparison with others. It is from employing these statistical methods to the analysis of standardized assessments that the area of school effectiveness has grown (for an overview and history of school effectiveness research, see Teddlie and Reynolds, 2000).

Carol Taylor Fitz-Gibbon initially set up large-scale monitoring systems for pre-university courses and these were extended by her and Peter Tymms to provide primary and secondary schools with measures of relative value-added feedback about their pupils (Taylor Fitz-Gibbon, 1997; Tymms, 1999; Tymms and Albone, 2002). These systems are run by the Centre for Evaluation and Monitoring (CEM) at Durham University, England. CEM's monitoring systems assess children at multiple points in their schooling, thus providing trajectories of growth. They were originally used by schools in England but have expanded into several countries (see www.cemcentre.org). Taylor Fitz-Gibbon advised the English government on setting up a national value-added system for its schools (Taylor Fitz-Gibbon, 1997). Similar models have evolved across the world, many in the USA (see, for example, Sanders and Horn, 1994). Value-added systems can pose a threat to teachers and head-teachers if the results are made publicly available in the form of published league tables of the type seen in the English media in recent years. This inevitably leads to stress within the profession and indeed of pupils themselves, a narrowing of the curriculum with teachers focussing entirely on the content of the tests and the de-motivation of pupils (National Union of Teachers, 2006). Teachers and schools do need high quality information but there needs to be an element of public trust and respect that this is being used in a professional way to improve pupils' outcomes.

Value-added feedback is also important for evaluating the impact of interventions and policies at a national level. For example, does a national policy to teach children to read using a systematic synthetic phonics programme significantly raise reading levels? Without a standardized assessment system to analyse the progress made by children, it is difficult to know. Once the impact of an intervention on pupils' outcomes has been established in terms of effect size (see for example Coe, 2002), this can be compared against the impact of other interventions and cost-benefit calculations performed.

Another use for standardized assessments is to investigate the importance of teachers, head teachers and districts with respect to pupils' progress. Effectiveness studies have tended to focus on the school as the unit of analysis but a study by Tymms et al. (2008) used standardized data to compare the effectiveness of districts, schools and teachers. The authors found that the district in which a child attended a school made virtually no difference to the amount of educational progress. The school made more of a difference but the most influential factor was the teacher. Knowing that it is effective teachers (see for example Nye et al., 2004) which make a difference to children's progress and outcomes rather than the head teacher or input from the district can influence decisions about resourcing in schools.

Advantages and limitations of standardized assessments

Having discussed some of the uses and values of standardized assessments, I now explore issues associated with different methods of conducting them.

Assessments of children can be made using a variety of methods. For example, if we wish to find out if children can perform a mathematical calculation or if they can read high-frequency words, we can ask them questions verbally, by computer or using the traditional pencil-and-paper format. Questions which have a single, defined, correct answer are relatively easy to mark with virtually no judgement about the quality of the response required. However, it is not appropriate to assess all areas of development by direct questioning. If we wish to learn more about a young child's behaviour, for example how well they interact with their peers or whether they can demonstrate sustained attention during a task, observing them in a natural setting over a period of time is likely to give a more reliable and valid result.

Each method has advantages and problems, yielding different amounts of information to different degrees of reliability, comparability and validity. Short questions with multiple choice answers are quick to administer and marking can be automated. Typically, tests of this format include many items and have high internal reliability but they have limitations; children are more likely to get an answer correct by chance than with constructed response items, they are often found to be biased towards boys (see for example Ben-Shakhar and Sinai, 1991) and since the answer options are limited in the information that they present, their focus can be narrow and not always elicit children's full understanding of concepts.

Assessment items requiring a constructed response, which is judged against a set of criteria, also have limitations. The judgements must be standardized if the results are going to be comparable. Newton (2009) investigated the reliability of the results from statutory national curriculum tests completed in England. He found that the marking of the mathematics test was the most reliable followed by science and considerably lower was writing. The mathematics test answers required the least interpretation by markers and the writing the most.

Assessing children's knowledge through observation alone has reliability issues. Firstly, a child may have sophisticated, in-depth knowledge but does not display it without being prompted. A young child might know how to perform complex mathematical computations but may be too timid to demonstrate that in classroom activities without prompting, or they may simply choose not to. An example of an assessment of children's knowledge and understanding that, it is suggested, should be conducted predominantly through observation of child initiated activities is the Early Years Foundation Stage Profile (EYFSP), which is a statutory assessment of children in Early Years Foundation Stage settings in England covering six areas of learning. The guidance for practitioners on completing the Profile stated that:

> Observational assessment is the most effective way of making judgements about all children's development and learning.
>
> (QCA, 2008, page 14)

> Practitioners need to ensure that they are observing children as a key way of understanding that they really know and can do. This is demonstrated most effectively when children are engaged in self-initiated activities. Because self-initiated activities

will take place within provision in which the adults have made decisions about which resources and equipment are available, it is important to clarify the definition of this.
(QCA, 2008, page 9)

Yet the guidance document does not provide evidence from well-conducted experiments to support the view that observations of self-initiated activities give more reliable information about what a child really knows and can do than other methods of assessment. At the present time, the assessment includes 117 scale points for which observations must be made and I would argue that to assess a class of up to 25 children in the recommended method is not an effective use of teachers' time and nor does it necessarily provide teachers with detailed information about their pupils' strengths and areas for development. It takes time to make detailed observations about a class of children and during that time the learning experiences that are afforded them might not be sufficiently tailored to their zone of proximal development. A recent independent review (Tickell, 2011) has called for the number of scale points in the EYFSP to be significantly reduced.

There is another problem which the guidance acknowledges: "There are some groups of children for whom this challenge needs particular consideration so that their attainment is not underestimated" (QCA, 2008, page 14). The groups of children which are listed are: (a) those with English as an additional language, (b) boys, (c) children with special educational needs and (d) children from minority groups. This is more than half of the population and a contradiction to the earlier statement that observational assessment is the most effective way of making judgements about all children's development and learning.

Problems with teachers' judgements are widely documented. Harlen (2005) suggested caution with regards to teachers' judgements of pupils' attainment and progress: "The findings of the review by no means constitute a ringing endorsement of teachers' assessment; there was evidence of low reliability and bias in teachers' judgements." Harlen referred to bias and this can be introduced when an assessor systematically downgrades an individual or group for construct irrelevant reasons. Several instances of bias in teacher assessments have been documented in relation to several factors, for example sex, ability, ethnicity, social class, age and behaviour. Harlen's systematic literature review of the evidence of reliability and validity of assessment by teachers used for summative purposes (2004) and Wilmut's investigation of the experiences of summative teacher assessment in the UK (2005) synthesized the findings of many studies.

A further example of bias in teachers' ratings in relation to children's ethnicity comes from a study by Sonuga-Barke et al. (1993). The authors investigated the relationship between teachers' ratings of hyperactivity and attention in groups of children classified as being of Asian or English origin, attending primary schools in one London borough. Teachers completed questionnaires and structured interviews to rate their pupils' behaviour. At the same time, objective measures of the activity and attention were taken. The teachers judged their pupils of Asian origin to be more inattentive and hyperactive than their peers of English origin. However, there was a discrepancy between the teachers' judgements and the scores derived from the objective measures for the children of Asian origin. The objective measures suggested no significant difference between the groups. The authors concluded that teachers appeared to overestimate the Asian children's levels of activity relative to those of the English children; a bias in their ratings.

The examples described so far have considered bias with groups of children in relation to those group characteristics which can be irrelevant to the construct being measured.

Another form of bias, sometimes referred to as the Halo Effect, occurs within subjects and can be a feature of the outcomes of assessments which are conducted through observation alone. Examples have been found across disciplines and are not limited to educational assessments (see Scorcher and Brant, 2002, and Rosenzweig, 2007 for examples in business and leadership). The Halo Effect occurs in educational assessment when a teacher rates a child as being competent in one subject area and because of the impression formed, she will also tend to rate the child as being equally competent in other areas such as motor development or personal, social and emotional development.

One example where the Halo Effect is evident is within the EYFSP described earlier. To illustrate this, 106 pupils' EYFSP scores from the six areas of learning which it covers (Language, Mathematics, Personal, Social and Emotional Development (PSED), Knowledge and Understanding of the World (KUW), Motor Development and Creative Development (Create Dev.)) were compared against each other and against their scores from the PIPS Baseline Assessment (described earlier) for Language and Mathematics. These children were assessed in the 2002/03 academic year. The EYFSP was conducted solely through observation and PIPS was conducted by asking each pupil questions in a standardized way by a computer-delivered program. The scores from the end of the first year at school of 106 children in three English primary schools were analysed and the correlations are shown in Table 13.1.

The correlations between EYFSP sections are all high. These areas of development are correlated to a certain extent, with the strongest association generally found between language and mathematics. The association between language or mathematics and motor development is generally weaker, for example Son and Meisels (2006) found correlations of $r = .40$ between the reading and visual motor skills, and $r = .20$ between the reading and gross motor skills of children in kindergarten when children were assessed with objective measures. Yet whilst the correlations between the EYPSP language and mathematics are high, as expected, the correlations between the EYFSP motor development and language or maths scores are much higher than expected. The correlations between the PIPS measures and EYFSP are high for language and maths, as would be expected, but lower between PIPS and the other EYFSP measured. This demonstrates a Halo Effect occurring within the EYFSP.

The EYFSP is an example of an assessment method which is at one extreme, relying predominantly on the observation of child-initiated activities, but the assessment of children's attainment and progress using a combination of teacher assessment and standardized objective assessments for the purpose of accountability is becoming a more widespread feature of national systems. Scotland has recently changed its national assessment system to align with its new curriculum (Curriculum for Excellence). In the guidance on assessment issued to all Scottish schools and councils (Scottish Government, 2010), a combination of teacher assessment by comparing pupils' attainment against national exemplars of standards along with standardized objective assessments is recommended. More recently, in 2011, the English government commissioned an independent review of testing arrangements at the end of the primary phase of education (referred to as the end of Key Stage Two). Evidence from many sources, including expert opinion, was gathered and the recommendation made to include a greater element of teacher assessment than currently occurs. A further recommendation was to consider the use of computer-delivered assessments, including diagnostic computer-adaptive programs (Bew, 2011).

Table 13.1 The Halo Effect in teacher ratings: data from the Early Years Foundation Stage Profile (EYFSP)

	EYFSP PSED	EYFSP Lang.	EYFSP Maths.	EYFSP KUW	EYFSP Motor Dev.	EYFSP Create Dev.	PIPS Lang.
EYFSP Lang.	0.81						
EYFSP Maths.	0.84	0.92					
EYFSP KUW	0.84	0.83	0.83				
EYFSP Motor Dev.	0.83	0.72	0.77	0.75			
EYFSP Create Dev.	0.80	0.82	0.79	0.85	0.81		
PIPS Lang.	0.65	0.82	0.80	0.74	0.61	0.66	
PIPS Maths	0.66	0.72	0.76	0.65	0.62	0.64	0.82

All correlations were significant at the 0.01 level (2-tailed).

Diagnostic computer-adaptive assessments are becoming more widespread and hold promise by producing detailed information about children's strengths and areas of difficulty that can be used to develop personalised education.[1] They are motivating for children, presenting questions that are within their zone of proximal development, and produce a more reliable measure especially for children at the high or low end of the ability range. I have given examples of the computer-adaptive assessments produced by CEM at Durham University, which are used on a large scale with hundreds of thousands of children using them each year and questions could be asked about them discriminating against children with additional support needs or with limited experience of ICT. We have investigated these possible issues and not found evidence of their presence. Moreover, we have received positive feedback about particular groups of children, for example, the indigenous children in Western Australia who, at the time of the report, had not been exposed to ICT-rich environments. Teachers reported the children's delight at the assessment format. Of course, as with any standardized assessment, care must be taken to eliminate bias and discrimination including ensuring fair access for children with a range of additional support needs such as sensory impairments or attentional difficulties. These assessments are valuable and flexible standardized tools whose uses are only just beginning to be realized in terms of their power to provide instant norm and criterion referenced feedback to both pupils and teachers.

Conclusions

Standardized educational assessment has many benefits and the chapter has discussed some examples. There are issues with how standardized assessments are conducted and despite the concerns expressed about observation methods, teachers do need a full picture of a child if they are going to cater for all their needs. This picture cannot realistically be achieved through objective assessments alone. A balance of assessment methods is required and there will always be a particular aspect of a child's behaviour or development elicited through a non-standardized method which is useful and important within the context of that individual. It is not only the type of assessment that matters but the way it is used.

Looking to the future, recent advances in computer-adaptive diagnostic assessments have the potential to provide efficient and reliable group assessments which probe children's knowledge and understanding in a detailed and appropriate way that has not been possible with more traditional group assessment methods, and to provide rapid feedback for improvement that is tailored to an individual's needs.

Notes

1   For a description of the development of a computer-adaptive diagnostic assessment of reading, see Merrell and Tymms (2006), and for a wide-ranging discussion of computer-adaptive testing for reading, see Chalhaub-Deville (2000)

References

Barkley, R. A. (1997). Behavioural inhibition, sustained attention, and executive functions: constructing a unifying theory of ADHD. *Psychological Bulletin, 121*, 65–94.

Ben-Shakhar, G. and Sinai, Y. (1991) Gender differences in multiple choice tests: the role of differential guessing tendencies. *Journal of Educational Measurement, 28*, 23–35.

Bew, Lord (2011) *Independent Review of Key Stage 2 Testing, Assessment and Accountability: Final Report.* Available at: www.education.gov.uk (accessed 2 July 2011).

Blatchford, P. and Cline, T. (1992). Baseline assessment for school entrants. *Research Papers in Education, 7*, 247–269.

Chalhoub-Deville, M. (Ed.) (2000). *Issues in Computer-Adaptive Testing of Reading Proficiency: Studies in Language Testing 10.* Cambridge: Cambridge University Press.

Coe, R. (2002) *It's the Effect Size, Stupid: What Effect Size is and Why It is Important.* Paper presented at the Annual Conference of the British Educational Research Association, Exeter, England.

Harlen, W. (2004). A systematic review of the evidence of reliability and validity of assessment by teachers used for summative purposes. In the Assessment and Learning Research Synthesis Group *Research Evidence in Education Library*. London: EPPI-Centre, Social Science Research Unit, Institute of Education.

——(2005). Trusting teachers' judgement: research evidence of reliability and validity of teachers' assessment used for summative purposes. *Research Papers in Education, 20*, 245–270.

Merrell, C. and Tymms, P. (2006) Identifying reading problems with computer-adaptive assessments. *Journal of Computer Assisted Learning, 23*, 27–35.

——(2010) Changes in children's cognitive development at the start of school in England 2001– 2008. *Oxford Review of Education.* iFIRST 1–13, available at http://www.informaworld.com/smpp/title~content=t713440173 (accessed 25 January 2012).

National Union of Teachers (2006) *Briefing: The Impact of National Curriculum Tests on Pupils.* NUT: London.

Newton, P. E. (2007). Clarifying the purposes of educational assessment. *Assessment in Education: Principles, Policy & Practice, 14*, 149–170.

——(2009). The reliability of results from national curriculum testing in England. *Educational Research, 51:2,* 181–212:

Nye, B., Konstantopoulos, S. and Hedges, L. V. (2004). How large are teacher effects? *Educational Evaluation and Policy Analysis, 26*, 237–257.

Qualifications and Curriculum Authority (2008) *Early Years Foundation Stage Profile Handbook*. London: HMSO

Rosenzweig, P. (2007). *The Halo Effect … and the Eight Other Business Delusions that Deceive Managers*. NY: Free Press.

Sanders, W. and Horn, S. (1994) The Tenessee Value-added Assessment System (TVAAS): mixed model methodology in educational assessment. *Journal of Personnel Evaluation in Education, 8*, 299–311.

Scorcher, M. and Brant, J. (2002). Are you picking the right leaders? *Harvard Business Review*, February.

Scottish Government (2010). *Curriculum for Excellence; Building the Curriculum 5; A Framework for Assessment*. Edinburgh: The Scottish Government.

Son, S-H, and Meisels, S. J. (2006). The relationship of young children's motor skills to later reading and math achievement. *Merrill-Palmer Quarterly, 52*, 755–778.

Sonuga-Barke, E. J. S., Minocha, K., Taylor, E. A. and Sandberg, S. (1993). Inter-ethnic bias in teachers' ratings of childhood hyperactivity. *Journal of Developmental Psychology, 11*, 187–200.

Taylor Fitz-Gibbon, C. (1996). *Monitoring Education: Indicators, Quality and Effectiveness*. Continuum: London.

——(1997). *The Value Added National Project: Final Report: Feasibility Studies for a National System of Value Added Indicators*. London: SCAA.

Teddlie, C. and Reynolds, D. (2000). *The International Handbook of School Effectiveness Research*. London: Falmer Press.

Tickell, C. (2011). *The Early Years Foundation Stage (EYFS) Review: Report on the Evidence*. Available at: http://media.education.gov.uk/assets/Files/pdf/T/The%20Tickell%20Review.pdf (accessed 2 July 2011).

Tymms, P. (1999). *Baseline Assessment and Monitoring in Primary Schools: Achievements, Attitudes and Value-added Indicators*. London, David Fulton.

Tymms, P. and Albone, S. (2002). Performance indicators in primary schools. In A. J. Visscher and R. Coe, *School Improvement Through Performance Feedback*. Lisse/Abingdon/Exton PA/Tokyo: Swetz & Zeitlinger (pp. 191–218).

Tymms, P., Merrell, C. and Jones, P. (2004). Using baseline assessment data to make international comparisons. *British Educational Research Journal, 30*, 673–689.

Tymms, P., Merrell, C., Heron, T., Jones, P., Albone, S. and Henderson, B. (2008). The importance of districts. *School Effectiveness and School Improvement, 19*, 261–274.

Wilmut, J. (2005). *Experiences of Summative Teacher Assessment in the UK; A Review Conducted for the Qualifications and Curriculum Authority*. London: QCA.

Wolfendale, S. and Lindsay, G. (1999). Issues in baseline assessment. *Journal of Research in Reading, 22*, 1–13.

Part XIV

What is the role of the modern educator in fostering moral values and virtues?

As I have argued elsewhere (Carr 1995, 1996), we need to resist the temptation – not least of social-constructivist or communitarian ethical theories – to regard virtues as expressions of local moral creeds, codes or customs. This is rather like identifying the art of good driving with obedience to this or that highway code ... But clearly, though good driving does clearly depend on observing *some* local code, it will have common procedural features in the context of quite different driving rules and custom from our own. But the same goes for moral virtues. To teach or educationally promote honesty, fairness, courage, tolerance or compassion is not necessarily, if at all, to indoctrinate in the values any particular local (ideological) perspective.

David Carr

But in talking about an "educated person" we are engaged in an evaluation of the sort of person he or she is – whether he or she has certain qualities. The aims of education are the expressions of those qualities which we wish to attribute to an "educated person". Such evaluations will always be controversial for they are necessarily based upon what we believe to be the distinctive qualities of being a person and of becoming one more fully.

Richard Pring

Chapter 28

On the educational value of moral virtues

Some lessons from ancient philosophy

David Carr

University of Edinburgh

Purposes of education, schooling, and teaching

If asked what education and schools are for, many would probably say that their purpose
is to provide the young with knowledge and skills required for effective functioning and
success in (an increasingly complex) society. If asked to specify such knowledge and skills
further, they might mention the (more or less useful) things that they had learned at
school – such as literacy and numeracy, history, physics, biology, woodwork, home
economics and physical education – perhaps adding (especially if they themselves had not
had these things at school) information and other technology and personal and social
(especially perhaps health and sex) education. Any such list could also include poetry,
music and religious education – though one could also guess that these might not be
mentioned quite so often. Again, if prospective or trainee teachers were asked what they
were ultimately hoping to teach, they would no doubt (if secondary teachers) mention a
particular subject (such as English, mathematics or physical education) or (if primary
teachers) a particular stage of child development (such as early years, lower primary or
upper primary). This is all well and good, so far as it goes: after all, schools (as social
institutions funded by tax payers) are responsible for equipping youngsters with individually
and socially useful knowledge and skills and primary and secondary school teachers do and
should want to teach what they take to be such knowledge and skills.

The problem here is not that there anything wrong with saying that it is the job of
schools and teachers to pass on knowledge and skills conducive to effective individual and/
or social functioning, success or flourishing, but that more needs to be thought and said
about what constitutes such success or flourishing if we are to avoid dangerously narrow or
attenuated conceptions of education and schooling. It is also arguable that this danger has
never been more clearly recognised than in the arguments of the founder of western
philosophy – Socrates – as recorded in the dialogues of Plato. To be sure, it is striking that
the first systematic ethical enquiries into the nature of human moral life, as attributed by
Plato to Socrates in such dialogues as *Gorgias*, *Protagoras*, *Meno* and *Republic* (Plato, 1961), are
actually driven by an essentially *educational* question about how human agents might best
live, how we might come to know that this or that possibility is a good or best life and
whether it is possible to teach such knowledge to others. Indeed, it is the present author's
view that Plato's *Gorgias* is one of the most profound and insightful essays on the philosophy
of education – here explicitly conceived as a central ethical concern – ever written; that it is
a work of enduring educational relevance (indeed, perhaps even more than in Plato's day),
such that it should be compulsory reading in contemporary teacher training.

Plato's *Gorgias*, like other Platonic dialogues, finds Socrates engaging critically with the views of those philosophers and theorists of his day usually known as the *Sophists* – here in particular with the famous sophist Gorgias. In today's terms, the ancient sophists may be regarded as forerunners of latter day market conceptions of education. They were effectively educational mercenaries who taught what they taught – which seemed to be almost anything that people might want to learn – for payment or profit. Their educational clientele were also well nigh exclusively the offspring – which in ancient Greece of course meant the male offspring – of aristocratic or otherwise well-to-do parents who desired such education or teaching as a means to worldly success, power and influence. Moreover, the means to power and success in the albeit limited political democracy of Athens (since it denied full or even partial civil rights to large sections of the population) seemed to be those skills needed for persuading others to support one's own interests in the Athenian democratic assemblies in which those of high social status participated. Thus, Gorgias argues that the most valuable of all human skills – of which he claims to be a distinguished teacher – is the art of *rhetoric* understood as fine speaking or effective persuasion. In the terms of modern popular psychology books, it is the art that enables one to win friends and influence people.

Is the good life having complete satisfaction of one's desires?

More precisely, in direct response to Socrates' basic question about what constitutes the good life, Gorgias argues that rhetoric is the most valuable of all human arts because it enables those who possess it to satisfy all of their deepest desires, not least their desires for power, wealth or sensual pleasure. On the view of Gorgias and other sophists it is obvious without need for demonstration that such personal-desire gratification is an unqualified good or benefit. How could a life in which individuals satisfied all their desires be other than completely happy and fulfilled (and a life of unsatisfied desires other than unhappily frustrated)? But it is this just this fundamental sophistical claim that Socrates sets out to refute in this great dialogue. Effectively, by re-evaluating or re-defining happiness or flourishing, Socrates denies that such basic desire gratification is either a necessary or a sufficient condition for a good life. It is certainly not sufficient, according to Socrates, because we can think of many powerful people – for example, great dictators or tyrants who are able to coerce others into giving them all they want – who may nevertheless not be enviable, in the sense of being the kind of people we should or would want to be (as in the parable of Gyges' ring). If the price of being able to satisfy all our desires is becoming a Ghengis Khan, Adolf Hitler, Josef Stalin, Saddam Hussein or Idi Amin, then there is at least a perspective from which such a price is far too high. In short, in a Gospel saying that may well owe much to Socratic/Platonic influence: "what doth it profit a man to gain the whole world and lose his soul"?

But since undue commitment to the gratification of basic desires is often associated with a kind of enfeeblement of moral character, it is not obvious that it is constitutive of or necessary for a flourishing life either. Thus, while having the capacity to achieve or satisfy all one's wants and desires is not necessarily destructive of all character or discipline – since such morally dubious characters as Ghengis Khan, Hitler and Stalin may have been men of iron will and firm resolve – it may lead to an infantile addiction to or dependence on more basic sensual pleasures that can undermine character. In this vein, Socrates argues that vicious tyrants and despots, far from being in control of their lives and destinies, are frequently mere slaves to irrational appetites, desires and impulses that they cannot control. He compares their dependence on insatiable desires to leaky buckets that need constant replenishing. Lacking the discipline of self-control, they cannot be said to act as genuine agents in the world: in this respect, they are far from having the self-possession characteristic of true human freedom and are more like spoiled children than free agents. Yet more, the intemperate desires and impulses towards which the undisciplined are inclined are themselves often destructive, not just of character, but of healthy human living and functioning. Insatiable addictions to the sensual pleasures of food, alcohol, drugs or unbridled sex are not just destructive of will and character but of the basic emotional, affective and somatic conditions of healthy human flourishing. Too much of anything can be bad for us. On this view, as J. S. Mill was to say later: "it is better to be Socrates dissatisfied, than a pig satisfied" (Warnock, 1970, p. 260).

In short, on Socrates' revised conception of happiness, one may have the capacity or resources to satisfy all one's desires without being counted happy (even if one mistakenly thinks that one is) and/or one may be happy without the satisfaction of *all* one's desires (since one may know full well that the satisfaction of all of these would not be good for one). Socrates argues – in the face of stiff opposition from Gorgias and his supporters – that there can be no genuine happiness of flourishing in the absence of autonomous human agency; that there can be no such agency failing the power to make choices that may entail control of or resistance to potentially unhealthy or enfeebling appetites or desires; and that such discipline or control requires rationally wise "second-order" discernment of what is or is not in our best (long- as well as short-term) interests as human agents. Effectively, what Socrates argues is that there can be no real human happiness or flourishing in the absence of *moral virtue* and that virtue requires a kind of knowledge of what is or is not humanly beneficial. Such knowledge is not mere acquaintance with facts or information about the world, or any kind of practical or technical skill, but a capacity for serious and profound critical reflection on the personal and social consequences of our actions in the world. Precisely, for Socrates, it is a kind of objective knowledge of the difference between right and wrong: it is a species of moral knowledge and it is focused, unlike rhetoric, on the discernment of *moral truth*.

To be sure, what Socrates (followed by Plato) precisely deplores about rhetoric is its disregard or unconcern for truth. For Gorgias and other sophists, it seems to matter hardly at all that what rhetoric sets out to persuade should also be true. Its worth is to be measured exclusively in terms of the extent to which it is effective in persuading others. The value of rhetoric is therefore that of a good advertisement. Just as it need not much matter to the advertiser whether "Dazzle" does actually wash whiter than any other soap powder, so long as the customer believes that it does and so buys it, so it does not matter whether what the rhetorician says is true as long as others are persuaded that it is true. Indeed, for Socrates, the potency of rhetoric clearly consists in its manipulation of emotions by means that deliberately seek to bypass the rational capacities of agents. To this extent good rhetoricians, advertisers and salesmen will often employ verbal or visual images that appeal directly to primal human desires: the heavy use of sexual imagery in modern advertising, of near naked female models to sell everything from chocolate bars to cars, is a prime example. Indeed, for Socrates and Plato, the emotions to which rhetoric (of which they took art to be a form) appeals are fundamentally irrational and therefore potential sources of temptation to error.

On the Socratic-Platonic view, then, there can be no sure route to the life that is worth living that does not involve the exercise of reason in pursuit of the knowledge of what is humanly good – that is also (for Socrates) identical with virtue. Since rhetoric bypasses reason and has no concern with truth, it cannot therefore count as a genuine form of knowledge or skill, cannot conduce to virtue and is humanly worthless. Socrates argues in *Gorgias* that rhetoric is not a genuine art or skill, but what he (disparagingly) calls a mere "knack". Distinguishing between the interests of body and soul, Socrates identifies knowledge and arts that benefit the body, such as medicine and gymnastics, and those that benefit the soul, such as justice and legislation. To these, however, he opposes practices such as cookery and cosmetics on the one hand and sophistry and rhetoric on the other. The trouble with cookery and cosmetics is that they pander to the appetites and promote false appearance, concealing disease or obesity and ignoring the need for genuine bodily health and fitness with which medicine and gymnastics properly deal. Likewise, sophistry and rhetoric (like advertising) appeal to egocentricity and vanity, promoting false flattery of the soul, rather than that true understanding of our own and other's interests that are the concern of justice and legislation. As cosmetics and cookery corrupt the body, so sophistry and rhetoric corrupt the soul. Moreover, Socrates argues that the user of rhetoric is no less liable to corruption than those he seduces. If a criminal uses rhetoric to swindle others, he cannot be counted at all fortunate if he is successful: on the contrary, it is better for his soul's health that he is caught, punished and forced to atone for his crimes.

Moral wisdom, virtue and education

But what lessons for contemporary education and schooling might be drawn from such Socratic opposition to sophistry and rhetoric? The first and most basic of Socratic points is that, since the good life cannot be conceived as a matter of gratification of any old appetites and desires, a good education has to be more than simply teaching means to satisfy such basic desires and appetites. Indeed, for Socrates and Plato, education must involve the rational evaluation and refinement of basic desires and appetites precisely in the content of wider reflection about individual and social benefit. But such wider personal and social reflection inevitably implicates education in the kind of enquiry into and teaching of moral and other *values* of which educationalists and teachers have often been extremely wary – precisely on the grounds that values are subjective and the teaching of them therefore potentially indoctrinatory. At the very least, however, it means that (theoretical and practical) reflection on education is at heart a form of *ethical* reflection – rather than (as modern educational theorists often seem to have thought) a form of social science.

Certainly, many philosophers have regarded values – construed as commitments to some conception of the good – as *subjective*. But this claim is variously questionable and would – in any extreme form – seem to rest on some conceptual conflation or confusion. To begin with, the term "subjective" may be taken to mean either "non-rational" or "personal". So-called non-cognitivist or sentimentalist moral philosophers, such as Hume (1969), have regarded value judgements as subjective in the sense of expressing no more than non-rational or sub-rational feelings, likings or tastes. But it is not at all plausible to reduce all or even any values to non-rational feelings in this way. On the contrary, since an agent may like or feel positive towards something (such as smoking) without regarding it as good, or regard something as good (such as strenuous exercise) without liking it, it seems that values – *as opposed* to mere tastes or likings – are precisely marked by appeal to reasoned justification: whereas I do not need to support my tastes for strawberries or toffee with reasons, I might well be expected to have supporting reasons for valuing dentistry or disvaluing smoking. Moreover, even though some of my values may be *personal* – in the sense of peculiar to myself or not widely shared by others – they need not necessarily be sub-rational like my taste for strawberries.

But just as values cannot all be reduced to the non-rational or sub-rational, so they cannot be reduced to the personal either. Although some of my perfectly rational values may be personal (in the sense of not required of others), clearly they are not all so. Indeed, many values are clearly impersonal in so far as widely prescribed or subscribed to on the basis of social obligation. Thus, I will usually drive on this or that side of the road as local law or custom dictates, on the grounds that this is conducive to the safety of all concerned. That said, as a rational agent, I do not drive on this or that side of the road simply out of respect for local custom or convention, but because I value good driving – which is not simply a local social or cultural value but (given the human condition) an absolute or universal one. In fact, most great moral philosophers have been ethical objectivists about at least some significant human values – though the reasons they have given for such moral objectivity have been many and varied. Thus, whereas Aristotle (1941) located the objectivity of moral virtues in natural features and needs of the human condition, Kant (1967) grounded the categorical imperatives of his moral law in the reciprocal features of rights-based justice and J. S. Mill (Warnock 1970) located right action in beneficial consequences.

Despite such differences, it should be clear enough that values are by no means largely, if at all, subjective in either non-rational or personal senses. To be sure, moral values are subject to debate or disagreement and people dispute endlessly over the propriety of extra-marital sex, abortion or capital punishment; but this is no less true of other disputes over so-called factual matters. Of course, it has often been said that the potential for rational evidence-based resolution in the case of factual disagreement is less available in the case of value disputes – which must always have a subjective (personal or non-rational) element. But this is not obviously so. It would seem – as moral philosophy has done much to show – that such fundamental questions of human value may be considerably clarified or illuminated through rational discussion (including conceptual analysis) and appeal to evidence regarding the brute facts of human weal and woe. What may be said here is that people are entitled to *endorse* this or that value regardless of reason or evidence – whereas they are less justified in continuing to believe that (say) the earth is flat in the face of contrary reason or evidence. But while this is not obviously true either (are racists entitled to continue subscribing to racism?), we should perhaps at least want to insist – in the spirit of Socrates – on universal educational entitlement to rational evaluation of all human values in hope of further reflective development of any and all human inclinations and desires.

The development of virtue as an intrinsic educational end

However, in opposition to the sophists, Socrates did not just argue for educational opportunity for normative evaluation or clarification of human inclinations, desires and values; he was more strongly arguing that education is properly and centrally concerned with actual moral formation in those objective values and virtues precisely neglected by the sophists. In pursuit of their own narrow careerist and mercenary professional agendas, the sophists failed as teachers or educationalists to cultivate that true wisdom, knowledge and understanding that would enable development of moral virtue in their pupils' souls. For Socrates, it is possible – via the rigorous educational (philosophical) reflection and argumentation that Plato labelled "dialectic" – to shape the soul (as physical exercise might shape the body) in that knowledge of human good and flourishing productive of virtuous character and conduct. Still, we should presently consider two common educational objections to this view. The first is an ancient problem about the relationship of moral knowledge (assuming there is such a thing) to moral motivation – of whether, precisely, moral knowledge or understanding is sufficient for virtue: the second is that of whether the teaching of moral virtues in present day (particularly culturally plural and liberal) democracies could ever be professionally required of justified.

With regard to the first issue, the view of moral development taken by Socrates and Plato was evidently rationalistic: Socrates appears to have held that all moral wrongdoing is the consequence of ignorance and that all an agent needs in order to act rightly is to appreciate the difference between good and bad conduct. But the view that (moral) knowledge is sufficient for right action is prey to the difficulty known as *akrasia* or "weakness of will", whereby it seems psychologically possible for agents to know what is morally better, yet to pursue what is worse. Indeed, moral wrongdoing seems all too often to be a matter of falling prey to temptations towards what we know full well we should resist. This problem has also beset most subsequent ethical theory – not least the various forms of moral rationalism of modern moral philosophy. It has also been an evident weakness of modern rationalistic accounts of moral education – notably the so-called cognitive developmental theories of Piaget (1932) and Kohlberg (1984) – that they have some trouble explaining how mere "cognitive" acquaintance with moral propositions or principles might ensure agents' obedience to what such propositions or principles enjoin. One modern response to this problem has been from so-called moral *non-cognitivists* or *sentimentalists* who have held that such propositions or principles are really just forms of affect, desires or pro-attitudes, in thin cognitive disguise.

In his *Republic* and elsewhere, while defending a thoroughgoing rationalist theory of moral knowledge, Plato clearly does appreciate the motivational problem. Moreover, Plato's solution to the problem inclines to a complex moral psychology according to which morality is a matter of the development of virtue, but virtue is not simply (as it seems to have been for his teacher Socrates) reducible to moral knowledge. For Plato, moral development is a matter of the cultivation of intellectual and *practical* capacities: as well as being able to reason rightly, moral agents need certain executive virtues of "spirit", "energy" or "initiative" that enable them to stick to any moral principles to which they may have more "intellectually" committed themselves. But Plato's solution to the *akrasia* problem seems less than satisfactory, since it is not at all clear how such ad hoc capacities as spirit and energy close the gap between moral intellect and agency. Why, after all, should spirit or intellect serve right moral reason rather than the "lower" (for Plato) demands of instinctual desire and appetite? Indeed, bad as well as good people may have much spirit and energy and such qualities may often serve the pursuit of dissipation and wickedness.

A much more satisfactory development of Plato's account of moral virtue is to be found in the ethics of his great pupil Aristotle (1941) who is the true founder of what has come to be known as "virtue ethics". Briefly, while Aristotle agrees with Plato that morality involves reason and knowledge, he also takes this to be a practical more than theoretical matter. While Aristotle takes moral agency to involve "cognitive" grasp of moral imperatives or principles, he also takes this to be part and parcel of the practical acquisition of practical habits or dispositions – such as honesty, justice, courage and temperance – independently justifiable on grounds of their evident contribution to human benefit. On Aristotle's naturalistic theory of ethics, the practical dispositions of moral virtue are needed for human agents to live well, and a certain kind of distinctively practical reason is needed to cultivate such dispositions. Thus, according to Aristotle, it is crucial to distinguish the practical reflection of what he calls *phronesis* or practical wisdom from the intellectual truth-seeking reflection of Plato's *dialectic* or other concepts of theoretical reason. However, practical wisdom – centrally concerned as it is with the proper ordering of natural human desires, emotions and appetites – cannot but be of intrinsic *educational* significance. There could be no education worthy of the name that neglected the cultivation of desires, emotions and appetites via the development of *phronesis*.

Can or should educators of today cultivate the moral virtues?

For Socrates, the "sophistical" focus on teaching the knowledge and skills that would enable gratification of basic human desires and appetites fatally neglected the key purpose of education to refine and cultivate such desires and appetites via deeper critical reflection on or evaluation of other (arguably "higher") possibilities of human flourishing. However, on Aristotelian development of the Socratic-Platonic conception of virtue as the key goal of human flourishing, it is not just needful for pupils to acquire any and all knowledge conducive to the development of moral virtue, but precisely to develop – via the cultivation of *phronesis* or practical wisdom – the various virtues of moral character themselves. Education cannot just be intellectual or academic education; it must also be concerned with promoting moral character of pupils. But how, one might ask, can this be justified or legitimated, or achieved if it can be legitimated, in modern (or post-modern) – particularly culturally plural liberal democracies – such as our own?

The key difficulty here – or at least that which is likely to be perceived as key – is the alleged indoctrinatory prospect or potential of such teaching. That said, in the long educational experience of this writer, this has often seemed more of a theoretical or "academic" problem than a professional or practical one. While it seems to have been widely and regularly assumed by past and present educational policy makers that teachers should promote morally positive dispositions and conduct on the part of pupils, this also seems to be the default position of most practising teachers. Indeed, in some field research into teachers' views on morals and values (conducted some years ago by the present writer and a university colleague), it was found that all the research participants, with few exceptions, more or less assumed that the teaching of moral values and virtues was part and parcel of their professional role (see Carr and Landon, 1998). The few exceptions were (a couple of) secondary specialist teachers of science who continued to insist – against majority opposition – that it was their job only to teach physics and chemistry and nothing else. Of course, statistics are not arguments: but the weight of contrary opinion here may well be taken as an indication that there is some error and/or confusion in any dissenting view.

I believe that there is both error and confusion. To begin with, it has often been argued that there is no such thing as value-free teaching: that even trying to dissociate the teaching of (scientific or other) knowledge from values, itself implies a significant (and dubious) value perspective. But if this is so, does this not make the potential for indoctrination in teaching moral character or virtues more acute? Surely, whatever we teach – not least in the way of moral education – must therefore involve the communication of contestable values. That might be so if we *had* to regard the teaching of morally good or virtuous character as contestable – or even as a matter of the teaching of *values*, at least in any very loaded sense here. But *is* the teaching of such virtues of (Aristotelian) moral character as honesty, fairness, self-control, courage, tolerance, care and compassion a matter of promoting contestable values?

There have certainly been highly influential theories of virtue that would seem to suggest that it is. Thus, for one celebrated example, the (allegedly Aristotelian) virtue theory of the distinguished modern moral and social theorist Alasdair MacIntyre (1981) seems to hold that moral virtues are locally formed in different "rival" cultural traditions, which means that what counts as a virtue in this social context might not count as a virtue – or might even count as a vice – in that rather different one. For MacIntyre, moral virtues are practice-sustaining dispositions and the practices they sustain are justified by diverse and even contrary traditions of moral reflection. But Macintyre here departs significantly from Aristotle in giving an unhelpfully "axiological" or "doxastic" account of virtue. That is, for MacIntyre, the identity of a virtue seems heavily dependent on people's local beliefs or values – which might determine whether (say) generosity or humility are to be counted as virtues (perhaps rather than vices). But for Aristotle, such virtue dispositions as temperance, courage and generosity are identified as reasonable means between unreasonable extremes of emotional or appetitive excess and defect: temperance avoids unreasonable extremes of self-denial and indulgence; courage of cowardice and recklessness; generosity of meanness and profligacy, and so on.

In this regard, Aristotelian virtues are morally *procedural* rather than substantive and we do not actually have to know what another person (whether Moslem, communist or atheist) actually values or believes in order to judge whether he is honest, just, courageous, temperate or compassionate: we only need to know that he is inclined to tell the truth, deal with others fairly, stand up for his principles even under threat, control his appetites or care for others. From this viewpoint, the language of virtue provides an effective cross-cultural currency of moral evaluation. As I have argued elsewhere (Carr 1995, 1996), we need to resist the temptation – not least of social-constructivist or communitarian ethical theories – to regard virtues as expressions of local moral creeds, codes or customs. This is rather like identifying the art of good driving with obedience to this or that highway code – from which we might conclude that good driving here (where people drive on the left side of the road) is different from good driving there (where they drive on the right). But clearly, though good driving does depend on observing *some* local code, it will have common procedural features in the context of quite different driving rules and custom from our own. But the same goes for moral virtues. To teach or educationally promote honesty, fairness, courage, tolerance or compassion is not necessarily, if at all, to indoctrinate in the values of any particular local (ideological) perspective.

I believe that this effectively answers the question of whether educators *can* teach moral virtues in the sense of avoiding indoctrination. It does not, of course, answer the no less pressing question of *how* teachers might teach virtue in school and classroom contexts. This is obviously a large question that cannot be here pursued in any depth in the remaining space. However, as I have indicated elsewhere, Aristotle had much to say about the issue of teaching, learning and cultivating virtues in his *Nicomachean Ethics*. Briefly, he identified three main processes necessary for the acquisition or cultivation of virtue. The first and most basic of these is practical training: children need encouraging in the actual practices of honesty, justice, temperance and so on and to be corrected when they fall short. The second process is moral exemplification: children need exposure to good moral (virtuous) example from parents, teachers and other guardians. This, of course, imposes a serious professional burden on teachers to be as far as possible morally serious people as well as effective instructors (see Carr, 2007). But the third and probably most important condition of virtue for Aristotle is the opportunity to develop the open reflection and deliberation required for the development of *phronesis,* practical wisdom. It also appears that for Aristotle, this could not be developed through any particular area of the school curriculum, but would require a broad liberal education – including, crucially, exposure to literature and the arts.

References

Aristotle. (1941). *The Nicomachean Ethics.* In R. McKeon (Ed.), *The Basic Works of Aristotle,* New York: Random House.

Carr, D. (1995). The primacy of virtues in ethical theory: Part I, *Cogito, 9,* 238–244.

——(1996). The primacy of virtues in ethical theory: Part II, *Cogito, 10,* 34–40.

——(2007). Character in teaching. *British Journal of Educational Studies, 55,* 369–389.

Carr, D. and Landon, J. (1998). Teachers and schools as agencies of values education: reflections on teacher's perceptions: part I: the role of the teacher. *Journal of Beliefs and Values, 19,* 165–176.

Hume, D. (1969). *A Treatise of Human Nature.* Harmondsworth: Penguin

Kant, I. (1967). *The Critique of Practical Reason and other Essays in the Theory of Ethics.* London: Longmans.

Kohlberg, L. (1984) *Essays on Moral Development: Volume I.* New York: Harper Row.

MacIntyre, A. (1981). *After Virtue.* London: Duckworth

Piaget, J. (1932) *The Moral Judgement of the Child.* London: Routledge and Kegan Paul.

Plato (1961) *Republic.* In E. Hamilton and H. Cairns (Eds.), *Plato: The Collected Dialogues.* Princeton: Princeton University Press.

Warnock, M. (Ed.) (1970). *Utilitarianism.* Collins: The Fontana Library.

Chapter 29

The pursuit of virtue as an aim of education

Richard Pring

Green Templeton College, University of Oxford

Watch your language

A *cri de coeur* has arrived from a head teacher of a highly successful small school in New York who is worried about the evaluation scheduled to take place of certain schools, assisted or led by the British firm of educational consultants. What will it mean for their highly successful and carefully thought out engagement with young people, many of whom suffer from the various forms of disadvantage often associated with inner city life? What will happen when the inspectors and evaluators enter with their lists of "performance indicators" to do "an audit", or when they check the "value addedness" from "before performance tests" to "after performance tests", or when they propose certain "efficiency gains"?

There are many ways in which the world of business has entered into the shaping of the aims and values, into the governance and, above all, into the language of education. The reaction to the perceived failure of schools has frequently been to run them more like private businesses (other than modern banks, one hopes!), and schools within the public domain are increasingly run by "for-profit" organisations, as indeed so are key educational services. Hence, there is a shift from the essentially moral language of education to that of the management theory that pervades the business world and profit-making.

But can schools be run like businesses?

Perhaps the most succinct and effective response to this question is given through the story related by Larry Cuban (2004) in his book *The Blackboard and the Bottom Line: Why Schools Can't Be Run Like Businesses*. The story might be abbreviated as follows. A successful business man, dedicated to improving public schools, told an audience of teachers: "if I ran my business the way you people operate your schools, I wouldn't be in business very long". Cross-examined by a teacher, he declared that the success of his blueberry ice cream lay in the meticulous way in which he selected his blueberries, sending back those which did not meet the high quality he insisted upon. To this the teacher replied:

> That's right … and we can never send back our blueberries. We take them rich, poor, gifted, exceptional, abused, frightened … we take them all. Every one. And that … is why it is not a business. It's a school.

> (Cuban, 2004, pp. 3–4).

But this is not a wholesale condemnation of any business involvement. The education of young people must embrace, as Dewey so clearly argued, preparation for living life outside the school which, of course, includes the world of work into which they are to enter. But for Dewey, as Cuban points out, "vocational" has the much broader sense than that of being trained for a specific occupation or specific role.

Cuban (2004) describes in detail the ways in which, over the course of a century or more, the business community has perceived its role in the shaping of the content, provision and organisation of what happens in schools. But more importantly, he gets beneath the description to analyse the reasons for this – the "logic of action", as he calls it. That is: clear goals or targets, regular measurement of performance in relation to those targets, public knowledge of the results of that measurement, parental choice in the light of that knowledge, competition between a range of providers, performance incentives (for example, performance related pay) and sanctions for failure. The underlying philosophy might best be expressed in the McKinsey formula (although Cuban does not make this point): what is real can be measured; what can be measured can be controlled. In some cases the "logic of action" takes us further – into vouchers, into for-profit schools and into the benefits from investment in "human capital", the economic consequences of which are put forward as an incentive to otherwise reluctant learners.

It is easy of course to develop an argument through the contrasting of extreme cases. There are clearly ways in which there need to be connections between the educational system and the economic context in which schools are preparing the next generation of citizens. Well-organised work experience can be educational through the development of understanding, personal qualities and relevant skills. The views of future employers are important as the teachers prepare young people for life after formal education is completed. All this is recognised. But there remain significant differences – as the interrogating teacher pointed out to the seller of blueberry ice cream. And the most important difference is the essentially moral purpose of education, an enterprise that is not and cannot be driven by the pursuit of profit. It is not that kind of thing.

The logic of action

The "logic of action" would seem to be quite straightforward. If I want to go to the shops and if bus no. 23 takes me to the shops, then it makes sense to get bus no. 23. The bus is the *means* for reaching the intended *end*. The two ("means" and "end") are only contingently related. It could be the case that, with a change of timetable, no. 23 would no longer be a means for reaching the end. Furthermore, as with all contingent relationships, it is an empirical matter (observation and experience) to show that getting the bus is a "means" to the intended "end".

Translating this simple piece of logic into educational contexts, one might say that going through certain exercises is a means of doing well in the examination and getting the required qualification. That can be demonstrated, especially if it is tested out on a large enough sample of students. Thus might arise a "science of teaching" – the gradual discovery of, through careful experiment on carefully selected samples of learners, "what works". To engage in such a science one would need to spell out the aims very precisely in terms of measurable targets – for example, getting so many Grade As in key subjects. They become the "end" to be reached. The most likely "means" of getting such grades can be shown to be the coaching in how to answer certain kinds of question. There is teaching to the test.

However, something suspiciously odd has happened here. First, the learners get bored and disengaged through the constant preparation for the tests. They have successfully "hit the targets", reached the intended "end", and yet question whether they have been educated. Indeed, the very "means" for reaching the defined "educational ends" seem, surprisingly, to have been mis-educational. They cause boredom and disengagement. They do not lead to that deeper understanding and that readiness and aspiration to continue with their learning. What seems to be not working is the logical separation of "means" from "ends" implicit within the "logic of action" that Cuban refers to.

This separation of "ends" from "means" in this way is, as argued by John Dewey (1916), a "false dualism" (p. 106). Being able to understand the mysteries of algebra is brought about by the doing of algebra, through the constant correction and guidance of the teacher. The "end" is embodied in the "means". There may well be "ends" which are externally related to the activity of thinking and working mathematically – for example, getting a prize. But the "end", which defines this activity (the "means") through which mathematical understanding is achieved, is logically related to the "means". Again, one might study the arts and humanities simply with a view to getting requisite qualifications – the "logic of action" in the first sense. But what makes the reading of this poem or the performance of that play the means to the educational end of understanding and appreciating the human condition is the continuity between the means and the end. The end is embodied in the means. They are not contingently related.

Therein lies a second "logic of action", namely, the pursuit of activities which embody the end (which itself might well evolve in the seeking of it) and which itself might require no justification in terms of some contingently related end. Such ends (the capacity to pursue mathematical reasoning, the better grasp of the human condition) are seen to be worthwhile in and of themselves. They are part of the "good life" as becomes a flourishing human being.

The ethical dimension of educational ends

The "logic of action" in the first sense does not raise, in itself, ethical issues. Success lies, not in the intrinsic value of what happens, but in the "effectiveness" with which the targets are reached. Books have been written on the "effective school" and much research undertaken, within the school improvement movement, into effective schools. The ends or targets themselves are introduced from outside the educational context – the proportion of students who reach Level 3 as that is measured, or the number who obtain five GCSEs at Grade C in certain core subjects. Such targets say nothing about the quality of learning, as might be reflected in the desire to carry on learning or in the transformation of how one lives and appreciates the world.

Such educational ends – the ones that are embodied in the many activities that, pursued successfully, relate to what counts as an educated person – require a very different kind of justification. There is a need to probe what are the qualities, understandings, aspirations and capacities that constitute being a person and indeed becoming one more fully. And that takes us into the realms of ethics – something rarely pursued in the school effectiveness and school improvement literature and policy. What is it to be a person, to live a distinctively human form of life, to flourish as a human being? Such questions, as in all ethical questions, will not receive a total consensus amongst the answers. These are philosophical questions that have stimulated massive debate over millennia. But although consensus will never be reached, the question is unavoidable since the qualities and capacities that constitute being a person are implicit in all educational choices – the subject matter to be taught, the pedagogical approaches to teaching, and the ethos generated in school and classroom to encourage learning.

On becoming a person

To become a person is a matter of learning – learning basic understandings of the physical, social and moral worlds one has entered into, learning how to adapt to and to cope with the physical and social environments one inhabits, learning what pursuits will bring deep and lasting satisfaction, learning how amidst all sorts of hardships one might attain a sense of personal dignity, learning how to take responsibility for the choices which shape one's life.

It is this capacity to be responsible for these choices and to deliberate (in the light of the wisdom of the past) what is a worthwhile form of life, which makes us distinctively human. Part of that learning does and should draw upon the inherited knowledge of the human condition gained from the sciences, the arts and the humanities, because these, in the words of Michael Oakeshott (1975/1990, p. 39), are:

> the voices joined, as such voices could only be joined, in a conversation – an endless unrehearsed intellectual adventure in which, in imagination, we enter into a variety of modes of understanding the world and ourselves ...

whereby we have come to understand the physical, social and moral worlds in which we grow. And that wisdom can be communicated by the good teacher to all young people, at different levels of complexity certainly, through the key ideas and modes of understanding that they embody – as Jerome Bruner (1960) so clearly attested.

There is a danger, however, that such an initiation into these different "voices in the conversation" becomes an end in itself – even a transmission of knowledge disconnected from the wider characteristics of personal development. Indeed, as is all too obvious, such knowledge and understanding can be used for bad ends – the pursuit of self to the detriment of other people, the gaining of power, the acquisition of personal wealth, the undermining of the public good. Being a person is to have the capacity and the propensity to see life – as it is and as it might become – as a whole, to deliberate on the aims and values which are worth pursuing, and to take on responsibility for one's actions and their consequences for the greater good of the community of which one is part.

Characteristic, therefore, of becoming a person more fully is a "different logic of action" from that described above. There is no clear "end" distinct from the "means" for attaining that "end". Rather is it a constant questioning of the "ends" or goals that are embedded in the life and activities in which one is engaged. Is the full-time dedication to stamp collecting really worthwhile? Of what value is the pursuit of historical scholarship? In what sort of activities might I find a high degree of fulfilment? Deliberation, rather than technical reasoning about the effectiveness of "means" to "ends", shapes the actions taken. And that deliberation responds and adapts to new experiences, to feelings of dissatisfaction with the status quo, to failed projects, to the questionings and criticisms of others, to challenges from similar contexts provided by literature, to understandings arising from scientific discovery, to examples of alternative life-styles, to enlightenment from the arts and the humanities. There is no formula to be invoked for settling the puzzles and questions. There is no end to the deliberations. It is a life-time task.

Such deliberation is prompted and enabled by the good teacher who is able to bridge the modes of understanding of the learner and the forms of experience embodied in the sciences, arts and humanities. Central to education, therefore, is the provision of opportunities for such deliberation to take place. Central, too, is the primary use of study of the sciences, arts and humanities as the resources upon which the teacher might draw in the pursuit of such deliberations. The teaching of the arts and the humanities is not a matter of transmitting knowledge for the sake of something else – a qualification, a place in the university, a good job – as is the case in the "logic of action" in the first sense. Rather it is an exposure to ways of thinking, valuing and appreciating which transform the learners' consciousness of the worlds in which they live.

An example from the arts

A typical class in the arts might be to introduce the students to a play, chosen because it explores powerfully some aspect of the human condition, relevant to the experiences, fears and hopes of the young people. Such an exploration would not only outline a situation but would engage the students and the teacher emotionally. If all goes well the class would not only see the world differently but also feel differently about it. It would not be just a matter of a cold analytic narration of a story – to be remembered for the examination but leaving the learner much the same as before.

Let us take, for example, the case (a real one) where the students are asked to discuss a quite simple proposition.

A young woman is about to get married to a man who is deeply in love with her. She likes him and respects him. But deep down she is in love with another, who terminated the friendship two years previously to marry another woman, by whom he now has a baby. When this man hears of the wedding preparations, he seeks out the young bride. He urges her to elope with him, abandoning his wife and child. She leaves behind a distraught and humiliated bridegroom and a lot of angry relatives. Put simply, were the man and the bride right in abandoning their responsibilities (wife and child), in breaking their promises (to marry the bridegroom), and in ignoring the wider misery to their families, in order to follow the path of "true love"?

Put like that, the story raises very simple moral questions. Should one break promises, especially ones made solemnly (as in marriage)? Should one abandon wife and child because one is in love with another? Should one pursue one's personal desires without regard to the wider social effect? A discussion amongst a group of 16/17-year-olds would normally conclude that what they did was wrong, although there will be some who would maintain that strong personal desire should overcome all else. But the moral rules seem to be generally clear.

Then one introduces them to Lorca's (1989) *Blood Wedding* – to the bride's anguished account or, indeed, justification to the mother of the now dead bridegroom (for, such were the passions, the elopement has resulted in the fight and the death of both the groom and seducer).

I went with him. And you would have gone too. I was a woman burning, covered in sores inside and out, and your son was a trickle of water which would give me children, land, health, but he was a dark river, full of branches, filling me with the murmur of its reeds, singing to me through clenched teeth. And I ran with your son, with your little boy of cold water, and the other one followed me with flocks of birds, so that I couldn't even walk, and my flesh filled with frost, the wounded flesh of a woman already withering, of a young girl burning. Listen to me well, I didn't want to, I didn't want to, do you hear? I didn't want to. Your son was all I ever wished for, and I didn't betray him, but the other one sucked me in with the force of the sea, and nothing could ever have stopped me from going … not ever, not even if I'd been old and all your son's children were holding me by the hair.

(Lorca, 1989, p.102)

She didn't want to, she didn't want to. But "the other one sucked me in with the force of the sea, nothing could ever have stopped me from going". The bride has returned to the bereaved, sorrowing mother-in-law, "for her to kill me", through letting it be known that she is still "clean", "no man has ever seen himself in the whiteness of my breasts".

And Leonardo in his final meeting in the woods with the bride, he protests, too, not his innocence, but the struggle and the forces within him.

My tongue is run through and through with sharpest glass, because I wanted to forget. And I put a wall of stone between your house and mine. It's true. You remember, don't you? And when I saw you pass by, I cast sand in my eyes. But my horse always took me to your door. And the silver pins of your wedding turned my blood black. And my flesh soured and grew thin with weeds. It's not me who's to blame, it's the earth itself, it's the scent of your breasts and of your hair.

(Lorca, 1989, p.91)

Or again, when Leonardo first meets the bride.

To burn in silence is the worst punishment we can inflict upon ourselves. What good did pride do me – what use was it pretending you didn't exist, leaving you to lie awake night in, night out? None … none at all. I burned all the more. Because you think things like that fade with time or that they can be locked away behind thick walls. And they can't. They can't. And when they reach their centre, they're unstoppable, like water rising in a deep well.

(Lorca, 1989, p.60)

But this is not a defence of his actions, just as the bride's protest was not a defence of hers. There is recognition of the heinousness of broken promises, of the disruption of a social order; there is deep remorse, a recognition of the righteousness of retribution – of the entitlement to punishment. Honour has to be satisfied, reputation made good.

And yet such moral passion and dilemmas are earlier placed within a context that makes one sympathetic to the suppressed passions of the bride. In introducing her to the bridegroom's mother the bride's father talks of her virtues.

What can I say about mine ...? She's up at three, with the morning star itself, to bake bread. Never speaks at all, unless spoken to first; as soft and gentle as wool, she embroiders all sorts of ... embroidery. And she can cut a rope with her teeth.

(Lorca, 1989, p. 49)

The discussion amongst the students changes – in direction and in substance, in understanding and in depth of feeling. Moral judgement is not so easy. It requires more than an application of rules, albeit reference to rules and principles remain. But there comes an appreciation, not simply of the passions as the driving force behind action, but of the root of those passions in the very nature of the beings themselves, in the deep urge for personal fulfillment. At the same time, those passions have to be understood within a wider context of responsibility and social relationships. That "understanding" requires a moral vocabulary, not simply of "oughts" and "desires", not simply of juxtaposing "wants" and "obligation", but also of "remorse", "retribution", "honour". The dramatic enactment of the deeper understanding of human conflict and emotion gives insight to those students that impartial, rational, analytic discourse simply cannot achieve.

The following conclusions might be drawn. First, the discussions are much more than mere swapping of opinions. They are rooted in the text. The one who sees no compromises with the promised undertaking has to respond to the bride's explanation. Literature and drama become a resource upon which the learners draw in order to make sense of their particular worlds.

Second, the passions and dilemmas, the sense of remorse, the difficulties of reconciliation, the sense of betrayal and of injustice, are the very stuff of human life – the graphic re-enactment of what is experienced in the lives of the young people themselves. The *educational* importance of drama or literature is that it makes explicit what is too often implicit and unexamined. It engages not just the reason through analysis but also the very emotions that embody the moral insights and dilemmas. Moreover, and more importantly, it does this through a form that distances the public debate from private revelation. The students can engage with something that is deeply personal, without exposing to public gaze that which is and should remain essentially private.

Third, moral traditions are embodied within a moral form of discourse, in a range of concepts that reflect an understanding of human nature and the relation of human beings to a social framework which shapes and sustains them. The good story reveals that moral life in all its complexity; it encapsulates the moral concepts through which that complexity has to be navigated; it acknowledges the principles to be followed and the human disposition (strengths and weaknesses) that interplay with those principles. It sets forth the scene, identifying the reference points, highlighting the dangers and weaknesses. It provides the basis for moral deliberation. But it will also respect that it remains just that – the deliberation that each, as a moral agent, cannot escape from.

Finally, therefore, at the heart of the educational task is, not the attainment of measurable targets (what would be the examination question and the scoring manual which would adequately test the impact of such deliberations on the young learners?), but the transformation of consciousness in the light of evidence and deliberation. And that transformation is more than a different kind of knowledge. It is an understanding that is integrated with appropriate emotions in regard to distinctively human conditions.

Where then are the virtues?

The aims of education, therefore, refer to that initiation into the different forms of learning through which come to understand the physical, moral, social, economic and practical worlds in which we live – an understanding of the human condition. Here I include the "practical worlds" so often neglected. As Michael Crawford (2009) argues in *The Case For Working With Your Hands*, "The disappearance of tools from our common education is the first step toward a wider ignorance of the world of artefacts we inhabit" (p. 1). But crucial, too, is that moral dimension in which young persons are enabled to foresee life as a whole, to think seriously about the life worth living, to recognise and to want to pursue excellence in the activities they are engaged in. Life is shaped at every level by the values one adheres to, even if these be but implicit. Let us call the caring about those values (for example, the readiness to examine them in the light of criticism, attending to alternative viewpoints, respecting the examples of others, or cherishing demanding ideals) "moral seriousness".

That moral seriousness is not something separate from the other dimensions we have referred to. The humanities and the arts are the very voices through which the human condition – its ideals and possibilities as well as its failures and weaknesses – is portrayed and made available to the new generation of learners. Nor is this moral dimension separable from the pursuit of practical capabilities or the more vocational pursuits, because these themselves have inbuilt values as to what are the appropriate standards to be embodied in practice. The good bricklayer is rightly proud of the elegantly constructed wall that he has built.

However, that moral dimension – the essential characteristic of becoming and being a person – is more than a matter of obeying the right rules of behaviour. Rather it is a matter of acquiring and developing the appropriate dispositions, both intellectual and moral. For example, the intellectual dispositions or virtues are essential to the serious engagement with, and pursuit of, knowledge. Understanding of whatever kind and at whatever level requires a concern for the truth – *honesty* in presentation of what one claims to know, *modesty* in terms of what one might achieve, *open mindedness* in the face of well-meant criticism of others, *patience* in the search for answers, *perseverance* in the often difficult task of solving a problem.

Such "virtues" are the dispositions to act appropriately in the pursuit of what one believes to be worthwhile. They are, as Aristotle argued, the middle way between two opposing tendencies, both of which would vitiate the search for understanding and knowledge. "Modesty", for example, is the disposition that militates against, on the one hand, that over-confident and exaggerated self-knowledge which closes the mind to criticism, and, on the other, the debilitating sense of failure that discourages any effort to make headway.

What might be referred to as the moral virtues are precisely these dispositions that enable one to live the distinctively human life, ensuring a proper balance between destructive extremes. "Courage" disposes one to pursue what is worthwhile despite setbacks and pain, and yet it shuns the foolhardiness that fails to recognize danger or faces dangers unnecessarily. The disposition to respect other persons reflects the perception of them as ends in themselves, not as objects in one's personal game and drama, whilst at the same time not blinding one to their faults.

Formal education, in its concern for the development of persons and helping each to acquire those qualities which make them distinctively human, cannot ignore this development of moral seriousness, that is, the development of the virtuous human being, reflecting on what is a life worth living, and disposed not only to take the question seriously but also to act accordingly. And such development requires attending to the emotions through which one sees, evaluates and acts upon the situations that confront one. In re-enacting Lorca's *Blood Wedding* the young people were facing explicitly, critically and deliberatingly, in the light of evidence put before them, graphic accounts of the human condition to which they could relate and from which they could not remain indifferent.

Conclusion

We have been seduced by the language of performance management, and come to see "education" therefore as a means to some end which would not be regarded as in itself educational – a qualification, a better job, more money. Education becomes but a means to an end, and a successful education is judged by its effectiveness in achieving that end, not by its moral worth.

That is the use of "education" in its purely descriptive sense. But in talking about an "educated person" we are engaged in an evaluation of the sort of person he or she is – whether he or she has certain qualities. The aims of education are the expressions of those qualities which we wish to attribute to an "educated person". Such evaluations will always be controversial for they are necessarily based upon what we believe to be the distinctive qualities of being a person and of becoming one more fully.

However, such controversies, if engaged in seriously, need to examine what kinds of learning are part and parcel of a distinctively human life and of flourishing within the world we inhabit. Such an examination will point to the different kinds of understanding and different sorts of practical capabilities through which young people are enabled to act intelligently within their different social and material contexts. Central to such acting are ability and dispositions to think seriously about the ways in which they engage with the world, enter into relationships, make a difference to the world, find deep satisfaction in the life they have chosen to follow, and develop a sense of dignity that will survive personal misfortune.

That is why the development of the appropriate virtues is central to the educational aims.

References

Bruner, J. (1960). *The Process of Education*. Cambridge, MA.: Harvard University Press.
Crawford, M. (2009). *The Case For Working With Your Hands*. London: Penguin Group.
Cuban, L. (2004). *The Blackboard and the Bottom Line: Why Schools Can't Be Run Like Businesses*. Cambridge: Harvard University Press.
Dewey, J. (1916). *Democracy and Education,* New York: The Free Press.
Lorca, F. (1989). *Blood Wedding*. London: Hodder and Stoughton.
Oakeshott, M. (1975/1990). A place of learning. In T. Fuller (Ed.), *Michael Oakeshott and Education*. London: Yale University Press.

Index

A-level 276–8
Abecedarian Project 152
academic skills 15–18, 143, 145–54, 159–66
achievement 264–5, 267, 276–80, 287
  gap 33–4, 146, 162, 165, 182
active learning 84–5
Adams, G. 31
addition 204–7, 209
adolescents 30, 40, 42–3, 45, 53
Adorno, T. 107
African Americans 32–3, 160–1, 166
aims *see* goals
akrasia 312
algebra 205–6, 318
Alliance for Childhood 112
alphabet 53–4, 126, 146–7, 149–51, 175–8, 184, 229–30, 233–4, 242
alphabetic principle 243–4, 247
analogs 199
analytic-synthetic method 232, 234
antibodies 42
anxiety 39–40, 45, 81, 129
approaches to learning (ATL) 128, 162
Archer, E. 289
Aristotle 3–4, 7, 311–15, 323
arithmetic 21–2, 127, 204–5
Arrow, A.W. 239, 241–9
arts 7, 10, 112, 315, 320, 323
Asia 51
Asians 210, 299
assessment 5, 17, 81, 276–7, 281, 285–90, 293–302, 317
asTTle 288–90
Athens 308

attachment 38, 40
attention 149, 162, 299
Attention Deficit Hyperactivity Disorder (ADHD) 294
attention-switching 127
Auckland 289–90
Australia 296, 301
Austria 204
autism spectrum 171
autonomy 7–8, 85

balance 159, 166
base systems 194, 205
baseline assessment 295, 297, 300
Basford, J. 107
Beals, D. 64
behavior 22, 30–1, 43, 129, 153, 294
Beijing 204, 208
Belsky, J. 29, 153
Bempechat, J. 265
Berger, N. 215, 217–26
Bermejo, V. 197
Bhutan 38
bias 299–300
Bielefeld Screening (BISC) 228
Biesta, G. 3, 7–9
Bildung 8
Bjorklund, D.F. 162, 166
Blair, C. 17
blocks 72–8, 83, 87, 209
Blood Wedding 320, 324
Bolivia 38
Bond, M.A. 66
Bonnett, M. 109–10, 112–13
books 49, 51–6, 59–66, 99

bootstrapping 200
Borneo 38
Bosch, B. 232
boys 17, 298–9
Bradley, L. 222
Brady, S.A. 244
braiding 124
brain 17, 40–2, 44–5, 97, 113–14, 116, 173, 266
breastfeeding 38, 40, 44–5
Britain 27–8
Brooks-Gunn, J. 43
Brosterman, N. 78
Brown, G.T.L. 285, 287–92
Bruner, J. 211, 319
Bryant, P. 191, 193–203, 222
Buckingham, D. 106
Building Blocks 77–8, 87
Burchinal, M.E. 32
Burkina Faso 38
Burma 38
Bus, A.G. 56, 222
business 316–17
Buxiban 275
Byrne, B. 241, 243

Cai, J. 206, 209
California 160, 275
Cambodia 38
cameras 97–8, 100
cardinality 194–9, 201
Carey, S. 199–200, 202
Carr, D. 305, 307–15
Cascio, E.U. 160
Cassidy, S. 251
causation 182, 217, 223, 264
center-based care 30–1
Centre for Evaluation and Monitoring (CEM) 295, 297, 301
Chall, J. 173–4
Chase, W.G. 20
cheating 288–9
Chen, E. 40
chess 19–23
Chicago Child-Parent Centers 30
Child Behavior Checklist 43
child-centredness 83, 85, 87, 99, 153–4

childcare 25, 27–34, 38–46
China 204–11
Chinese 53, 62, 230
Chinese Room Argument 82
Chinese-Americans 210
Chow, B.W.-Y. 62
Chutes and Ladders 83
civic aims 7–8
class level effects 278
Clements, D.H. 69, 71–80, 87
cognition 19–24, 125–7, 181
cognitive decentration 230, 234
cognitive entry skills 242–4, 246–7
communication 97–8, 100–1, 109–10, 138, 161
communicative function 268–9
competencies 7, 23, 81, 84–5, 87, 98, 101–2, 223
comprehension 172–4, 177, 181, 184–6, 232, 242
computational models 250
computer-adaptive programs 300–2
computers 78, 97, 99–102, 107, 110, 112, 114–15
Congo, Republic of 38
Connelly, V. 242, 244
Connor, C.M. 164, 174, 246
consensus xi
Constrained Skills Theory (CST) 149–50
constructivism 83, 85, 314
contextual guessing 246
conversations 59–61, 64–6
Cooper, H. 276, 278, 282
correlational studies 60, 147–9, 182, 221, 227
correspondence relations 193
cortisol 39–45
Cost, Quality, and Outcome Study 31
counting 193–202, 205
Cowan, R. 198
Cramer, C. 42
cramming 275
Crawford, M. 323
cross-sectional studies 264–5, 270
Cuban, L. 316–18
culture 5, 9, 64–5, 101, 103, 113, 204, 210–11, 276, 314

curiosity 81, 84, 234, 277
curriculum materials 206–9
Cutspec, P.A. 63

Dahlin, B. 1, 3–12
Damasio, A. 110
Daniels, H. 198
daycare *see* childcare
De Marco, A. 25, 27–38
Deardoff, J. 44
debate x–xi
decoding 146–7, 164, 171, 173–7, 181–8,
    219, 232, 242–7
deep processing 288
deliberation 319–20, 322
Deming, W.E. 296
democracy 4–5, 7–9, 308
Denmark 29
depression 39–40
desires 308–13, 320, 322
Dettmers, S. 279
developmental approach 162–3
developmental psychology x–xi, 133, 228
developmental violence 106
developmentally appropriate practice
    (DAP) 76
Dewey, J. 317–18
Dhuey, E. 160–1, 166
dialectic 312–13
dialogic reading 52, 55–6, 60–5, 151
DiCicca, P. 152–3
didactic teaching 165
digital media 93, 95–104, 301
    inappropriateness 105–16 *see also* ICT
Ding, M. 208
disability 162, 217
dispositions 13–18, 100–2, 128, 323–4
diversity x–xi
division of labor 241
Dobrich, W. 59
Doddington, C. 110
Dogon 38
domain-specificity 23
Downing, J. 229
Dr. Seuss 54
drama 322–3
drill 14–15

Dufau, S. 251
Duncan, G.J. 149–50
Durand, M. 222
Durham University 295, 297, 301
DVDs 98–9
dyslexia 177, 186, 217–19

Early Childhood Education Review 151
Early Childhood Longitudinal Study-
    Kindergarten (ECLS-K) 152, 161–2
Early, D.M. 165
Early Head Start 30
Early Years Foundation Stage Profile
    (EYFSP) 298–300
economy 3–4, 6, 317
eczema 42
Edelstein, W. 218
education for reality 3, 9–10
Education Reform Act 8
effectiveness 296–7, 318
Ehri, L.C. 169, 171–80, 222, 231, 243,
    250, 252
Einstein, A. 9, 81, 106
elaborative talk 64–5
Elder, L. 244
Elkind, D. 109, 112, 115–16, 161
Ellenbogen, M.A. 39
Elley, W.B. 187
Elliott, J. 261, 275–84
Else-Quest, N. 187
embodiment 110
emergent reading 171
emotions 153–4, 161–2, 270, 279, 309
    emotional support 164–5 *see also*
        feelings
empathy 7, 110
ends *see* goals
England 234, 275, 277–8, 281, 293–8,
    300
English 54–5, 62, 146–7, 177–8, 185, 187,
    205, 227, 231, 242, 252–3, 299
Enlightenment 7–8
environment-dependency 244, 246–7
epigenetic imprinting 41
Epstein, J.L. 261, 263–74
equality 207
ethics 318–19 *see also* morals

Europe 8, 28, 51, 63–4, 210, 218
European Commission 3
everyday life 100
exams *see* assessment
executive functioning 127, 266, 294
expectations 287–9
expertise x–xi
explicit phonics 250–9
extended family 38
external causes 172–3, 178
externalizing problems 129, 153
EyeToy 100

family values 27
far transfer 23
Farrow, S. 277–8
fatalism 115
feedback 288–9, 297, 301–2
feelings 13, 15, 310 *see also* emotions
feminism 107
Fielding-Barnsley, R. 243
fine motor 129–30
Fisher, K 69, 81–92
Fitz-Gibbon, C.T. 276–8, 296–7
flashcards 243
Fletcher-Flinn, C.M. 239, 250–60
flourishing 307–9, 313, 318, 324
formal instruction 16–18, 123, 171, 173,
    178
foundational experiences 74–5
foundational skills 172
Foy, J.G. 61
fractions 86, 205–6, 209
France 29
free play 43, 61, 74–6, 78, 83, 85–7
freedom 3–6, 8
Freeman, N.H. 197
French 279
Freud, S. 10
Froebel, F. 71, 78
Frydman, O. 196
fulfilment 3, 10
Fuller, R.B. 78
functional risks 164
functionalism 6
Fuson, K 197
Future of Children 33

Gaskins, I.W. 176
Geary, D.C. 204
Gelman, R. 194–8, 201–2
Gelman, S.A. 198
geometry 74, 76, 85, 87
German 177, 222, 227, 231, 233
Germany 8, 187, 219, 228, 232–4, 278–9
Ghengis Khan 308
gifts 72
Gingell, J. 3, 5, 9
Ginsburg, H.P. 87
girls 17, 44, 54, 63
Glotin, H. 251
GNP 6
goals 7–9, 317–19 *see also* purposes
Goethe, J.W. von x, 185
Golinkoff, R.M. 69, 81–92
good life 4, 6, 308, 310, 318
Goodman, K.S. 246
Gorgias 307–10
Gough, P.B. 243
Grainger, J. 251
graphemes 175–6, 231, 233, 243, 245
gratification 265, 308, 310, 313
Great Depression 27
Gréco, P. 198, 202
Greece 3–4, 308
Greenfield, S. 109
Groenveld, M.G. 43
Groot, A. de 19–24
gross motor 129, 300
guided play 85–7
Gullo, D.F. 159
Gunnar, M. 41, 43
Gur, T. 243

Habermas, J. 107
Hagwon 275
Hair, E. 161–2
Halo Effect 300–1
Hamre, B.K. 163
Han, X. 208
happiness 307–9
Harlen, W. 299
Harris, A. 176
Harris, L.R. 290
Hattie, J. 285, 287–92

Head Start 30–1, 64–6, 160, 162, 166
Head Start Impact Study 151–2
health 130, 161–2, 166
Healy, J.M. 109, 112–13
Hearing, Listening, Learning (HLL) 222
Hedegaard, M. 136
Heidegger, M. 107, 109–10, 112, 114
higher order thinking 165
Hindman, A.H. 121, 123–32
Hinton, M. 110
hippocampus 40–1, 44
Hirsh-Pasek, K. 69, 81–92
Hispanics 64, 160
Hitler, A. 308
homework 210, 261, 263–71, 275–82
Hong Kong 52–3, 55, 62, 204, 210
hormones 39–41
House, R. 93, 105–20
Howard-Jones, P. 97
Howes, C. 165
Hufton, N. 281
Hughes, K. 159
Hughs, D. 174
Hulun Buir Fantasy Children's Choir 204
human capital 317
human condition 323–4
humanism 8
humanities 320, 323
humanity 106–8, 116, 162, 319
Hume, D. 310
hyperactivity 299
hyperlexic reading 171
hypothalamic-pituitary-adrenocortical
    (HPA) axis 39–44

ICT see digital media
ideology critique 108
Ijzendoorn, M.H. van 56, 222
imagination 7
immaturity 162, 166, 294
immune system 42
income see socio-economic status
India 55
individualization 124
individuation 199–201
information processing 219–20, 223
inhibition 127, 294

inhuman 108, 110, 116
intellectual goals 15–18
interaction 65–6, 101
interactive homework 269
interests 5
internal causes 172–3, 178
internalizing problems 129
interpersonal skills 128–9
intervention research 62–6, 150–3, 182–3,
    221–2, 233
Iran 38
Isle of Man 277

Jacobson, M. 176
Janes, H. 65
Japan 210, 275
Jong, P.F. de 245
Juel, C. 174, 182, 243
Juku 275
Justice, L.M. 63

Kale, P. 78
Kant, i. 8, 311
Karrass, J. 63
Katz, L. 1, 13–18
Kentucky 281
Kermani, H. 65
Kirschhock, E.-M. 229
Kisilevsky, B.S. 45
knowledge 13–14, 100, 307, 309–10,
    312–13, 323
Knowledge Sources theory 254–9
Kohlberg, L. 312
Korea 55, 276
Krajewski, K. 223

labour market 6, 27, 33
Lakoff, G. 110
Landerl, K. 220
language 9, 185, 204, 277, 316
    phonological awareness 228–9,
        233–4
    preschool/kindergarten 146–7, 150,
        154
    school readiness 124–6
    shared book-reading 45, 51–6, 59–60,
        62–5

language comprehension skills (LCS)
    see comprehension
Laos 38
Latinos 66
laws 3–5
league tables 297
learner-dependency 243–4, 246–7
learning 3, 241–2, 319
    trajectories 76–8
lectures 208
letter knowledge 219–20, 223, 253–6
Lever, R. 63
Levin, D.M. 114
lexicalised phonological recoding 254,
    256–9
Li, X. 208
Li-Grining, C.P. 162
liberalism 3, 5, 7–10
Liberman, I.Y. and A.M. 241
Lillard, A. 187
literacy 15, 73, 75
    digital media 98–9, 111
    instruction 241–3, 247
    phonological awareness 217–21, 223,
        227, 233–4
    preschool/kindergarten 145–52, 154,
        163–4, 178
    school readiness 124, 126
    shared book-reading 53, 56, 59, 61,
        63–6
literature 315, 322
Löffler, I. 231
logic 136, 138–9
logic of action 317–18, 320
London 299
London, A.S. 34
long-term memory 21–4
longitudinal studies 17, 182–3, 217–23,
    229, 231, 265, 269–70, 282
Lonigan, C.J. 143, 145–58
Lorca, F. 320–2, 324
love 10, 320
Lundberg, I. 221–2, 228
Luria, A. 133–6, 138
Lyotard, J.-F. 107–8, 116

Ma, L. 206, 209

McBride-Chang, C. 49, 51–8
McDowall, S. 290
MacIntyre, A. 314
McPake, J. 93, 95–104, 107
Mali 38
Mann, V. 61
Manolitsis, G. 174
Maori 287
Marcon, R. 87, 143, 159–68
marketization 4, 95
Marx, H. 218
Marx, P. 232
Marxism 6
maternal bond 44–5
maternal employment 27–30
mathematics 110, 127
    assessment 294–5, 298
    homework 268, 271, 277–9
    preschool/kindergarten 69, 71–8, 81–8,
        149, 151–4
    primary school 191, 193–202, 204–11,
        219, 223
mathematization 74–6
Matthew effects 54, 182–4
meaning 3, 10, 20–1, 109
    mathematics 83, 88
    preschool/kindergarten 146, 148, 176,
        181
    school readiness 125–6, 135
means and ends 317–18
measurement 317
Meisels, S.J. 300
memory 15, 19–24, 81–4, 127, 165,
    171–3, 175–6, 205
Mercer, N. 137
Merleau-Ponty, M. 110
Merrell, C. 285, 293–304
meta-analysis 63, 147–9, 184–5, 218,
    221–2
meta-cognition 137
meta-communication 138
Metsala, J. 61
migration 222, 233
Mill, J.S. 309, 311
Minden-Cupp, C. 174, 243
Minnesota, University of 44
minorities 30, 32–3, 74

mobile phones 95, 97, 101
modernity 105–6, 108–10, 112–13
Mol, W.E. 63
Mongolia 204
monitoring progress 296
monkeys 44
Montessori schools 187–8
moral panics 106–7, 116
morals 309–15, 318–20, 322–3
    moral seriousness 323–4
Morrison, F.J. 121, 123–32, 164, 173
mothers 27–9, 293
motivation 56, 84, 87–8, 128, 153, 163,
    234, 265–7, 280–1, 297, 312
motor development 129
Muhlenbruck, L. 277
multiplication 21–2
Munich Longitudinal Study on the
    Genesis of Individual Competencies
    (LOGIC) 219–21
music 138–9, 204

narcissism 114
narrative 64, 134, 139
Nation, K. 251
National Assessment of Education Progress
    (NAEP) 145–6, 209
National Center for Early Development
    and Learning (NCEDL) 164–5
National Early Literacy Panel (NELP)
    147–51
National Education Goals Panel 161
National Mathematics Advisory Panel 81
National Reading Panel 245
Naydler, J. 107–8, 113, 116
Netherlands 280, 296
Neuman, S.B. 160
neuroendocrine responses 39–45
neurology 17, 97
New Zealand 188, 250, 253–4, 287–90,
    296
Newborn Hearing Screening Programme
    293
Newton, P.E. 293, 298
Ni, Y. 191, 204–14
NICHD Study of Early Childcare 31–3
Nicholson, T. 242

Nicomachean Ethics 315
Nintendo 100
non-parental childcare 27–34, 38–46
nonlexical phonological recoding 252,
    255, 257–8
North Korea 38
Norway 280
null hypothesis 181, 187–8
number 194–202
numeracy 15
Nunes, T. 191, 193–203
nursery see preschool
Nursery World 107
Nussbaum, M. 7

Oakeshott, M. 319
objectivity 9, 299–300, 309, 311
O'Hara, M. 107
Olson, D.R. 139
one-to-one correspondence 196–8,
    201–2, 207
operational skills 100–1
oral language 53, 61–3, 146–8, 150–1, 218
ordinality 195, 200
orthography 185–6, 227, 230–1
outcomes 7, 39, 43, 145
oxytocin 45

Paine, L. 208
paradigmatic mode 134, 139
parallel individuation 200–1
parallelism 75–6
parental leave 29
parenting 33, 44, 51, 56, 59, 210, 266–9,
    279–80
Parr, J.M. 290
Pasifika 287
patriarchy 107
Performance Indicators in Primary Schools
    On-entry Baseline Assessment
    (PIPS-BLA) 295, 300
Perry Preschool Study 31, 152
Phillips, B.M. 143, 145–58
Phillips, D.A. 31
philosophy x, 81–2, 105, 107–9, 307
phonemes 175–7, 228–31, 233–4
phonics 239, 241–5, 247, 250–9

phonological awareness 126, 215, 217–23, 227–34
  preschool/kindergarten 146–7, 149–51, 172–3
  reading instruction 242, 244, 247, 250
  shared book-reading 61–2, 65
Phonological Core Deficit Model 146
phonological information processing 218–19
photographs 100–1
phronesis 313, 315
physical activity 100, 129
Piaget, J. 193–6, 198, 201–2, 230, 234, 312
Pianta, R.C. 163
Plato x, 3, 307–10, 312–13
play 15–16, 18, 43, 65, 277
  digital media 99, 101–2
  mathematical development 71–2, 74–6, 78
  preschool/kindergarten 159, 162–3, 166
playful learning 81–8
Plowman, L. 93, 95–104, 107
political function 268–9
Politics 3
Portuguese 177
positivism 181, 188
Post, T. 86
Postman, N. 109
Poulter, T. 107
poverty *see* socio-economic status
power 6
Pramling, 121, 133–42
Pramling Samuelsson, I. 121, 133–42
Pratt, C. 72
pre-kindergarten 164–6
precautionary principle 105, 115–16
precocious reading 171, 174
prefrontal cortex 127, 266
Preschool Curriculum Evaluation Research Consortium (PCERC) 152–4
pretend reading 171
primary school 104, 137–8, 191, 276–8
Pring, R. 305, 316–24

print skills 62–5, 126, 146–7, 149–51, 171, 229–31, 234
problem solving 19–24, 84–5, 194, 205
process 7, 32
professional development 102, 208
Program for International Student Assessment (PISA) 5–6, 187, 210, 276, 278–9
progress 95, 113
Progress in International Reading Literacy Studies (PIRLS) 5–6, 233
Project Approach 16, 18
pseudowords 252–3, 256–7
public lessons 207–8
purposes 1, 3–10, 13–18, 307 *see also* goals

qualification 7–10, 317–18, 320, 324
quantitative relations 193–5, 202

Ranschburg, P. 217
rationality 310–12
Raver, C.C. 162
reading 239, 241–6, 250–9
  assessment 294–5
  digital media 99, 111
  homework 276–8
  phonological awareness 217–23, 227–9, 231–4
  preschool/kindergarten 145–51, 153, 169, 171–8, 181–8
  shared book-reading 49, 51–6, 59–66
reality 9–10
Reason x, 8
reasoning 84, 88, 110, 134–40, 195
recoding 219, 250–8
Reed, E. 108–9
Reese, E. 49, 59–68
refrigerator art 16, 18
relational judgements 193, 195, 197–9, 207
relative value-added 297
religion 8
reminiscing 61, 64–5
Renninger, K.A. 84
Republic 312
researchers x–xi, xiv
rhetoric 308–10
rhymes 228, 230, 234

Rockwell, N. 28
Roisman, G.I. 43
Romantics 8
Rønning, M. 280
Roos, J. 232
Rosie 28
Roskos, K. 160
Rossoni, E. 45
rote learning 21–2, 81, 165
Rovine, M.J. 29
Rozak, T. 107
Russell, J.L. 160–1
Russia 275–6, 281

Säljö, R. 135
Sanders, C. 110–11
Sarama, J. 69, 71–80, 87
Sardello, R. 110–11
Sarnecka, B.W. 198
scaffolding 85, 135–8, 140, 154,
    165–6
Scandinavia 29
Scarborough, H. 59, 124, 172, 244
Schaal, B. 45
Schneider, W. 215, 217–27, 232–3
Schöler, H. 232
school readiness 16–17, 39, 121, 123–30,
    133–40, 161–2, 165
school's readiness 137–9
Schwartz-Salant, N. 114
science x–xi, 277–8, 313, 317, 319–20
Scotland 104, 244, 296, 300
screen technology 111, 114–15
Searle, J. 82
second language 51, 55, 279
secondary school 208, 276–7, 281
Seek the Shapes 85
self-reflection 9
self-regulation 17, 83, 128, 154, 162–3,
    166, 265
self-teaching hypothesis 251–2
Sénéchal, M. 63, 124
sense-making 85, 139
senses 108–12
sets 193–202
Seymour, P. 177, 244
Shakespeare, W. 185

Shanahan, T. 148
Share, D.L. 243, 245, 251–2
shared book-reading 49, 51–6, 59–66,
    124, 151
Showronek, H. 218
Siberia 38
Sigman, A. 25, 38–48, 114
Sim, S. 116
Simon, H.A. 20
Simple View of Reading (SVR) 146
Siraj-Blatchford, J. 107–8, 114
Skibbe, L.E. 166
snowball effect 184, 188
socialisation 5–9, 128–9
socio-economic status (SES) 16, 96, 233
    homework 279–81
    mathematics 73–4, 87
    non-parental childcare 30–3, 39–40
    preschool/kindergarten 146, 150, 178,
        185–6
    school readiness 136–7
    shared book-reading 56, 60, 62–4
Socrates 307–13
Son, S.-H. 300
Sonnenschein, S. 66
Sonuga-Barke, E.J.S. 299
Sony 100
Sophian, C. 198
sophists 308–13
South East Asia 275
Soviet Union 133, 275
Spaemann, R. 3, 9–10
Spain 55
Spanish 66, 177
specific language impairment (SLI)
    222
speech 45, 228, 230, 234
spelling 176, 217–23, 227–34, 242
spirituality 8–10
Sputnik 275
stages of development 173–4
Stainthorp, R. 174
Stalin, J. 308
Standish, P. 3, 7
Stanovich, K.E. 217, 223
state 3–6, 8–9
state-independent schools 4–5

State-Wide Early Education Programs (SWEEP) 165
Steiner, R. 106, 109, 112, 188
Stengard, C. 218, 220
Stenius, F. 40
Stephen, C. 93, 95–104, 107
Stephenson, K.A. 54
Stipek, D.J. 153
stories 250
stress 39–44, 280
students 266–7
Su, S. 84
subjectification 7–9
subjectivity 310–11
sublexical relations 243–4, 246
subtraction 193–4, 205–7, 209
Suggate, S.P. 169, 181–90
suitcase problem 183, 186
Sumatra 38
Sumner, M. 41
Sweden 29, 137
Sweller, J. 1, 19–24
Switzerland 279
syllables 228–30
syllogisms 134–5
synthetic approaches 232–3

Tafa, E. 174
Taipei 208
Taiwan 275
Tapscott, D. 107
targets 317–18, 322
Teachers Involve Parents in Schoolwork (TIPS) 269–70
teaching to the test 318
technology 93, 95–104, 106–7, 109, 113–16 see also digital media
teddy bears 16
television 98, 103, 178, 204
tests see assessment
text-centred approach 250, 257
textbooks 206–8, 210
Third International Mathematics and Science Study (TIMSS) 278–81
Thompson, G.B. 239, 250–60
Thorndike, E. 72
toddlers 38, 44, 59, 128

Tonga 38
transition 133, 137–40
Trautwein, U. 276–9
Trends in Mathematics and Science Study (TIMSS) 5–6
Tunmer, W.E. 239, 241–9
Turkmenistan 38
two basics 205
Tymms, P. 261, 275–84, 294, 296–7

UK 8–9, 293, 295–6, 299
unconscious 113
understanding 13–14, 22, 100, 322–4
US 9, 234, 297
 homework 268, 275–6, 279, 281
 mathematics 71, 73, 81–2, 84, 205–10
 non-parental childcare 27–9, 31, 33–4
 preschool/kindergarten 159–61, 165, 173
 shared book-reading 52, 64

Valtin, R. 215, 227–38
value-added systems 297
values 27, 29, 310–11, 313–14, 323
Van Voorhis, F.L. 261, 263–74
Vandell, D.L. 43
Venezky, R.L. 245
verbal information processing speed 219–20
Vernon-Feagans, L. 25, 27–38
Victoria, University of 228
Vienna Boys' Choir 204
Vietnam 38
violence 97
virtues x, 305, 307–15, 323–4
vocabulary 242, 246–7, 254–9, 294–5
 phonological awareness 233–4
 preschool/kindergarten 151, 164, 172–8, 185–6
 shared book-reading 51–6, 60, 62–5
vocational aims 7–8
Vreeburg, S.A. 40
Vygotsky, L. 136

Wagemaker, H. 54
Waldorf schools 188
Wasik, B.A. 66

Waynforth, D. 40
Weber's law 199
West 7, 29, 38, 210
West Africa 38
What Works Clearinghouse (WWC) 151
Whitebread, D. 107
Whitehurst, G.J. 146, 161
whole child 71, 166
whole-language approaches 246–7
Wii 100
Wilce, L.S. 243
Wilmut, J. 299
Wimmer, H. 220
Winch, C. 3, 5, 9
Wittgenstein, L. 107
Wolfgang, C.H. 87
women 27–9, 34

Wong, V.C. 151
words 228–30
    reading skills 172, 175–6, 184–5,
        256–7
    recognition 242, 245
work 27–9, 265
working memory 97, 127, 219, 223, 234
World War II 28
Wright, F.L. 78
writing 171, 177, 233–4, 290, 298
written language acquisition *see* print skills
Würzburg training program 222, 233
Wynn, K. 200–1

Yelland, N. 115

Ziegler, J.C. 251